BREAD
in Half the Time

BREAD
in Half the Time

Use Your Microwave and
Food Processor to Make Real
Yeast Bread in 90 Minutes

LINDA WEST ECKHARDT and
DIANA COLLINGWOOD BUTTS

Illustrations by Dolores R. Santoliquido

Crown Publishers, Inc., New York

♦KATIE,
KATHERINE,
and BETTY
Women who work, make a
home, and inspire us to keep
trying new ideas

Grateful acknowledgment is made to Narsai David for permission to use his recipe for Narsai David's Light Rye.

Copyright © 1991 by Linda West Eckhardt and Diana Collingwood Butts
Illustrations copyright © 1991 by Dolores R. Santoliquido

Published by Crown Publishers, Inc., 201 East 50th Street, New York, New York 10022. Member of the Crown Publishing Group.

CROWN is a trademark of Crown Publishers, Inc.

Manufactured in the United States of America

Design by Lauren Dong

Library of Congress Cataloging-in-Publication Data

Eckhardt, Linda West,
     Bread in half the time : use your microwave and food
     processor to make yeast bread in ninety minutes
     / Linda West Eckardt and Diana Collingwood Butts.—1st ed.
        p.   cm.
     Includes index.
     1. Bread. 2. Microwave cookery.   I. Butts, Diana Collingwood.
     II. Title.
     TX769.E226   1991
     641.8′15—dc20   91-6285
                                                                                      CIP
     ISBN 0-517-58154-X

     10 9 8 7 6 5 4 3 2 1

     First Edition

◆ CONTENTS

Preface   vii
Acknowledgments   viii
Introduction   1
    How to Use This Book   3
    Ingredients   4
    Equipping the Half-Time Kitchen   15

PART ONE: MICRO-RISE BAKING: YEAST BREADS IN TWO HOURS OR LESS USING THE MICROWAVE AND THE FOOD PROCESSOR

The Micro-Rise Method   29
1. Basic Breads   49
2. Fitness, Health, and High-Fiber Breads   75
3. Breakfast and Brunch Breads   94
4. Hors D'Oeuvres, Toasts, Croutons, and
   Salad Breads   121
5. Bagels, Baguettes, Breadsticks, Buns, and Rolls   137
6. Pizza, Focaccia, Flatbreads, and Filled Breads   165
7. Soup and Sandwich Breads   190
8. Festive Sweet, Holiday, Dessert, and High-Tea
   Breads   207

PART TWO: HOME-BAKED BREAD IN THE BREAD MACHINE

Bread Machine Basics   239
9. Basic Breads   251
10. Fitness, Health, and High-Fiber Breads   260
11. Breakfast and Brunch Breads   266
12. Hors D'Oeuvres, Toasts, Croutons, and Salad
    Breads   275
13. Bagels, Baguettes, Breadsticks, Buns, and Rolls   281
14. Pizza, Focaccia, Flatbreads, and Filled Breads   293
15. Soup and Sandwich Breads   308
16. Festive Sweet, Holiday, Dessert, and High-Tea
    Breads   319

Appendix   334
Index   338

◆ PREFACE

Making bread has long been an act of meditation. From the time when farm women with eight children found a precious 15 minutes of privacy while kneading the daily bread to modern-day Zen monks for whom the work of baking itself is an act of prayer, making bread is more than simply the production of food for the table.

Dedicated bakers get a pained expression on their faces when we describe our new craft of baking bread that employs the latest in kitchen tools and equipment. Perhaps the cause of their pain is the fear that the meditative aspect will be lost.

Heretical as it sounds, you can yet experience that still, small moment of peace that comes from kneading an aromatic mound of dough in a patch of sunlight on a well-worn wooden board, even if you trade off the time spent in hand kneading by giving that job over to a food processor that will accomplish the work in 60 seconds flat. Really. Despite the whirling food processor, the humming microwave, and the radiant electric oven, the 90 minutes or so you'll need to make, raise, and bake bread can provide a quiet, contemplative time. We know. We've been enjoying this island of peace in our lives for almost a year now.

It has long been taken as gospel that in order for bread to taste good, it needs a long time to rise. With only a few caveats, we challenge that belief. We believe you can produce a loaf of bread that will have a rich, round, well-developed flavor, and it won't take all day to do it.

So, we say to all you naysayers and old-time bakers, try it. Make bread a half-dozen times using our new methods, and we believe you'll see that baking Bread in Half the Time feeds the soul as well as the body. Even if we do employ the latest in kitchen equipment.

Linda West Eckhardt
Diana Collingwood Butts

◆ ACKNOWLEDGMENTS

For helping *Bread* rise and grow from the merest yeasty idea, we sincerely thank our editor, Erica Marcus, who kept the concept on track and knew the right questions to ask.

We also thank Lauren Dong, who designed this book with such vision and such verve. Our thanks also go to Randy Rourke, who photographed breads for the cover, and to Dolores Santoliquido, who illustrated the text. Thanks also go to Nancy Maynes, Laura Starrett, Jane Rutman, Etya Pinker, and all the other folks at Crown who got excited about *Bread in Half the Time*.

We particularly wish to thank our agent, Mildred Marmur, who continues to guide us through the wilds with such care and wisdom.

We also thank our friends in the business, who offered support, encouragement, and aid. Thanks go to Narsai David and Nach Waxman, who gave us the benefit of their wisdom. And to Julia Child for her words of encouragement. This book would not have been possible without the cooperation of our friends in the food industry. To the folks at Amana, Black and Decker, Braun, Panasonic, Red Star, Sanyo, Sassafras, Seiko, Welbilt, and Zojirushi, we say thanks for the use of the modern-day kitchen wizards that make it possible to create bread in half the time.

We particularly wish to thank Fleishmann's Yeast for the enthusiastic support they offered for this new yeast bread craft.

Saving the best for last, we thank our families for being involved in the shopping, cooking, cleaning, testing, tasting of endless kinds of breads. To Larry and Joe, our good husbands, we couldn't have done it without you. Also to the neighbors and friends who eagerly tasted breads, thanks from both of us and stick around. That aroma wafting out of our kitchens these days comes from dessert. Wanna taste? Come on over.

Linda and Diana

◆ INTRODUCTION

What *is* Bread in Half the Time? It's bread baked using our Micro-Rise process, or made in one of those newfangled bread machines. In the Micro-Rise process, the kneading is done in 1 minute by a food processor, the dough is quickly proofed in the microwave using Micro-Rise techniques, then baking is done in the conventional oven.

For owners of bread machines, recipes are included in Part Two that require nothing more than combining ingredients into the mixing/baking pan, pressing a few buttons, then taking out a finished loaf of bread. The features, versatility, and capabilities of the various machines are discussed in the introduction to Part Two.

Every commercial baker uses a "proofing" cabinet to scientifically control heat and humidity for a predictable dough-rising time. When you use the microwave to raise dough, you are employing the same basic technique. Bread machines use a computer and sensor to do the same thing. These new technologies make it possible to calculate accurately how long it will take to make, raise, and bake yeast breads. Granted, bread making may become more science than art when you use these new techniques, but bread dough is still a living thing, somewhat temperamental, and has enough personality to make the job interesting.

If you're using a bread machine, the delayed timer makes it possible to put the ingredients into the machine before you go to bed, set the timer, then wake up to the tantalizing fragrance of fresh baked bread. Using the Micro-Rise method, you can have bread for brunch out of a conventional oven in just over an hour. Either way, you get a house that smells like home, hot bread for breakfast, and a great start on a new day.

You can also make high-fiber, low-fat, no-cholesterol breads at home. Perhaps your doctor has advised you to modify your diet in order to avoid additives, to alleviate food allergies, or simply to be a healthier person. The only way to *really* know the ingredients in the bread you eat is to make it at home. Using the Micro-Rise method, or a bread machine, you can make pure, wholesome breads with ease.

You'll find a wonderful collection of recipes here for aromatic breads that go with hearty soups. We've also included crunchy crostini, fragrant bruschetta, traditional and new pizzas, calzone, and bread salads.

Whole meals wrapped in breads are a staple around the world. We've tried various ethnic sandwiches to see what works. We found you can freeze meat-filled steamed buns, then have them ready to thaw, raise, and bake for a party. This new technique can be used to plan ahead, doing work in little snatches. For example, say you eat out at a Chinese restaurant, and you get an extra order of good barbecued pork to take home. Next day, make the buns (see page 304) using a bread machine. Shape, fill them with the pork, and freeze them, and you're halfway to a good, spontaneous party.

We weren't too sure how fruits would react to this quick method, but we found fruit and nut breads popped right up, almost out of the pan, fragrant and tempting. We did discover that machine kneading tends to chew fruits and nuts, so they must be kneaded in by hand at the end of the machine kneading process unless your food processor has a dough hook or plastic dough blade. Otherwise, fruits and nuts simply vanish into the dough when processed with a metal blade.

We know time is highly valued around holidays when it seems there is never enough to go around. The Micro-Rise method solves the dilemma of how to make holiday breads when you have even less time than usual. We had lots of fun trying these. We found great choices for a centerpiece bread that makes a party festive. Some really showy, flashy-looking breads are found in the chapter "Festive Sweet, Holiday, Dessert, and High-Tea Breads." Also in this chapter you'll find that for afternoon tea you can make an exquisite home-baked bread.

We adapted traditional recipes, ethnic recipes, regional favorites, and new ideas to the Micro-Rise method and to the bread machine process. We had to tinker with the proportions of flour to liquids to achieve a dough that would knead by machine; raise in our new-age proofing cabinet, the microwave; then bake in the oven. With a few exceptions, we found acceptable taste development, size, and lift that met rigorous standards, and most of all, we discovered making bread the Micro-Rise way is fun.

We've decided the microwave oven, food processor, and bread machine are our toys. These small electrics of the nineties fitted out with their own electronic brains to do some of our thinking and hard work are full of delight. Ever see a kid with a Betty Crocker toy oven heated with a light bulb? Making mud pies? That's how we feel. Baking the Micro-Rise way just doesn't seem like work. It seems like play, with a little Silicon Valley magic thrown in.

The bad news is you still have to do the dishes. We did consciously try to cut down steps and procedures so that you wouldn't have a full sink at the end of the baking time. We came to appreciate the new rhythm of working in the kitchen that the microwave encourages. We found we did have just enough time to clean up as we went along during the brief periods the dough was rising. We also had time to call out spelling words, iron a blouse, read a chapter of *Jane Eyre*. Flip through *HG*. Whatever we wanted to do.

We encourage you to try these new kitchen techniques. We've learned so much about baking in writing the book. We wish you equal good luck and fun in the kitchen.

HOW TO USE THIS BOOK

The book is divided into two parts. The first part has recipes for use with a food processor, microwave oven, and conventional oven: the Micro-Rise process. (Before you begin baking, turn to pages 29–35 for a complete run-down on this process.)

Micro-Rise recipes are accompanied by tips, hints, go-withs, and ancillary recipes, found in the sidebars and, occasionally, after the main recipe.

The second, smaller part of the book consists of recipes for use with bread machines. We have tested recipes for both 1-pound and 1½-pound machines and have given proportions for both, where appropriate. For recipes that use only the dough cycle of the machine—the machine is used to knead and raise the bread dough, which is then removed, formed, raised, and baked in a conventional oven—we usually give one recipe quantity. (Alternate proportions aren't needed here because you can make either a pound or pound and a half of dough in any bread machine, as long as the final rise is not in the machine and the baking takes place in a conventional oven.)

Take care, when using the regular bread machine recipes, to use the proportions suitable to your particular machine. If you're not sure whether you have a 1-pound machine or a 1½-pound model, check your owner's manual. Another way to tell is this: if the recipes in the booklet that came with your machine call for about 2 cups of flour, you have a 1-pound machine; if the recipes call for 3 or more cups of flour, you have a 1½-pound model.

◇   ◇   ◇

There is, necessarily, a lot of crossover from chapter to chapter: you'll find sandwich suggestions, for example, in several different chapters, depending on the primary bread. For ease of use, we encourage you to study the index and to note cross-referenced recipes and ideas.

INGREDIENTS

Breads are made up of a combination of flour, liquid, leavening, salt, sugar, and sometimes eggs and/or fats. Additionally, cheese, fruits, nuts, spices, or herbs may be added for flavor.

Flours

One good reason to bake at home is that you can control the flours you use to get the best results.

One reason ordinary commercial bread has that odd wallpaper-pasty odor, shrinks, and loses its shape as it stands in the kitchen is that it may be made with inferior flour. Baking at home, you are ahead of the game before you start simply by using better flours.

Wheat flour contains proteins that, when added to liquids and kneaded, create an elastic substance called gluten, which provides the cell structure in yeast breads to make them rise and stay up after baking.

Although, botanically, there are more than thirty-thousand varieties of wheat, in baking we are concerned with only two: hard and soft. Hard wheat is grown on the high plains—Montana, the upper Midwest, and the Southwest. Deaf Smith County, Texas, where Linda grew up, is noted for producing some of the best hard wheat in the nation. Soft wheat comes from the milder climates of the middle and eastern United States, with Illinois and Indiana harvesting the most soft wheat.

Hard wheat contains more gluten-forming protein than soft wheat and is best for yeast breads. Soft wheat flours, lower in gluten but higher in starch, are better used for fine-textured cakes, quick breads, and biscuits. Somewhere in the middle of the gluten scale are pastry flours, ideal for pies and tarts.

So-called all-purpose flours are varying mixtures of hard and soft wheats, milled to be used for all baking. If you're expecting the best results, however, you'll be happier if you use specialized flours. Modern milling methods have removed the necessity of sifting flour, and, in our experience, local mills or grocery store house brands seem to work just as well as nationally known brand names. What is important, however, is to know the *type*, rather than the brand, of flour you're buying.

Bread flour: "Bread flour" is the shorthand term for high-protein, enriched, bromated, white flour made from hard wheat that is high in gluten. Dough that's elastic and strong results, making a sturdy web to hold the carbon dioxide gases released by yeasts, thus yielding the most volume to the dough. Commercial bakers like bread flour not only for its gluten properties, but also because they believe it creates better-tasting bread. Breads made with bread flour will be flavorful, light, strong, and well risen. Bread flour has 13 to 14 percent protein content compared with 10.5 percent for all-purpose flour, so it's better for you too.

Bread flour absorbs more liquid than all-purpose flour. Our recipes have been tested with bread flour and call for it. If you're substituting all-purpose flour you may have to make some adjustment in the flour-liquid ratio, holding back a couple of tablespoons of liquid in the initial mixing process so that you don't end up with a too-sticky dough.

The potassium bromate that is added to "bromated" bread flour is what manufacturers call a dough conditioner. First used by commercial bakers to help dough stand up to machine kneading, it is particularly valuable to use bromated bread flour if you are using a food processor or bread machine to knead dough. You'll get more volume and a better texture. You'll find breads have a tender crumb and a finer grain when made with bromated bread flour.

Unbleached white flour: Our second choice for bread making is made from a combination of hard and soft wheat. All freshly milled "white" wheat flour is a pale tan color and must be whitened before use. *Unbleached* flour is allowed to age for several months, during which time natural oxidation causes the flour to whiten, whereas *bleached* white flour is chemically whitened. Unbleached flour has the added advantage of a slightly higher protein content than bleached all-purpose, plus it retains the vitamin E that is leached out during chemical whitening. The aging process used with unbleached flour also improves the bonding characteristics of gluten, giving you stronger, more elastic doughs that will produce breads with higher volume.

All-purpose enriched white flour: The most common commercially milled white flour, it is, by law, vitamin enriched to replace nutrients lost in the milling and chemical bleaching process. A combination of hard and soft wheat, it can be used in any recipe calling for white flour. But because it is a "one-size-fits-all" blend, the results will not be as rewarding, whether you're making a cake or a loaf of bread. Use bread flour for bread. Cake flour for cake. You'll get the best results.

Instant-blending flour, sold in shaker cans, is made from flour that's been combined with water, then dried and pulverized into an instant-blending powder. Splendid for soups and sauces, it is not suitable for bread baking.

Self-rising flour, all-purpose flour combined with baking powder and salt, is sometimes used for biscuits, but it isn't suitable for yeast-bread baking or recommended for quick breads because the leavening can be out-of-date.

Gluten flour is a high-protein wheat flour that is practically starch free. You'll find controversy over its use. Occasionally used by itself for low-carbohydrate diet bread, gluten flour is mainly used to lighten heavy doughs, such as rye or whole wheat. The problem with gluten flour is that there are poorly defined standards for its production, so that what you buy in Minnesota as gluten flour may vary from what is sold in Florida. The gluten flour we have used here in Oregon has been a boon to our bread baking. We find that the addition of a tablespoon of gluten flour per cup of heavy flour will create a dough that rises as nicely as a hot-air balloon on a May morning. You may have to make a fine adjustment in the liquids when adding gluten flour to a recipe, but feel free to add it to lighten any whole-grain bread.

Whole wheat flour: Milled from the entire wheat kernel, the best kind to buy—from a nutritional standpoint—is stone-ground (see illustration page 76). Stone grinding is an ancient process that crushes the entire wheat berry; endosperm, bran, germ, and husk between heavy stones turned by waterpower, and this flour retains all the taste and nutrition of the wheat berry. No artificial nutritional enrichment is added. If you are lucky enough to have access to stone-ground whole wheat flour, you will find it heavier than commercial whole wheat flour. Commercial whole wheat flour is a recombination of parts from milling: white flour, germ, and bran. The presence of bran reduces gluten development. Breads made with all whole wheat will be heavier than those made with white flours. Stone-ground whole wheat flour is more perishable than chemically treated white flour. Buy only what you can use in a short time and store in a cool place—the refrigerator or freezer in the summer.

For more on storing flours, see page 7.

Graham flour: Finely milled whole wheat flour that includes the bran, graham flour was developed by—guess who—Dr. Sylvester Graham, a Presbyterian minister who, during the early part of the nineteenth century, advocated it for its ability to cure intemperance. In Graham's book *Treatise on Bread and Breadmaking*, he advocated not only whole wheat flour but also loose clothing, fruits and vegetables in the diet, and sleeping in fresh air. Even though temperance may not be the goal in the nineties, we must agree the old preacher was on to something for a healthy life.

Rye flour is made from rye berries and is available in light, medium, and dark. Boxed rye from the supermarket is generally medium and may be used in any recipe in this book. Dark pumpernickel flour is sometimes available and is simply rye that's coarsely ground with bran particles and husk left in. This creates that almost black, chewy Eastern European–style bread. If you can't find pumpernickel flour, you can use a combination of rye, white, and cornmeal to approximate the taste and texture (see recipe page 68). You'll find rye doughs sticky, tacky, sometimes downright sullen. Although rye is high in protein, it is low in gluten, creating breads that are quite dense. Mixing rye with wheat flour, using half again as much wheat as rye, will create a lighter loaf. A tablespoon or so of gluten flour will lift a rye loaf as well.

Semolina flour: Pale yellow and granular, this flour is made from the endosperm of durum wheat. Durum, or hard, wheat is milled, removing the bran from the berry before grinding into flour. When the largest particles of the endosperm detach, they're known as semolina. Pulverized, this endosperm makes a fine flour. Generally found in pasta, semolina is also used for Mediterranean breads.

Other grains: Cracked wheat, wheat germ, whole wheat berries, and buckwheat, or kasha, are sometimes added to bread dough for taste and nutritional reasons. Remember to soak wheat berries so they don't dislodge your fillings. Buckwheat, which is a Russian grain usually found in blini and buckwheat cakes, may be ground in a blender and gives a splendid taste when added to whole wheat bread.

Potato flour: Sometimes labeled potato starch, potato flour is made from cooked potatoes that are dried, then ground into a flour that will ferment rapidly and, when added to wheat flour, will create a dough that rises quickly.

Cornmeal: Use either white or yellow, but try to buy stone-ground meal that contains the flavorful and nutritious corn germ.

STORING FLOURS

Flours absorb objectionable odors and love to make a home for fluttering kitchen insects, so it is most important that you buy fresh flours and store them properly.

Shop in a store that has a high turnover. Flour purchased at a neighborhood convenience store is most likely to be old and weird tasting. If you can locate a grocer who stocks baker's supplies in bulk and seems to cater to home *boulangers*, by all means get your baking supplies there. Look for date codes on boxed flours.

Once you have the flour home, repackage it in an airtight, opaque canister and store in a cool cabinet. We sometimes recycle glass jars with good seals, remembering to store the flour in a cabinet that is dark as well as cool, since the jars are transparent. If you buy a large supply of flours, say from a mail-order house, you can double wrap the flour in plastic freezer bags and store it in the freezer for more than a year without loss of flavor or utility.

If you buy a variety of flours and repack them when you get home, be sure to leave some sort of identifying label in the flour. More than once, we've placed flour in a tin and were sure we'd never forget what it was, only to stare in wonderment at it 6 months later with no memory of its origin. This leads to interesting, never-to-be-replicated mystery breads, but only for those who are true swashbuckling bread adventurers. They can all be grouped under the heading of "God knows breads."

Professional bakers look at flour with a more discerning eye than the rest of us. They're quick to point out that flour you bring into the house will sometimes seem lumpy, sometimes as dry as house dust. The absorbent property of flour means that flours you buy—even if they're the same brand and type—may not always contain the same amount of moisture. This is why you may have to adjust the ratio of flour to liquid in a recipe. The pros don't measure by volume but by weight to account for this variation in moisture content. But we home bakers just limp along, adjusting our recipes rather than hauling out the kitchen scales.

When Linda's grandmother bought flour for use on a ranch 75 miles from the nearest store, she bought it in 100-pound sacks. Even on the desiccated high plains of Kansas, weevils would hatch in the flour and flutter about the kitchen. Grandmother's solution to weevils was to sift them out of the flour and press on. If you find weevils in flour you buy, just stick the flour in the freezer for 48 hours or so and kill the little suckers. Then sift and press on. Diana does what Heloise recommends. She sticks a couple of bay leaves in the flour. Apparently bugs hate bay leaves as much as Dracula hates garlic. When you examine flour that's been stored awhile, you can tell if you have bugs if you notice that the flour moves: it's resettling into spaces made by the bugs' movement.

Liquids

Plain water, milk, beer, and sometimes yogurt or cooking water from potatoes or dried fruits are all used to moisten the flour (thereby activating the gluten) and to activate the yeast. When using the food processor to knead breads, remember that eggs, cottage cheese, oils, soups, honey, molasses, or any other viscous additions must all be considered part of the liquid.

Warmed liquids begin both the gluten and yeast activation processes more quickly. For our method, adding the liquid to a food processor bowl full of dry ingredients, we like to say use liquids the temperature of hot tap water (about 120°F to 130°F). This means water so hot you can barely hold your hand under it. Remember never to pour really hot liquids (over 140°F) directly onto yeast or you will kill it. Always mix yeast thoroughly with flour and other dry ingredients before pouring in hot liquids. Yeast, however, being the temperamental beast that it is, will also shrink in the presence of cold liquids and refuse to work at all.

The microwave is a perfect device for warming most any liquid called for in a recipe. About a minute, with the oven set on high or 100 percent power, will raise a cup of most refrigerated liquids to that hot tap water temperature (about 120°F).

Yeast breads made with water as the only liquid tend to have a crisp brown crust and an intense grainy flavor. These breads, French bread, for example, are always best if eaten the day they are made, for they have poor keeping qualities. Milk in breads creates a creamier texture and a loaf that will last longer.

You may run across old recipes that call for scalding milk. Raw milk requires heating because it contains an organism that breaks down gluten. Unless you're using milk from a cow in your backyard, you never need scald milk. If you do use scalded raw milk, remember to cool it down to about 120°F before adding it to the bread dough, or you'll kill the yeast.

Nonfat dry milk plus water has been found to improve the cell structure of breads and cause them to have a stronger web and a sturdier lift than breads made with homogenized milk instead. You can always substitute regular milk for nonfat dry milk plus water in recipes: For each 2 tablespoons of nonfat dry milk plus ½ cup water (or whatever liquid the recipe calls for) you can substitute ½ cup regular milk. Using whole milk in these cases, you can expect a slightly smaller, more dense loaf. Add nonfat dry milk to the other dry ingredients, then add the appropriate amount of warm water.

The first bread machine recipes always called for nonfat dry milk for its strengthening characteristics. Through testing and experimentation we have been able to accommodate the particular demands of the bread machines so that every recipe doesn't require dry milk.

Evaporated milk is a good choice for bread baking in that it produces a creamy loaf with a slight caramel undertone to the taste. If you dilute this milk with half water, it will perform much like homogenized milk in the loaf.

Buttermilk makes a marvelous tangy bread. If you're not in the habit of buying it, you can always sour a cup of milk by adding 1 teaspoon plain vinegar to it, or keep powdered buttermilk on hand. One cup water plus ¼ cup dried buttermilk equals 1 cup liquid buttermilk. Using the food processor, simply add the dried buttermilk with the other dry ingredients, then add the appropriate amount of hot tap water.

Any kind of milk added to bread dough counteracts some of the acidity produced by the fermentation of yeast and can result in doughs that require a slightly longer rising time.

If you buy yeast in bulk, you can quickly determine if it's outdated by proofing it. Combine 1 tablespoon yeast with ¼ cup warm (105° to 115°F) water and ½ teaspoon sugar. Stir and let dissolve for about 5 minutes. If the liquid bubbles and swells, the yeast is active.

If you've made the horrifying discovery that your yeast is dead after a batch of dough has stubbornly refused to rise and lies petulant in the bottom of the bowl, don't despair. By adding fresh yeast, you can simply start over, without wasting the ingredients in the bread dough (see page 36).

To bring the dough back to life, using yeast you are *sure* is alive—because you have proofed it as described above—add this yeast mixture to the dough and incorporate by rekneading in the food processor for another minute. You will probably have to add a tablespoon or so of flour to achieve the proper smooth, satiny texture that a well-kneaded ball of dough should have. Now, you simply proceed to microrise again, as described in the recipe.

If, like us, you occasionally forget to reduce the setting on the microwave to the appropriate microrise power and you kill the yeast in the dough in the first rising, you can likewise salvage the dough by adding more proofed yeast, rekneading in the food processor, and microrising again, using the proper reduced microwave power setting.

Yeast

The leavening in breads that makes them rise and become lighter than the original dough, yeast is a living fungus that feeds on the starch in flour and on sugar, giving off carbon dioxide gas and alcohol that is then trapped in the glutenous web made by the flour and water. When well-risen bread dough is put into a hot oven, the yeast gives off one last push, raising the bread up to 25 percent higher still. Then the heat kills the yeast. Bakers call this *oven spring*.

Commercial yeast comes in several forms. Active dry yeast is by far the most common. Sold in foil packs containing 2½ teaspoons each—or enough for one or two 1-pound loaves of bread—this stable yeast was developed during World War II for the convenience of the army.

Dehydrated yeast cells, living but dormant, become active in the presence of warm water, flour, and sugar. Yeast can be used without sugar; it then feeds off the flour alone, but the taste will not be as well developed.

Fifty-percent-faster active dry yeast is a hybrid developed in answer to queries from the public for faster bread. This genetically engineered yeast is not only a different strain from regular active dry yeast, it is also more finely ground. It is ideal for use in the food processor. The method of combining yeast with the dry ingredients, then adding a 120°F liquid, was developed for this type of yeast. However, using a food processor to blend and knead dough, we find these two types of yeast interchangeable, both in measure and method. You needn't fret if you can't find 50-percent-faster yeast. You may have to make some modest adjustment in the time allotment using active dry yeast. Dough will, at times, take a little longer to rise in the microwave, although the time differences are slight.

Bread machine makers recommend active dry yeast for use in machine-made breads. Consult your owner's manual for suggestions on interchanging yeasts in the bread machine. Fleischman's RapidRise Yeast is the most readily available of the 50-percent-faster-yeasts, and we have had great success with it. We have also tested some splendid European instant-yeast strains that are available through mail order from Williams Sonoma (see appendix, page 337) or through specialty stores in major cities. These yeasts give a reliable quick rise to breads of all kinds.

Both active dry and 50-percent-faster active dry yeasts are found in foil packs, in jars, and in bulk wherever bread supplies are sold. The packs and jars are date coded. Check the code and buy only what you can use before the yeast is outdated. Store dry yeasts in the refrigerator.

The original yeasts were wild and are now seen in what we know as sourdough (see pages 258–259 for more on sourdough). The first commercial yeasts were sold in fresh cakes, each ⅗-ounce cake being equivalent to 2½ teaspoons active dry or 50-percent-faster active dry. Although we know bread mavens who swear this compressed fresh yeast produces a better-tasting loaf, we can't taste it. Compressed fresh yeast keeps only about 2 weeks in the refrigerator. If you'd like to try it, take care to purchase yeast that's within its pull date and use it promptly. Throw out any that has lost its nice tan color or become gray or moldy looking.

Brewer's yeast is not a leavening agent. Sold in natural and health food stores for nutritional purposes, don't try to substitute it for baker's yeast.

Salt

Salt strengthens the web made by gluten and controls the action of yeast as well as adds flavor to the breads. If you make salt-free bread, it will be less stable, really light, and can taste bland and flavorless. Ordinary table salt is what we've used to test these recipes. If you prefer kosher salt, you may find you need to add up to a third more to achieve the same taste. The usual ratio of salt to flour is ¼ teaspoon salt for 1 cup flour.

If you're on a salt-free diet, experiment by adding herbs, seeds, or other tasty spices to your favorite loaf of bread. Remember to start with a small amount of additive.

Sugar

Not only does sugar add a sweet taste to breads, but it also feeds the yeast. So even in breads that don't seem sweet at all, you're likely to see some sugar in the list of ingredients. Once yeast feeds on sugar, it ferments, forming the gas that makes bread rise. Sugar also makes a tender bread and contributes to a good grain and texture as well as to a golden brown crust. For variety and color, you may substitute maple syrup, honey, brown sugar, or molasses for sugar (see page 14).

Do not use confectioners' sugar in baking. The small amount of cornstarch it contains to prevent caking will throw off the measurement and lend a peculiar taste to baked goods.

Nonsweet white breads usually have from 1 to 2 tablespoons sugar just to feed the yeast. Sweet doughs may have up to ¼ cup per loaf of bread.

Eggs

Eggs contribute flavor, color, nutritional value, and a richness to bread that cannot be duplicated by any substitution. In this book all recipes call for grade-A large eggs unless otherwise indicated. A large egg measures about ¼ cup in volume. If you'd like to add eggs to improve the nutritional content of your bread, remember to displace a like volume of the other liquid in the recipe.

If you are concerned about cholesterol, you can substitute a like volume of egg white, that is, ¼ cup egg white to substitute for every egg called for in the recipe. The resulting bread will not have the golden hue or the rich taste that egg yolks contribute but will be free of the cholesterol that egg yolks contain.

One simple way to warm up an egg is to cover the unopened egg with hot tap water and allow it to stand a few moments before cracking it into the other ingredients. In most recipes, though—unless several eggs are called for—it's OK to add refrigerated eggs to the dry ingredients.

If you wish to halve an egg in a recipe you're reducing, break it into a cup, whisk a moment, then measure off half: about 2 tablespoons. Give the rest of it to the cat, or save it to glaze the loaf.

To store leftover egg whites, place them in a covered jar in the refrigerator for up to 5 days. For longer storage, you may freeze them in an airtight container for up to 3 months.

Egg yolks require more careful storage, or they'll develop a hide as tough as boot leather. Place them in a small container, cover with a little water, then cover tightly. They'll keep 3 or 4 days in the refrigerator. Yolks don't freeze well.

To separate eggs, work with cold eggs to prevent the yolk from breaking. Using a knife or the edge of a bowl, crack the egg, then either pass the yolk from shell to shell, letting the white fall into a waiting bowl, or—more foolproof but gooshy—drop the egg into the palm of your hand and allow the white to drip through your fingers. If you are separating several eggs, use two small bowls for breaking and separating the eggs and one bowl for collecting the whites. Work with one egg at a time, breaking it and separating the yolk and white into the two bowls. Only after you have successfully separated the egg, pour the white into the third bowl. Because the bad news is that one drop of egg yolk mixed in with the egg white will prevent the whites from whipping up to even a froth. If a yolk breaks into the white, just dump the whole thing in with the yolks and don't count that egg. You can always have scrambled eggs for supper.

Fat

Even though fat has become an abominable notion in the nineties, a small measure of fat in bread makes a big difference in taste and texture. Fats in all foods carry flavors, and this certainly holds true for bread.

Fats make breads softer, giving them a delicate crumb, and a lovely golden crust. They also help breads to keep. Any recipe you see that is laden with fat is likely to produce bread that stays moist and mold-free for up to a week, if properly stored. Think about fat-free French bread. It's only good the day it's made.

Butter, vegetable shortening, oils from the most flavorless cooking oil through olive oil and up to a punchy walnut oil make valuable contributions to breads. With the exception of highly flavored oils, fats in breads are interchangeable, measure for measure, whether liquid or solid. We frequently call for canola oil, which is made from rapeseed and is cholesterol free. If you can't find it, substitute any vegetable oil.

We prefer unsalted butter because it makes a fresher, sweeter product and also because it gives you more control over the total amount of salt in the recipe. We've specified unsalted butter in all the recipes. If you're using regular salted butter, you might want to back off on the salt called for in the recipe just a bit.

Old loathsome lard makes some of the best country breads there are. If you can buy good, fresh lard, by all means try it in a hearty whole-meal bread. The taste and crumb will be marvelous.

Solid vegetable shortening can be used in any recipe, measure for measure, as a substitute for butter. You'll lose that buttery taste, and yellow cast to the crumb, but the same tenderness will remain.

Always taste fats before adding to make sure they're not rancid. Nothing can ruin a loaf of bread quicker than old oil.

About Substitutions

You'll notice we usually specify bread flour rather than all-purpose or unbleached white flour. Eckhardt's cardinal rule for cooking is *Never let the lack of an ingredient stop you from trying a recipe. SUBSTITUTE.* Who knows, you might invent a better recipe than the one you read about in the cookbook.

What this means is if you don't have bread flour, experiment. Use what's on hand: unbleached white, all-purpose, what have you. The differences between flours are too subtle to let not having the specified kind hold you back. (To learn more about flours, refer to "Ingredients" on page 4).

We've also differentiated between the types of yeast called for in the Micro-Rise process and in the bread machine recipes. Although we call for 50-percent-faster yeast for micro-rising and regular active dry yeast for the bread machines, do not hesitate to substitute. (To learn more about yeasts, see page 10.) In the Micro-Rise process, yeasts are interchangeable, measure for measure, although there are subtle differences in the time and lift you'll get with each yeast.

If you wish to use 50-percent-faster yeast in a bread machine, consult your manufacturers' instructions. Bread machines are programmed to use active dry yeast and, like Hal in *2001*, your machine's computer can become confused if you deviate from the norm. Each manufacturer deals with this issue in a different way.

Many of our recipes call for sugar (see page 11), but we often substitute maple syrup, honey, brown sugar, or molasses. Remember maple syrup and honey are twice as sweet as sugar, and only half the volume of either should be used to replace sugar in a recipe. Brown sugar or molasses can be substituted measure for measure. Reduce other liquids in the recipe if you're using liquid sweeteners.

Eckhardt's rule also applies to equipment. If you don't have a pan of the size called for in a recipe, use what you have. Who knows? You might make a more dazzling-looking loaf than we ever dreamed of. The only caveat about bread pans is that if you use a metal pan, you can't put it in the microwave oven for the final rising.

We encourage you to read about ingredients, about equipment, about the technique. Making bread the Micro-Rise way is a new craft, and it's something like switching from a typewriter to a word processor. The more you understand about the basic principles before you start, the more pleased you'll be with the outcome.

EQUIPPING THE HALF-TIME KITCHEN

When Linda's grandmother traded in the trusty black wood cookstove that had dominated her kitchen for a sleek, white natural-gas range, it was an event in the family.

This grandmother was a famous cook in western Kansas and had actually started out her married life in a prairie dugout with the same black, fire-breathing behemoth set square in the middle of the only room in the house. As a bride, she had tamed that wood stove, turning out fantastic cakes, breads, biscuits, pies, sometimes using cow chips she had gathered herself for fuel. So a kitchen range that could be fired up with just the turn of a dial seemed like a miracle.

She got up early to start the dinner. Looking at the sleek, white, art nouveau, thirties-style gas range, she felt like the very picture of a modern housewife.

Bustling around, she got everything together, got the bread kneaded, the turkey stuffed, the pie crusts rolled.

It was time to bake. She smiled fondly at her gleaming new stove. She turned the dial. Simple. Then, fumbling around for a match—looked like Grandpa had taken off with the matches again to light his pipe in the backyard—she fussed around and finally dug one out of the catchall drawer.

Then she opened the oven door and arranged the turkey on the shelf. Maybe there was room for a loaf of bread too. She placed the loaf thoughtfully. Just right. Now she'd start to cookin'.

Scratching the long kitchen match against the bottom of her shoe, she moved her hand toward the open mouth of the new white oven. *Boom!*

Grandmother found herself sitting on the other side of the kitchen. The windows had blown out. The turkey had become a wet bomb that had exploded all over the kitchen: walls, floor, ceiling. Her eyebrows were singed off. The smell of burning hair was everywhere. Grandmother had a lot to learn about gas.

New kitchen appliances may not knock you on your can, but they do require some getting used to. We made quite a few leaden doorstop loaves before we refined the Micro-Rise technique, using a food processor and microwave oven, into a reliable system that would work again and again to produce a glistening, light loaf of bread.

The thing that threw us was that the computer-driven machines in our kitchens called for different skills than we had when we started.

Mainly, you have to tune yourself up. Kneading with a food processor takes only a minute. Raising bread in the microwave takes only fifteen. You need to get yourself into this new rhythm of kitchen chores. The basic thing to learn is that kneading goes fast, raising goes fast, and you must be ready to do the next step.

Think of it as learning to do the tango. Once you relax, listen to the music, master the steps, and find the right partner, you'll never be content just to walk.

Here's what we learned about our new partners, the equipment necessary for the half-time kitchen.

Buying a Food Processor

Almost 20 years ago, Cuisinart made a fundamental change in the way we worked in the kitchen. We learned to chop, to purée, to grate, and to knead using this kitchen wonder. But food processors have proliferated, mutating over time, until the choices in the store make it difficult to make a decision.

What kind of food processor do you need to knead? First of all, choose a heavy-duty machine that is capable of turning heavy dough for at least a minute. We also prefer a large bowl, at least an 8-cup capacity (which will handle a dough made with more than 4 cups of flour). It is, however, possible to knead dough (2 cups plus) in a small heavy-duty food processor with a 4-cup capacity bowl, like the early-model Cuisinart. You may have to divide the dough and knead it in parts, but then you can knead the dough balls together by hand after each part has had a minute in the machine.

The Braun Multipractic Deluxe food processor has proved to be a workhorse for us. It has an enormous bowl, a variable-speed motor, and a capacity for handling more than 4 cups of flour in the heaviest, most sluggish dough. It's also a good buy, because standard equipment includes a set of adjustable disks for shredding and slicing, as well as a whisk attachment and a heavy-duty kneading blade and dough hook. Our only quarrel with this machine is that the wide feed tube is hard to figure out. Looks like you need an engineering degree to manage it. Once Linda got it assembled wrong and shot shreds of cabbage all over the kitchen instead of into the bowl—shades of grandmother.

We also have run the legs off a Cuisinart, which is powerful, quiet, and reliable. With its 1-horsepower motor it can handle the heaviest doughs. However, our quibble with this machine is that after a while the drive shaft reams out the blade fitting and will seize, making it impossible to remove the blade from the base of the processor. One friend of ours boxed up her Cuisinart and sent it back to Connecticut, with food in the bowl, because she couldn't get the blade off the drive shaft nor could she remove the bowl from the base of the machine. Now that is frustrating.

One of the changes that's taken place in the food processor business is that many sizes are now for sale. We have loved a small 3-cup capacity Black & Decker ShortCut food processor. For grating cheese, chopping onions, or kneading 2 cups of flour into dough for a pizza crust, this little ShortCut is well named. Not only is it easy to use, but, because it is small, it is easier to clean. A breeze to rinse out, not too big for the countertop or dishwasher, a real honey in the kitchen.

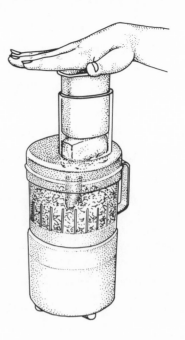

Most food processors come with a plastic dough blade as well as a steel blade. The plastic blade seems to work best for short pastry and dough. It is heaven for pie crust. But in our experience the plain old steel blade works best for kneading yeast doughs. We use a plastic dough blade or metal dough hook only for fruit-studded doughs because the fruits will remain whole while being kneaded.

Which Microwave Should You Buy?

Although we considered ourselves to be old hands with microwave ovens when we started this project, we learned a lot—the hard way. Between us, we must have made enough dough bricks to build a house. What we were doing was cooking the yeast, and the dough wouldn't rise. We had a time figuring out how to set our microwave ovens low enough to use them as proofing cabinets.

We believe we've refined the Micro-Rise system so that you'll get bread, not bricks, the first time out. But you'll have to have the right microwave oven to do it. (Instructions for figuring out your microwave oven's correct Micro-Rise setting appear on page 35.)

Strangely enough, the smaller the microwave, the harder the job is. A 400-watt microwave oven with only two settings cannot be used. The lowest setting on this machine is too hot and will cook the yeast. You can get by with a 500-watt oven, but you'll probably have to use the lowest setting, and you may even have to reduce the heating time to *2 minutes* instead of 3.

You need to choose a microwave oven with infinitely variable power settings or, at least, power settings in increments of ten. A machine with only five power settings may or may not work.

We suggest an infinite-setting, 1-cubic-foot capacity (or larger), 600- to 700-watt microwave oven with a carousel to prevent hot spots. You'll have the greatest control and flexibility with this large-capacity oven.

But even if you restrict yourself to these features, the machines are far from standardized, and there are vast differences from brand to brand and model to model in terms of directions, explanations, capacities, and capabilities.

Diana's Panasonic expresses the power settings in wattage. If you set such a machine at 200–250 watts, it's just right for the micro-rise system. Linda's Quasar expresses power settings in percentages. For her machine a setting of 20 percent power, called "low," is maximum for our technique.

We learned very quickly that one microwave's "defrost" is another one's "cook." Don't listen to the words. Listen to the numbers. Get out your instruction book and read. And get out your dough and experiment.

We went to a local retailer who sells a dozen different brands and tried out various machines and read different manuals. It was amazing to see the differences in the way ideas were expressed and in the suggestions given.

Whenever we could find any reference to raising dough in the microwave oven, we found the instructions to be inadequate and sometimes just plain wrong. We called up the Microwave Institute and were told that there is so little standardization from brand to brand that even the institute cannot come up with standard instructions for maintaining a setting as low as that required to raise yeast dough.

We knew we were plowing new ground.

Ovens

On the conventional oven front, we prefer electric over gas because the heat is more even and the results are more predictable. Whatever oven you have, we suggest you buy an independent thermometer to check against the thermostat. It is not uncommon for ovens to be off by as much as 50°F. Professional kitchens have their ovens calibrated monthly. It's simpler for the home cook to make adjustments using a thermometer.

Most breads bake best if placed in the middle part of the oven or above. The heat is greatest at the bottom of the oven and radiates up. Don't use a cookie sheet that covers the whole shelf in the oven either, or you'll interfere with the air circulation.

Some recipes call for you to heat the oven as high as 500°F, then turn the oven down as soon as you put the bread inside. This will help to get a crisp, beautiful crust.

Whenever you're beginning to bake, arrange the shelf in the oven before you preheat, and open the oven door as little as possible to place the bread inside. If you have a glass door in your oven, turn on the light inside and look through the glass rather than opening the oven door to check on the bread's progress. Aha. Caught you. Yes. You'll have to clean off that glass if you mean to look through it. Every time you must open the oven door to check on the bread, add 5 minutes to the cooking time to make up for the time lost from that blast of cold air you allowed into the oven.

Work Space

Fortunately, it doesn't take much space to make bread, even if you are using machines. A 24-inch square will suffice to knead and shape the dough into loaves or rolls. A 12-by-6-inch place on your countertop will accommodate most food processors. If you're really cramped for space, hang the microwave on the wall. Attach shelving securely to the studs and get that appliance up and out of the way.

The work surface can be made from a variety of materials. Our very favorite is marble. In one kitchen we have a real marble countertop. In the other, a higgledy-piggledy rectangular scrap of marble about 14 by 18 inches that came from a tombstone maker.

Marble provides a cool dispassionate surface that makes both kneading and rolling doughs a joy. Unless bread dough is unnecessarily tacky, it won't stick or lose the shape you create.

Our second-favorite choice for bread making is wood. We have a large butcher-block surface that also works estimably for kneading, rolling, cutting, and shaping dough.

Formica works quite well, although it will nick and cut if you're using a knife, sharp biscuit cutter, or dough scraper with too much alacrity.

Stainless steel is the surface of choice for commercial bakers because it passes all health department regs and because it's a clean, cool surface. We yearn for a piece of stainless countertop and plan to include it in the next kitchen remodeling job.

The only remaining caveat about the work surface is its height. Thirty-six inches is the standard height of most countertops. If you are a standard person this may be well and good, but here's how to tell if this is the right height for you.

Extend your arms and rest the heels of your hands on the edge of the countertop. If your arms feel comfortable in this position, 36 inches is the right height for you. (Think of yourself as a clock that reads four o'clock. Your head is the 12. Your hands are the 4.)

If you're taller, you may find a standard countertop too low. In this case you'd do well to invest in a piece of maple butcher block an inch or so thick to give you a countertop surface that's the right height.

If you're shorter than average, you may find you have to bend your arms too much to get the palms of your hands on the countertop. What can you do short of sawing off the cabinets? Stand on a sturdy wooden box that lifts you up high enough so you can extend your arms. Wear high heels. Do *something* to get yourself up there so you'll be comfortable in your own kitchen.

Utensils

When it comes to which utensils to use for the Micro-Rise process, one simple principle obtains: Use things that can go from the food processor to the microwave, from the microwave to the oven, and from anything into the dishwasher. If you've cut your kitchen time in half, the last thing you want is a sinkful of dirty dishes. We tried hard to streamline all operations so that you'd have as few items to wash as possible.

We did buy some special equipment for the Micro-Rise process. We also made use of some old friends we've had for years.

Knives: We've invested in several bread knives. One that cost more than $50. Granted it works like a charm, but so does the Ginsu knife we ordered from late-night television. The idea is to have a long enough knife with the kind of serrated edge that looks like moons. Allow the bread to cool, then gently saw it apart. We're ashamed to admit it, but we even got out the sixties gewgaw from old weddings: the electric knife. It works admirably to cut homemade bread.

Ovenproof glass measures: One of the most useful things for the microwave and food processor you can own is a set of three nested glass liquid measures. A 1-cup, 2-cup, and 1-quart glass measure will provide you with both mixing and cooking utensils that can go into the microwave and out. The handle stays cool, the lip is useful for pouring, and—because the measures are transparent—you can watch through the window of your microwave to see what's happening. Is the water boiling? Has the butter melted? Did the dough rise? We use these measures constantly.

Ovenproof glass measures are useful for the food processor as well. Pouring liquids through the feed tube is made easy by hooking the lip of the glass measure over the top, then slowly drizzling in the liquid. You can easily control how slowly you wish to add the liquids in this way, watching the dough absorb the liquid, so that you don't add too much and make a batter instead of a dough. And, if you need to heat the liquid before adding it to the flour, you've got a piece of equipment that goes into the microwave and over to the food processor with no trouble at all.

Baking Equipment

Our main aim here is to have pans that can be used both in the microwave for micro-rising and in the conventional oven. We prefer ovenproof glass and are especially smitten with Pyrex's new Clear Advantage, which is a coated glass that requires no greasing. Breads pop right out of the pan after cooking. Quite amazing. Really.

Plastic microwave ovenware that can go from the microwave to the conventional oven works too. We love our Rubbermaid tube pan for making bubble loaf.

You can always substitute a metal pan where we've used a glass one, but you'll have to do the final rise in a warm draft-free place rather than in the microwave oven.

Rummaging through our pantries, here's what we found:

2 ovenproof glass loaf pans, 8½ × 4½ × 2½ inches
1 ovenproof glass cookie sheet
1 rectangular ovenproof glass baking dish, 13 × 9 × 2 inches
1 rectangular ovenproof glass baking dish, 11 × 7 × 1½ inches
1 round 3-quart ovenproof glass casserole dish
2 round 9-inch ovenproof glass cake pans
1 round 9-inch ovenproof glass pie pan
1 9-inch round metal springform pan
1 microwavable plastic tube pan
1 microwavable plastic muffin tin, 6 cups each, ½-cup capacity
Clay bakers: La Cloche, loaf pan, pizza stone

Baking with Clay

We recommend the use of clay for the Micro-Rise process. These utensils can go from the microwave into the oven, and will give excellent baking results.

We've just discovered the joy of baking on a stone rather than in a baking pan. You can use unglazed quarry tiles or a pizza stone for this purpose. The way it works is this: you preheat the oven with the stone or tiles in place on a middle rack or just above for at least a half hour before placing the bread in the oven to bake.

Form the loaf for its final rise on a surface sprinkled heavily with cornmeal so that you can slide it off onto the hot baking stones. You can buy a wooden pizza peel (see below) or use a cookie sheet with no sides, or even a plain old piece of cardboard. The idea is to have a surface that's so smooth and flat the bread will slide right off onto the hot cooking stone. This takes some practice but makes a crust you'll never forget. If you wish to micro-rise the bread a second time, choose a flat surface that is microwavable and will fit into the microwave. We've had good luck with the back side of a glass cookie sheet sprinkled with cornmeal. It fits in the microwave, and with the lip turned down instead of up, it gives you that ball-bearing-slick surface you need to slide the bread onto the hot baking stones.

Another way to combine micro-rising with the baking stone is to use parchment paper: line the floor of your microwave (or the rotating disk) with parchment paper, sprinkle with flour, and place the shaped dough directly on the paper. Micro-rise. Then carefully slide the paper onto a peel (or piece of cardboard) that has been sprinkled with cornmeal. Then carefully slide the risen dough *and paper* onto the hot stone. In 10 minutes you should be able to pull the paper right out from under the bread. Do so, but be careful you don't burn yourself.

When placing the pizza stone in the oven, allow the back of the stone to touch the back wall of the oven so that when you shovel the bread onto the hot stone, it can't slide off the back and create a disaster on the oven floor.

Pizza stone: The even heat distribution and moisture absorption you get from baking on a pizza stone produce the very best baking results—crisp, golden crusts and a texture to the bread that is even, fine, and sturdy. Available from cookware stores, some take-out pizza places, or by mail (Sassafras Enterprises, Inc., 1622 W. Carroll Avenue, Chicago, Illinois 60612), a pizza stone is made from clay that's been fired at temperatures over 2,000°F and can withstand the hottest oven temperature: It can also withstand freezing temperatures and can be used in the microwave. Don't use a clay baker of any kind over an open flame, however. That will break it. And all clay utensils will break from thermal shock. Don't place a hot stone in cold water or on a marble slab. Conversely, don't transfer a clay baker from the freezer directly to a hot oven. This is old-fashioned unglazed clay, not new-age Pyroceram. Some pizza stones are sold in metal racks that also go into the oven.

You never need to grease a pizza stone. The cornmeal you've placed on the pizza

peel (see "Pizza Peel," below) will transfer with the bread or pizza to the stone. To clean, soak the *cool* pizza stone in plain water and scrape off food with a metal spatula or wire brush. No need to use soap. It could leave an aftertaste. Air dry the stone and place it in the oven, or store it in the pantry. The stone will change color with use, but this will not affect its utility.

You can, if you wish, lift the pizza on the stone out of the oven and serve it directly from the stone. Remember that the stone retains heat a long time and will continue to cook the crust some, even after it's removed from the oven. If you're eating outside, this can be a distinct advantage in that it will keep the pizza hot. However, that same heat retention also means you can burn your fingers for a good while. Be careful.

If you lift a hot pizza stone out of the oven, take care that you don't set the rack over a fine wood surface. There's enough heat still in the stone to discolor and ruin the finish of your dining room table. Place the hot stone over protected furniture only.

You can cut a pizza right on the pizza stone without worry about scratching or marring the surface.

Quarry tiles: Buy unglazed tiles from a cookware store, catalog, tile store, or lumberyard. Get enough to make at least a 16-inch square in the oven. Arrange the tiles on an oven rack placed in the middle of the oven. Preheat for at least 30 minutes before placing the bread on the hot baking tiles.

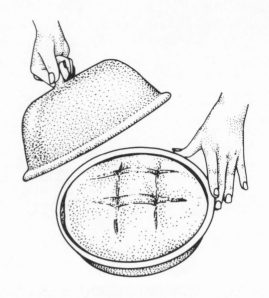

Clay baker: Sassafras (see address under "Pizza stones," above) makes a wonderful clay baker called La Cloche that can be used to imitate a French baker's oven. You can cook high, round loaves of French country bread (see page 69) in this wonderful clay bell. We adore it. Sassafras also sells clay bakers in the traditional loaf shape and in rounds.

Pizza peel: A wooden paddle, thin as a shingle—and really rather fragile—is the tool of choice to shovel bread onto hot quarry tiles or a pizza stone. You can also use the peel to remove baked bread from the oven.

Sprinkle the peel generously with cornmeal—organic ball bearings—and give the bread a trial shake before you open the oven door to make sure the bread will slide freely from the peel.

If you're using the peel for pizza, here are a couple of tricks we've learned. Place the stone or quarry tiles against the back wall of the oven so that when you shovel the pizza into the oven, it doesn't get a chance to fly off the back end of the stone.

If you're putting round things on top of the pizza, say whole black olives or cherry tomatoes, leave them off until the pizza is in the oven. It's one of those old laws of physics. Break that inertia by jerking the pizza off the peel and the edible balls just won't stop. They'll roll off the pizza and wind up on the bottom of the oven to burn and make a terrible mess.

The other thing to remember when using a peel is that if you have a hole in the pizza dough, so that liquids can seep through, they'll make a glue spot and that damn pizza will not move. One drop of tomato sauce on that peel and the pizza sticks like hot chewing gum.

To keep the peel in good condition, don't get it wet. Don't rest it on a hot surface—like the top of the kitchen range. It will chip. It will crack. Don't cut pizza on it or leave it in the oven with pizza on it to keep warm. It warps. Use it to shovel pizza in and out of the oven, then wipe if off with a barely damp cloth and hang it to store, so that its razor-thin edge is protected.

If you can fit a jerry-rigged peel in the microwave, you can micro-rise breads or pizzas for the final rise. Otherwise, just place the peel with the bread loaf or pizza in a warm, draft-free place for the final rise.

Water sprayer: Most loaves of bread that are cooked on a stone or on clay call for a crisp, golden crust. To get the jump on that crust, leave the dough uncovered for the final rise, and spritz the loaf with water just before placing it on the hot stone in the oven. A clean plastic spray bottle filled with plain water can be used for this.

Spritz the oven, too, five or six times during the first 10 minutes of the baking process to imitate the steam found in commercial bakers' ovens. If you're baking on cookie sheets and don't have a pizza stone or quarry tiles, spritzing water into the oven will help you approximate results the pros get. Even if you are cooking on a stone, a spritz of water crisps the crust. Open the oven just a crack and shoot the water into the top portion of it, closing the oven door as quickly as possible, so as not to cool it unnecessarily (see illustration page 48).

MICRO-RISE BAKING UTENSILS

Nested dry measuring cups: ¼ cup to 1 cup
Liquid measuring cups: 1 cup, 2 cup, 1 quart
Set of measuring spoons
Rubber and metal spatulas
Wire whisk or balloon whisk
Pizza-cutting wheel
Palette knife for spreading icing and fillings
Razor blade or sharp knife for slashing the tops of dough
Kitchen shears
Lemon zester
Dough or pastry scraper
Paint or pastry brush for spreading butter and glazes
Oven thermometer
Kitchen timer
Heavy rolling pin
Large wire rack

Parchment paper (baker's parchment)

Plastic wrap

Waxed paper

Tea towels

Oven mitts and hot pads

Nonstick spray

12-inch ruler

Doughnut cutter

Mechanical carousel (if not built-in on your microwave)

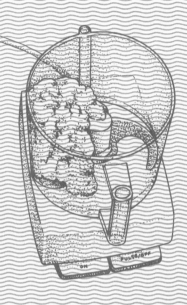

Micro-Rise Baking: Yeast Breads in Two Hours or Less Using the Microwave and the Food Processor

WHAT IS THE MICRO-RISE METHOD
FOR BAKING BREAD?

With the Micro-Rise method for baking bread, you can approximate the results that professional bakers get, using machines you have in your kitchen.

To learn this new craft of baking bread, you begin by adapting some traditional procedures for handling dough, where *hand* is the operative word, and let machines do some of the work. The food processor will knead the dough in a minute; the microwave oven will raise it in less than half the time it takes traditionally; the conventional oven will bake the bread as usual. The Micro-Rise method for baking bread takes 2 hours or less, with no more than 20 minutes' active work on your part. Decide to make bread at six, and you can have hot bread on the table for dinner at eight. It's that simple.

When you make yeast breads, you combine flour(s) with liquid and yeast, then transform these inert ingredients into a new, living creature that takes on a shape, texture, and taste through the process of kneading, fermentation, and baking.

Kneading releases the gluten in the flour so that the molecules can form a web to hold the gases released during fermentation. This in turn makes it possible for you to form the dough into fantastic and not so fantastic shapes that will endure even after exposure to the high heat in the oven.

Machine kneading improves the cell structure of yeast dough and makes a stronger dough for you to work with. Microwave raising takes some of the guesswork out of the fermentation process.

A professional baker kneads dough in a big Hobart mixer, then raises bread in a proofing cabinet where temperature and humidity are controlled and monitored. Then the baker bakes bread in a big Blodgett convection oven that may have steam injection as well. Using your food processor, microwave, and regular oven, borrowing professional techniques and secrets from the masters, you can learn to bake as well as many professionals.

MICRO-RISE BAKING: AN OUTLINE

Here are some general directions before you get started. First of all, look at your food processor. If you have a heavy-duty, small, 4-cup size, you can make one loaf that calls for no more than 2 cups of flour, or you can knead larger volumes of dough in parts. If you have a larger 8-cup size, you can make two loaves and use up to 3½ cups of flour.

Read your microwave directions. Then read the section called The "Appropriate Micro-Rise Setting" (see page 35). There you'll learn how to find the setting you'll use to raise the dough. Different brands give these settings different names. But the main idea is not to kill the yeast with too much heat. Finally, you will bake the bread as usual in the conventional oven.

We're going to walk you step-by-step through the machine-kneading and micro-rising processes. But first, here's an outline of the whole procedure:

Food Processor Mixing and Kneading of Bread Dough

1. Combine yeast with flour, salt, and sugar(s) in the bowl of the food processor fitted with the steel blade. Pulse to mix and aerate the dry ingredients. Add fats and pulse to mix until fats disappear.

2. Combine liquids in a glass measure and raise to the temperature of hot tap water (120°F) in the microwave set on high power (usually under a minute).

3. With the food processor motor running, add all the liquids to the flour mixture, holding back the last tablespoon or so to see if the dough will form a ball. Once the dough does form a ball that cleans the sides of the bowl, process for 60 seconds. Add the last portion of liquid only if necessary.

4. Remove the dough from the processor bowl, knead by hand a few seconds, then form into a ball. With your thumbs, punch a hole to form a donut shape. Remove the steel blade from the processor; place the dough doughnut back into the bowl. Cover loosely with a damp tea towel or microwavable plastic wrap. You can place this bowl directly into the microwave oven for rising.

Micro-Rising Bread Dough:
Learning the 3-3-3-6 Method

5. Position an 8-ounce glass of water in the back of the microwave, and reduce the power to the appropriate micro-rise setting (see page 35). Place the dough in the microwave and heat for 3 minutes. Let the dough rest in the oven for 3 minutes. Then heat again for 3 minutes. Let rest for 6 minutes. (The total time is 15 minutes.) By now, the bread dough should have doubled in bulk. If not, let it raise in the microwave, undisturbed, a few more minutes.

6. Remove the dough to a lightly floured work surface. Punch down the dough. Cover the dough with the processor bowl and let it rest a few minutes while you prepare the cooking pans. Then form into the desired shape for baking and place in the prepared pan. Without covering the dough, raise it to double in bulk. If you've used a microwave-safe cooking pan, place the shaped dough in the microwave and repeat step 5. Otherwise, raise in a warm, draft-free place.

7. Meanwhile, preheat the conventional oven as called for in your recipe. Soon your bread will be ready to go into the oven to bake as directed.

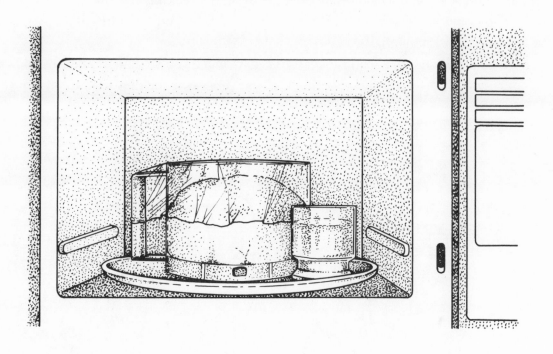

Using the Food Processor to
Knead Yeast Dough

Although we found recipes that called for different methods of combining the ingredients in the food processor bowl, we found—through trial and error—that the most reliable way is to place the dry ingredients in the bowl fitted with the steel blade, then pulse to mix. This aerates the flour and thoroughly mixes flour with salt, sugar, and yeast. Think of it as new-age sifting. Now, add the fat, pulse to mix until the fat disappears into the flour. Then with the motor running, pour in the liquid through the feed tube, holding back the last portion to see if the dough will form a ball.

When the dough balls up and rides the blade around, cleaning the sides of the bowl as it goes, you have just the right ratio of flour to liquid. You can make minor adjustments by adding flour or liquid by the tablespoon through the feed tube, keeping an eye on the dough ball as you go to see if it's cleaning the sides of the bowl.

At the end of the kneading period, open the lid and pinch up a piece of the dough. It should feel warm, tacky, elastic, satiny, and soft. Kind of like baby fat. If the dough is sticky, it's too wet. If it's hard, like a cannonball, you haven't added enough liquid. You can make fine adjustments either by kneading in more flour by hand, in case the dough is too wet, or for a too-hard dough by first breaking the dough ball into four pieces, then adding more liquid through the feed tube and kneading it in by machine to soften up the cannonball.

Kneading dough in a food processor is easy. Once you've done it a few times, you'll wonder how you ever got along without a food processor for this job.

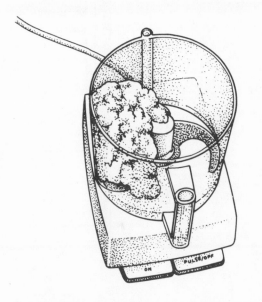 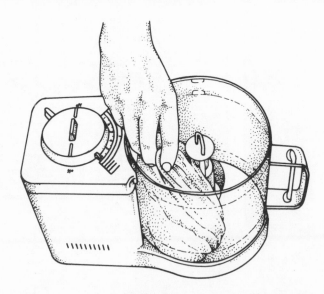

We caution that if you plan to add ingredients that you wish to be able to see in the finished product, such as raisins, pine nuts, fennel seeds, or basil leaves, don't try kneading them using a steel blade in your processor. They'll vanish. Knead in fruits, nuts, seeds, and leaves at the end, by hand, and you'll get those lovely little explosions of taste and texture in the final bread. If your food processor has a dough hook as the Braun has, you can knead fruits and nuts in by machine. The hook won't chew up the whole food additions.

If you begin kneading dough in the machine and the lights flicker, or the machine groans in complaint or jumps all over the counter, you've overloaded the bowl. Some machines have an automatic overload switch and will stop when the motor overheats. But you shouldn't wait for that. If you hear the motor lugging, stop, remove half the dough, and knead it in parts. A good rule of thumb is that the volume of the dough should never come up past the halfway mark in the bowl.

Once you've started counting to 60 for the single minute's kneading, turn the processor off promptly at the count of 60. The main drawback to machine kneading is that there's a risk of overkneading, which will result in a dry, coarse-textured bread.

One advantage to machine kneading, besides the fact that it is fast, is that you can work with a softer dough than you can by hand. You'll get better gluten development, and more lift to the breads, because you are better able to incorporate liquids into flour with the blade of the food processor than with your hands.

At the end of the kneading period, you can tell if you have the right ratio of flour to liquids when you remove the dough ball from the machine. The ball of dough should almost have cleaned the bowl. The cleaner the bowl, the more ideal is the ratio of flour to liquids.

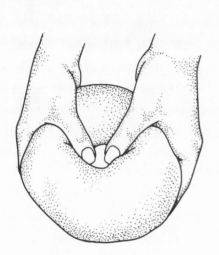 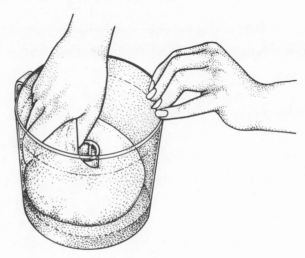

One of our earliest *Eureka!* discoveries about the Micro-Rise process was how well the food processor bowl works as a microwave rising bowl. After you've kneaded the dough, remove it and the steel blade from the machine, knead the dough by hand a few moments, form into a ball, then pull the dough into a doughnut shape by punching your thumbs through the center of the ball, then replace in the food processor bowl. You don't need to grease the bowl as you do when you make bread the old-fashioned way. If the dough is the right consistency, it will rise up in that food processor bowl as if that's what the bowl were designed for.

Cover the bowl loosely with a damp tea towel or plastic wrap and you're ready to micro-rise. The doughnut shape of the dough makes it easy for the microwaves to bombard the cells with life-giving energy to raise the dough right up in the food processor bowl.

But what if you don't own a food processor? Can you still use the Micro-Rise method? With certain modifications, yes. We both own Kitchenaid mixers with a dough hook and have found that machine does an admirable job of kneading dough. It takes 5 minutes, rather than 1 minute, to knead 3 cups of flour, yeast, plus liquid into dough, but you'll have a well-kneaded dough at the end of that period. Now, place the dough in a microwavable bowl, cover and micro-rise.

And should you want to work off your frustrations, or simply meditate, you can knead dough by hand. Fifteen minutes by the clock will equal a minute's machine time. We are the first to admit that it might be 15 minutes well spent. That warm, yielding dough, the yeasty aroma, the floury hands. It's an experience you ought to try.

Using the Microwave Oven to Raise Dough

Before you become a micro-rise master, you'll have to make some practice loaves. We'd suggest you begin with No Pain Ordinaire (see page 52). Follow the instructions up to the point of micro-rising the dough. Now you're going to figure out how to use your particular microwave oven as a proofing cabinet. If you have an instant or dough thermometer, get it out. If you have the owner's manual that came with your microwave oven, that may be a help too in determining the capacity of your oven. By experimentation, you will find the ideal setting for using your particular microwave oven to micro-rise yeast doughs. Now, refer to the box on page 35.

(We learned early on that the great equalizer was that 8-ounce glass of water. If you put a glass of water into the microwave oven and set the oven at 10 percent power, the water should pull off enough energy to bombard the dough to make it rise.)

The "Appropriate Micro-Rise Setting"
◇ A Simple Test ◇

1. Determine the wattage and capacity of your microwave. Read the instruction book. If you can't find the book, look for the serial number on the plate on the back or bottom of the machine.

- 600- to 700-watt microwave ovens can be set somewhere between 10 percent and 35 percent power, or around 250 watts, to micro-rise dough.
- 500-watt ovens usually will require the lowest setting, 10 percent power.
- Small-cavity ovens, regardless of the wattage, may require the lowest setting, 10 percent power, and may require a shortened heating time, 2 minutes.

2. Make a recipe of No Pain Ordinaire (see page 52), following the instructions up to micro-rising the dough. For the first test, *set your microwave oven at 10 percent power*, then raise the dough as directed. At the end of the first 15-minute rise, look at the dough. Did it double in bulk? Pull the dough out of the food processor bowl. Is it too hot to handle? Can you hold the dough in your hand comfortably? Take the dough's temperature if you like. It should read no more than 112°F. Ideally, the dough should be about 110°F.

3. If the dough is too cold, make adjustments in your microwave setting, punch the dough down, and repeat the test. If you found the dough too cool, under 100°F, raise the setting to 20 percent power for the second raising. If the dough was too hot, drop the time back to 2 minutes. If the dough doesn't rise at all the second time, excessive heat has killed the yeast. Add more yeast (see page 10), turn the microwave down a notch, and start over.

4. In testing your microwave oven, begin with the lowest setting and work your way up. This saves you from making doorstops instead of loaves you can eat. (See below for further discussion.)

We got the best results using a 700-watt, 1.1-cubic-foot oven with ten power settings. We set this Panasonic oven on 245 watts, called "defrost," or 35 percent, and used the 3-3-3-6 method to micro-rise the dough.

We tested many recipes with equally good results using a Quasar 700-watt, 1.35-cubic-foot oven with 70- to 700-watt infinite slide-control power settings. We set this microwave oven on 20 percent power, called "low." Anything higher than that cooked the yeast. We used a Whirlpool 650-watt, 1-cubic-foot oven with ten power settings. The setting for 30 percent worked perfectly. We also used a 500-watt, 0.6-cubic-foot Amana microwave oven by setting the machine on the lowest setting, 10 percent power.

What we noticed was that the smaller-capacity oven, with the lower wattage, demanded the lowest setting. Those microwaves have less space to bang around in in a small oven and will jostle the molecules in the bread dough more, heating it up faster. Watch it, or in a small-cavity oven, you'll have a fatal overheating.

If your microwave set on the lowest setting, or 10 percent power, overheats the dough at 3 minutes, try dropping the cooking cycle back to 2 minutes. Cook 2 minutes, rest 4 minutes, cook 2 minutes, and rest for 7 minutes. Pull the dough from the bowl. It should feel comfortably warm, never more than 112°F.

If you wish to raise dough outside the microwave oven, there are some good choices. Linda uses the top of the range while it's preheating. Diana has a built-in wall oven, so she's likely to take bread or sourdough starter to the closet in her house where the hot-water heater lives. (You talk about a warm, draft-free place.)

We've also heard stories of other places to raise bread quickly. One woman who uses an enormous Bosch mixer to knead dough, raises several loaves at one time by placing the bread dough on a heating pad wrapped in newspaper on the kitchen counter. Others use a conventional oven that's been preheated for 1 minute to 120°F, then turned off.

We got a letter from one woman who raises bread in her clothes dryer. Neither of us would dare try it. Sure as we placed bread dough in a warm preheated dryer, some other family member would come along behind us and throw in wet tennis shoes.

WHAT IF I'VE KILLED THE YEAST?

If you pull that dough out of the microwave oven and it's as hot as the proverbial hot potato, you don't have to throw the whole thing out and start over. You just need to add new yeast.

Make a mixture of an equal amount of yeast, as called for in the original recipe, say 2½ teaspoons, combined with ½ cup flour, 1 tablespoon sugar, and enough water to make a paste. Mix thoroughly with a fork, then machine knead this back into the original dough.

Now begin again. Micro-rise on a lower setting of your microwave oven. If you have set your oven at the lowest setting, have reduced the cooking time from 3 minutes to 2, and still cooked the yeast, forget it. Raise the dough in a warm, draft-free place instead.

"OR UNTIL DOUBLED IN BULK"

Although this phrase is used repeatedly in this and most bread books, the truth of it is you can tell the dough has risen to almost double simply by looking at it. The volume should be about double what it was when you placed the dough in the microwave. The dough will be humped up, the surface should be smooth and satiny, with gas bubbles visible just under the surface and around the sides. Or, use the easy finger-poke test. Poke your finger into the dough at the end of the stated rising period. If the dough springs back, it needs to rise some more. If the hole remains, the dough has risen sufficiently. In some cases, say when you're using whole grains or heavy flours, the dough will never actually be doubled in bulk. By and large, the darker the dough, the less likely that it will actually double in bulk. (See "Ingredients," page 4), for a detailed discussion of various flours and their rising properties.)

Bake Until Done

Breads can be tested for doneness three ways. First, insert a cake tester, wooden or metal skewer, or thin-bladed knife in the center of the loaf or one of the rolls to be tested. If it comes out clean or with a dry crumb attached, it is done. Second, you can test a yeast bread by tapping it with your knuckle. If the bread sounds hollow all the way through, it is more than likely done. Third, the internal temperature of most yeast breads is 200° to 210°F when done. This can be checked by inserting an instant-reading thermometer into the middle of the loaf after the loaf has been in the oven for the minimum recommended baking time. We think the knuckle test is the best choice for yeast breads.

Tapping bread is something like thumping watermelons. If you don't know what you're doing, you feel like a fool thumping away, listening intently, wondering what in heaven's name you're supposed to be hearing. Think of it this way. One of the main things that happens when you bake bread is that the liquids inside evaporate. If you thump a loaf that's done, it sounds hollow—because it mostly is. Tap a loaf that's still wet inside, and it gives off a dull thud. Don't ask us what to do about watermelons. It took us nearly a year to figure out about bread. We'll work on melons next year.

We occasionally remove a loaf of bread from a glass loaf pan only to discover that it's not done quite enough to suit us. We then simply place the loaf back in the oven directly on the rack to cook for 5 minutes or so. This not only finishes baking the loaf but improves the crust.

High-Altitude Baking

The higher you are, the easier it is to raise breads. At 5,000 feet, use only half the yeast called for in most recipes. We live and work at 1,000 feet, and the amount of yeast called for in our recipes reflects this altitude.

Making Bread in the Half-Time Kitchen

If you're an old hand at baking bread, we would like to point out a few differences between our process and the traditional one. For greatest lift and best results, bread doughs should be softer than those kneaded by hand (see page 32). When you have the proportion of flour to liquid exactly right, the ball of dough will lift out of an almost clean food processor bowl.

If the dough is too wet, it will stick to the sides of the food processor as you knead it. If the dough is not wet enough, it will form a globe as solid as a cannonball.

After you've kneaded the dough, pinch up a piece of it. The dough should feel warm, satiny, elastic, and soft. Your fingers should not stick to it.

After you micro-rise the dough for the first time, lift it out of the processor bowl and notice the temperature of the dough. If it feels too hot to handle, your microwave oven is probably set too high. The dough, after micro-rising, should feel warm as your best friend's forehead, provided your best friend doesn't have a fever. We don't think you need to resort to thermometers to check this out, but if you have an instant thermometer or a dough/oven thermometer, the temperature of a micro-risen dough should be no more than 112°F.

Storing Bread

Although we're the first to admit that homemade bread seldom gets stored in our kitchens, we have discovered that an old-fashioned bread box works like a charm. We found one from the thirties, a lovely art nouveau stainless steel number, that seems to keep bread forever. We're hunting thrift shops for its companion. If you're storing bread, be sure to cool it thoroughly first, then wrap in paper or plastic wrap, tie, fold, or twist shut, and keep in a cool, dark place. Although some people recommend the refrigerator, we find that it not only dries out bread, but can give it an off-taste. If you're planning to store bread for more than 2 or 3 days, we believe the freezer works best. If you know in advance you'll only be using the bread a slice at a time, cut it before you freeze it. Don't expect bread to keep more than a month in the freezer.

Reheating Bread

The first choice for reheating bread is the oven. Either a conventional oven or even a toaster oven. Wrap the bread in foil, place in a 350°F oven for a few minutes, then feel the bread to see if it's hot. Five minutes will usually do it.

One old-fashioned way to heat bread is to place it in a brown paper bag (free of inks that might contain toxic heavy metals). Twist it closed, then run tap water over the outside of the bag before placing it in the preheated oven. This will not only heat bread, but will rehydrate dried-out bread.

You can use the microwave to reheat bread provided you are careful. Overdo it and you've turned that bread into a tooth-breaking brick. Reheat single servings of bread wrapped in paper towel on 50 percent power for 15 seconds. Feel it. Is it hot enough? If not, repeat for another 15 seconds. When using the microwave to reheat, always divide the bread into serving-sized pieces. If you attempt to reheat a whole loaf, you're likely to harden the edges before the bread is heated through.

You can use the microwave to thaw frozen bread by following the same technique, except up the time to 30 seconds.

Giving the Spirit Shape

Bread can be made from the simplest ingredients: flour, salt, yeast, water. The fascinating aspect of making bread comes in learning techniques for making these simple ingredients transform themselves into myriad shapes, textures, tastes, and aromas.

The Micro-Rise method eliminates some of the time usually required for making bread, but still, if you want to enjoy the possibilities that breadmaking offers, borrow techniques from professional bakers for the raising, shaping, and baking of dough. You'll get the satisfaction of handmade bread and still save time.

Recipes in this book occasionally have a single rise, most usually two rising periods, and occasionally even three or four. The fermentation that takes place with each additional rising period changes the taste and texture of the bread.

You will also find variation in that some recipes call for the making of a micro-rise sponge. In the old days, when cake yeast was the most commonly available commercial yeast product, Grandmother mixed this yeast with flour and water into a batter and let it stand overnight before beginning to make bread. This batter rose and became light and spongy.

We like the finish of bread that comes from making a batter-thick sponge in the food processor, then micro-rising it, usually for a simple sequence of 3 on, 3 off, before adding the remaining ingredients to make the dough. This seems to jump start the fermentation process and improve the taste of many bread recipes with which we've experimented.

Regardless of the shape you want, you'll get the best results if at the end of the first or second micro-rise you follow this general procedure for forming dough into loaves. First, test to be sure the dough has risen properly:

• Poke the dough with your forefinger; if the dough has risen sufficiently, the indentation your finger makes will remain.

- If you're making bread using whole grains, the dough will not rise as high as dough made from bread flour. But you can still indent the dough with your finger, and it will still feel elastic, and when properly risen, the indentation will remain.
- Finally, if you pinch up a piece of the dough, it will feel spongy and light.

If you let the dough relax a few minutes before its final shaping, it will hold its shape better for the final rise. On a lightly floured surface, punch the dough down, cut into the number of pieces you'll be shaping for the final rise, then let the dough rest while you prepare the pans. Now's the time to grease those pans or sprinkle a pizza peel with cornmeal.

SHAPING BREAD DOUGH

Although we've given instructions for some basic shapes with the recipes, you can get a lot of variety by shaping the dough into different forms. Besides, that's the fun part. Hold the warm, elastic dough in your hands. Inhale the tantalizing fragrance. Take a little bite of the dough. Watch the dough take shape as you manipulate it on the board and into the pan. Bread is like the very spirit of nourishment, and it can take on a thousand forms.

To form a standard loaf: Using your palms, and fingers, flatten the dough into an oval about three times the width of the baking pan. Fold over the edges, as if you were making an envelope, folding the first side over to the center from the outside, and the second side over that. Place the loaf in the pan, seam side down, ends tucked under. This will give you a loaf that is higher in the middle and rounded on top.

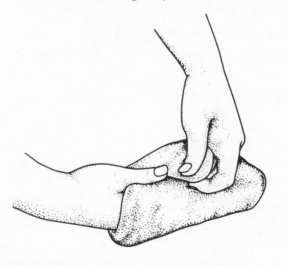

To form a high round loaf: Hold the dough in your left hand and begin folding it under with your right hand, making a mushroom cap, always tucking the dough toward the bottom center. Fold and rotate the dough at least ten times, so that you have a very compact, smooth mushroom-shaped dough ball.

Now lay the ball of dough sideways on a lightly floured surface, with the mushroom cap facing left. Place your cupped hand on the mushroom, and, applying pressure, skid the dough toward you. This will tighten and firm the dough ball. Turn and skid the dough at least ten times.

Tuck the end—which now looks like a whirlpool—under, and place the round ball on the prepared baking sheet, ready for its final micro-rise.

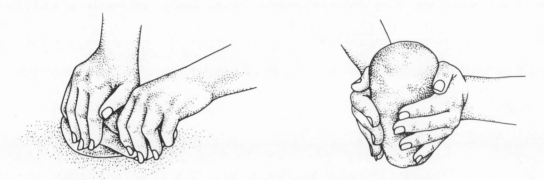

Pinwheel loaf: If you like buttery bread, use the plain bread or whole wheat recipe and make a savory pinwheel. Flatten the dough into a long rectangle as wide as the baking pan. Butter the dough. You can also sprinkle the dough with sweet or savory additions. Fresh herbs. Seeds. Cinnamon and sugar. Black pepper and cheddar. Use your imagination. Roll the dough evenly, then place it seam side down in the baking pan with the ends flat against the pan, not turned under.

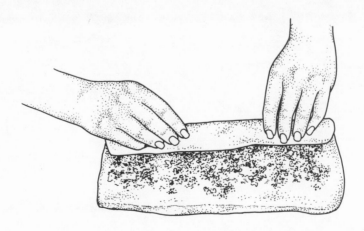

Pull-apart bread: Divide the dough into an even number of small roll-sized pieces. Shape each piece into a ball, coat it with melted butter, then pack it into the loaf pan, making a single row of balls for a small pan, and a double row for a larger pan. When the dough rises, each section should be about the thickness of a generous slice. Serve the bread warm, and pull the sections apart with a fork. The glowing bouquet of home-baked bread will fly up your nose.

Marble loaf: Make a recipe of white bread and a recipe of your favorite whole-grain bread, let them rise separately the first time, then form into a pair of two-toned marble loaves. Divide each recipe into four parts, then form into eight strands. Using two strands each of the two different kinds of dough, about half again as long as the pan you're using, lay two on top of the other two, checkerboard fashion, then twist. Place the bread in the pan with the ends flat against the ends of the pan, not turned under.

Coiled loaf: We particularly recommend this shape with rye breads. Pat the dough into a rectangle about twice the length of the diameter of a 9-inch cake pan, 18 by 5 inches, then fold in half, lengthwise. Roll up and place in the pan with the open side of the fold down. Pinch the end to fasten so the coil won't unroll. Brush generously with butter to keep the edges separate.

Baguette: Flatten the dough into an 8-inch oval. Fold the dough in half lengthwise by bringing the far edge of dough down over the near edge. Seal the edges by pressing the seam with your extended thumbs. Now roll the dough a quarter turn up, so the seal is on top. Again, flatten the dough into an oval. Press a trench along the center of the dough, fold the dough in half toward you again, and this time seal the edges by pressing

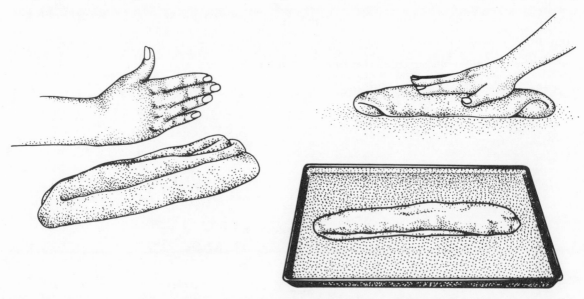

with the heel of your hand. Now roll the dough back and forth, sliding your hands along the length, making a long, 16-inch sausage roll. Place the dough, sealed side down, on a baking sheet or pizza peel for the final rise. Just before baking, make three quick, deep slashes in the top, holding the knife at a 45-degree angle.

Italian bread: Roll the dough into a 15-by-10-inch rectangle. Roll, jelly-roll style, until you have a 15-inch-long loaf. Taper the ends and stretch the loaf an inch or so. Pinch the seam to seal, and roll the loaf onto a prepared baking sheet, seam side down. Once the dough has risen, cut three or four deep diagonal slashes, holding the knife at a 45-degree angle.

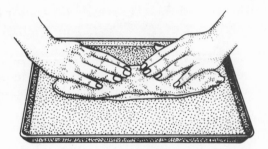

Braided loaf: For challah or any other dough of your choice, shape the dough into three equal 16-inch-long ropes by rolling on a floured surface. Lay the three ropes beside one another, then braid beginning in the *center* and working to the ends. Press each end firmly together and tuck under.

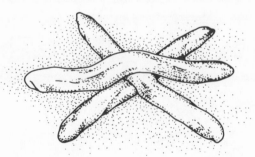
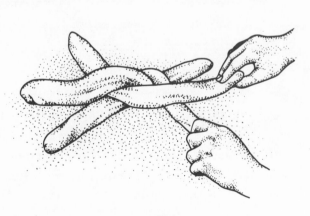

Take any of the roll recipes in this book and make them yours by forming the dough into different shapes. Here are some choices that assume you're working with dough made from 3 cups of flour. Make the rolls using the Micro-Rise process or the dough setting of a bread machine. The final shaping and rising can be done using the Micro-Rise method, or you can raise the rolls in a warm, draft-free place. Remember that because rolls are smaller than loaves, they raise quickly. Any of these rolls bake in a 400°F preheated oven for about 15 minutes, or until browned.

Knots: Divide the dough into a dozen equal pieces, then roll each piece into a 6-inch-long rope. Carefully tie each rope into a knot and arrange on a greased cookie sheet. Brush with melted butter. Cover to raise.

Crescents: Roll the dough into a 9-inch circle. Cut the circle into 12 wedges. Roll each wedge from the wide side to the point, curve the ends, and place the crescents on a lightly greased cookie sheet, with the point on the bottom. Cover to raise.

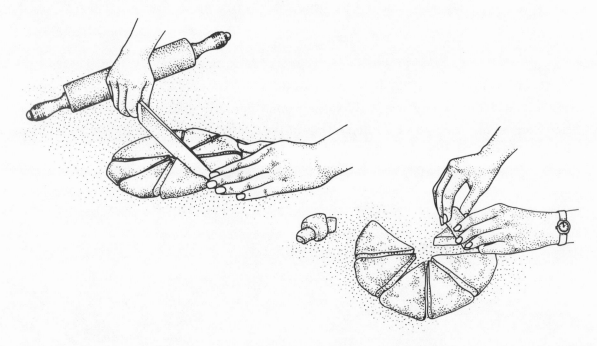

Pan rolls: Divide the dough into sixteen equal pieces. Form each piece into a ball by pulling the dough over your fingers, turning the ball, and tucking the dough under until you have a mushroom with a flat bottom. Dip each roll in melted butter, then arrange the rolls, flat side down, in an 8-by-8-inch baking pan, sides touching, and let them rise until doubled.

Pinwheels: Roll the dough into a 10-by-12-inch rectangle. Cut the dough into thirty 2-inch squares. Arrange on a lightly greased baking sheet, leaving an inch between the rolls. Cut each square from the corner to the center, 1-inch deep. Now you have eight points. If you wish, fill the center of each roll with a teaspoon of raspberry jam, or raisins and nuts. Fold every other point in to the center and press down. Brush with melted butter or egg glaze and allow to rise until double.

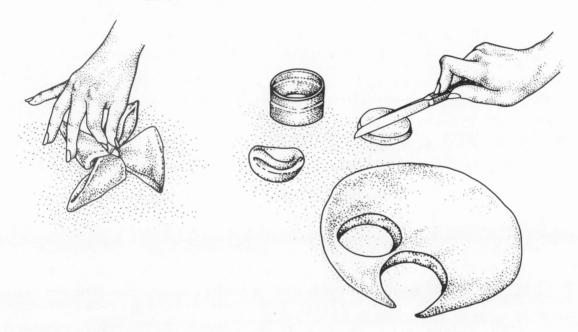

Parker House rolls: Roll the dough ½ inch thick. With a floured 2¾-inch cutter, cut circles. Knead the trimmings and cut more. Dip both sides into melted butter, then using a sharp knife dipped in flour, make a deep crease across the middle of each roll. Fold in half, and press edges together lightly. Arrange closely in rows, sides touching; cover and let them rise until doubled.

Cloverleaf rolls: Grease 24 muffin cups. Divide the dough into 24 equal pieces. Divide each piece into three small marble-size balls and place in the muffin cups. The dough shouldn't come more than a third of the way up the side of the cups. Brush tops with melted butter, cover, and let rise until doubled.

Fantans: Grease 18 muffin cups. Roll out the dough ⅛ inch thick. Brush the dough with melted butter. Now, using a pizza cutter, cut strips 1½ inches wide. Stack the strips at least eight layers deep. With a string or fishing line, cut off pieces about 1½ inches wide. Place the rolls in the prepared muffin cups, the cut edges up. Brush with melted butter. Let them rise until doubled in bulk.

Palm leaves: Sprinkle the work surface with a mixture of ½ cup turbinado sugar and 1 teaspoon ground cinnamon. Roll half the dough into a 6-by-18-by-¼-inch strip. Fold the two ends to the center so that you have a 6-by-9-inch sheet of dough. Fold again, bringing the ends to within ½ inch of the middle. Now roll the dough so that the fold is on the side. Cut into ¼ inch thick "palm leaves." Repeat this process with the remaining half of the dough, remembering to sprinkle the work surface with sugar and cinnamon first. Place the leaves on an ungreased baking sheet and allow them to rise.

Cinnamon snails: Grease 18 muffin cups. Roll the dough into a ¼-inch-thick rectangle. Spread generously with soft butter. Sprinkle with turbinado or brown sugar, ground cinnamon, chopped nuts, raisins, or citrus zest. Roll the dough, jelly-roll fashion, from the long side. Cut 1-inch-thick snails and place them in the prepared muffin cups. Brush with additional butter, sprinkle with more sugar, and allow them to rise until doubled before baking.

Finishing the Loaf

There are many ways to get different finishes on loaves of bread or rolls. You can decide whether you prefer a soft or crispy crust, whether you want the bread crust crunchy or buttery. Glazed or dull. Seeded or floured. There are many choices.

The simplest solution is to do nothing. Bread will come out of the oven with a crisp, dull finish and a lovely pale gold-brown color.

If you've added whole seeds, nuts, herbs, or other special flavoring ingredients, borrow a trick from professional bakers. Mist the risen dough with plain water or brush with an egg-white glaze, then sprinkle the top heavily with the same seed or nut that's in the bread. Not only does this make the bread look good, it prepares the taster for the flavor and texture of the bread. If you've used several seeds and nuts, you can either mix them, or you can place them on the bread in parts, or make a design.

We saw a terrific-looking loaf the other day, billed as prairie bread, that was simply a whole wheat, free-form, round loaf topped with an egg wash and a mixture of green pumpkin seeds, poppy seeds, and sesame seeds. The loaf was a mouth-watering, glazed mahogany round glistening with green, black, and tan seeds. The finish was what set this loaf apart from a plain loaf of whole wheat bread.

Another great-looking finish is achieved by rubbing whole-grain flour into a coarse cloth—say, terry cloth—then placing the cloth on top of the loaf as it rises for the final time. Remove the cloth, slash the loaf, and bake. This gives you that wonderful grainy, dusted look so appropriate on country-style high, round loaves with cross-hatching.

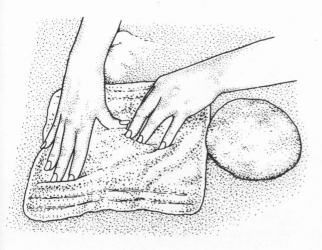
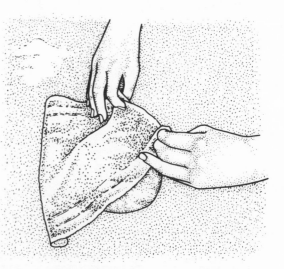

To slash loaves of bread, choose a very sharp knife or razor blade, hold it at a 45-degree angle, and make quick, sure, deep slashes in the bread after it's risen and just before baking. We make these slashes after we've sprinkled the top of the loaf with seeds or glazed or floured it. That way, the slashes stand out in an even more stark way.

For a soft crust, after baking rub the loaf all over with butter or margarine while the bread's still hot. The butter will melt and soften the crust, also adding a wonderful rich taste.

For a crisp crust, like you find in French bread, mist the oven with plain water several times during the first 10 minutes of baking. Don't open the oven wide. Just open it a crack and shoot the water to the top of the oven where it can fall down over the bread.

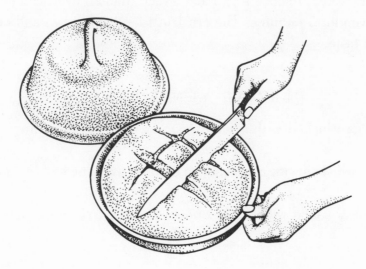

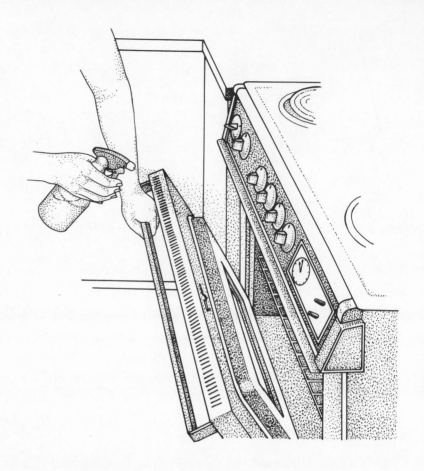

FOR CRUSTIER CRUSTS

If you love heels and crusts of bread the best, bake bread in a glass loaf pan; then when the bread is baked, remove it to a metal rack, dab all over with heavy cream, and replace in the oven for 5 minutes. The crust will be deep brown and crunchy and will have the richest taste.

GLAZING YEAST BREADS

1. Whole egg whisked with a tablespoon of water gives a shiny, medium-brown glaze.
2. Egg yolk whisked with a tablespoon of milk gives the shiniest mahogany-brown glaze.
3. Egg white whisked with a tablespoon of water gives a caramel shine.

1 ◆ BASIC BREADS

No Pain Ordinaire 52

Pane all'Olio 54

Pain de Mie 56

Anita's Sour Faux 58

Buttermilk Bread 60

Idaho Potato Bread 61

Challah 63

Our Daily Bread 65

Poppy-Seed Bread 66

Black Bread 68

French Country Bread in a Cloche 69

Deaf Smith County Wheat Bread 72

Uncle Larry's Beer Bread 73

Baking is a craft you can learn best by doing. Kneading bread dough in the food processor and micro-rising bread dough before baking in the conventional oven make the craft easier to master than ever before.

All yeast breads require the same sequence of tasks—whether made using a big bowl and your two good hands or the most modern equipment for kneading, raising, and baking.

The idea is to take flour, yeast, liquid, sometimes sweeteners and salt, then knead them to release the gluten in the flour so that a web will form to hold the gases that bubble up from the fermentation of the yeast. By following this sequence of tasks, you can create a light loaf of bread the old cowboys called wasps' nests.

Some breads require only one rise, most require two, and some require three. If, for some reason, you've allowed a dough to overrise, you can always punch it down and let it rise again. The taste of bread improves with every rising. In our method, most breads call for only two risings, but we've found that if we have the time to let the bread rest on the countertop after the first rise, even for 10 minutes, before the final shaping, we seem to get a better-tasting loaf of bread.

We've also discovered that you can make a sponge using half the flour and liquid with all the yeast, then micro-rise the sponge for about 6 minutes, 3 minutes on and 3 minutes off. This additional raising period seems to help flavors develop better.

Here is the sequence for making bread:

1. Combine flour with other dry ingredients, then add fat.
2. Add yeast and warmed liquids.
3. Mix and adjust flour-to-liquid ratio until the dough forms a ball.
4. Knead the dough to release the gluten and change the character of the dough into a smooth, satiny, elastic, soft ball.
5. Raise the dough for the first time until doubled in bulk.
6. Punch the dough down, then reknead a moment to release all gas bubbles.
7. If desired, raise an intermediate time in a ball or doughnut shape.
8. Deflate the dough, reknead a moment, form into a ball, and let the dough rest while you prepare the pans. (Allowing the dough to rest a few moments will permit the gluten to relax fully before you shape the dough for final rising and baking.)
9. Raise the dough for the final time to nearly double in bulk. Add glazes, seeds, slashes, or any other finishing touches before baking.

10. Bake until done.
11. Cool and store the bread.

To get started, we suggest you try No Pain Ordinaire (see page 52). It's easy. It's quick. It's Bread in Half the Time for sure.

Standard for a Perfect Loaf of Basic Bread

After you've baked your first loaf of bread, look it over. The top should be well rounded, with an even dark brown color. While the loaf is cooling, notice the gas bubbles on the edges of the bread. They should be fairly uniform in size.

Once the bread has thoroughly cooled, cut into it. The holes in the bread should be small and uniform in size from top to bottom. The interior should be soft and moist and easy to pull apart. The aroma should be yeasty and rich. If you've added nuts, raisins, or other fruits or seeds, they should be evenly distributed throughout the loaf.

Reheating bread in the microwave is simple when you follow 2 easy steps. First, always wrap the bread in a paper towel to absorb the excess moisture so it doesn't become steamy and rubbery. Second, don't microwave for more than 15 seconds on 50% power, or you will cook the bread again. If you prefer to reheat in the conventional or toaster oven, try wrapping the bread in aluminum foil then heating for 5–10 minutes in a preheated 350°F oven.

◇ **Half-Time Jams** ◇

Like all vegetables and fruits cooked in the microwave, jams processed this way retain their fresh flavor and color. Microwave energy heats from all sides, not just the bottom; therefore, the sugar does not scorch and needs little stirring. We recommend using powdered fruit pectin for thickening, since the fruit juices do not have time to evaporate in the short cooking time. Remember to use a large, deep casserole, because the juices boil up high. Watch the jam closely. Remove all casseroles from the microwave with pot holders, and lift off the lid away from you to avoid steam burns.

All jars and lids should be sterilized in a hot-water bath or washed in a dishwasher and taken directly from the dishwasher while hot. The United States Department of Agriculture recommends processing the filled and sealed jars in a water bath for 5 minutes before cooling and storing.

Strawberry Jam
◇ **Made Easy** ◇

*Makes approximately 8 cups
in 30 minutes*

*5 C. strawberries, washed,
hulled, and crushed*

NO PAIN ORDINAIRE

Makes 1 standard loaf in 1 hour

Good for the evening breadbasket, and the leftovers make excellent French Milk Toast (see page 109) the next morning. Children love it morning, noon, or night.

3 C. bread flour	*1⅛ C. (1 C. plus 2*
1½ tbsp. sugar	*tbsp.) hot (120°F)*
1 teas. salt	*tap water*
4 teas. 50% faster	*Unsalted butter or*
active dry yeast	*margarine, for a softer*
1½ tbsp. unsalted butter	*crust (optional)*
or margarine	

1. Fit the processor bowl with the steel blade. Combine and pulse to mix the flour, sugar, salt, yeast, and butter or margarine.

2. With the motor running, pour the hot water through the feed tube.

3. When the dough leaves the side of the bowl and forms a ball, knead with the machine running for 60 seconds.

4. Remove the dough and the steel blade from the bowl. Knead the dough a few seconds by hand, adding flour as necessary if it feels sticky. Form the dough into a ball. With your thumbs, punch a hole to form a doughnut shape and replace in the processor bowl. Cover loosely with a damp tea towel or microwavable plastic wrap.

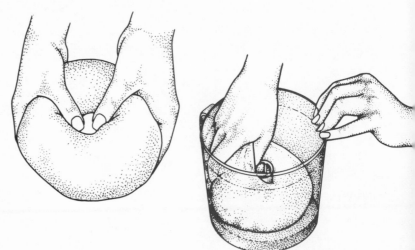

5. Place the processor bowl in the middle of the microwave. Set an 8-ounce glass of water next to it. To micro-rise, lower the microwave power to the appropriate micro-rise setting (see page 35). Heat for 3 minutes. Rest for 3 minutes. Heat for 3 minutes. Rest for 6 minutes or until dough has doubled in bulk. Meanwhile, lightly grease an 8½ × 4½ × 2½-inch glass loaf pan.

6. Remove the dough from the microwave and the processor bowl. Punch down and knead by hand a few seconds on a lightly floured surface. Shape into a loaf (see page 40) and place in the prepared loaf pan. Position the bread off-center in the microwave and the glass of water in the middle of the microwave. Repeat step 5. Meanwhile, preheat the oven to 400°F.

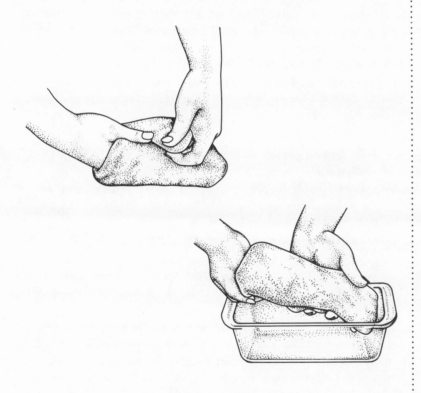

7. Place the bread on the middle rack in the preheated oven. Bake for 20 to 25 minutes or until the loaf sounds hollow when lightly tapped.

8. Remove the loaf from the pan and let it cool on a rack. For a softer crust, immediately rub the top of the loaf lightly with butter or margarine.

1¾-oz. box powdered fruit
    pectin
6½ C. sugar

1. Place the crushed strawberries in the bottom of a deep 3-quart casserole. Gradually add the fruit pectin, stirring well. Cover and microwave on 100% power 8 to 11 minutes, or until the mixture reaches a full rolling boil.

2. Add the sugar and stir well. Uncover; microwave on 100% power 8 to 11 minutes, stirring after 5 minutes until the mixture reaches a full rolling boil. Boil for 1 minute. Skim off any foam, and stir jam for 5 minutes before ladling into hot, sterilized jars. Wipe off the jar rims and seal with hot, sterilized lids or melted paraffin.

Golden Peach
◇ Jam ◇

Makes approximately 7 cups
in 30 minutes

5 C. peeled, pitted, and
    crushed ripe peaches
2 tbsp. fresh lemon juice
1¾-oz. box powdered fruit
    pectin
5 C. sugar

1. Place the peaches in a deep 3-quart casserole. Gradually add the lemon juice and pectin. Stir well. Cover and microwave on 100% power for 8 to 11 minutes or until the mixture comes to a full rolling boil. Stir for 30 seconds.

2. Add the sugar and stir well. Uncover and microwave on 100% power 7 to 10 minutes, stirring after 4 minutes until the jam reaches a full rolling boil. Boil for 1 minute. Skim off any foam, stir for 5 minutes, and ladle into hot, sterilized jars. Wipe off the jar rims and seal with hot, sterilized lids or melted paraffin.

We love this bread so much, we sometimes make a larger recipe and divide it into two *bâtard*-sized loaves. You could also make one long baguette. If your food processor can't handle this much dough, pull half of it out, and machine knead the dough in 2 pieces.

Makes 2 bâtards in 2 hours

4½ C. bread flour
  4 teas. 50% faster active
    dry yeast
1⅔ C. hot tap water (120°F)
2½ teas. salt
1½ teas. sugar
1½ tbsp. fruity olive oil

◇ **Muffuletta** ◇

Serves 6 in 5 minutes

This New Orleans sandwich originated early in the twentieth century. Drippy but delicious. Heaven with Pane all'Olio.

  1 C. pimiento-stuffed green
    olives, chopped
  1 C. Kalamata or other
    black olives, chopped
½ C. fruity olive oil
  4 oz. jar pimientos, chopped
½ C. fresh parsley, minced
  2 oz. tin anchovy fillets,
    minced
  2 tbsp. capers, drained
  2 cloves garlic, minced
  1 tbsp. fresh minced
    oregano or 1 teas. dried
Salt and freshly ground black
pepper to taste
  1 loaf or 2 bâtards Pane
    all'Olio
  4 oz. thinly sliced Italian
    salami
  4 oz. thinly sliced provolone
  4 oz. thinly sliced
    mortadella

PANE ALL'OLIO

Everyday Italian Olive Oil Bread

Makes 2 large rolls or 1 medium loaf in 2 hours

This is real bread, with a crisp, golden crust, a fine texture, and a sturdy web that will stand up to cheese or a smear of sweet butter.

Method is all here, for the list of ingredients couldn't be more basic. A micro-rise sponge to begin helps to develop the taste; then the use of traditional shaping and baking techniques, borrowed from the Italian bakers who invented this bread, helps you to approximate breads found only in Italian village bakeries.

For the best results, bake the loaves on tiles or a pizza stone (see pages 21–25), preheated 30 minutes. If you don't have either, bake the loaves on cookie sheets and mist the oven with water 5 or 6 times during the baking process to improve the crispness of the crust. Don't be alarmed by the long cooking time. It helps develop the crust and really won't burn the bread.

  3 C. bread flour,
    divided
2½ teas. 50% faster
    active dry yeast
  1 C. hot tap water
    (120°F), divided

  2 teas. salt
  1 teas. sugar
  1 tbsp. fruity olive oil

1. In the processor bowl fitted with the steel blade, add half the flour, all the yeast, and half the hot water. Process for 60 seconds.

2. Remove the steel blade, cover the bowl loosely with a damp tea towel or plastic wrap, and place the bowl in the microwave. Position an 8-ounce glass of water in the microwave, reduce the power to the appropriate micro-rise setting (see page 35), then micro-rise the sponge by heating for 3 minutes, then resting for 3 minutes.

3. Replace the steel blade in the processor bowl, place bowl back on the base of the food processor, and add remaining dry ingredients. Then, with the motor running, add remaining liquids, holding back the last small portion of the water to see if the dough will form a ball.

4. Process until the dough begins to leave the side of the bowl, forming a ball. Add the last tablespoon or so of liquid only if necessary. Knead 60 seconds, with the motor running, adding flour as necessary if the dough seems sticky. Pinch up a piece of the dough. It should feel soft, tacky, smooth, elastic, and warm.

5. Remove the dough and the steel blade and prepare to micro-rise. On a lightly floured surface, knead the dough by hand a few seconds. Form the dough into a ball. With your thumbs, punch a hole to form a doughnut shape, then replace in the processor bowl. Cover loosely with a damp tea towel or plastic wrap. Place the dough in the microwave.

6. With the water in place in the back of the microwave, and the setting still at the appropriate micro-rise setting, heat for 3 minutes. Rest for 3 minutes. Heat for 3 minutes. Rest for 6 minutes or until the dough has risen to about double in bulk.

7. Remove the dough to a lightly floured surface and knead by hand a few seconds. Divide the dough in 2 pieces, cover with the processor bowl, and let it rest for 5 minutes.

8. Preheat the oven with the pizza stone in place on the middle rack for 30 minutes at 450°F. Sprinkle a pizza peel (see page 24) or cardboard generously with cornmeal. Now, shape each piece into a cigar-shaped roll 7 to 8 inches long, fat in the middle, and tapered at both ends. Alternately, make one 12-inch cigar-shaped loaf (see page 40 for shaping hints). Place the rolls on the peel or cardboard for their last rising. Micro-rise, uncovered, repeating step 6, or raise in a warm, draft-free place until nearly doubled in bulk.

9. When the rolls have nearly doubled in bulk, make a single, deep slash at a 45-degree angle in the top of each one using a razor blade or sharp knife. Spritz the rolls with plain water. Give the rolls a trial shake before you open the oven door to make sure they'll slip onto the hot stone easily.

10. Slide rolls from the peel or cardboard onto the hot stone on the middle rack in the preheated oven and bake for 12 minutes at 450°F, then reduce temperature to 375°F and continue baking 45 minutes more.

11. Remove golden rolls immediately to a rack to cool. Wrap in a brown paper bag to store. This bread is best eaten the same day it's made.

1. Combine first 9 ingredients and season this olive salad to taste with salt and pepper. Cover and refrigerate overnight to allow flavors to marry.

2. To serve, first drain olive salad and reserve the oil. Slice the bread horizontally, forming a top and bottom. Remove centers of bread, leaving a 1-inch shell. Brush inside of shell with reserved olive oil dressing. Spoon half the olive salad into bottom half of the shell. Layer salami, provolone, and mortadella over. Spoon remaining salad into the top half of the bread shell, then close it quickly—like a clam. Wrap in plastic wrap, weight it with 5 pounds (say a 5-pound sack of sugar), and refrigerate at least a half hour. Can be made up to 6 hours ahead.

3. Cut the sandwich into thick slices, spear each sandwich with a bamboo skewer, and serve. This is a 2 paper napkin treat. Don't forget to pass the napkins.

Anchovy-Garlic
◇ Crostini ◇

Makes 24 hors d'oeuvres in 10 to 15 minutes

When the pantry holds a can of anchovies and yesterday's bread, the hors d'oeuvres are almost ready.

> 20 anchovy fillets, drained
>   2 cloves garlic, peeled
>   1 tbsp. fresh lemon juice
> Freshly ground black pepper to
>   taste
> ¼ C. olive oil
>   6 slices Pain de Mie
> Olive oil, for brushing on slices
>   3 tbsp. minced red onion,
>   for sprinkling on top

Garnish
Lemon wedges

1. Place the anchovies and garlic in the bowl of a food processor. Process until the anchovies are a paste and the garlic is chopped fine. Add the lemon juice and pepper. Continue to process while *very slowly drizzling* the olive oil through the feed tube. Process until all ingredients are the consistency of thick mayonnaise (about 10 seconds).

2. Lightly brush both sides of the bread slices with olive oil and place on a baking sheet. Toast under the broiler for 2 to 3 minutes or until lightly browned. Turn the slices over and spread with the anchovy-garlic paste. Return to the broiler and broil for an additional 3 to 5 minutes or until the topping bubbles and sizzles. Sprinkle with the finely chopped onion. Slice each piece of bread into 4 triangles. Serve immediately garnished with lemon wedges.

PAIN DE MIE

Pullman Loaf

Makes 1 standard loaf in 1 hour and 30 minutes

Pain de Mie, the French white sandwich bread, is used for making professional-looking canapés, appetizers, and fancy sandwiches. The bread is firm, close-grained, and fairly rectangular. The top is weighted while the bread is baking to give the bread true rectangular shape. Before the age of microwaves it took hours, plus you needed special pans. We have used a standard 8½ × 4½ × 2½-inch glass pan, then topped it with a larger 6½ × 9½-inch glass casserole, to make our Pain de Mie mold. You will also need a microwavable something to weight the top glass casserole. We used professional pie weights, but dried beans (you will not be able to eat them later) or a brick will do.

>   1 C. tepid milk,   2 teas. 50% faster
>   divided   active dry yeast
> 2½ C. plus 3 tbsp. bread   1½ teas. salt
>   flour   3 tbsp. unsalted butter
>   1 teas. sugar

1. Heat the milk in a glass measure to lukewarm (110°F) about 30 seconds on high power in the microwave. In the processor bowl fitted with the steel blade, add 1 cup of the flour, sugar, yeast, and ¾ cup of the milk. Process for 10 seconds to blend. Remove the steel blade from the processor bowl and place the bowl in the microwave to micro-rise the sponge. Set an 8-ounce glass of water next to it.

2. Lower the microwave power to the appropriate micro-rise setting (see page 35), and heat for 3 minutes. Rest for 3 minutes. Remove the processor bowl from the microwave. Place the processor bowl back on the base and fit with the steel blade. Add to the sponge the remaining 1½ cups plus 3 tablespoons bread flour, salt, and butter. Process until well blended, about 10 seconds.

3. With the machine running, *drizzle the milk very slowly* into the dry ingredients, holding back the last portion of liquid to see if the dough will form a ball.

4. Process until the dough begins to leave the side of the bowl, forming a ball. Add the last of the liquid only if necessary. With the machine running, knead for 45 seconds,

adding flour as necessary if the dough seems sticky. Pinch up a piece of the dough. It should feel soft, tacky, smooth, elastic, and warm.

5. Remove the dough and the steel blade, and prepare to micro-rise. On a lightly floured surface, knead the dough by hand a few seconds. Form dough into a ball. With your thumbs punch a hole to form a doughnut and replace in the processor bowl. Cover loosely with a damp tea towel or plastic wrap. Place the dough in the microwave.

6. With the 8-ounce glass of water in the back of the microwave and the microwave power still set at the appropriate micro-rise setting as in step 2, heat for 3 minutes. Rest for 3 minutes. Heat for 3 minutes. Rest for 20 minutes or until the dough has doubled in bulk. Meanwhile, lightly grease an 8½ × 4½ × 2½-inch glass loaf pan. Cut a perfectly smooth piece of aluminum foil 2 inches larger all around than the bread pan. Lightly grease the shiny side and set aside.

7. Remove the dough to a lightly floured surface, punch down, then knead by hand a few seconds. Form the dough into a loaf (see page 40) and place the dough into the pan. Using your knuckles, press the top of the dough flat and snugly into the corners. Cover the loaf loosely with clear microwavable wrap (not a tea towel, as you will not be able to see what is happening in the microwave). Preheat the oven to 425°F.

8. Place the loaf off-center in the microwave and an 8-ounce glass of water in the middle. With the microwave power still at the appropriate micro-rise setting, heat for 3 minutes, then rest for 3 minutes. The dough should rise three-fourths of the way up the side of the pan and no farther. Remove it when it gets to this point. If it still needs a little more volume, heat again for 3 minutes.

9. When the dough has risen sufficiently, remove it from the microwave and remove the plastic wrap. Cover the top of the pan with the aluminum foil, greased shiny side down. Place a 6½ × 9½-inch casserole dish on top and add weights to it.

(continued)

Makes 20 servings in 20 minutes

This year for our Fourth of July buffet, we made an Old Glory Sandwich using day-old Pain de Mie. We made the sandwich 4 hours before our Independence Day celebration began, then held it in the refrigerator so the flavors would marry. The durned thing tasted so good we had a few offers of marriage ourselves once the bachelors got the cream cheese wiped off their chins.

First we cut off the crusts, then sliced the bread horizontally into 5 equal pieces. We lightly coated both sides of each slice with butter, then arranged the fillings.

We used a layer of minced red onion, then a layer of shrimp pâté from the deli, then a layer of well-peppered red tomato slices, then a layer of deli salmon pâté, then a layer of thinly sliced cucumbers.

Once we'd layered the sandwich, we iced it with soft cream cheese. Now that we had a white-iced brick shape, we decorated it to look like a flag by piping cream cheese around the base, then making red stripes using minced red bell pepper and a field of blue using raw blueberries. We piped stars of cream cheese onto the blue field using a cake decorator.

We kept the minced red bell pepper in neat stripes by laying chopsticks on the iced surface, then pressing the bell pepper down in the row. Carefully, we lifted the chopsticks and voilà! Parallel, straight stripes of red.

We served the sandwich by slicing it vertically so that each person got a colorful ribbon sandwich filled with bright, punched up flavors. You could choose a layer of hard-cooked egg or a layer of caviar for this sandwich. Yum.

◇ Melba Toast ◇

Makes toast in 1 hour

Melba toast, the thin crackerlike bread used as a base for caviar, as bread for those dieting, and as teething biscuits for babies, can be made from day-old Pain de Mie.

Trim the crust from the bread and slice 1/16 inch thick. Layer the slices on a large baking sheet, overlapping slightly, and bake them in a preheated 275°F oven for 30 minutes. Turn the bread over and bake an additional 30 minutes or until crisp, slightly curled, and pale gold in color. Remove and cool. Store the toast in plastic bags or an airtight container. Melba toast in a tin makes a good gift.

◇ Garlic Spread ◇ For French Bread

Makes 1/2 cup spread in 2 hours

No book would be complete without a recipe for everyone's favorite, garlic bread.

- 1/2 C. (1 stick) unsalted butter, room temperature
- 1 clove garlic, peeled and crushed
- 1 tbsp. finely chopped fresh parsley (optional)
- 2 tbsp. freshly grated Parmesan
- 1 loaf Free-Form French Baguette or Anita's Sour Faux

1. Thoroughly combine the butter, garlic, parsley, if using, and Parmesan in a small bowl. Allow to sit at room temperature for 1 hour. Thirty-five minutes before serving, preheat the oven to 375°F.

2. Meanwhile, slice the bread into 1-inch-thick slices, cutting *to* the bottom of the loaf but *not* all the way through. Gently separate the slices and spread both sides

10. Place the loaf carefully on the middle rack of the preheated oven and bake for 40 minutes. Test to see if the loaf is done by tapping with your knuckles; it should sound hollow. Bake for an additional 5 minutes if needed.

11. Turn the bread out onto a rack to cool. The flavor and texture will improve if the bread is allowed to sit for 12 to 24 hours before using. Store cooled bread in a plastic bag or an airtight container.

For canapés the crust should be evenly trimmed from the entire loaf and the bread sliced thinly (this will be very easy to do if the loaf has had at least 12 hours to sit). The pieces can then be used as is or shapes can be cut with canapé cutters or cookie cutters, or cut geometric shapes with a sharp knife.

ANITA'S SOUR FAUX

Yum!

Makes 2 small loaves in 2 hours

The addition of a little rye flour to a standard French bread recipe gives it that sourdough bite that begs for Brie. These baguettes are best baked on a pizza stone or oven tiles.

- 3 C. bread flour, divided
- 2 1/2 teas. 50% faster active dry yeast
- 1 1/4 C. hot tap water (120°F)
- 1/2 C. rye flour
- 2 teas. salt

1. In the processor bowl fitted with the steel blade, combine half the bread flour with all the yeast and half the hot water. Process for 60 seconds.

2. Remove the steel blade from the bowl, cover the bowl loosely with a damp tea towel or plastic wrap, and place the bowl in the microwave. Lower the microwave power to the appropriate micro-rise setting (see page 35), place an 8-ounce glass of water inside, and micro-rise the sponge by heating it for 3 minutes, then resting it for 3 minutes.

3. After the sponge has become bubbly and light, put the bowl back on the base of the food processor, replace the steel blade, and add the remaining ingredients—bread flour, rye flour, salt, and the water. Drizzle the water in with the motor running, a little at a time, holding back the last portion of liquid to see if the dough will form a ball.

4. Process until the dough begins to leave the side of the bowl, forming the ball. Add the last liquid only if necessary. Knead 60 seconds, adding flour by the tablespoon, through the feed tube, as necessary if the dough seems sticky. Pinch up a piece of the dough. It should feel soft, tacky, smooth, elastic, and warm.

5. Remove the dough and the steel blade and prepare to micro-rise. On a lightly floured surface, knead the dough by hand a few seconds. Form dough into a ball. With your thumb, punch a hole to form a doughnut shape and replace in the processor bowl. Cover loosely with a damp tea towel or plastic wrap. Place the dough in the microwave.

6. With the 8-ounce glass of water in the back of the microwave, and the power on the appropriate micro-rise setting, heat for 3 minutes. Rest for 3 minutes. Heat for 3 minutes. Rest for 6 minutes or until the dough has risen to about double in bulk.

7. Remove the dough to a lightly floured surface and knead by hand a few seconds. Form into a ball, cover with the food processor bowl, and allow the dough to rest for 10 minutes.

8. Meanwhile, sprinkle a pizza peel (see pages 21–25) generously with cornmeal. With a pizza stone in place on the middle rack, preheat the oven to 450°F for at least 30 minutes.

9. Cut the dough in 2 equal pieces. Shape the dough into 16-inch-long baguettes (see page 42), and place on the prepared pizza peel. Raise until almost doubled in bulk, uncovered, repeating step 6 or using a warm, draft-free place.

10. When the dough has nearly doubled in bulk, make 3 deep diagonal slashes at a 45-degree angle in the tops of the loaves, using a razor blade or sharp knife. Mist with plain water, and bake on the hot stone in the preheated oven 10 minutes, then reduce heat to 375°F and continue baking 30 minutes more or until evenly browned.

11. Remove immediately to a rack to cool. Wrap in a paper bag to store. This bread is best eaten the same day it's made.

of each slice with the butter-garlic mixture. Re-form the slices into a loaf and place the loaf on a piece of aluminum foil large enough to wrap it completely. Place the wrapped loaf on a baking sheet and bake on the middle rack of the preheated oven for 25 minutes. Unwrap and serve at once.

Let us Break Bread Together— ◇ The French Way ◇

From the cradle, every French child is taught *le respect du pain*. In other words—don't waste the bread. Remember, the French Revolution began over bread. Take only what you can eat. When sliced bread is presented, if you can only eat a half piece, tear the slice in two.

If Madame makes bread pudding from the leftovers, act grateful. Even if you hate the stuff.

And when a long baguette is presented at the dinner table, you *break* off just what you require. Why break? A French etiquette book, *Regles du Savoir-Viver* (*Rules of Etiquette*), by Mme. Baronne Staffe, makes it plain—in a Gallic sort of way—"Pieces could, under the effort of the knife, jump into the eyes of the guests" or, the gods forbid, "on uncovered shoulders."

Mme. Baronne wrote her rules for Gallic behavior in 1889, but things are slow to change in France.

The French also disapprove of using bread to sop up the sauce. And, *ça ne se fait pas*, never make dough balls out of bread even in the excitement of discussing the Revolution. A fatal *faux pas*, say our French guides to fine dining.

Just so you'll know, the French also disapprove of loud talking, guffawing, drinking too much, and other displays of loss of control. Good thing they make good bread.

Yum!

BUTTERMILK BREAD

Makes 2 standard loaves in 1 hour and 30 minutes

The tang of buttermilk blended with a little sugar makes this the bread you wish your grandmother had known how to make. You'll notice this is a 2-loaf recipe calling for a lot of flour. If your food processor can't knead all this dough at once, pull out half and take 2 minutes to knead the dough in 2 parts, then knead it back together by hand.

1 tbsp. 50% faster
  active dry yeast
3 tbsp. sugar
5 C. bread flour
2 teas. salt
¼ teas. baking soda
1 C. hot tap water
  (120°F)
1 C. buttermilk
⅓ C. shortening

Glaze
  1 egg, lightly beaten

Sesame, caraway, or
  poppy seeds, for
  sprinkling on top
  (optional)

1. Fit the processor bowl with the steel blade. Combine and pulse to mix the yeast, sugar, flour, salt, and baking soda.

2. Combine in a 2-cup measure the hot water, buttermilk, and shortening. With the motor running, pour the liquid through the feed tube.

3. When the dough leaves the side of the bowl and forms a ball, knead with the machine running for 60 seconds.

4. Remove the dough and blade from the bowl. Knead the dough by hand a few seconds, adding flour as necessary if the dough is too sticky. Form dough into a ball. With your thumbs, punch a hole to form a doughnut shape and replace in the processor bowl.

5. Cover the bowl loosely with a damp tea towel or microwavable plastic wrap and prepare to micro-rise.

6. Place an 8-ounce glass of water in the middle of the microwave and set the processor bowl of dough beside it. Lower the microwave power to the appropriate micro-rise setting (see page 35). Heat for 3 minutes. Rest for 3 minutes. Heat for 3 minutes. Rest for 6 minutes or until doubled in bulk.

7. Remove the dough from the processor bowl, punch down, and knead by hand a few seconds. Turn the processor bowl over on top of the dough and let it rest about 10 minutes.

8. Meanwhile, preheat the oven to 375°F. Grease two 8½ × 4½ × 2½-inch glass loaf pans. Cut the dough into 2 pieces. Shape into 2 loaves (see page 40) and place in the prepared pans. Cover the pans loosely with towels.

9. Replace the pans in the microwave. Place the glass of water in the center and the pans off-center. Repeat step 6.

10. Just before baking, carefully brush the tops with the beaten egg and, if desired, sprinkle with the seeds (poppy, caraway, or sesame). Wipe away any egg that touches the glass pan (it sticks!). Discard leftover egg. Bake in the preheated oven 40 to 50 minutes, or until the loaves are golden brown and tap hollow on the bottom.

11. Remove the breads from the pans. Cool on a rack. Wrap in aluminum foil to store.

At the end of the cooking period, if the bread seems moist on the bottom, remove the bread from the pan, and place the loaf back in the oven on the bare rack for 5 minutes or so to ensure a crisp crust.

IDAHO POTATO BREAD

Makes 2 standard loaves in 2 hours

Fabulous!

Here's an old recipe with a new twist. No more boiling and mashing the potato the old-fashioned way. Just cook the potato in the microwave and "mash" it by processing in the food processor. Potatoes have been added as a dough conditioner by bakers who wanted to make a tender crumb and a more flavorful loaf.

One 4–5-oz. russet potato
5 C. bread flour
3 tbsp. sugar
1½ teas. salt
3½ teas. 50% faster active dry yeast

5 tbsp. unsalted butter, cut into tablespoon-sized pieces
¾ C. reserved potato water
½ C. milk

For extra flavor and crispness, try substituting ½ cup potato flour (potato starch) for 1 cup of the flour. The amount of liquids remains the same.

1. Peel and quarter the potato. Place the potato in a 4-cup microwavable measure and add enough water to cover. Microwave the potato uncovered on high power for 5 to 6 minutes or until a fork pierces the potato easily. While the potato is cooking, organize your ingredients, and grease well two 8½ × 4½ × 2½-inch glass loaf pans. *(continued)*

2. Remove the potato from the water and place it in the processor bowl fitted with the steel blade. Reserve the potato water.

3. Pulse the potato about 5 seconds or until it looks mashed. Remove the processor lid and add the flour, sugar, salt, yeast, and butter to the potato. Pulse to mix the dry ingredients.

4. In a 2-cup measure combine the reserved potato water and the milk. With the motor running, add all of the potato water–milk mixture except for about 1 tablespoon. The dough should leave the side of the bowl and form a ball. If it doesn't, gradually add the remaining 1 tablespoon of liquid ingredients, and the dough will form a ball. With the machine running, knead for 60 seconds.

5. Remove the dough and the steel blade from the bowl. Knead the dough by hand a few seconds, adding flour as necessary if the dough seems sticky. Form dough into a ball. With your thumbs, punch a hole to form a doughnut shape and replace it in the processor bowl. Cover the bowl loosely with a damp tea towel or microwavable plastic wrap. Place the processor bowl in the middle of the microwave.

6. To micro-rise, set an 8-ounce glass of water in the microwave and lower the microwave power to the appropriate micro-rise setting (see page 35). Heat for 3 minutes. Rest for 3 minutes. Heat for 3 minutes. Rest for 20 minutes or until dough has doubled in bulk.

7. Remove the dough from the microwave and the bowl. Punch down and knead by hand a few seconds on a lightly floured surface. Divide the dough in half and shape each half into a loaf (see page 40). Place the loaves, seam side down, in the prepared pans. Place the loaves off-center in the microwave and the 8-ounce glass of water in the middle of the microwave. Repeat step 6. Meanwhile, preheat the oven to 375°F.

8. Place the bread on the middle rack of the preheated oven. Bake 35 to 45 minutes or until the loaves are a golden brown and sound hollow when tapped.

9. Remove the loaves from the pans and cool on a rack. Wrap in aluminum foil to store.

CHALLAH

Makes 1 braided loaf in under 2 hours

A classic challah, richly braided egg bread, made by Jewish women as an act of meditation and in the service of God, is one of the most rewarding breads we know of.

Orthodox Jewish bakers pinch off a marble-sized piece of the dough and offer it up as a sacrifice by burning it in the fire. Lovingly braided, this bread is a joy to look at as well as to eat. We like it best when cooked on a stone (see pages 21–25). This produces the most even mahogany-colored crust and a tender, moist crumb that's so good we have to hide the leftovers if we want enough to make bread pudding (see page 233).

> A Book of Verses underneath the Bough,
> A Jug of Wine, a Loaf of Bread—and Thou
> Beside me singing in the Wilderness—
> Oh, Wilderness were Paradise enow!
>
> —Edward FitzGerald
> *The Rubáiyát of Omar Khayyám*
>
> ◇

1 teas. sugar
¾ C. hot tap water (120°F)
1 tbsp. 50% faster active dry yeast
3 C. bread flour
½ teas. salt
1 large egg
2 tbsp. unsalted butter or margarine, room temperature

Glaze
1 egg yolk plus 2 tbsp. water

Sesame or poppy seeds, for sprinkling on top

1. In a glass bowl combine the sugar, water, and yeast. Add half the flour and stir to mix, forming a sponge.
2. Place this sponge in the microwave oven, lower the microwave power to the appropriate micro-rise setting (see page 35), and place an 8-ounce glass of water in the back of the oven. Heat for 3 minutes, then rest the dough for 3 minutes or until spongy and light.
3. In the processor bowl fitted with the steel blade, combine the remaining flour with salt and pulse to mix.
4. Open the top and add the egg, butter or margarine, and sponge; process.
5. When the dough leaves the side of the bowl and forms a ball, knead for 60 seconds, adding additional tap water as necessary if dough seems too stiff.
6. Remove the dough and blade from the bowl. Knead the

(continued)

dough by hand a few seconds, adding flour as necessary if dough seems sticky. Form dough into a ball. With your thumbs, punch a hole to form a doughnut shape and replace in processor bowl. Cover loosely with a damp tea towel or microwavable plastic wrap and prepare to micro-rise.

7. With the glass of water in the back of the microwave and the microwave power still set as in step 2, place the dough in the microwave. Heat for 3 minutes. Rest for 3 minutes. Heat 3 minutes. Rest 6 minutes or until the dough is about doubled in bulk.

8. Remove the dough from the processor bowl, punch down, and knead by hand a few seconds. Cover the dough with the processor bowl and allow the dough to rest 10 minutes.

9. Meanwhile, lightly grease a glass baking sheet. Preheat the oven to 350°F. If you're baking the Challah on a stone, place the stone on the middle rack of the oven and allow 30 minutes preheating time.

10. Form dough into a braid by dividing it into 3 equal pieces, then roll each into a long strip about 1 inch in diameter. Form the 3 pieces into a fat braid (see page 43) beginning in the middle and braiding outward, then pinching top and bottom ends under neatly. Place on the prepared baking sheet or pizza peel (see page 24).

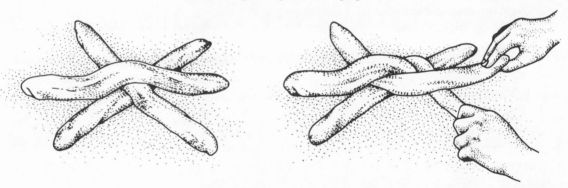

11. Place in the microwave and repeat step 7. Alternately, place in a warm, draft-free place to rise until nearly doubled in bulk.

12. Just before baking, brush the top with a mixture of egg yolk and a couple of tablespoons of cold water. Sprinkle generously with sesame or poppy seeds and bake on the middle rack in the preheated oven, preferably on a stone, about 40 to 50 minutes or until a luscious golden color.

13. Remove to a rack to cool. Store in plastic wrap.

OUR DAILY BREAD

Makes 1 standard loaf in under 2 hours

Great for kids' school sandwiches, wonderful toasted for breakfast. Keeps well.

3 C. bread flour, divided
1 tbsp. 50% faster active dry yeast
1½ C. hot tap water (120°F)
1 tbsp. molasses
2 tbsp. honey

⅓ C. rolled oats
2 tbsp. yellow cornmeal
½ C. whole wheat flour
Pinch ground cinnamon
1 teas. salt
3 tbsp. canola oil or other vegetable oil

1. In a glass bowl combine 1 cup of the bread flour and yeast with the water, molasses, and honey, forming a sponge.

2. Place this sponge in the microwave oven, lower the microwave power to the appropriate micro-rise setting (see page 35), and place an 8-ounce glass of water in the back of the oven. Heat for 3 minutes, and rest the dough for 3 minutes or until spongy and light.

3. In the processor bowl fitted with the steel blade, combine the remaining bread flour with the rolled oats, cornmeal, whole wheat flour, cinnamon, and salt, then pulse to mix.

4. Open the top and add the oil and the sponge. Process.

5. When the dough leaves the side of the bowl and forms a ball, knead for 60 seconds, adding additional tap water as necessary if dough seems too stiff.

6. Remove the dough and the blade from the bowl. Knead the dough by hand a few seconds, adding flour as necessary if dough seems sticky. Form dough into a ball. With your thumbs, punch a hole to form a doughnut shape and replace in processor bowl. Cover loosely with a damp tea towel or microwavable plastic wrap and prepare to micro-rise.

7. With the glass of water in the back of the microwave and the microwave power set as in step 2, place the dough in the microwave. Heat for 3 minutes. Rest for 3 minutes. Heat 3 minutes. Rest 6 minutes or until the dough is about doubled in bulk.

8. Remove the dough from the processor bowl, punch down, and knead by hand a few seconds. Cover the dough
(continued)

Potted Shrimp, Leek, and Dill ◇ on Toast ◇

Serves 4 in 20 minutes, plus 3 hours for marination

Cut thick slices of Our Daily Bread, toast on both sides, then cover with generous spoonfuls of this spread. Garnish with a sprig of fresh dill, and it's high tea.

¼ C. (½ stick) unsalted butter or margarine
3 medium leeks (white parts), chopped finely
¼ C. finely chopped shallots
1 pound medium shrimp, shelled and deveined
½ C. sour cream or plain low-fat yogurt
2 tbsp. minced fresh dill

Garnish
Dill sprigs
Salt and freshly ground black pepper to taste

1. In a 10-inch skillet melt half the butter or margarine and sauté the leeks and shallots until tender, about 10 minutes. Remove from the skillet and set aside.

2. Melt remaining butter or margarine in the skillet and cook the shrimp just until pink, about 4 minutes. Remove the shrimp and pan juices to the processor bowl fitted with the steel blade. Chop coarsely, then add cooked leeks and shallots, sour cream or yogurt, and 2 tablespoons dill. Process to form a rough puree. Adjust seasonings with salt and pepper.

3. Pack into a crock, garnish with dill sprigs, cover, and refrigerate at least 3 hours and up to 2 days before serving. Makes a great teatime sandwich filling.

with the processor bowl and allow the dough to rest 10 minutes.

9. Meanwhile, lightly grease a glass loaf pan 8½ × 4½ × 2½-inches. Preheat the oven to 375°F.

10. Form the dough into a loaf (see page 40) and place in the prepared loaf pan. Position in the microwave and repeat step 7. Alternately, place in a warm, draft-free place to rise until nearly doubled in bulk.

11. Just before baking, spritz the top with plain water. Bake on the middle rack in the preheated oven about 40 to 50 minutes or until a luscious golden color.

12. Remove to a rack to cool. Store in plastic wrap.

POPPY-SEED BREAD

Makes 1 standard loaf in 2 hours

Bread for the true poppy seed lover, the cut surface is flecked with smoky blue seeds producing a slightly nutty flavor. Because the bread is dense, it takes more time to rise. Best served the day it's baked. Try it with cream cheese and served alongside peppered strawberries.

½ **C. poppy seeds**
1 **C. whole wheat flour**
2¼ **C. bread flour**
3 **tbsp. gluten flour**
1 **teas. salt**
3 **teas. 50% faster active dry yeast**

2 **tbsp. unsalted butter**
¾ **C. milk**
¼ **C. honey**
1 **large egg, room temperature, beaten lightly**

1. Fit the processor bowl with the steel blade. Combine and pulse to mix the poppy seeds, flours, salt, yeast, and butter.

2. Measure the milk into a 2-cup microwavable measure and heat on high power in the microwave for 1 minute or until it is the temperature of hot tap water, about 120°F. Add the honey and egg to the warm milk.

3. With the motor running, add all but 1 tablespoon of the milk mixture to the seed-and-flour mixture. The dough should leave the side of the bowl and form a ball. If it doesn't, gradually add the remaining 1 tablespoon of liquid ingredients, and the dough will form a ball. Knead for 60 seconds.

4. Remove the dough and the steel blade from the bowl. Knead the dough by hand a few seconds on a floured surface and form dough into a ball. With your thumbs, punch a hole to form a doughnut shape. The dough will seem fairly stiff. Place in the processor bowl. Cover loosely with a damp tea towel or microwavable plastic wrap. Place the processor bowl in the middle of the microwave.

5. Set an 8-ounce glass of water in the microwave and prepare to micro-rise. Lower the microwave power to the appropriate micro-rise setting (see page 35). Heat for 3 minutes. Rest for 3 minutes. Heat for 3 minutes. Rest for about 30 minutes. The dough should have doubled in bulk; if not, let it rest, undisturbed, in the microwave a few more minutes.

6. Grease well an 8½ × 4½ × 2½-inch glass loaf pan. Remove the dough from the microwave and processor bowl. Punch the dough down and knead by hand a few seconds on a lightly floured surface. Shape into a loaf (see page 40) and place in the prepared pan. Preheat the oven to 375°F.

7. Place the bread off-center in the microwave and an 8-ounce glass of water in the middle of the microwave. With the microwave power still at the appropriate micro-rise setting, repeat step 5 except rest for 20 minutes. The bread should now be even with the top of the pan. If not, let it rest a few more minutes in the microwave.

8. Bake the bread on the middle rack of the preheated oven for 25 to 30 minutes, or until it sounds hollow when tapped lightly.

9. Turn the bread out onto a rack and let it cool. Wrap in aluminum foil to store.

Try a piece of this bread with a dish of spring's first fresh strawberries, sliced and seasoned lightly with just-ground pepper and a few sprinkles of sugar. Let the berries sit 30 minutes or so, and they will become juicy and sweet!

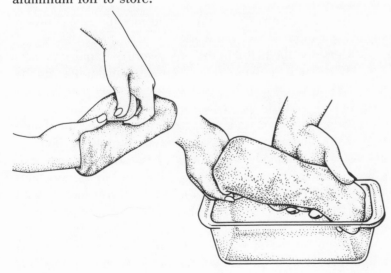

Eggs with Frizzled
◇ Pastrami on Rye ◇

Serves 4 in 15 minutes

1 *clove garlic, minced*
1/2 *pound sliced pastrami*
4 *tbsp. (1/2 stick) unsalted*
  butter
4 *eggs*
Salt and freshly ground black
  pepper to taste
4 *thin slices Jim Beard's*
  Black Beard
Dijon mustard

Parsley sprigs

1. In a 10-inch skillet sauté the garlic and pastrami in 1 tablespoon of the butter over medium-high heat until golden and frizzled, about 2 minutes. Remove from the skillet and set aside.

2. In the same skillet, over low heat, add the remaining butter and fry the eggs as you like them: over easy, sunny-side up. Your choice. Season to taste with salt and pepper.

3. Toast and spread bread with mustard, then arrange on dinner plates; top roast with pastrami and eggs. Garnish each plate with a sprig of parsley.

BLACK BREAD

Makes 1 round loaf in 2 hours

Jim Beard applauded innovative technique. We revised his favorite black bread and made it oh so simple. This bread should always be sliced thin, is heaven with seafood, and makes divine sandwiches. It keeps well if wrapped in plastic and refrigerated. We like it because it's not too sweet.

1/4 *C. yellow cornmeal*
1/4 *C. cold water*
1/2 *C. strong black*
  coffee
1 1/2 *teas. unsalted butter*
1 *teas. salt*
3/4 *teas. caraway seeds*
1 1/2 *teas. Dutch process*
  unsweetened cocoa
1 *tbsp. 50% faster*
  active dry yeast

1 1/2 *tbsp. brown sugar*
1/4 *C. warm water*
1 *C. dark rye flour*
1/2 *C. whole wheat flour*
1 *C. unbleached white*
  flour

Glaze
1 *egg white plus 2*
  tbsp. cold water

1. Mix cornmeal and cold water thoroughly in a small glass bowl.

2. In a 2-cup glass measure, heat the coffee to boiling in the microwave set on high power (about 1 1/2 minutes).

3. Pour the boiling coffee over the cornmeal mixture and stir until thick. Then add butter, salt, caraway seeds, and cocoa. Stir to mix.

4. In a 2-cup glass measure stir to mix the yeast, brown sugar, and warm water. Set aside.

5. Combine the flours in the processor bowl; pulse to mix.

6. With the processor motor running, pour liquids into the flour. When the dough leaves the side of bowl and forms a ball, knead with the motor running for 60 seconds.

7. Remove the dough and steel blade from the bowl. Knead the dough by hand a few seconds, adding flour as necessary if the dough is too sticky, then form the dough into a ball. With your thumbs, punch a hole to form a doughnut shape and replace in the processor bowl. Cover loosely with a damp tea towel or microwavable plastic wrap and prepare to micro-rise.

8. Place an 8-ounce glass of water in the back of the microwave. Lower the microwave power to the appropriate

micro-rise setting (see page 35). Place the dough in the microwave. Heat for 3 minutes. Rest for 3 minutes. Heat 3 minutes. Rest 6 minutes or until doubled in bulk.

9. Remove the dough from the processor bowl, punch down, and knead by hand a few seconds. Form into a ball. Invert the processor bowl over the dough and allow it to rest 10 minutes.

10. Preheat the oven to 375°F. If you're cooking on a stone (see pages 21–25), place the stone on the middle rack and preheat at least 30 minutes. With yellow cornmeal dust a glass 8-inch pie plate or pizza peel (see page 24).

11. Form the dough into a ball and place in the pie plate or on the pizza peel. Place the dough in the microwave and repeat step 8, or raise in a warm, draft-free place until almost doubled in bulk.

12. Just before baking, brush the dough top with a mixture of egg white and 2 tablespoons cold water. Bake on the middle rack in the preheated oven about 50 to 60 minutes or until the loaf taps hollow. Beard says this bread is better overdone than underdone. Be patient.

13. Cool on a rack. Store in plastic wrap in the refrigerator.

FRENCH COUNTRY BREAD IN A CLOCHE

Makes 1 large round loaf in 2 hours

The burning question here is: Can technology equal the power of the French farmwife's forearm? We took Paula Wolfert's heavenly tourte recipe—it takes a French farm wife 2 days and a lot of hand kneading to create a big, splendid, dense, round, crosshatched, golden loaf—and knocked the time back to 2 hours and the work down to a manageable level. Did we get a good loaf of bread? We think so. Try it yourself.

The bread requires more than double the amount of flour we can knead comfortably in our large Braun food processor. Normally, we try to limit the flour to 3 cups, but this recipe called for a total of 8 cups. We learned from doing this recipe that all you have to do if you wish to machine knead a lot of

(continued)

Wine that maketh glad the heart of man: and oil to make him a cheerful countenance, and bread to strengthen man's heart.

—Psalms 104:15

◇

Toast thick slices of this dense country bread topped with a thin coating of fruity olive oil and a sprinkling of *herbes de Provence*. Serve with goat cheese or a crisp, cold salad.

Alternately, top thick slices of the bread with tapenade (page 171) and slice into bite-sized fingers. Or, make a quick lunch topping.

Black Olive
◇ Pesto ◇

Makes 1½ cups in 10 minutes

1 C. pitted black olives
¼ teas. red pepper flakes
2 large cloves garlic, peeled
2 shallots, peeled
1 teap. fresh thyme leaves
   or ½ tsp. dried
1 teas. red wine vinegar
½ C. fruity olive oil

Combine all ingredients except oil in the food processor bowl fitted with the steel blade and pulse until you have a minced mixture. Stir in the oil. Spoon on toasted country bread or use a few tablespoons on servings of just-cooked hot pasta. The pesto will keep in the refrigerator for up to a week.

Fabulous! 9

dough is divide the dough, then knead each 3- to 4-cup portion for a minute, then knead the smooth, elastic, satiny dough balls together by hand.

We cooked the free-form round loaf in a clay baker called La Cloche (see page 24), which produced a picture-perfect loaf. Alternately, you can bake the loaf on a cookie sheet or preheated stone (see pages 21–25), misting the oven with water from time to time, to get a crisp crust.

We adore this clay baker because not only does it improve the taste and texture of the bread, it also can be used in the microwave for the final micro-rise.

In Wolfert's version, a starter is begun a day or two before you make the bread. We used a micro-rise sponge and added plain yogurt to get that rich, tangy flavor. This bread keeps 3 or 4 days and is the bread of choice with rich winter soups, as a basis for sandwiches, or simply great with a piece of cheese and a glass of wine.

2 T

2½ teas. 50% faster
   active dry yeast
1 C. warm tap water
~~1 C. bread flour~~ *○ About 6½*
5½ C. bread flour
1 C. whole wheat flour
½ C. rye flour (optional)

1 tbsp. salt
1 C. plain low-fat
   yogurt
1 C. hot tap water
(120°–130°F)

1. In a 2-cup glass measure or bowl, combine the yeast with 1 cup water and flour. Stir to mix with a fork, then place in the microwave set at the approximate micro-rise power (see page 35). Place an 8-ounce glass of water in the back of the microwave. Heat for 3 minutes; rest for 3 minutes.

2. Meanwhile, in a large bowl, measure out flours and salt. Stir to mix.

3. In a 2-cup glass measure, heat plain yogurt in the microwave (45 seconds on high power) to about 120°F, and combine with 1 cup hot tap water. Whisk together with a fork.

4. In the food processor bowl fitted with the steel blade, combine half the flour mixture, half the sponge, and half the yogurt water.

5. Process until the dough begins to leave the side of the bowl. Knead 60 seconds, adding flour as necessary if the dough seems sticky or additional tablespoons of water if the dough seems stiff. Pinch up a piece of the dough. It should feel soft, tacky, smooth, elastic, and warm.

6. Remove the dough to a lightly floured surface, then repeat steps 4 and 5 with the other half of the ingredients. Knead the 2 balls of dough together by hand and prepare to micro-rise. Remove the steel blade from the processor bowl. Form dough into a ball. With your thumbs, punch a hole to form a doughnut shape and replace in the processor bowl. Cover loosely with a damp tea towel or plastic wrap.

7. At the appropriate micro-rise power, as in step 1, heat for 3 minutes. Rest for 3 minutes. Heat for 3 minutes. Rest for 6 minutes or until the dough has risen to about double in bulk.

8. Remove the dough to a lightly floured surface and knead by hand a few seconds. Form into a large ball and place on a cookie sheet or clay baking dish generously sprinkled with cornmeal.

9. Micro-rise, repeating step 7, or raise dough in a warm, draft-free place until nearly doubled in bulk, about 1 hour. Meanwhile, preheat the oven to 450°F.

10. When the dough has nearly doubled in bulk, make deep crosshatch slashes at a 45-degree angle in the top with a sharp knife or razor blade. Spritz the top of the loaf with water.

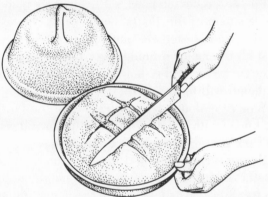

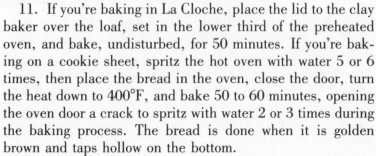

11. If you're baking in La Cloche, place the lid to the clay baker over the loaf, set in the lower third of the preheated oven, and bake, undisturbed, for 50 minutes. If you're baking on a cookie sheet, spritz the hot oven with water 5 or 6 times, then place the bread in the oven, close the door, turn the heat down to 400°F, and bake 50 to 60 minutes, opening the oven door a crack to spritz with water 2 or 3 times during the baking process. The bread is done when it is golden brown and taps hollow on the bottom.

12. Remove the loaf to a metal rack to cool. Wrap in plastic wrap to store. This bread keeps 3 or 4 days.

To toast sesame seeds in the micro-wave, place the seeds in a small custard cup and heat on high power for 1 minute. Stir and heat on high for 1 more minute or until the seeds are toasted to taste.

About Whole
◇ Wheat ◇

Whole wheat flour is made in 2 ways. Five thousand years ago the Egyptians discovered they could make flour from raw wheat kernels by grinding the wheat berries between enormous stones, turned by waterpower. Until the nineteenth century this was the only way wheat flour was made—by stone grinding.

If you've ever seen a commercial flour mill, you might wonder why it is 3 or 4 stories tall. That's because the wheat is poured in at the top and run through a series of steel rollers. Air is blown through the flour as it falls, and the lightweight bran is lifted off. Wheat germ and other by-products, called "shorts," are separated out. For whole wheat flour, they're blended back in at the end of the process using an arithmetic ratio of white flour to bran and other by-products.

Although the controversy rages over which whole wheat flour is more nutritious, the most important thing to remember is that whole wheat flours of all kinds are more perishable than white flours. If you buy flour from bulk supplies, pinch up a piece of the flour. It should taste sweet, never bitter. If you buy packaged flour, see if it is date coded, and buy the freshest flour you can find.

Buy only what you can use within a month or so. Store whole wheat flour in a cool, dark place. The refrigerator or freezer are ideal if you live in a hot, humid climate.

DEAF SMITH COUNTY
WHEAT BREAD

Makes 1 standard loaf in 1 hour and 10 minutes

Butter, honey, and seeds are the heart and soul of this wheat bread. It is fast and one of the best-tasting wheat breads to come out of our kitchens.

1½ C. bread flour
1½ C. whole wheat flour
1 teas. salt
4 teas. 50% faster active dry yeast
2 tbsp. honey
1½ tbsp. unsalted butter or margarine
1½ tbsp. toasted sesame seeds

1 C. hot tap water (120°F)

Glaze
1 egg white, beaten until frothy

Sesame seeds, for sprinkling on top (optional)

1. Fit the processor bowl with the steel blade. Combine and pulse to mix the flours, salt, yeast, honey, butter or margarine, and toasted sesame seeds.

2. With the motor running, *very slowly drizzle* the hot water through the feed tube, holding back the last portion to see if the dough will form a ball.

3. When the dough leaves the side of the bowl and forms a ball, knead with the machine running for 60 seconds. Add the last portion of liquid only if necessary.

4. Remove the dough and the steel blade from the bowl. Knead the dough a few seconds by hand, adding flour as necessary if it seems sticky. Form the dough into a ball. With your thumbs, punch a hole to form a doughnut shape and place in the processor bowl. Cover loosely with a damp tea towel or microwavable plastic wrap. Place the processor bowl in the middle of the microwave.

5. Set an 8-ounce glass of water in the microwave. To micro-rise, lower the microwave power to the appropriate micro-rise setting (see page 35). Heat for 3 minutes. Rest for 3 minutes. Heat for 3 minutes. Rest for 6 minutes or until the dough has doubled in bulk.

6. Meanwhile, grease well an 8½ × 4½ × 2½-inch glass loaf pan and preheat the oven to 375°F.

7. Remove the dough from the microwave and the processor bowl. Punch down and knead by hand a few seconds on a floured surface. Shape into a loaf (see page 40) and place in the prepared pan. Brush the loaf lightly with the beaten egg white to cover and sprinkle with the sesame seeds, if desired. Discard any remaining egg white. Be careful not to let the egg white run down the sides of the loaf or the bread will stick to the pan. Place the bread off-center in the microwave and an 8-ounce glass of water in the middle of the microwave. Repeat step 5.

8. Place the bread on the middle rack in the preheated oven. Bake for 25 to 30 minutes or until the loaf sounds hollow when tapped.

9. Remove the loaf from the pan and cool on a rack. Wrap in aluminum foil to store.

UNCLE LARRY'S BEER BREAD

Makes 1 standard loaf in 1 hour and 30 minutes

Uncle Larry loves beer—and bread. So he combined the two and reinvented this terrific bread. We adapted his recipe for the food processor. This bread has just one rising period and is especially easy. What Uncle Larry may not know is that the very first yeast "light" breads were made by mixing home-ground wheat with home-brewed ale 5,000 years ago, but we won't tell. He thinks he invented this stuff.

2 C. bread flour	2 teas. salt
1¾ C. medium rye flour	1 teas. caraway seeds
2 tbsp. honey	½ teas. minced fresh
1 tbsp. unsalted butter or margarine	garlic or ¼ teas. garlic powder
3 teas. 50% faster active dry yeast	1 C. beer, your favorite brand

1. Fit the processor bowl with the steel blade. Combine and pulse to mix the flours, honey, butter or margarine, yeast, salt, caraway seeds, and garlic or garlic powder.

2. Measure the beer into a 2-cup microwavable measure. Heat the beer to the equivalent of hot tap water (120°F) in the microwave, set on high power, for about 1 minute.

(continued)

This bread, which is chewy and moist, is ideal for a buffet table served with a wedge of sharp cheese, or use it toasted and buttered as the base for this earthy mushroom delight.

Crostini with Mushroom and ◇ Tarragon Cream ◇

Serves 6 in 50 minutes

6 *large mushrooms, cleaned and sliced*
¾ *teas. salt*
1 *C. whipping cream*
1 *teas. dried tarragon, crumbled*
6 *toasted and buttered beer bread slices*

Place all the ingredients except bread slices in a large heavy skillet over moderate heat. Bring to a boil. Reduce the heat and simmer, stirring occasionally until the cream is thick and the color is a rich caramel, about 30 to 40 minutes. Place the toast on individual serving plates and spoon cream and mushrooms over. Serve immediately.

3. With the processor motor running, *very slowly drizzle* the beer through the feed tube, holding back the last small portion. When the dough leaves the side of the bowl and forms a ball, knead for 60 seconds with the machine running. Add the last liquid portion only if necessary.

4. Grease well a microwavable 8-inch round cake pan. Remove the dough from the bowl. Knead the dough by hand a few seconds on a lightly floured surface, adding flour as necessary if the dough is too sticky. Form the dough into a ball and place loosely in the prepared pan. Flatten only *slightly*. Cover the dough loosely with microwavable plastic wrap that has been lightly sprayed with nonstick vegetable oil spray. Set the dough aside to rest for 10 minutes.

5. Place the bread off-center in the microwave and set an 8-ounce glass of water next to it.

6. To micro-rise, lower the microwave power to the appropriate micro-rise setting (see page 35). Heat for 3 minutes. Rest for 3 minutes. Heat for 3 minutes. Rest for 26 minutes or until doubled in bulk. Meanwhile, preheat the oven to 375°F.

7. Remove the plastic wrap and place the bread on the middle rack of the preheated oven and bake for 35 to 40 minutes or until medium brown.

8. Remove the bread from the pan to a rack to cool slightly. This bread is best served warm. Wrap any leftovers in aluminum foil to store.

2 ◆ FITNESS, HEALTH, AND HIGH-FIBER BREADS

Low-Fat Buttermilk Biscuits 77

Whole Wheat–Style Dinner Rolls 78

Cracked-Wheat Bread 79

Gloria's Whole-Meal Bread 81

Irish Barley-Wheat Bread 82

Apple Butter Bread 84

Carrot-Currant-Wheat Berry Bread 86

Featherweight White Bread 88

Oat Bran–Oatmeal Bread 89

White Bread—Salt Free 91

Gold Dust Loaf 92

We'd like to begin this chapter by telling you what you won't find here contrary to what you're likely to find in commercially sold "health and diet" breads. You won't find any nondietary cellulose. Whenever you begin reading labels on prepared foods, remember that you can read "cellulose" as "sawdust" and frequently be right on.

Much as we believe in keeping weight at a reasonable level, we think sawdust belongs on the sawmill floor, not in the bread, thank you. We like our dietary fiber to come from whole wheat bran and choose whole wheat flour to make bread that contains this important nutritional component.

What we've offered here are wonderful, nutritious choices for breads that will give you maximum nutrition with minimum damage in the high-fat, high-sodium, high-guilt department.

The Wheat Industry Council points out that a single slice of commercially prepared whole wheat bread offers a bonanza in nutrition of the carbo-loading variety. Thirty-eight percent starch, 38 percent water, 10 percent protein, 5.5 percent fiber, 4.5 percent fat, 2 percent sugars, and 2 percent minerals. When you begin baking yourself, you can control those proportions even more.

Need to eliminate salt? Do it. Wish to avoid sugars or fats? Cut them out. Want to up your intake of complex carbohydrates? Start with good, wholesome bread. Many times, the bread can be practically a whole meal in itself.

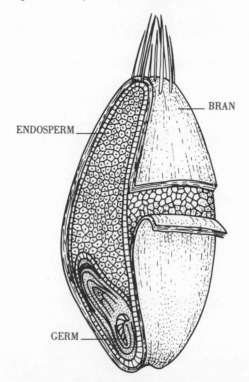

ENDOSPERM

BRAN

GERM

LOW-FAT BUTTERMILK BISCUITS

Makes 1 dozen biscuits in 45 minutes

Anyone who ever decided to watch her weight knows you have to give up biscuits. However, using buttermilk and yeast, we've come up with a low-fat, low-cholesterol version that is ready for the table in less than 45 minutes, flaky and tender, there for breakfast when you are.

2 C. bread flour
1 teas. baking powder
1 teas. salt
2 tbsp. all-vegetable shortening
⅔ C. low-fat buttermilk

1 tbsp. sugar
1 tbsp. 50% faster active dry yeast
2 tbsp. water
Milk for brushing on top

1. In the processor bowl fitted with the steel blade, combine the flour, baking powder, and salt. Pulse to mix.

2. With the motor running add the shortening. Process 10 seconds.

3. Heat the buttermilk to lukewarm in a glass measure in the microwave set on high power (about 40 seconds). Meanwhile, preheat the oven to 425°F.

4. Stir sugar, yeast, and water into the warm buttermilk.

5. With the processor motor running, add the yeasty liquid to the ingredients in the processor bowl and mix *just until the dough forms a ball* (3 to 5 seconds). Turn off motor and use a rubber spatula to remove dough to a lightly floured surface. Don't worry if it seems a little sticky. Just sprinkle on a bit of flour if necessary.

6. Knead by hand 2 or 3 times, then pat into a round form ¼-inch to ½-inch thick. Cut out the biscuits with a cutter or a glass dipped in flour—from 1½ to 2½ inches in diameter.

7. Lightly grease a glass cookie sheet and place biscuits atop. Brush the tops lightly with milk.

8. Micro-rise the biscuits by placing them in the microwave oven. Set an 8-ounce glass of water inside. Then lower the power to the appropriate micro-rise setting (see page 35). Heat for 3 minutes. Let rest 3 minutes.

9. Bake in a preheated oven until golden brown, about 10 to 15 minutes. Serve hot. Biscuits should be eaten the day they are made.

If you like biscuits crisp and brown all over, leave space around each biscuit on the baking sheet. If you prefer biscuits brown on top but soft and white on the sides, crowd them in the pan.

To further reduce the fat, place biscuits on an ungreased nonstick baking surface, such as Pyrex Clear Advantage (see page 21).

If you like what we like, southern biscuits, cut them ¼ inch thin and small enough to be eaten in a bite or two. For Yankee biscuits, pat the dough about ½ inch thick, and cut them into larger circles.

Don't reknead the leftover dough; just pat it out, roll smooth, and cut as desired. You can make impromptu cinnamon snails from these by patting the dough out thin, sprinkling with cinnamon, sugar, and butter, then rolling into a jelly roll and cutting into ¼-inch-thick snails. Cook on a separate heavily buttered sheet. Try not to worry about fat.

For a healthful breakfast, top these low-fat biscuits with applesauce, then dust with cinnamon. No guilt, no gain. For a satisfying lunch, cut the biscuits the size of silver dollars, sprinkle generously with black pepper and bake as usual. Punched up flavor, punched up pleasure.

Although white breads and white flour have gotten a lot of bad press from born-again nutritionists, the fact is that breads and biscuits made with white flour are also nutritious. Although whole wheat breads have somewhat more fiber and somewhat more vitamins and minerals than breads made from white flour, white breads provide certain nutrients in greater supply than one would find in whole wheat.

For best nutrition, eat a broad diet that includes both whole wheat and white breads. And whatever you do, don't give up your biscuits.

Exchange!
    Try exchanging whole wheat flour for up to half of the white flour called for in recipes for home-baked breads.
    Other grains that can be successfully exchanged are buckwheat flour, wheat bran, rolled oats, and cornmeal. In a recipe that calls for 3 cups of white flour, you can exchange 1 cup rolled oats, ½ cup buckwheat flour, ½ cup wheat bran, or ½ cup cornmeal for an equal amount of the other flour.

WHOLE WHEAT–STYLE DINNER ROLLS

Makes 8 rolls, just enough for a small dinner party, in 2 hours

Whole wheat flour combined with low-fat cottage cheese makes a moist, chewy roll. Great with fall soups and winter stews.

¾ C. low-fat cottage cheese	1 large egg
1 tbsp. unsalted butter	2¼ C. whole wheat flour
2 teas. honey	2 tbsp. gluten flour
½ teas. molasses	1 tbsp. 50% faster active dry yeast
¼ teas. salt	¼ C. lukewarm water

1. Fit the processor bowl with the steel blade. Combine and process to mix the cottage cheese, butter, honey, molasses, salt, and egg. Remove the steel blade and place the bowl in the middle of the microwave. Heat on high power for 70 to 80 seconds or until the mixture is just warm (120° to 130°F). Remove the bowl from the microwave and replace the steel blade. Place the bowl back on the processor base.

2. Add to the processor bowl the flours and yeast. Process for 10 seconds. With the machine running, very slowly drizzle just enough of the ¼ cup water into the flour mixture so the dough forms a ball that cleans the sides of the bowl and rides the blade around. Process until the dough turns around the bowl 25 to 30 times.

3. Remove the dough from the processor to a lightly floured surface. Knead several times, adding flour as necessary if the dough seems sticky. Form the dough into a ball. With your thumbs, punch a hole to form a doughnut shape and place it back in the processor bowl. Cover loosely with a damp tea towel or microwavable plastic wrap. Place the processor bowl in the middle of the microwave.

4. Set an 8-ounce glass of water next to it. Lower the microwave power to the appropriate micro-rise setting (see page 35). Heat for 3 minutes. Rest for 3 minutes. Heat for 3 minutes. Rest for 40 minutes or until the dough has doubled in bulk. Meanwhile, lightly grease a glass baking sheet.

5. Remove the dough from the microwave to a lightly floured surface. Punch the dough down and lightly knead to remove air bubbles. Shape the dough into 8 equal-sized balls and place on the prepared baking sheet. Cover the rolls loosely with a damp tea towel or microwavable plastic wrap.

6. Micro-rise repeating step 4, except rest the dough for 20 minutes or until the rolls have doubled in bulk. Meanwhile, preheat the oven to 375°F.

7. Remove the rolls from the microwave and bake on the middle rack of the preheated oven for 15 minutes or until the rolls are nicely browned.

8. Remove from the pan to a rack. Serve warm with unsalted butter. Wrap in a plastic bag to store. These rolls are best eaten the same day as made.

CRACKED-WHEAT BREAD

Makes 2 loaves in 1 hour and 30 minutes

There is nothing like wheat bread toasted in the morning. Try this with some sweet, sun-ripened fruit of the season or an all-fruit spread.

2 *C. water*
½ *C. medium-grind cracked wheat (this is also known as bulgur)*
1 *tbsp. plus 2 teas. 50% faster active dry yeast*
1 *teas. sugar*
⅓ *C. instant nonfat dry milk solids*
4 *tbsp. gluten flour*
3½ *C. whole wheat flour*
1 *C. bread flour*

1¼ *teas. salt*
¼ *C. (½ stick) unsalted butter, cut into tbsp.-sized pieces*
¼ *C. cold tap water*

Glaze
1 *large egg, lightly beaten*

1 *tbsp. medium-grind cracked wheat, for sprinkling on top*

(continued)

We have found gluten flour to be a godsend in giving whole-grain breads that extra little nudge needed to raise in the microwave. Add approximately 1 tablespoon per cup of flour in your bread recipes to improve texture and elasticity and to help the bread rise. You can buy gluten flour in health food and specialty food markets and some supermarkets.

1. In a microwavable 4-cup measure, bring 2 cups water to a boil (approximately 4 minutes). To the boiling water, add the ½ cup cracked wheat. Set aside to cool while preparing the rest of the recipe.

2. Fit the processor bowl with the steel blade. Combine and pulse to mix the yeast, sugar, nonfat dry milk, gluten flour, other flours, salt, and butter. Add the cooled cracked wheat and pulse to blend. With the machine running, *very slowly drizzle* the ¼ cup water through the feed tube, holding back the last small portion to see if the dough will form a ball.

3. When the dough leaves the side of the bowl and forms a ball, knead with the machine running for 45 seconds. Add the last portion of water only if necessary.

4. Remove the dough and the steel blade from the bowl. Knead the dough by hand a few seconds, adding flour as necessary if the dough is too sticky. Then form the dough into a ball. With your thumbs, punch a hole to form a doughnut shape and replace in the processor bowl.

5. Cover the bowl loosely with a damp tea towel or microwavable plastic wrap and prepare to micro-rise. Place the processor bowl in the middle of the microwave.

6. Place an 8-ounce glass of water in the microwave. Lower the microwave power to the appropriate micro-rise setting (see page 35). Heat for 3 minutes. Rest for 3 minutes. Heat for 3 minutes. Rest for 6 minutes or until the dough has just about doubled in bulk.

7. Remove the dough from the processor bowl to a lightly floured surface, punch down, and knead by hand a few seconds. Set the dough aside to rest.

8. Grease two 8½ × 4½ × 2½-inch glass loaf pans. Cut the dough into 2 pieces. Shape into 2 loaves (see page 40) and place in the prepared pans. Do not cover the pans. Do not add a glass of water to the microwave for the second rising.

9. Replace the pans in the microwave. Micro-rise by repeating step 6. Meanwhile, preheat the oven to 375°F.

10. Just before baking, carefully brush the tops with the beaten whole egg and sprinkle with the cracked wheat. Bake on the middle rack in the preheated oven 40 to 45 minutes, or until the loaf is nicely browned and it sounds hollow on the bottom when tapped.

11. Remove the bread from the pans to a rack to cool. Wrap in aluminum foil to store.

GLORIA'S WHOLE-MEAL BREAD

Makes 1 loaf in 1 hour and 30 minutes

Here's a recipe from the days when Gloria made bread to last a week and laboriously hand kneaded 3 loaves at a time. You can make one perfect loaf in a food processor.

1 tbsp. 50% faster active dry yeast	1 teas. salt
½ C. hot tap water (120°F)	¼ C. canola oil
2 tbsp. honey	4 oz. (½ cup) plain low-fat yogurt
1 C. bread flour	⅓ C. total *any or all of the following:*
½ C. high gluten white flour	*Sesame or poppy seeds, rolled oats,*
1½ C. whole wheat flour	*chopped nuts,*
½ instant nonfat dry milk	*raisins, dates*

1. In a glass bowl combine the yeast, water, and honey. Set aside.

2. Fit the processor with the steel blade and pulse to mix the flours, dry milk, and salt.

3. Add the oil and yogurt to the yeasty liquid, then pour into the flours with the motor running.

4. When the dough leaves the side of the bowl and forms a ball, knead for 60 seconds.

5. Remove the dough from the bowl to a lightly floured surface. Remove the dough blade. Knead seeds, rolled oats, nuts, raisins, or dates into the dough by hand, adding flour as necessary if the dough is too sticky, then form into a ball. With your thumbs, punch a hole to form a doughnut shape. Place in the processor bowl. Cover loosely with a damp tea towel or microwavable plastic wrap and prepare to micro-rise.

6. Place an 8-ounce glass of water in the back of the microwave. Lower the microwave power to the appropriate micro-rise setting (see page 35). Place the dough in the microwave. Heat for 3 minutes. Rest for 3 minutes. Heat 3 minutes. Rest 6 minutes or until the dough has just about doubled in bulk.

(continued)

Whole Meals from ◇ Gloria ◇

- Toast a thick slice of Gloria's bread, then rub it with garlic and top with thick slices of tomato, basil leaves, and mozzarella. Drizzle with a little fruity olive oil, then run under the broiler until cheese is bubbly.

- Mash equal parts cream cheese and goat cheese together, then chop in a generous portion of fresh garlic, green onions and tops, and fresh parsley. Slather onto bread and top with a slice of cucumber and a sprig of parsley.

- Toast a thick slice of bread, then butter and top with a slice of your favorite pâté. Serve with cornichons.

- Float a thick slice atop your favorite country soup, say bean with bacon or French onion. Dust with Parmesan and run under the broiler until hot and bubbly.

- Whip together sweet butter, garlic, parsley, and fresh herbs of your choice, then smear generously onto slices of Gloria's.

- PB&Js are raised to new heights beginning with Gloria's. Use chunky all—peanut butter and all-fruit spreads of your choice for a lunch-box special that kids won't throw behind the refrigerator.

7. Remove the dough from the processor bowl to a lightly floured surface, punch down, and knead by hand a few seconds. Then cover the dough with the processor bowl and let it rest 10 minutes.

8. Dust a glass 8-inch pie plate with yellow cornmeal. Preheat the oven to 350°F.

9. Form the dough into a slightly flattened ball and place in the pie plate. Put it in the microwave and repeat step 6.

10. Just before baking, spritz the dough with plain water, then sprinkle the top generously with more of the seeds, oats, nuts, raisins, or dates you put in the bread.

11. Bake on the middle rack in the preheated oven about 30 to 40 minutes until golden brown and the bread taps hollow.

12. Turn out on a rack to cool. Wrap in foil to store.

IRISH BARLEY-WHEAT BREAD

Makes 1 loaf in 2 hours

The goodness of whole wheat flour and barley combine with low-fat cottage cheese to make a high-rising, nutty-flavored loaf. Cooking grains is no last-minute decision, so don't forget to allow 30 minutes to cook the barley.

½ C. warm water, divided	*2 C. bread flour*
½ C. low-fat cottage cheese	*1 tbsp. 50% faster active dry yeast*
¼ C. honey	*1 large egg*
2 tbsp. unsalted butter or margarine	*1¼ C. whole wheat flour*
½ teas. salt	*¼ C. rolled oats*
¼ C. barley, cooked and cooled (follow package directions for plain, cooked barley)	*Unsalted butter or margarine, melted, for brushing on top*

1. Fit the processor bowl with the steel blade. Combine and process to mix ¼ cup of the warm water, the cottage

cheese, honey, butter or margarine, and salt. Remove the steel blade and place the bowl in the middle of the microwave. Heat on high power for 70 seconds until the mixture is just warm (120° to 130°F). Remove the bowl from the microwave and replace the steel blade. Place the bowl back on the processor base.

2. Add to the processor bowl the cooked barley, bread flour, yeast, egg, whole wheat flour, and rolled oats. Process for 10 seconds. With the machine running, very slowly drizzle just enough of the remaining ¼ cup of warm water into the flour mixture so the dough forms a ball that cleans the sides of the bowl. Process until the dough turns around the bowl 30 times.

3. Remove the dough and the steel blade from the processor bowl, and place the dough on a lightly floured surface. Knead several times, adding flour as necessary if the dough seems sticky. Form the dough into a ball. With your thumbs, punch a hole to form a doughnut shape and place it back in the processor bowl. Cover loosely with a damp tea towel or microwavable plastic wrap. Place the processor bowl in the middle of the microwave.

4. Set an 8-ounce glass of water in the microwave. Lower the microwave power to the appropriate micro-rise setting (see page 35). Heat for 3 minutes. Rest for 3 minutes. Heat for 3 minutes. Rest for 30 minutes or until the dough has doubled in bulk. Meanwhile, lightly grease an 8½ × 4½ × 2½-inch glass loaf pan.

5. Remove the dough from the microwave to a lightly floured surface. Punch the dough down and lightly knead to remove air bubbles. Shape the dough into a loaf (see page 40) and place into the prepared pan. Cover the pan loosely with a damp tea towel or microwavable plastic wrap.

6. Place the pan off-center in the microwave with the glass of water and micro-rise by repeating step 4. Rest for 10 minutes or until the dough has risen 1 inch above the top of the pan. Meanwhile, preheat the oven to 350°F.

7. Remove the dough from the microwave and bake on the middle rack of the preheated oven for 35 to 40 minutes or until the loaf is nicely browned and it sounds hollow on the bottom when tapped.

8. Remove from the pan to a rack to cool thoroughly. Brush the top of the loaf with melted butter or margarine. Wrap in a plastic bag to store.

Whole-Grain Breads: Read the ◇ Label ◇

Try to get the most from every slice of bread and every muffin, biscuit, cake, and cookie that you eat. Your goal should be 2 grams of dietary fiber per slice of bread and per muffin or biscuit. Irish Barley-Wheat Bread has 3 grams of dietary fiber per slice. Most bread companies do not list the amount of dietary fiber on their labels. Your best choice is for the first ingredient listed on the label to be 100 percent whole wheat. Wheat flour, the first ingredient found on most labels, is white flour. Don't be fooled by the brown color of the bread; some companies add caramel coloring so the bread appears to be whole wheat.

Makes 2 cups in 20 minutes

Like all fruits and vegetables cooked by the microwave, jellies, jams, and preserves retain their crisp, fresh flavor in addition to a clear, bright color. As with stove-top cooking, they boil up high, so be sure to use a large, deep micro-wavable casserole.

> 5 large *Granny Smith apples (any tart apple will do)*
> ½ *C. apple juice*
> ½ *C. firmly packed dark brown sugar*
> 1½ *teas. ground cinnamon*
> ⅛ *teas. ground allspice*
> ⅛ *teas. ground cloves*
> 1 *tbsp. orange juice*

1. Wash the apples well and remove the stems and cores. Halve the apples and then quarter each half. Place the apples and the apple juice in a large microwavable casserole. Cook the apples, covered, on high power for 8 minutes. Reduce the heat to medium and cook, covered, for 7 minutes or until the apples are very soft and will easily go through a strainer.

2. Mash the fruit through a strainer or ricer, discarding skins and seeds. Add the brown sugar, spices, and orange juice. Heat on high, uncovered, for 2 minutes or until boiling. Let cool. Store in the refrigerator up to two weeks.

APPLE BUTTER BREAD

Makes 1 loaf in 1 hour and 45 minutes

One nice thing about apple butter is that it's the spread that can be made year-round in your microwave—fast—now. Use either our homemade version, which is a little on the spicy side, or try your favorite commercial variety. If you're using the commercial variety, remember to warm it, close your eyes, inhale, and you can see the apple squeezin's being pressed in the orchard on a crisp October day.

> 1 *C. warm water, divided*
> 1 *teas. sugar*
> 1 *tbsp. 50% faster active dry yeast*
> 2½ *C. bread flour, divided*
> ⅓ *C. apple butter*
> 1 *C. whole wheat flour*
> 2 *tbsp. unsalted butter, room temperature and cut in half*
>
> 1 *tbsp. honey*
> ½ *teas. salt*
> ¼ *C. toasted wheat germ*
> ¼ *teas. ground cinnamon*
>
> **Glaze**
> 1 *egg, beaten with 1 teaspoon water*

1. In the food processor bowl fitted with the steel blade, combine ½ cup of the warm water, sugar, yeast, ½ cup of the bread flour, and apple butter. Process for 10 seconds to blend. Remove the steel blade from the processor bowl and place the bowl in the microwave.

2. Set an 8-ounce glass of water next to it. Lower the microwave power to the appropriate micro-rise setting (see page 35), and heat the sponge for 3 minutes. Rest for 3 minutes.

3. Remove the processor bowl from the microwave. Place the processor bowl back on the base and fit with the steel blade. Add the remaining 2 cups bread flour, whole wheat flour, butter, honey, salt, wheat germ, and cinnamon and process until well blended, about 10 seconds.

4. With the machine running, very slowly drizzle just enough of the remaining ½ cup warm water into the flour mixture so the dough forms a ball that cleans the sides of the

bowl. Process until the dough turns around the bowl 25 times. (If this is too much dough for your machine, after it has formed a ball, divide the dough in half and process each half separately.)

5. Remove the dough and the steel blade from the processor bowl. Form the dough into a ball. With your thumbs, punch a hole to form a doughnut shape, adding a little flour as necessary if the dough seems sticky, and place it back in the processor bowl. Cover loosely with a damp tea towel or microwavable plastic wrap. Place the processor bowl in the middle of the microwave.

6. Set an 8-ounce glass of water in the microwave. With the microwave power still set at the appropriate micro-rise setting, as in step 2, heat for 3 minutes. Rest for 3 minutes. Heat for 3 minutes. Rest for 20 minutes or until the dough has doubled in bulk. Meanwhile, lightly grease a glass baking sheet.

7. Remove the dough from the microwave to a lightly floured surface and punch down. Form the dough into an 8-inch round loaf and place it on the prepared baking sheet. Cover loosely with waxed paper. Place the dough in the microwave. Repeat step 6 except rest for 15 minutes or until the dough has doubled in bulk. Meanwhile, preheat the oven to 425°F.

8. Remove the dough from the microwave and brush with the beaten-egg glaze. Bake the loaf on the middle rack of the preheated oven for 10 minutes. Lower the heat to 375°F and bake for 20 more minutes or until the loaf sounds hollow when tapped.

9. Remove the loaf from the baking sheet to a rack to cool. Serve with additional apple butter. Wrap in aluminum foil to store.

Testing for ◇ Doneness ◇

Breads can be tested for doneness 3 ways. First, insert a cake tester, wooden or metal skewer, or thin-bladed knife in the center of the loaf or one of the rolls to be tested. If it comes out clean or with a *dry* crumb attached, it is done. Second, you can test a yeast bread by tapping it with your knuckle. If the bread sounds hollow all the way through, it is more than likely done. Third, the internal temperature of most yeast breads is 200° to 210°F when done. This can be checked by inserting an instant-reading thermometer into the middle of the loaf after the loaf has been in the oven for the minimum recommended baking time. We think the knuckle test is the best choice for yeast breads.

CARROT-CURRANT-WHEAT BERRY BREAD

Makes 1 loaf in 2 hours

One way to get whole wheat is to use *whole wheat*. Whole wheat berries, that is, the secret ingredient to this delicious crunchy carrot-colored bread that helps satisfy the urge for sweet stuff when you're on a diet and provides maximum nutrition with every bite. If you've been asked to restrict salt, this is one bread you can leave it out of without a flavor loss. Great for breakfast, or for lunch-box lunches when spread with cream cheese and sprinkled with additional raisins and cinnamon.

Using the sponge method adds a step to making the bread, and about 15 minutes' time, but it helps to make it lighter by jump starting the yeast.

1 C. water	2 tbsp. molasses
¼ C. whole wheat berries	2 medium carrots
¼ C. currants	2 tbsp. canola oil
2½ teas. 50% faster active dry yeast	1 C. bread flour
1¾ C. whole wheat flour, divided	1 teas. salt (optional)
¾ C. water, divided	¼ teas. ground cinnamon
	¼ teas. ground nutmeg
	¼ C. nonfat dry milk

1. In a 2-cup glass measure, combine 1 cup water and wheat berries. Raise to a boil in the microwave set on high power, and boil for 10 minutes. Remove from the microwave, add currants, cover, and set aside.

2. Meanwhile, in a 2-cup glass measure, make a sponge by combining the yeast, ½ cup of the whole wheat flour, ½ cup of the water, and 2 tablespoons molasses. Whisk together with a fork, cover loosely with a damp tea towel or plastic wrap, and prepare to micro-rise.

3. Lower the microwave to the appropriate micro-rise setting (see page 35), and place an 8-ounce glass of water in the back of it. Place the sponge in the microwave and heat for 3 minutes, then rest 3 minutes.

4. Meanwhile, in the processor bowl fitted with a fine-shredding disk, shred the carrots. Now replace the shredding

disk with the steel blade and add oil, remaining whole wheat flour, bread flour, salt if desired, cinnamon, nutmeg, and dry milk. Pulse to mix.

5. Add the sponge to the processor bowl and process until the dough forms a ball, leaving the side of the bowl. Add reserved water as necessary to form a warm, soft, tacky, elastic dough. Process for 60 seconds.

6. Turn the dough out onto a lightly floured surface. Drain wheat berries and currants and knead them into the dough by hand. Form the dough into a ball. With your thumbs, punch a hole to form a doughnut shape, replace in the processor bowl, cover with a damp tea towel or plastic wrap, and prepare to micro-rise.

7. Place the dough in the microwave oven still set at the appropriate micro-rise setting, with the glass of water still in the back. Heat for 3 minutes. Rest for 3 minutes. Heat for 3 minutes. Rest for 6 minutes or until almost doubled in bulk.

8. Meanwhile, generously grease a standard 8½ × 4½ × 2½-inch glass loaf pan. Preheat the oven to 375°F. Once dough has doubled in bulk, place on the lightly floured surface, punch down, and form into a loaf (see page 40). Put the dough in the loaf pan and raise one final time—either micro-rise, repeating step 7, or raise in a warm, draft-free place.

9. Once the bread has risen almost double, spritz the top with water and place it on the middle rack in the preheated 375°F oven to bake 35 to 40 minutes or until golden brown. For the last 5 minutes or so of baking, you may wish to take it out of the pan and place it in the oven on the bare rack to get a crispier crust.

10. Remove to a rack to cool. Wrap in plastic wrap to store. This bread keeps well.

The wheat berry is a veritable storehouse of nutrition. Each tiny seed contains 3 distinct parts that are separated in the milling process to make flour.

Eighty-three percent of the wheat kernel's weight is called endosperm. That's what makes white flour. The endosperm also contains the greatest share of protein, carbohydrates, iron, and B-complex vitamins, including riboflavin, niacin, and thiamin.

The bran represents almost 14½ percent of the kernel's weight. The bran contains B-complex vitamins, trace minerals, and indigestible cellulose that we call dietary fiber.

The wheat germ, although only 2½ percent of the kernel's weight, contains important trace minerals and B-complex vitamins. You can buy wheat germ separately, and it is included in whole wheat flour.

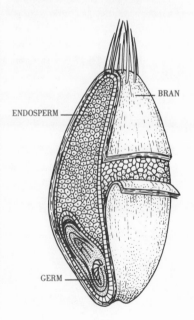

When dining out or shopping for a low-calorie bread, choose breads from the following list, since they are usually lower in fat and calories:

- French or Italian breads, whose recipes usually call for no fat at all. These are best eaten the same day as made, because fat in bread acts as a preservative and the shelf life for these breads is usually no more than 24 hours.
- Pita breads, which are wonderful stuffed with vegetables and thinly sliced low-calorie cheeses and deli meats. (See page 188.)
- Whole-grain crackers or flatbreads, which can be topped with high-fiber bean dips or other low-calorie, high-fiber fare.
- Bagels, known to dieters everywhere as a choice that provides maximum chewy taste and minimum diet damage since they are made with no fat. One skinny publicist we know noshed her way through college on a bagel diet that kept her waistline down and her energy level up.

FEATHERWEIGHT WHITE BREAD

Makes 1 loaf in under 2 hours

For the calorie-conscious consumer we offer our version of diet bread. Light as a feather and versatile to boot. It's a toasting bread, a sandwich lover's dream, and can be made into low-fat croutons or used as a base for hors d'oeuvres.

3 C. bread flour
1½ tbsp. sugar
1½ teas. salt
2 tbsp. nonfat dry milk solids
1 tbsp. butter or margarine, room temperature

2 teas. 50% faster active dry yeast
1 C. warm tap water (110°F)

1. In the processor bowl fitted with the steel blade, add all ingredients except the water. Process for 10 seconds to blend.

2. Pour the warm water into a liquid measure. With the motor running, *drizzle the water very slowly* into the dry ingredients, holding back the last portion of liquid to see if the dough will form a ball.

3. Process until the dough begins to leave the side of the bowl, forming a ball. Add the last of the liquid only if necessary. With the machine running, knead for 60 seconds, adding flour as necessary if the dough seems sticky. Pinch up a piece of the dough. It should feel soft, tacky, smooth, elastic, and warm.

4. Remove the dough and the steel blade and prepare to micro-rise. On a lightly floured surface, knead the dough by hand a few seconds, then form dough into a ball. With your thumbs, punch a hole to form a doughnut shape and replace in the processor bowl. Cover loosely with a damp tea towel or plastic wrap. Place the dough in the microwave.

5. Place an 8-ounce glass of water in the back of the microwave. Lower the microwave power to the appropriate micro-rise setting (see page 35). Heat for 3 minutes. Rest for 3 minutes. Heat for 3 minutes. Rest for 20 to 30 minutes or until the dough has doubled in bulk. Meanwhile, lightly grease an 8½ × 4½ × 2-inch glass loaf pan.

6. Remove the dough from the microwave and the processor bowl. Punch down and knead by hand a few seconds on a lightly floured surface. Shape into a loaf (see page 40) and place in the prepared loaf pan. Cover the dough with plastic wrap sprayed with nonstick vegetable spray, or use a waxed-paper tent. Place the bread off-center in the microwave and the glass of water in the middle of the microwave. Repeat step 5 until the dough has risen 1 inch above the top of the pan. Meanwhile, preheat the oven to 375°F.

7. Place the bread on the middle rack in the preheated oven. Bake for 30 to 35 minutes or until the loaf sounds hollow when lightly tapped.

8. Remove the loaf from the pan and let it cool on a rack. Wrap in aluminum foil to store.

OAT BRAN–OATMEAL BREAD

Makes 1 loaf in 2 hours

Oat bran and oatmeal together turn bread into a creamy-textured loaf that seems so rich you need only a little butter to help you savor the taste and aroma. You can also make this bread without salt. Without the salt the bread will rise faster, so make sure you don't let it rise more than 1 inch above the top of the pan or it may collapse.

1 C. warm tap water, divided	*¼ C. rye flour*
	¼ C. whole wheat flour
⅓ C. quick rolled oats	*1½ C. bread flour*
1 tbsp. 50% faster active dry yeast	*¼ C. oat bran*
	½ teas. salt (optional)
1 teas. sugar	*2 tbsp. gluten flour*

1. In the processor bowl *without* a blade, pour ¾ cup of the water and place in the microwave. Heat on high power for 2 minutes or until the water just begins to boil. Remove from the microwave and add the rolled oats. Stir in the butter and let cool to lukewarm.

(continued)

Using Nonwheat ◇ Flours ◇

When mixing nonwheat flours in a recipe, a good rule of thumb is to use just a little of the nonwheats, because most of them are blander tasting than wheat. When included with whole wheat flour they usually make the loaf heavier and not as flavorful. Try adding sprouts from the nonwheats, such as rye sprouts, or lightly cooked cereals, because the dough-gluten structure of the bread can support more grains than flour.

◇ Goldenrod Eggs ◇

Serves 4 in 20 minutes

The traditional Easter morning breakfast at the Eckhardt household makes use of uneaten Easter eggs and the best bread we've got.

> 4 *hard-cooked eggs, peeled*
> *and separated*
> 2 *tbsp. unsalted butter or*
> *margarine*
> 2 *tbsp. unbleached white*
> *flour*
> 4 *slices thick bread*
> 1 *C. milk*
> Salt and freshly ground black
> *pepper to taste*
> 1 *raw egg yolk*
> 1 *tbsp. fresh lemon juice*

Garnish
> *Fresh parsley*

1. Using a fork, crumble the cooked egg yolks and set aside. Dice the egg whites and reserve separately.

2. In a medium saucepan, over medium heat, raise the butter or margarine to foam, then add the flour and make a light roux, stirring constantly, about 2 minutes. Meanwhile, toast the bread and butter it, then arrange slices of toast on breakfast plates.

3. Slowly add the milk to the roux, stirring constantly, and cook until the sauce has thickened, about 5 minutes. Season to taste with salt and pepper.

4. In a glass measure, whisk the raw egg yolk together with the lemon juice. Add the hot white sauce, by the tablespoonful, whisking after every addition, then when you have a half cup of the sauce mixed in, pour the whole business back into the saucepan and cook another minute or so, until the

2. Fit the processor bowl with the steel blade. Add the yeast; sugar; rye, whole wheat, and bread flours; oat bran; salt; and gluten flour. Process for 10 seconds to blend.

3. Pour the remaining ¼ cup warm tap water in a liquid measure. With the machine running, *drizzle the liquid very slowly* into the dry ingredients, holding back the last portion of liquid to see if the dough will form a ball.

4. Process until the dough begins to leave the side of the bowl, forming a ball. Add the last of the liquid only if necessary. Knead with the machine running for 60 seconds, adding flour as necessary if the dough seems sticky. Pinch up a piece of the dough. It should feel soft, tacky, smooth, elastic, and warm.

5. Remove the dough and the steel blade and prepare to micro-rise. On a lightly floured surface, knead the dough by hand a few seconds, then form dough into a ball. With your thumbs, punch a hole to form a doughnut shape and replace in the processor bowl. Cover loosely with a damp tea towel or plastic wrap. Place the dough in the microwave.

6. Position an 8-ounce glass of water in the back of the microwave. Lower the microwave power to the appropriate micro-rise setting (see page 35). Heat for 3 minutes. Rest for 3 minutes. Heat for 3 minutes. Rest for 20 minutes or until doubled in bulk.

7. Lightly grease an 8½ × 4½ × 2½-inch glass loaf pan. Remove the dough to a lightly floured surface and knead by hand a few seconds. Form the dough into a loaf (see page 40) and place into the prepared pan. Cover the loaf loosely with plastic wrap spritzed lightly with nonstick vegetable-oil spray or with a waxed-paper tent and place the loaf off-center in the microwave with an 8-ounce glass of water in the middle of the microwave.

8. Repeat step 6 except to rest for 30 minutes or until the dough has risen to the top of the pan. Meanwhile, preheat the oven to 375°F.

9. Bake the loaf on the middle rack of the preheated oven for 45 minutes or until the loaf is golden brown and sounds hollow when tapped on the bottom.

10. Remove from the pan to a rack to cool. Wrap in aluminum foil or a plastic bag to store.

WHITE BREAD—SALT FREE

Makes 1 loaf in 1 hour and 15 minutes

At first, we thought salt-free bread would have to be bland. But it really doesn't. It does, however, seem to be an acquired taste. Try adding salt-free herbs, lime zest, or a dash of red pepper for punched-up flavor.

Salt controls the leavening action of yeast, and without that control, bread raises in no time flat. Don't let the bread raise more than 1 inch over the top of the pan before baking, or it may collapse on itself.

3½ C. bread flour	1 tbsp. grated orange
1 tbsp. 50% faster active dry yeast	zest
	1 tbsp. sugar
2 tbsp. unsalted butter or vegetable oil	1⅛ C. hot tap water (120°–130°F)

1. In the processor bowl fitted with the steel blade, add the flour, yeast, butter or oil, orange zest, and sugar. Process for 10 seconds or until the ingredients are well blended.

2. Pour the hot water into a glass liquid measure. With the motor running, *drizzle the liquid very slowly* into the dry ingredients, holding back the last portion of liquid to see if the dough will form a ball.

3. Process until the dough begins to leave the side of the bowl, forming a ball. Add the last of the liquid only if necessary. Knead with the machine running for 60 seconds, adding flour as necessary if the dough seems sticky. Pinch up a piece of the dough. It should feel soft, tacky, smooth, elastic, and warm.

4. Remove the dough and the steel blade and prepare to micro-rise. On a lightly floured surface, knead the dough by hand a few seconds, then form dough into a ball. With your thumbs, punch a hole to form a doughnut shape and replace in the processor bowl. Cover loosely with a damp tea towel or plastic wrap. Place the dough in the microwave.

5. Place an 8-ounce glass of water in the back of the microwave. Lower the microwave power to the appropriate micro-rise setting (see page 35). Heat for 3 minutes. Rest for 3 minutes. Heat for 3 minutes. Rest for 15 minutes or until

(continued)

sauce is smooth, hot, and golden. It should not boil. Remove from the heat and stir in diced egg white.

5. To serve, pour the sauce over toast, sprinkle with egg yolk, garnish with parsley, and serve. Happy Easter.

Even when you have a machine to do all the work, a large breadboard is something worth owning. Use it *only* for breads so that it doesn't pick up any strange tastes or smells and transfer them to your bread. Keep it clean and dry so that it does not warp or crack (the same holds true for your pizza peels; see page 24). A wet towel placed between the board and the countertop will keep it from slipping. Give yourself plenty of space to work in, preferably in front of a window with a view. Enjoy.

the dough has risen to double in bulk. Meanwhile, lightly grease an 8½ × 4½ × 2½-inch glass loaf pan.

6. Remove the dough to a lightly floured surface and knead by hand a few seconds. Form into a loaf (see page 40) and place in the prepared pan. Cover the loaf with a waxed-paper tent and place the loaf off-center in the microwave with an 8-ounce glass of water in the middle of the microwave.

7. Repeat step 5 except rest until the dough is approximately 1 inch above the top of the pan. Meanwhile, preheat the oven to 400°F.

8. Bake the loaf on the middle rack of the preheated oven for 30 minutes or until the loaf is golden brown and sounds hollow when tapped on the bottom.

9. Remove from the pan to a rack to cool. Wrap in aluminum foil or a plastic bag to store.

GOLD DUST LOAF

Makes 1 round loaf in 2 hours

When you need a bread that can stand up and be counted, this is it. The delicate yeast flavor combined with the crunch of the millet is a wonderful balance. The texture is firm and the nutritional value is boosted by adding 2 whole grains, millet and cornmeal. Serve with your favorite broth-based soups, such as chicken noodle or barley beef.

1½ C. bread flour, divided	½ C. whole wheat flour
1 tbsp. 50% faster active dry yeast	⅓ C. millet
	⅓ C. cornmeal
¾ C. warm water, divided (105°– 115°F)	2 tbsp. vegetable oil
	1 teas. salt
3 tbsp. honey, divided	Whole wheat flour, for dusting on top

1. In the processor bowl fitted with the steel blade, add ½ cup of the bread flour, yeast, ½ cup of the water, and 1 tablespoon of the honey. Process for 10 seconds to blend. Remove the steel blade from the processor bowl and place the bowl in the microwave.

2. Set an 8-ounce glass of water next to it. Lower the microwave power to the appropriate micro-rise setting (see page 35), and heat the sponge for 3 minutes. Rest for 3 minutes. Remove the processor bowl from the microwave. Place the processor bowl back on the base and fit with the steel blade. Add the remaining bread flour, honey, whole wheat flour, millet, cornmeal, oil, and salt and process until well blended, about 10 seconds.

3. Pour into a glass liquid measure the remaining ¼ cup of warm water. With the machine running, *drizzle the liquid very slowly* into the dry ingredients, holding back the last portion of water to see if the dough will form a ball.

4. Process until the dough begins to leave the side of the bowl, forming a ball. Add the last of the water only if necessary. Knead 40 seconds, adding flour as necessary if the dough seems sticky. Pinch up a piece of the dough. It should feel soft, tacky, smooth, elastic, and warm.

5. Remove the dough and the steel blade and prepare to micro-rise. On a lightly floured surface, knead the dough by hand a few seconds, then form dough into a ball. With your thumbs, punch a hole to form a doughnut shape and replace in the processor bowl. Cover loosely with a damp tea towel or plastic wrap. Place the dough in the microwave.

6. Position an 8-ounce glass of water in the back of the microwave. With the microwave power still set at the appropriate micro-rise setting as in step 2, heat for 3 minutes. Rest for 3 minutes. Heat for 3 minutes. Rest for 20 minutes or until doubled in bulk.

7. Lightly grease a microwavable glass baking sheet. Remove the dough to a lightly floured surface and knead by hand a few seconds. Form into an 8-inch-diameter ball and place on the prepared baking sheet. Dust the top lightly with whole wheat flour and score the top by holding a sharp knife at a 45-degree angle to the bread and cutting a ticktacktoe pattern. Lightly spray a piece of plastic wrap with nonstick vegetable-oil spray and cover the dough with the wrap.

8. Place the dough in the microwave. Repeat step 6. Meanwhile, preheat the oven to 375°F.

9. Bake the loaf on the middle rack of the preheated oven for 30 minutes or until the loaf is golden brown and sounds hollow when tapped on the bottom.

10. Remove from the baking sheet to a rack to cool. Serve warm. Wrap in aluminum foil or in a plastic bag to store.

Choose Your ◇ Crust ◇

Three types of crust you may choose include: First, au naturel, which means you simply do nothing. What you see is what you get, some shade of brown, gold, or pale tan. Second choice is a shiny crust. A shiny crust is usually achieved by lightly brushing on an egg beaten with 1 tablespoon water. Sometimes rolled oats or seeds are then sprinkled on. Be generous, the most gorgeous, drop-dead breads are heavily seeded or have had heavy doses of fresh, chopped herbs applied. Be sure to cover the whole exposed area of the loaf or it will look terrible. A soft, fat feather is the best brush and will not puncture the dough as you brush, causing it to deflate. Laurel of *Laurel's Kitchen* suggests using a fringed cloth table napkin. Third is what we call the Wheat First! crust. Similar to the au naturel, you usually use it on a round loaf bread. Bakeries love this flashy finish that's easy to achieve. Lightly dust the surface of the loaf with whole wheat or bread flour, then score the loaf with the famous ticktacktoe pattern or just slashes. If some of the flour disappears during baking, have no fear, let the loaf cool and then redust with flour lightly.

3 ◆ BREAKFAST AND BRUNCH BREADS

Honey-Swirl Raisin Bread with Glaze 96

Lauren's Cinnamon Sugar Monkey Bread 98

Cinnamon Pinwheel Bread 100

Crumpets 102

English Muffins 103

English Muffin Loaf 104

Hot Anise Sweet Bread 106

Hawaiian Sweet Bread 108

French Milk Toast 109

German Coffee Cake 110

Cinnamon Roll Coffee Cake 112

Austrian Plunder Brot 114

Baked Cinnamon Sugar Doughnuts 116

Cinnamon Sugar Crullers 118

Pigs in a Blanket 119

No other meal demands bread in the way that breakfast does. From the simplest slice of toast served with jam to the most ornate sideboard groaning with breakfast delights, the one food item we need to include is grain. And grain in the form of bread is the ultimate convenience food.

We have included recipes that can be made in less than an hour. We have included recipes where the work is done the night before. The one thing these recipes have in common: they're designed to meet the needs of nineties diners. Delicious, nutritious breads that taste good and will help you to jump start your day.

From pigs in a blanket to monkey bread, the choices here are fun to make, will fill your kitchen with the heady aroma of yeast bread, and will provide solid nutrition for you and your family. Have a great breakfast.

HONEY-SWIRL RAISIN BREAD WITH GLAZE

Makes 1 standard loaf in 2 hours

Raisin bread appeals to the child in all of us. We anticipate the first cut into the loaf; the aroma overtakes us; the beauty and symmetry of the swirl shines forth. Spangled with raisins, slathered with honey and cinnamon, this is a true comfort food: mother in a loaf.

2½ C. bread flour	½ teas. ground cinnamon
3 tbsp. unsalted butter, room temperature	½ C. soft seedless raisins (see page 231)
2 tbsp. sugar	
¾ teas. salt	
2½ teas. 50% faster active dry yeast	**Glaze**
1 large egg, room temperature	½ C. confectioners' sugar
½ C. buttermilk	2 teas. orange juice or 1 tbsp. sour cream
2 tbsp. honey	

1. In the processor bowl fitted with the steel blade, add the flour, butter, sugar, salt, yeast, and egg. Process for 10 seconds or until the ingredients are well blended.

2. Pour the buttermilk into a glass liquid measure. Raise to room temperature by heating in the microwave, set on high power, for 20 seconds. With the processor motor running, *drizzle the warm buttermilk very slowly* into the dry ingredients, holding back the last portion of liquid to see if the dough will form a ball.

3. Process until the dough begins to leave the side of the bowl, forming a ball. Add the last of the buttermilk only if necessary. Knead with the machine running for 50 seconds, adding flour as necessary if the dough seems sticky. Pinch up a piece of the dough. It should feel soft, tacky, smooth, elastic, and warm.

4. Remove the dough and the steel blade and prepare to micro-rise. On a lightly floured surface, knead the dough by hand a few seconds, then form dough into a ball. With your thumbs, punch a hole to form a doughnut shape and replace

in the processor bowl. Cover loosely with a damp tea towel or plastic wrap. Set the dough in the microwave.

5. Place an 8-ounce glass of water in the back of the microwave. Lower the microwave power to the appropriate micro-rise setting (see page 35). Heat for 3 minutes. Rest for 3 minutes. Heat for 3 minutes. Rest for 20 minutes or until the dough has risen to double in bulk. Meanwhile, lightly grease an 8½ × 4½ × 2½-inch glass loaf pan.

6. Remove the dough to a lightly floured surface and knead by hand a few seconds. Press or roll the dough out to a rectangle measuring approximately 8 × 10 inches. Drizzle the honey over the dough. Sprinkle the cinnamon evenly over the dough. Dapple evenly with raisins. Starting on the short side, carefully roll the dough into a jelly roll. Place in the prepared pan. Cover the loaf with a waxed-paper tent and place the loaf off-center in the microwave with an 8-ounce glass of water in the middle of the microwave.

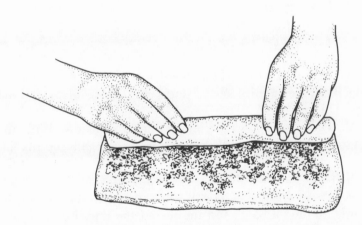

7. Repeat step 5 except rest for 20 minutes or until the dough is 1 inch above the top of the pan. Meanwhile, preheat the over to 375°F.

8. Bake the loaf on the middle rack of the preheated oven for 40 minutes or until the loaf is golden brown and sounds hollow when tapped on the bottom.

9. Remove from the pan to a rack to cool. When cooled, mix the confectioners' sugar and juice or sour cream together to form a glaze. Drizzle over the cooled loaf. Wrap in aluminum foil or a plastic bag to store.

Earl Grey's
◇ Cinnamon Toast ◇

Serves 2 in 10 minutes

Brew yourself a fine pot of Earl Grey tea. Call your best friend and invite her for tea. While the tea is steeping, thoroughly mix 2 tablespoons confectioners' sugar with ¼ teaspoon ground cinnamon. Toast 2 slices of fresh bread and lightly butter. Allow the butter to melt. Sprinkle generously with the cinnamon sugar. Serve warm and enjoy with your friend.

"I can't believe *that!*" said Alice.

"Can't you?" the Queen said in a pitying tone. "Try again: draw a long breath and shut your eyes."

Alice laughed. "There's no use trying," she said: "one *can't* believe impossible things."

"I dare say you haven't had much practice," said the Queen. "When I was your age, I always did it for half-an-hour a day. Why sometimes I've believed as many as six impossible things before breakfast."

—Lewis Carroll
Through the Looking-Glass

LAUREN'S CINNAMON SUGAR MONKEY BREAD

Makes 1 large loaf in 2 hours

Lauren, a very good cook for six years old, says this is how monkeys would make bread if they could. Small balls of sweet yeast dough, coated with butter and cinnamon sugar. A loaf made of doughnut holes.

3 C. bread flour
2½ teas. 50% faster active dry yeast
⅓ C. instant nonfat dry milk solids
1 tbsp. unsalted butter or margarine
1 teas. salt
2 tbsp. sugar
1 C. hot tap water (120°–130°F)

Cinnamon-Sugar Coating
¼ C. (½ stick) unsalted butter or margarine, melted
¾ C. sugar combined with 1¼ teas. ground cinnamon

1. In the processor bowl fitted with the steel blade, add the flour, yeast, dry milk, butter or margarine, salt, and sugar. Process for 10 seconds to blend.

2. Pour the hot water into a liquid measure. With the motor running, *drizzle the water very slowly* into the dry ingredients, holding back the last portion of liquid to see if the dough will form a ball.

3. Process until the dough begins to leave the side of the bowl, forming a ball. Add the last of the liquid only if necessary. With the machine running, knead for 45 seconds, adding flour as necessary if the dough seems sticky. Pinch up a piece of the dough. It should feel soft, tacky, smooth, elastic, and warm.

4. Remove the dough and the steel blade and prepare to micro-rise. On a lightly floured surface, knead the dough by hand a few seconds, then form dough into a ball. With your thumbs, punch a hole to form a doughnut shape and replace in the processor bowl. Cover loosely with a damp tea towel or plastic wrap. Place the dough in the microwave.

5. Set an 8-ounce glass of water in the back of the microwave. Lower the microwave power to the appropriate micro-

rise setting (see page 35). Heat for 3 minutes. Rest for 3 minutes. Heat for 3 minutes. Rest for 20 to 30 minutes or until the dough has doubled in bulk. Meanwhile, lightly grease an 8½ × 4½ × 2½-inch glass loaf pan.

6. Remove the dough to a lightly floured surface and knead by hand a few seconds. Line up your ingredients in the following order on the countertop: (1) dough, (2) melted butter or margarine, (3) cinnamon sugar, and (4) the pan. Tear off walnut-sized pieces of dough and form into a ball. Dip the dough into the melted butter or margarine and then into the cinnamon-sugar mixture. Place the balls in the pan randomly in 2 layers. Drizzle any remaining butter or margarine over the assembled loaf and sprinkle with any remaining cinnamon sugar.

7. Place the loaf off-center in the microwave and an 8-ounce glass of water in the middle. Repeat step 5 except rest for 10 minutes or just until the dough reaches the top of the pan. Meanwhile, preheat the oven to 375°F.

8. Bake the loaf on the middle rack of the preheated oven for 30 minutes or until a skewer inserted in the middle of the loaf comes out clean.

9. Let the loaf rest on a rack in the pan for 10 minutes before removing, because the loaf is fragile when hot. Carefully loosen from the sides of the pan with a sharp knife and invert onto a serving platter. Serve warm. Wrap in aluminum foil or in a plastic bag to store.

Alternately wrap the pieces of monkey dough around small pieces of fruit before dipping in the butter and cinnamon-sugar mixture. One large apple, cored, peeled, and cubed, works nicely. Bake until the fruit is soft and just pierces with a sharp knife or skewer.

Skillet Breakfast ◇ Bread Pudding ◇

Serves 4 in 10 minutes

Begin with leftover Cinnamon Pinwheel or other good quality white bread.

- *1 tbsp. unsalted butter or margarine*
- *2 C. cubed bread, cut crouton size*
- *1 large egg*
- *1 C. milk*
- *1 tbsp. instant nonfat dry milk solids*

Confectioners' sugar, for dusting on top, or honey or jam

1. In a 10-inch skillet over medium heat, heat the butter or margarine until foamy, then sauté the bread cubes until lightly browned.

2. Meanwhile, in a 2-cup glass measure, combine remaining ingredients and whisk to mix with a fork.

3. Remove the skillet from the heat, quickly pour in the milk mixture, and stir to mix. Lower the heat to the lowest setting, return the skillet to the heat, and cook until all the liquid is absorbed and the custard has set, just 2 or 3 minutes.

4. Cut into 4 pieces and serve dusted with confectioners' sugar or with honey or jam.

CINNAMON PINWHEEL BREAD

Makes 1 standard loaf in 2 hours

A combination of hard and soft wheat flours gives this bread a soft, fine, cakelike texture.

- *2 C. bread flour*
- *1 C. cake flour*
- *2 tbsp. sugar*
- *1 teas. salt*
- *2½ teas. 50% faster active dry yeast*
- *¼ C. (½ stick) unsalted butter*
- *1 C. less about 2 tbsp. milk*
- *1 large egg*

Filling

- *3 tbsp. cold unsalted butter, cut into bits*
- *1 large egg, whisked and divided*
- *2 tbsp. ground cinnamon, divided*
- *¼ C. turbinado sugar, divided*

1. In the processor bowl fitted with the steel blade, add the flours, sugar, salt, and yeast. Pulse to mix. Now, cut butter in finely, and pulse to blend so that it almost disappears.

2. In a glass measure, heat the milk in the microwave to about 120°F (about 45 seconds on high power), then add the egg. Whisk together with a fork, then, with the motor running, gradually pour the liquids slowly into the dry ingredients, holding back the last couple of tablespoons of liquid to see if the dough will form a ball.

3. Process until the dough begins to leave the side of the bowl, forming a ball. Add the last portion of liquid only if necessary. Knead 60 seconds, adding flour as necessary if the dough seems sticky. Pinch up a piece of the dough. It should feel tacky, smooth, elastic, and warm.

4. Remove the dough and the steel blade and prepare to micro-rise. On a lightly floured surface, knead the dough by hand a few seconds, then form dough into a ball. With your thumbs, punch a hole to form a doughnut shape and replace in the processor bowl. Cover loosely with a damp tea towel or plastic wrap.

5. Place an 8-ounce glass of water in the back of the microwave. Lower the microwave power to the appropriate micro-rise setting (see page 35). Heat for 3 minutes. Rest for

3 minutes. Heat for 3 minutes. Rest for 6 minutes or until the dough has risen to about double in bulk.

6. Remove the dough to a lightly floured surface and knead by hand a few seconds. Form into a doughnut shape again (as described in step 4), replace in the processor bowl, and raise again in the microwave, repeating step 5.

7. Grease generously a standard 8½ × 4½ × 2½-inch glass loaf pan. Preheat the oven to 375°F.

8. Once the dough has risen a second time, punch down, and roll into a rectangular shape about 10 × 12 inches. Spot with pieces of cold butter and chop this in, using a pastry scraper (dough blade). Now, paint the dough with all but 2 tablespoons of the whisked egg and chop that in. Spread cinnamon and turbinado sugar over, holding back a hefty pinch of each for the top. Now roll up, jelly-roll fashion, beginning at the 10-inch side. Gently place the dough into the prepared loaf pan, seam side down, and let it rise one final time, either in the microwave, repeating step 5, or in a warm, draft-free place, until the dough is nearly doubled in bulk.

Serves 1 in 10 minutes

Toast and butter a couple of thick slices of leftover Cinnamon Pinwheel Bread (or other rich whole wheat or white bread). Then place the hot toasted bread in a wide soup bowl and sprinkle with sugar.

While the bread is toasting, heat a cup of milk in the microwave, about a minute set on high power, add a whiff of vanilla, then pour over the toast in the bowl. If you have a sick child in the house, make and feed Grandmother's Milk Toast to that child, one spoonful at a time. You'll be amazed at how that kid perks up.

Some grandmothers—who don't approve of sugar—poach an egg and slip it into the milk toast, seasoning the whole thing with freshly ground black pepper. This will heal children of all ages.

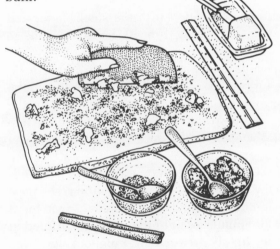

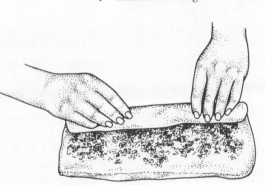

9. When the dough has risen, brush with reserved egg to make a glaze, taking care not to allow any to run down the sides of the pan (it sticks). Make 3 deep, diagonal slashes in the top with a sharp knife or razor blade. Sprinkle top with the reserved cinnamon and turbinado sugar.

10. Bake on the middle rack in the preheated oven 25 to 30 minutes or until evenly browned.

11. Remove immediately to a rack to cool. Wrap in plastic to store. This bread keeps up to a week, properly stored.

Cooking on the griddle is a good choice for a lot of fast breakfast breads: pancakes, crumpets, English muffins, and French toast. All are cooked quickly on the hot surface of a griddle and require very little fat.

Breads cooked on the griddle make a wonderful hot stick-to-your-ribs winter breakfast, and in the summer they are a marvelous partner to fresh fruits and berries.

CRUMPETS

Makes 1 dozen crumpets in 1 hour and 15 minutes

The best crumpets are full of holes and very spongy. Crumpets are a batter bread, a kind of yeast pancake, served toasted, spread with butter, and topped with honey or jam. You will need 3-inch crumpet rings, or you might try clean tuna fish or pineapple cans with the tops and bottoms cut out. A griddle or large skillet is used to bake the crumpets.

2 C. unbleached white flour
1 teas. salt
1 teas. sugar
2½ teas. 50% faster active dry yeast
1½ C. warm milk (115°F)

¼ C. warm tap water (115°F)
½ teas. baking soda
¼ C. warm water, for dissolving soda

1. In the processor bowl fitted with the steel blade, add the flour, salt, sugar, and yeast. Process for 10 seconds to blend.

2. Measure the milk and water into a 2-cup liquid measure. With the motor running, pour the liquids slowly into the dry ingredients. Process until the batter is smooth. Pour the batter into a large microwavable bowl and cover with a damp tea towel or plastic wrap.

3. Place the batter in the microwave. Place an 8-ounce glass of water in the back of the microwave. Lower the microwave power to the appropriate micro-rise setting (see page 35). Heat for 3 minutes. Rest for 3 minutes. Heat for 3 minutes. Rest for 20 minutes or until the batter has tripled in volume. Meanwhile, lightly grease your crumpet rings.

4. When the batter has tripled in volume, remove it from the microwave and dissolve the baking soda in the water. Immediately add it to the batter and stir the batter down. Cover the batter and let it rest for 20 minutes. Preheat the griddle on medium heat. The griddle is hot enough when a drop of water flicked onto it leaps off, screaming.

5. Place your rings on the griddle and pour a scant ¼ cup of batter into each. Cook for approximately 8 minutes or until the tops of the crumpets are no longer shiny and they are

◇ **Eggs Sardou** ◇

Serves 4 in 30 minutes

One of New Orleans's grand egg dishes and one of our favorites.

2 C. *fresh spinach leaves, stems removed, and steamed*
8 *small fresh artichoke bottoms, steamed, or good-quality canned, warmed*
1 *recipe Microwavable Hollandaise with Lemon or Lime*
8 *large eggs, poached*
4 *English Muffins, split and toasted*

spongy when lightly pressed with your finger. If you cannot cook all the crumpets at once and need to reuse the rings, be sure to lightly grease the rings again before baking the next batch. Toast the crumpets and serve at once with butter and your favorite jam.

ENGLISH MUFFINS

Makes 1 dozen muffins in 1 hour and 30 minutes

Nicely browned on the outside with a few flecks of cornmeal, and tender like a biscuit on the inside, an English muffin slathered with butter and your favorite topping makes breakfast an event. A griddle or large skillet is used to bake the muffins.

3½ C. unbleached white flour	3 tbsp. vegetable oil
1 tbsp. 50% faster active dry yeast	½ C. warm water (115°F)
1½ teas. salt	1 C. warm milk (115°F)
1 tbsp. sugar	

1. In the processor bowl fitted with the steel blade, add the flour, yeast, salt, sugar, and oil. Process for 10 seconds to blend.

2. Measure the water and milk into a 2-cup liquid measure. With the motor running, pour the liquids into the dry ingredients. Process just until the dough forms a mass around the blade. *Do not knead.* The dough will be very soft.

3. Remove the dough and the steel blade and prepare to micro-rise. On a lightly floured surface, knead the dough by hand a few seconds and then form dough into a ball. With your thumbs, punch a hole to form a doughnut shape and replace in the processor bowl. Cover loosely with a damp tea towel or plastic wrap. Place the dough in the microwave.

4. Position an 8-ounce glass of water in the back of the microwave. Lower the microwave power to the appropriate micro-rise setting (see page 35). Heat for 3 minutes. Rest for 3 minutes. Heat for 3 minutes. Rest for 20 minutes or until the dough has doubled in bulk.　　　　　　*(continued)*

1. Warm 4 plates in a 175°F oven for 10 minutes. Keep steamed spinach, artichoke bottoms, and hollandaise warm in the oven with the plates.

2. To assemble, put 1 split English muffin on each plate. Add ½ cup steamed spinach divided equally on the muffin. Top the spinach with an artichoke bottom, and place 1 poached egg on the artichoke bottom. Cover each portion with hollandaise. Serve this with New Orleans café au lait and you'll understand why we think the New Orleans breakfast is the best.

Microwavable Hollandaise with ◇ Lemon or Lime ◇

Makes 1 cup in 5 minutes

½ C. (1 stick) unsalted butter
3 egg yolks, beaten
1½ tbsp. fresh lemon or lime juice
1 tbsp. water
1 teas. grated lemon or lime zest

1. In a 4-cup microwavable measure, heat butter in the microwave on high power for 1 minute or *just until* melted. *Do not overheat.*

2. Add the egg yolks, lemon or lime juice, and water; whisk until smooth. Heat on medium power 1 minute, then whisk well until the curdled texture becomes smooth. If the sauce has not thickened enough, heat on medium for 30 seconds more. Whisk in lemon or lime zest. This recipe can be successfully doubled if you like more hollandaise on your eggs.

Here are some dandy toasts to make using English Muffin Loaf or your favorite whole wheat or white bread—try Gloria's Whole-Meal (see page 81) or Our Daily Bread (see page 65). If you're of English extraction, you may wish to toast the bread first, before making these toasts. That will get you a crisp, dry, flavored toast. If, however, you prefer the comfort of a lightly toasted bread with a soft middle, begin with thick slices of bread.

Classic
◇ Cinnamon Toast ◇

Preheat the broiler in your oven. Generously butter thick slices of bread, then sprinkle with white sugar and cinnamon. Place bread slices on a cookie sheet and run them under the broiler until bubbly and browned.

Green-Chili
◇ Cheddar Toast ◇

Preheat the broiler in your oven. Lightly butter thick slices of bread, then cover with thin slices of cheddar. Top with a dollop of chopped green chilies. Place bread slices on a cookie sheet and run them under the broiler until bubbly and browned.

Honey-Pecan
◇ Toast ◇

Preheat the broiler in your oven. Combine an equal measure of honey with pecan pieces and stir to mix. Lightly butter thick slices of bread, then spread with honey-pecan mixture. Place on a cookie sheet and run them under the broiler until bubbly and browned.

5. Lightly sprinkle a microwavable baking sheet with cornmeal. When the dough has doubled, remove the dough to a lightly floured surface. Pat or roll the dough until it is about ⅓ inch thick. Using a 3-inch round biscuit cutter, cut out the muffins and place them on the prepared baking sheet. Cover the muffins with waxed paper and place them back in the microwave. (Don't reroll the scraps for muffins because they'll be tough. Unless, of course, you're using scraps for hush puppies. Dogs don't seem to mind tough muffins.)

6. Repeat step 4. Meanwhile, preheat a griddle to medium heat until a drop of water jumps off.

7. Lightly grease the griddle when hot and place the muffins on the griddle. Cook for 10 minutes on the first side and 5 minutes on the other.

8. Split the muffins in half before serving and butter. Serve warm with Fresh Berry Jam (page 143) if you like. Store leftover muffins in a plastic bag or an airtight container. They will keep refrigerated up to a week.

ENGLISH MUFFIN LOAF

Makes 1 loaf in 1 hour

English muffins in a loaf, made in under an hour using only a food processor and a microwave, make breakfast a great beginning. The loaf will be pale and close grained and is meant to be toasted. We like the toast buttered, dusted with Parmesan and paprika, for a half-time lunch needing only a slice of Beefsteak tomato and a cup of tea to round out the menu.

2½ C. bread flour
1 tbsp. sugar
1 teas. salt
⅛ teas. baking soda
2½ teas. 50% faster active dry yeast

1 C. skim milk
¼ C. water
Cornmeal, for dusting on top

1. Attach the steel blade to the processor bowl. Combine in the processor bowl the flour, sugar, salt, soda, and yeast. Pulse twice to mix.

2. Combine the milk and water in a 2-cup glass measure and heat in the microwave at full power for 1 minute or until very warm (125° to 130°F).

3. With the processor motor running, pour the warm liquids into the flour mixture, then process to mix. Add additional flour as needed, up to a cup, through the feed tube, until the dough leaves the side of the bowl and the mixture forms a ball. Knead with the machine running for 45 seconds.

4. Generously grease and lightly dust with cornmeal a microwavable bread pan. Remove the dough from the processor bowl, knead by hand a few times, then form into a loaf (see page 40), and place in the pan. Dust lightly with cornmeal. Cover with a damp tea towel or plastic wrap, and prepare to micro-rise.

5. Place an 8-ounce glass of water in the back of the microwave. Place the covered bread dough in the microwave. Lower the microwave power to the appropriate micro-rise setting (see page 35). Heat for 3 minutes. Rest the dough for 3 minutes; heat 3 minutes; then rest the dough for 6 minutes or until doubled in bulk.

6. To bake, microwave the loaf in the oven set on 100 percent power, 6 minutes and 30 seconds. Take the bread from the microwave and rest in the pan 5 minutes. Remove to a rack to cool. The surface of the loaf will be pale and slightly rounded on top. Once the bread has cooled some, slice thin, then toast and butter. Great with orange marmalade or raspberry jam.

7. If you prefer a brown loaf, you may follow directions up to the point of baking, then place the dough in an ovenproof bread pan and bake in the conventional oven. Place the pan on the middle rack in a cold oven, set to 400°F, then bake for 25 to 30 minutes or until brown. Remove to a rack immediately to cool. Best eaten the day it's made.

Banana–Peanut ◇ Butter Toast ◇

Preheat the broiler in your oven. Spread a thin layer of peanut butter on a thick slice of bread, then arrange sliced banana over all. Drizzle with honey, then place on a cookie sheet and run under the broiler until bubbly and browned.

◇ Toast Cups ◇

Preheat the oven to 400°F. Cut thin slices of English Muffin Loaf, Pain de Mie (see page 56), or your favorite soft-bodied white or wheat bread. Trim the crusts, then flatten the bread with a rolling pin. Brush each slice lightly with butter or margarine.

Lightly butter muffin cups. Press a square of flattened bread into each cup. Bake in the preheated oven for 10 minutes or until toasted and golden.

Now fill each cup with a heaping tablespoon of your favorite filling: scrambled eggs with smoked salmon, fruit-flavored yogurt, fresh fruit of the season, or cottage cheese sprinkled with sesame seeds. Use your imagination. What do you like for breakfast?

Here's Lookin' at ◇ You, Kid ◇

Using a small cookie cutter or glass, cut a hole from the middle of a thick slice of English Muffin Loaf or other white or brown bread.

In an 8-inch skillet, heat a tablespoon of butter or margarine until foamy, then place the bread with the hole in it in and toast on one side. Turn the bread over and break an egg into the hole. Cook just until the yolk begins to set, then flip it over and cook a moment on the second side. Serve at once.

For a Mexican Christmas morning, serve Hot Anise Sweet Bread along with steaming cups of Mexican hot chocolate, seasoned with cinnamon, and Huevos con Salsa.

Huevos Con
◇ Salsa ◇

Serves 1 in 10 minutes

In buttered glass ramekins, place a tablespoon of fresh salsa, then a raw egg. Cover with a dollop of sour cream, and set in a hot-water bath. Place in a preheated 350°F oven and cook just until set, about 5 minutes. Serve immediately.

HOT ANISE SWEET BREAD

Makes one braided loaf in 1 hour and 30 minutes

Not only is this bread aromatic and delightful for brunch when spread with orange Neufchâtel cheese, it makes a lovely bread to bake and give away for a Christmas gift.

½ *cup water*
½ *C. golden raisins*
3 *C. bread flour*
¾ *teas. salt*
½ *C. sugar*
2½ *teas. 50% faster active dry yeast*
½ *C. evaporated milk*

¼ *C. (½ stick) unsalted butter*
2 *large eggs, whisked, reserving 1 tbsp. for glaze*
1 *teas. anise extract*
½ *teas. lemon zest*

1. Boil water in a glass measure in the microwave set on high power (about 3 minutes). Pour boiling water over raisins and set aside.

2. Fit the processor bowl with the steel blade and add flour, salt, sugar, and yeast. Pulse to mix.

3. Pour the milk into a glass measure and heat in the microwave to 120° to 130°F (about 30 seconds set on high), then add butter; egg, reserving 1 tablespoon for glaze; anise extract; and lemon zest. Whisk together. With the processor motor running, gradually pour liquids into the dry ingredients, holding back the last portion to see if the dough will form a ball.

4. Process until the dough begins to leave the side of the bowl, forming a ball, using the last portion of liquid only if necessary. Knead 60 seconds, adding flour as necessary if the dough seems sticky.

5. Remove the dough and the steel blade and prepare to micro-rise. Drain the raisins, and knead them into the dough by hand for a few seconds, then form dough into a ball. With your thumbs, punch a hole to form a doughnut shape and replace in the processor bowl. Cover loosely with a damp tea towel or plastic wrap.

6. Place an 8-ounce glass of water in the back of the microwave. Set the dough in the microwave. Lower microwave power to the appropriate micro-rise setting (see page 35). Heat for 3 minutes. Rest for 3 minutes. Heat for 3

minutes. Rest for 6 minutes or until the dough has risen to about double in bulk.

7. Remove the dough to a lightly floured breadboard and knead by hand a few seconds. Divide into 3 equal pieces. Roll each piece into a 12-inch strand, then set the dough aside to rest for 5 minutes or so.

8. Butter generously an 8½ × 4½ × 2½-inch glass loaf pan. Preheat the oven to 375°F. Braid strands together, then place the dough in the pan, tucking loose ends under, and micro-rise, repeating step 6, or raise in a warm, draft-free place until nearly doubled in bulk. Meanwhile whisk a teaspoon of water into the reserved egg for a glaze.

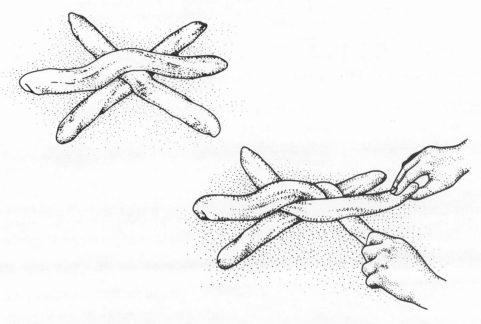

9. When the dough has nearly doubled in bulk, glaze with the egg wash, taking care not to allow any to run down the sides into the pan (it sticks).

10. Bake on the middle rack in the preheated oven about 40 minutes or until evenly browned. Remove immediately to a rack to cool. Serve warm cut into thin slices. Makes great toast. Store in plastic wrap.

Tropical
◇ Bread Pudding ◇

Serves 6–8 in 75 minutes

6 *C. cubed Hawaiian Sweet*
  Bread
1 *C. sweetened flaked*
  coconut
20-*oz. can crushed*
  pineapple, drained, or 2½
  C. fresh, pureed in
  blender
1½ *C. hot milk (heat on high*
  power in microwave for 90
  seconds)
⅓ *C. macadamia nuts,*
  coarsely chopped
2 *tbsp. unsalted butter,*
  melted
2 *eggs*
¾ *C. sugar*
1 *teas. vanilla extract*
1 *teas. rum extract*
  (optional)
¼ *teas. salt*

1. **Preheat the oven to 350°F.**
In a large mixing bowl combine the
bread cubes, coconut, pineapple,
hot milk, nuts, and butter.
2. In a separate bowl, beat the
eggs and add the sugar, vanilla extract, rum extract (if using), and
salt. Mix until thoroughly blended,
then add to the bread mixture and
blend well.
3. Grease well a 2-quart glass
baking dish. Pour the mixture into
it and stir to distribute the ingredients thoroughly. Bake uncovered in
the oven for 1 hour or until a knife
inserted in the center comes out
clean and the top begins to brown.
Allow to cool and serve slightly
warm or chilled.

HAWAIIAN SWEET BREAD

Makes 1 loaf in 2 hours

This Hawaiian bread can trace its roots back to the whaling
ships' galleys. The sailors were always looking for a bread
that was a good "keeper" (wouldn't go stale or spoil easily).
We like it made into French toast (see page 109 for French
Milk Toast) or try the leftovers in Tropical Bread Pudding.

3 *C. bread flour*
3 *teas. 50% faster*
  active dry yeast
1½ *teas. salt*
3 *tbsp. sugar*
1 *teas. vanilla extract*
¼ *C. instant nonfat dry*
  milk solids
¼ *C. (½ stick) unsalted*
  butter, cut into
  tablespoon-sized
  pieces

½ *C. hot tap water*
2 *large eggs, room*
  temperature
1 *tbsp. unsalted*
  butter, melted, for
  brushing on crust

1. Fit the processor bowl with the steel blade. Add the
flour, yeast, salt, sugar, vanilla, nonfat dry milk, and butter
to the processor bowl. Pulse to blend well and incorporate the
butter into the dry ingredients.
2. Combine in a 2-cup measure the hot water and eggs.
With the motor running, *pour the liquid mixture very slowly*
through the feed tube, holding back the last portion to see if
the dough will form a ball. When the dough leaves the side of
the bowl and forms a ball, knead with the machine running
for 45 seconds. Add the last portion of liquid only if needed.
3. Remove the dough and the steel blade from the processor bowl. On a lightly floured surface, knead the dough by
hand a few seconds, adding flour as necessary if the dough
seems sticky.
4. Form the dough into a ball. With your thumbs, punch
a hole to form a doughnut shape and replace in the processor
bowl. Cover the bowl loosely with microwavable plastic wrap.
Place the processor bowl in the middle of the microwave.

5. Set an 8-ounce glass of water in the microwave. To micro-rise, lower the microwave power to the appropriate micro-rise setting (see page 35). Heat for 3 minutes. Rest for 3 minutes. Heat for 3 minutes. Rest for 30 minutes or until doubled in bulk.

6. Grease well a glass 9-inch pie plate. Remove the dough from the processor bowl; knead by hand a few seconds on a lightly floured surface. Form the dough into a ball and place in the prepared pie plate. Flatten only *slightly*. Cover loosely with microwavable wrap. Place the bread in the microwave off-center with a glass of water in the middle of microwave. Repeat step 5.

7. Place the bread on the middle rack in a *cold* conventional oven and set the oven temperature to 375°F. Bake for 35 to 40 minutes or until the bread is nicely browned and sounds hollow when tapped.

8. Turn the bread out of the pan and onto a rack to cool. Brush the hot bread with the melted butter and let cool. To store, wrap in a plastic bag.

FRENCH MILK TOAST

Makes 10 slices in 20 minutes

This family favorite will get them to the table on time. Remember to serve the toast on warmed plates with warm syrup.

3 eggs, well beaten	*1 teas. vanilla extract*
5-oz. can evaporated milk	*10 bread slices (any kind of white bread will do)*
¼ C. sugar	
½ teas. ground cinnamon	*Unsalted butter, for frying*

1. Mix the eggs, milk, sugar, cinnamon, and vanilla. Dip the bread into the mixture, turning to coat both sides.

2. Brown in the butter on a hot preheated griddle, turning only once.

We use a coffee grinder to grind stick cinnamon. The aroma is wonderful and you get a sweet spiciness that you won't get with the commercial ground-cinnamon varieties. A separate grinder is recommended so that the flavors of coffee and cinnamon do not intermingle.

Serves 6–8 in under 2 hours

Ideal for parties, because all the work is done the day before, this light bread-and-custard concoction makes a splendid buffet centerpiece for breakfast. Add apple slices, blanched asparagus tips and ham, or pears if you wish.

6 *slices good-quality white*
  or whole wheat bread
Salt and freshly ground black
  pepper to taste
1½ *C. grated melting cheese*
  (sharp cheddar, Gouda,
  provolone, Monterey Jack)
1½ *C. milk*
1 *teas. Worcestershire sauce*
6 *eggs, gently whisked*
¾ *teas. dry mustard*
Whiff of paprika

1. Arrange bread slices in a single layer in a glass baking dish 10 × 4 × 2 inches. Season to taste with salt and pepper, then sprinkle with grated cheese. (Add thin slices of fruit or ham here instead of cheese if you wish.)

2. Combine the milk, Worcestershire sauce, and eggs and whisk to blend, sprinkle with dry mustard and paprika, then carefully pour over the arranged bread slices. Cover and refrigerate at least 6 hours, or overnight.

3. Place the dish in a larger ovenproof pan, pour water up to 1 inch on the sides, then put it in a cold oven. Set the oven temperature to 350°F, and bake 1 hour or until the custard is puffy and golden.

GERMAN COFFEE CAKE

Makes two 9-inch cakes in under 1 hour and 30 minutes

The Italians dimple flatbreads with their fingers, then sprinkle the tops with savory additions. The Germans use the same technique, except they make a sweet yeast dough, top with sour cream, then sprinkle the dimpled top with sugars and fruits. Either way, it's an easy, quick everyday yeast bread that takes to the Micro-Rise method like the proverbial duck to . . .

Try adding dried fruits to this topping for some variety. Apricots, prunes, or peaches would be lovely, cut into fine dice and placed on the bread dough underneath the sour cream or yogurt topping. You could also try nuts: walnuts, pecans, macadamia nuts chopped coarsely. The explosion in flavors—yeasty bread, soft sour cream, and cinnamon sugar crystals—makes breakfast worth getting up for.

3 *C. bread flour*
½ *teas. salt*
2 *tbsp. sugar*
2½ *teas. 50% faster*
  active dry yeast
5 *tbsp. butter,*
  softened, cut into
  pieces
⅔ *C. hot milk*
  (120°–130°F)
1 *large egg*

Topping
½ *C. turbinado sugar*
1 *teas. ground*
  cinnamon
⅛ *teas. salt*
⅔ *C. sour cream or*
  plain low-fat yogurt

1. Fit the processor bowl with the steel blade. Add the flour, salt, sugar, and yeast, then pulse to mix. With the motor running, drop in the soft butter by pieces and blend thoroughly.

2. Heat the milk by placing it in a glass measure, then in the microwave oven set on high power for about 40 seconds. (Stick your finger in to test. Should be like hot tap water.) Whisk the egg into the hot milk, using a fork, then with the processor motor running, slowly pour liquids into the dry ingredients, holding back the last portion to see if the dough will form a ball.

3. Process until the dough begins to leave the side of the

bowl. Add the last portion of liquid only if necessary. Knead 60 seconds, adding flour as necessary if the dough seems sticky.

4. Remove the dough and the steel blade and prepare to micro-rise. Knead the dough by hand a few seconds, then form the dough into a ball. With your thumbs, punch a hole to form a doughnut shape and replace in the processor bowl. Cover loosely with a damp tea towel or plastic wrap. Set the dough in the microwave.

5. Place an 8-ounce glass of water in the back of the microwave. Lower microwave power to the appropriate micro-rise setting (see page 35). Heat for 3 minutes. Rest for 3 minutes. Heat for 3 minutes. Rest for 6 minutes or until the dough has risen to about double in bulk.

6. Remove the dough to a lightly floured surface and knead by hand a few seconds. Divide into 2 pieces. Roll into 8-inch disks, each about ½ inch to ¾ inch thick, then set the dough aside to rest for 5 minutes or so.

7. Butter generously two 8-inch round glass pie plates. Preheat the oven to 375°F. Place the dough in the pie plates, press down slightly, then micro-rise, repeating step 5, or raise in a warm, draft-free place until nearly doubled in bulk.

8. Meanwhile, combine the first 3 topping ingredients in a small bowl by mixing together sugar, cinnamon, and salt.

9. When the dough has nearly doubled in bulk, dimple the dough with your fingertips, spoon on a thin layer of sour cream or yogurt, then sprinkle generously with the sugar-cinnamon-salt topping.

10. Bake on the middle rack of the preheated oven about 25 minutes or until the breads are deeply brown and the crust on the bottom is hard.

11. Turn breads out onto a rack to cool. Serve by slicing into thin pie-shaped wedges. Best if eaten the day they're baked.

Coffee cake is best if eaten the same day it's baked. For a wonderful Orange Sunshine coffee cake, simply substitute orange juice for half the milk, delete the cinnamon, and add grated zest from half an orange to the filling.

CINNAMON ROLL COFFEE CAKE

Makes 1 large coffee cake under 1 hour

Looking like a giant bear claw, this rich cinnamon-flavored coffee cake makes a terrific Sunday morning breakfast with *caffe latte* and fruit of the season.

3¼ C. bread flour
¼ C. sugar
1 teas. salt
1 large egg
1 C. hot tap water
2 tbsp. 50% faster active dry yeast
1 tbsp. sugar
2 tbsp. butter or margarine, softened

½ C. walnut pieces
½ C. raisins
¼ C. brown sugar
½ teas. ground cinnamon

Glaze
1 C. confectioners' sugar
1 tbsp. cold milk
¼ teas. vanilla extract

Filling
1 tbsp. butter or margarine, softened

1. In the processor bowl fitted with the steel blade, combine the flour, sugar, and salt. Pulse to mix.

2. In a 2-cup glass measure lightly beat the egg, then combine with the hot tap water, yeast, and sugar.

3. With the processor motor running, slowly add the butter and yeasty liquid to the dry ingredients, holding back the last portion of the liquid to see if the dough will form a ball.

4. When the dough leaves the sides of the bowl and forms a ball, knead with the motor running for 60 seconds. Use the last portion of liquid only if necessary.

5. Remove the dough from the bowl to a lightly floured surface, then knead by hand a few seconds, adding flour as necessary if the dough seems sticky. Flatten into a 14 × 10-inch rectangle.

6. Spread the dough with the filling of butter, walnuts, raisins, brown sugar, and cinnamon.

7. Roll up the dough from the long side, and seal seams by pinching together. Place seam side down on a greased, glass baking sheet. Form the dough into a crescent shape. Cut slits using a sharp, wet knife, 1½ inches apart and ⅔ through the

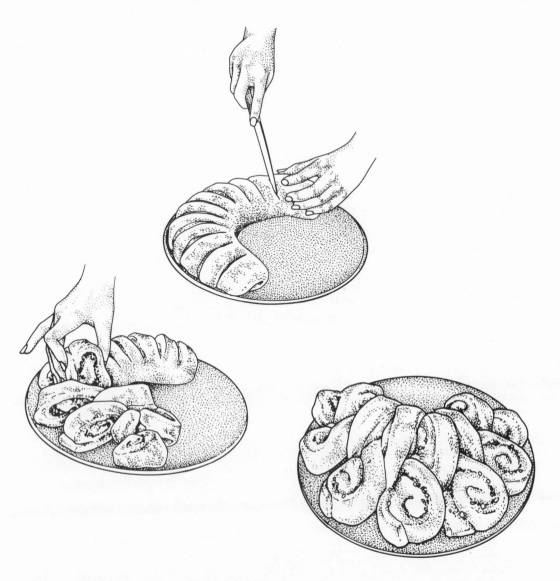

dough. Alternating sides, pull the cut pieces out. Cover loosely with waxed paper and prepare to micro-rise.

8. Lower the microwave power to the appropriate micro-rise setting (see page 35). Place the dough in the microwave beside an 8-ounce glass of water. Heat for 3 minutes. Rest for 3 minutes. Heat 3 minutes. Rest 6 minutes or until just about doubled in bulk. Meanwhile, preheat the oven to 375°F.

9. Bake on the middle rack in the preheated oven until golden brown, about 20 minutes. Remove to a rack to cool.

10. Mix the glaze ingredients in the processor bowl, then drizzle atop the cooling bread. Store in plastic wrap.

Once you've made this bread, you may wish to make variations. Top with a sprinkling of turbinado sugar, or poppy seeds, or cinnamon sugar for breakfast. Dapple with cheddar cheese and green chilies for lunch.

◇ **Scalloped Eggs** ◇

Serves 4 in 30 minutes

A good choice for a brunch buffet, this dish begs for Canadian bacon and a good-quality bread to begin with.

- 4 tbsp. (½ stick) unsalted butter or margarine
- 2 C. good-quality bread crumbs
- 8 hard-cooked large eggs, peeled and sliced

Salt and freshly ground black pepper to taste

Whiff of cayenne pepper

- 2 tbsp. just-snipped chives or 1 tbsp. dried
- 1 C. milk

1. Preheat the oven to 400°F. Butter a 9-inch glass pie plate.
2. In a 10-inch skillet, over medium heat, raise butter to a foam, then add bread crumbs and cook, stirring, until crumbs have absorbed all the butter and are golden, 2 or 3 minutes.
3. Spread half the crumbs over the bottom of the pie plate. Arrange egg slices over them, season to taste with salt, pepper, and cayenne. Sprinkle with chives. Pour milk evenly over the egg slices. Sprinkle the top with remaining bread crumbs.
4. Bake in the preheated oven for about 25 minutes. Serve hot, cut in pie-shaped wedges.

AUSTRIAN PLUNDER BROT

Makes 1 medium braided loaf in 1 hour and 30 minutes

A rich, light, buttery bread that begs for the best preserves you have in the larder. This yellow braided bread looks a lot like challah and is not only delicious for breakfast, but also a stunning addition to a dinner table.

- 3 C. bread flour
- ½ teas. salt
- 3 tbsp. sugar
- 2½ teas. 50% faster active dry yeast
- ½ C. (1 stick) unsalted butter, divided in 2 pieces, then cut into bits
- ½ C. milk
- ¼ teas. vanilla extract
- 1 teas. lemon zest
- 1 large egg plus 1 large egg yolk

1. Fit the steel blade into the processor bowl and add flour, salt, sugar, and yeast. Pulse to mix. Add ¼ cup of the butter, cut into bits, and process thoroughly to mix.
2. In a glass measure, heat the milk in the microwave to 120° to 130°F (about 30 seconds, set on high power), then add vanilla and lemon zest.
3. Combine the egg and egg yolk and whisk with a fork to mix, then reserve 1½ tablespoons of the mixture for an egg wash topping. Pour the remaining egg mixture into the hot milk and whisk together.
4. Gradually pour in liquids with the processor motor running, holding back the last portion to see if the dough will form a ball.
5. Process until the dough begins to leave the side of the bowl. Add the last portion of liquids only if necessary. Knead 60 seconds, adding flour as necessary if the dough seems sticky. This makes a very soft dough.
6. Remove the dough and the steel blade and prepare to micro-rise. Knead the dough by hand a few seconds, then form the dough into a ball. With your thumbs, punch a hole to form a doughnut shape and replace in the processor bowl. Cover loosely with a damp tea towel or plastic wrap.
7. Position an 8-ounce glass of water in the back of the microwave. Place the dough in the microwave. Lower the

microwave power to the appropriate micro-rise setting (see page 35). Heat for 3 minutes. Rest for 3 minutes. Heat for 3 minutes. Rest for 6 minutes or until the dough has risen to about double in bulk.

8. Remove the dough to a lightly floured surface and punch down, then knead by hand a few seconds. Divide the dough into 3 equal pieces. Roll each piece out into a strand about 12 inches long, then flatten and dot the length of each strand with pieces of the reserved butter. Fold the dough over the butter to cover, making 3 long, rounded strands. Let the strands rest for 5 minutes or so.

9. Grease generously a standard 8 × 4 × 2-inch glass loaf pan. Preheat the oven to 375°F. Braid the 3 strands together by beginning in the middle, laying the strands on top of each other like spokes on a wheel. Then braid each end. Place the braid in the loaf pan, tucking under the loose ends. Micro-rise, repeating step 7, or raise in a warm, draft-free place until nearly doubled in bulk.

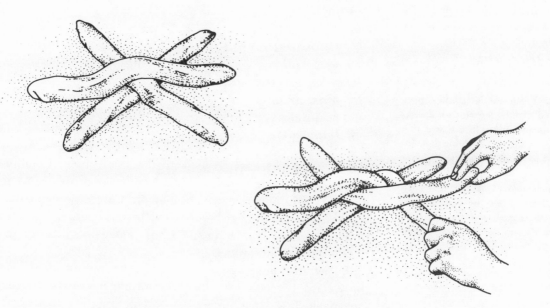

10. Meanwhile, whip together the reserved egg with 1 teaspoon water. When the braid has risen, brush on the egg wash, taking care that it doesn't run down the sides (it sticks).

11. Bake on the middle rack in the preheated oven 35 to 40 minutes or until evenly golden brown. Remove immediately to a rack to cool. Serve warm. Wrap in plastic wrap to store.

◇ Jelly Doughnuts ◇

Makes 1 dozen doughnuts in 2 hours and 30 minutes

Old-fashioned jelly doughnuts can be made from the Baked Cinnamon-Sugar Doughnuts recipe with just a few simple alterations and the addition of 2 ingredients.

  1 recipe Baked
      Cinnamon-Sugar
      Doughnuts
  2 C. blackberry, raspberry,
      grape, or other jelly
Confectioners' sugar, for
      sprinkling on top

1. Make the doughnuts according to directions except cut out the doughnuts with a 3-inch round cutter that has no hole in the middle. Bake according to directions. Do not shake with the cinnamon-sugar mixture.

2. Fill a cake-decorating bag (fitted with a tip with about a ¼-inch hole in the end) with the jelly. When the doughnuts have cooled slightly, pierce each doughnut on the side with a sharp, thin knife, making a 1-inch incision. Insert the tip of the decorating bag into the incision and gently squeeze a small amount of jelly into each doughnut. Place the filled doughnuts on a rack and sprinkle with confectioners' sugar. Serve immediately.

BAKED CINNAMON SUGAR DOUGHNUTS

Makes 1 dozen doughnuts in 2 hours

You say you gave up doughnuts when you started eating less fat? We developed this recipe after requests for a nonfried doughnut for children and those on a low-fat diet. A sponge begins the flavor development in these doughnuts. Take your time. Do not rush this dough, be sure it has doubled in volume before going on to the next step, and the result will be a nice light, warm doughnut.

  1 C. lukewarm water
      (approximately
      100°F)
  3 teas. 50% faster
      active dry yeast
  1 tbsp. sugar
  ¾ C. bread flour
  ¼ C. instant nonfat dry
      milk solids
  ½ teas. ground nutmeg
  ½ teas. ground
      cinnamon
  ¾ teas. salt

  1 large egg
  ¼ C. vegetable oil
2¼ C. bread flour
  7 tbsp. (½ C. minus 1
      tbsp.) sugar

Glaze
  2 tablespoons butter,
      melted
  ½ C. sugar
  ½ teas. ground
      cinnamon

1. Fit the processor bowl with the steel blade. Combine and pulse to mix the water, yeast, 1 tablespoon sugar, ¾ cup flour, dry milk, nutmeg, and cinnamon. Carefully remove the steel blade from the bowl and cover the bowl with a damp tea towel or microwavable plastic wrap. Place the bowl in the middle of the microwave.

2. Set an 8-ounce glass of water in the microwave. Lower the microwave power to the appropriate micro-rise setting (see page 35). Heat the sponge for 3 minutes. Rest for 3 minutes. Heat for 3 minutes. Remove the bowl from the microwave and remove the plastic wrap. Replace the steel blade in the bowl and position the bowl back on the processor base.

3. Add the salt, egg, oil, 2¼ cups flour, and 7 tablespoons sugar to the bowl. Replace the lid and process just until the dough forms a ball. *Do not knead.* Remove the steel

blade. The dough will be sticky. With the back of a spoon, smooth the dough into a doughnut shape in the bowl. Cover the bowl loosely with a damp tea towel or plastic wrap and place in the middle of the microwave. Place an 8-ounce glass of water next to it.

4. With the microwave power still set on the appropriate micro-rise setting, heat for 3 minutes, rest for 3 minutes, heat for 3 minutes, and rest for 30 minutes or until the dough has doubled in bulk.

5. Lightly grease a glass microwavable baking sheet. After the dough has doubled in bulk, remove the dough from the microwave and the processor bowl to a lightly floured surface. Sprinkle the dough with just enough additional flour to make it manageable, and knead; the dough will be very soft. Roll or pat the dough out to a thickness of ½ inch. Cut out 10 doughnuts and place on the prepared baking sheet. Reroll the scraps and cut out the remaining two. Place on the prepared baking sheet. Cover loosely with a damp tea towel or micro-wavable plastic wrap.

6. Place the doughnuts in the microwave with the 8-ounce glass of water next to them, and repeat step 4 except rest for 5 minutes or until doubled in bulk. Meanwhile, preheat the oven to 375°F.

7. When the doughnuts have doubled in bulk, remove them from the microwave, discarding the plastic wrap. Place the doughnuts on the middle rack in the preheated oven. Bake for approximately 12 to 15 minutes or until light brown in color.

8. Remove the doughnuts from the oven and baking sheet to a rack to cool. Brush the hot doughnuts with the melted butter. Place the sugar and cinnamon in a clean brown paper bag and add the doughnuts 3 at a time, giving a good shake to cover the doughnuts with the cinnamon-sugar mixture. Serve immediately.

The critical period in matrimony is breakfast-time.

—Sir Alan Patrick Herbert
Uncommon Law

◊

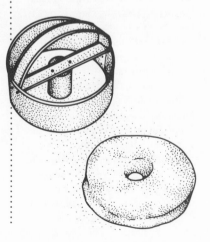

Breakfast Frittata with Parmesan ◇ and Parsley ◇

Serves 6 in 30 minutes

A good choice for a brunch buffet, this frittata tastes as good at room temperature as it does hot.

½ C. (1 stick) butter, divided in 2 parts
2 C. bread crumbs
10 large eggs
Salt and freshly ground black pepper to taste
2 teas. fresh Italian parsley, minced
¾ C. freshly grated Parmesan

Garnish
Fresh parsley sprigs

1. Preheat the oven to 350°F. In a 10-inch ovenproof skillet, melt half the butter and add the bread crumbs. Cook and stir until the crumbs are golden. Remove the skillet from the heat and set aside crumbs in a bowl. Wipe out the skillet with a paper towel.

2. Gently whisk together the eggs; season to taste with salt and pepper. Stir in the parsley. Over medium-low heat, melt the remaining butter in the skillet and add half the bread crumbs. Then carefully pour in the eggs. Cook without stirring just until the eggs have begun to set. (Don't overcook. Just takes a minute or two.)

3. Place the skillet in the preheated oven and cook another 2 minutes. Now dust the top with the remaining bread crumbs and the Parmesan. Bake another minute, just until set, then remove from the oven, loosen the edges, and slide onto a flat serving plate. Cut into wedges to serve, and garnish with additional fresh parsley sprigs.

CINNAMON SUGAR CRULLERS

Makes a baker's dozen crullers in 1 hour

Best if eaten the same day, crullers are yet another version of sweet fried dough. Dunk one in a cup of hot steaming coffee. Delicious.

2 C. bread flour
3 tbsp. instant nonfat dry milk solids
1 tbsp. sugar
2½ teas. 50% faster active dry yeast
½ teas. salt
¼ teas. ground cinnamon
¼ teas. vanilla extract
1 large egg
½ C. hot tap water (120°–130°F)

3 tbsp. butter, softened, cut into bits
Vegetable shortening, for deep-frying

Coating
3 tbsp. sugar
½ teas. ground cinnamon

1. In the food processor fitted with the steel blade, combine the flour, dry milk, sugar, yeast, salt, and cinnamon. Pulse to mix.

2. Combine in a glass measure the vanilla, egg, and hot tap water. Whisk together with a fork. With the motor running, gradually pour liquids into the flour mixture. Then add bits of butter.

3. Process until the dough begins to leave the side of the bowl, forming a ball. Knead 60 seconds, adding flour as necessary if the dough seems sticky.

4. Remove the dough and the steel blade and prepare to micro-rise. Knead the dough by hand a few seconds, then form dough into a ball. With your thumbs, punch a hole to form a doughnut shape and replace in the processor bowl. Cover loosely with a damp tea towel or plastic wrap.

5. Place an 8-ounce glass of water in the back of the microwave. Lower the microwave power to the appropriate micro-rise setting (see page 35). Heat for 3 minutes. Rest for 3 minutes. Heat for 3 minutes. Rest for 6 minutes or until the dough has risen to about double in bulk.

6. Remove the dough to a lightly floured breadboard and knead by hand a few seconds. Divide into 13 equal pieces

and set the dough aside to rest for 5 minutes or so.

7. Lightly grease a cookie sheet. Working with 1 piece of dough at a time, roll each piece into a 12-inch-long rope, then fold the rope in half and twist it 3 or 4 times, pinching the loose ends together. Arrange crullers on the cookie sheet in a row, weighing down the pinched ends with something handy—say a rolling pin—so that the twists won't come undone. Mist crullers with water, then cover and micro-rise, repeating step 5, or raise in a warm, draft-free place until nearly doubled in bulk.

8. Meanwhile, in a paper bag combine the coating of 3 tablespoons sugar and ½ teaspoon cinnamon. Measure shortening into a 10-inch skillet and melt so that the shortening is 2 inches deep. Heat the shortening to 370°F. You'll find it's best to use a thermometer so that you get the temperature just right. Too cool fat will make soggy crullers. Too hot will burn them before they're cooked through. If you don't have a deep-fat thermometer, cook only 1 cruller at first and adjust the temperature as necessary. When the oil is the proper temperature, fry the cruller about 1½ minutes, allowing it to become golden on a side before you turn it. The second side will become golden in something under a minute.

9. Remove cooked crullers with tongs to paper bag and shake to coat with cinnamon-sugar mixture. Serve immediately.

PIGS IN A BLANKET

Makes 16 sausage-filled rolls in under 1 hour

These little piggies, made with only one micro-rise, are ready for the brunch buffet in less than an hour. Serve with butter and honey and a side of curried fruit for a Sunday morning you won't soon forget.

3 C. bread flour	2 large eggs
2 tbsp. sugar	¾ C. hot tap water
1½ teas. salt	½ pound (8) breakfast
5 teas. 50% faster	sausage links
active dry yeast	Sesame or poppy seeds,
2 tbsp. unsalted butter	for sprinkling on top
or margarine	(continued)

The groaning sideboard of a Creole brunch is never complete without a casserole dish of Curried Fruit. Following that strange paradox of hot foods for hot countries, this dish is best made in June when stone fruits are sweet and ripe for the picking. Make the fruit with canned or frozen fruits only if you're desperate. If you really want to go all out for the buffet, add a bowl of whipped cream flavored with no sugar at all, just a jigger of brandy.

Pit all the fruit before you combine. Don't worry if you can't find every fruit on this list. Just substitute an equal measure of whatever perfect fruits you can find at the produce market.

Serves 8 in 50 minutes

1 C. *pitted Bing cherries*
1 C. *sliced fresh peaches*
1 C. *sliced fresh pineapple*
1 C. *halved fresh apricots*
2 *medium bananas, peeled
   and sliced*
½ C. *brown sugar*
2 *tbsp. cornstarch or
   arrowroot*
1 *tbsp. curry powder (or to
   taste)*
¼ C. (½ *stick*) *unsalted
   butter, melted*

1. Cut fruits into large pieces and combine in a large mixing bowl. Generously butter a 2-quart casserole dish. Preheat the oven to 350°F.

2. Combine brown sugar, cornstarch or arrowroot, and curry powder. Stir melted butter into fruits and toss to mix. Then sprinkle brown sugar–cornstarch–curry mixture over all and toss again. Turn mixture into prepared casserole dish.

3. Bake in the preheated oven for 30 minutes. Cool 10 minutes or so before serving.

1. In the processor bowl fitted with the steel blade, add flour, sugar, salt, and yeast. Pulse to mix. Now, cut butter or margarine in finely, and pulse to blend so that it almost disappears.

2. Separate one egg; set white aside. Combine in a glass measure the hot tap water and the remaining egg and egg yolk. Whisk together with a fork, then with the motor running, *drizzle the liquids very slowly* into the dry ingredients, holding back the last portion of liquid to see if the dough will form a ball.

3. Process until dough begins to leave the side of the bowl, forming a ball. Add the last portion of liquid only if necessary. Knead 60 seconds, adding flour as needed if the dough seems sticky. Pinch up a piece of the dough ball. It should feel soft, tacky, smooth, elastic, and warm.

4. Remove the dough from the processor bowl to a lightly floured surface, and knead by hand a few seconds. Cover the dough with the processor bowl and let it rest 5 minutes. Meanwhile, in a 9-inch glass round cake pan, arrange the 8 sausage links, and partially cook them in the microwave, set on high power, for 3 minutes. Then cut each link in 2 pieces, and drain off excess fat from the pan and reserve. Return the sausages to the pan, and place on a cool surface (marble is wonderful) to cool the pan and the sausages.

5. Divide the dough into 16 equal pieces. Form into balls, then flatten each into a disk. Roll each disk around a piece of cooling sausage, then arrange, seam side down, in the cake pan, sides touching. Beat the reserved egg white until foamy and brush over the rolls, taking care that none runs down the sides (it sticks). Sprinkle the rolls with poppy or sesame seeds. Place the rolls in the microwave.

6. Prepare to micro-rise. Place an 8-ounce glass of water in the back of the microwave. Lower microwave power to the appropriate micro-rise setting (see page 35). Heat for 3 minutes. Rest for 3 minutes. Heat for 3 minutes. Rest for 6 minutes or until the rolls have risen to about double in bulk.

7. Meanwhile, preheat the oven to 425°F. When the dough has nearly doubled in bulk, bake in the preheated oven about 20 minutes or until the rolls are a deep golden brown.

8. Remove immediately to a rack to cool. Serve hot with butter and honey. Wrap in plastic wrap to store. Heat leftovers the next day a few moments in the oven or toaster oven for best results.

4 ◆ HORS D'OEUVRES, TOASTS, CROUTONS, AND SALAD BREADS

Parmesan-Basil Toast 123

Popping Pitas 124

Country Bread with Pears, Hazelnuts, and
    Gorgonzola 126

Country Raisin-Walnut Bread 128

Seasoned Crouton Bread 130

Tuscan Toasts 132

Crete Bread 134

French Bread Salad 135

We don't entertain with full-scale dinner parties as often as we used to. Inviting people over to sample our latest find in a good Oregon wine along with some interesting foods to be eaten out of hand is about all we have time for.

Here's where homemade bread can really become the centerpiece of the moment. Not only that, we have suggestions in this chapter that begin with leftover French bread.

If you want cooking to be part of your entertainment, we highly recommend Popping Pitas (see page 124), a bread that hollows out, blows up right before your eyes as you look in the oven, and comes out ready for the table in less than 10 minutes. This hollow puff of golden bread tastes so good with a smear of tapenade (see page 171), caponata, or fresh tomato salsa.

Some of the breads in this chapter are hearty enough to be lunch. Add a wedge of cheese, a glass of wine, a piece of fruit. You're set.

And don't forget to try other parts of the book for appetizer breads. Pizza, cut into small squares, is terrific out of hand. Italian Loaf Rustica (see page 172) is a taste you'll remember. Even the most basic No Pain Ordinaire (see page 52) when toasted and sprinkled with Parmesan and black pepper makes a terrific quick appetizer.

One tip we'd like to pass on is this: almost any sandwich bread complete with fillings and dressings can be tossed together into a salad to feed a crowd. Not long ago we served Muffuletta (see page 54) as a salad by cutting the French baguette into crouton cubes, then tossing with the meats, cheese, olives, olive oil, vinegar, and spices. A new look, but an old, familiar taste. The serving bowl was empty at the end of the party.

PARMESAN-BASIL TOAST

Makes hors d'oeuvres for 8 in 25 minutes

Make this toast using whatever fresh herbs you have, ad-libbing it. Serve with a bracing red wine, and antipasti that could include black and green olives, Italian red peppers, carrot and celery sticks, rolled anchovies with capers. Who wants dinner?

1 day-old loaf French-style bread (Pane al Olio, Sour Faux, Hands-off French Bread)
1 tbsp. fruity olive oil
½ C. cream cheese
½ C. mayonnaise
1 small red onion (about ½ cup when minced)
1½ oz. Parmesan (about ½ C. when grated)
½ C. fresh basil leaves, chopped

2 tbsp. freshly snipped chives or 1 tbsp. dried
1 tbsp fresh oregano leaves, crushed, or 1 teas. dried
1 teas. Worcestershire sauce
Shot of Tabasco
Whiff of cayenne pepper
Generous sprinkling of paprika

1. Preheat the oven to 350°F. Slice the bread in half, lengthwise, and place on a cookie sheet. Brush the loaf lightly with olive oil.

2. Warm the cream cheese (for 30 seconds in the microwave set on 100% power), then combine with the mayonnaise. Whisk together with a fork.

3. Using the steel blade, place the onion in the food processor and mince. Then replace with the grating disk and grate Parmesan into the bowl. Replace the steel blade and add fresh herbs: basil, chives, oregano, what have you. Pulse to chop and mix. Measurements of herbs can be "to taste."

4. Add the cream cheese and mayonnaise to the food processor bowl. Then add Worcestershire, Tabasco, and cayenne. Pulse to mix.

5. Spread the herbed cheese on the bread, dust generously with paprika, then bake in the preheated oven until bubbly and browned, about 15 to 20 minutes. Cool a moment, then slice with a serrated knife into thick trapezoid shapes.

Composed Salad of Italian Roasted Red and Green ◇ Peppers ◇

Serves 4

4 large green bell peppers
4 large red bell peppers

Salt and freshly ground black pepper to taste
Hard-cooked eggs, chopped
Anchovies
Capers
Niçoise olives
Red onion, chopped

Parsley Vinaigrette
Juice and zest of half a lemon
¼ C. fruity olive oil
2 cloves garlic, pressed
¼ C. minced fresh parsley

1. Roast whole peppers on a tray under the broiler set on high heat, turning often until the skins blister and blacken. Pop the hot peppers into a plastic bag, twist it shut, and allow them to sweat for 20 minutes.

2. Working over a bowl to catch the juices, rub the blistered skins off with your hands. Cut peppers into thirds; remove and discard seeds and membrane. Reserve the pepper juices.

3. On a serving plate arrange the peppers along with the eggs, anchovies, capers, olives, onion, and any other parts of the composition you may want to ad-lib.

4. Whisk together the vinaigrette, adding back the reserved pepper juices. Drizzle over composed vegetables, and season to taste with salt and pepper.

Half-Time
◇ Caponata ◇

Makes 1 quart in 45 minutes

Although this doesn't take long to put together, it tastes best if its allowed to stand overnight. Make it in 45 minutes the day before you want to serve—if you can wait that long. Try it with Anita's Sour Faux (see page 58) or other toasts.

2 medium eggplants
1 pound fresh Italian plum tomatoes (2 C.)
1½ C. fruity olive oil
1 large sweet yellow onion
1 medium red onion
2 large ribs celery
2 large cloves garlic
¼ C. minced fresh parsley
½ C. chopped black olives
2 tbsp. capers, drained
¼ C. red wine vinegar
1 tbsp. brown sugar
2 tbsp. tomato paste
Salt and freshly ground black pepper to taste

¼ C. toasted pine nuts (see page 185)

1. Place whole eggplants in the microwave and cook on high power until soft, about 20 minutes. Remove from the microwave, cut in half, and allow them to cool.

2. Meanwhile, in the food processor bowl fitted with the steel blade, chop the tomatoes, then set aside.

3. In a medium saucepan, heat ½ cup of the olive oil. While it's heating finely chop both onions in the food processor, then sauté in the olive oil until the onions are soft but not brown. Stir in the celery and garlic. Continue cooking 5 minutes over medium heat, stirring until everything is soft and tender.

POPPING PITAS

Makes 3 loaves in 1 hour and 15 minutes

If the social kitchen best describes your household, then this bread's for you. An Italian-style pocket bread full of hot air, it bakes in 5 minutes. Invite guests and children to participate in making this showy appetizer, which is served warm with antipasto and a smooth red wine. Pull a chair over to the oven so the children can watch it "explode" right before their eyes. Use for pita sandwiches, too.

1 C. warm water (110°F), divided
2 teas. 50% faster active dry yeast
3 C. bread flour, divided
⅛ C. (2½ tbsp.) fruity olive oil

½ teas. dried oregano
½ teas. salt
Olive oil, for brushing on hot loaves
Freshly grated Parmesan, for sprinkling on hot loaves

1. In the food processor bowl, with the steel blade, combine ¾ cup of the warm water, yeast, and ¾ cup of the bread flour. Process for 10 seconds to blend. Remove the steel blade from the processor bowl and place the bowl in the microwave.

2. Set an 8-ounce glass of water in the microwave. Lower the microwave power to the appropriate micro-rise setting (see page 35) and heat the sponge for 3 minutes. Rest for 3 minutes. Remove the processor bowl from the microwave. Place the processor bowl back on the base and fit with the steel blade. Add the remaining 2¼ cups flour, olive oil, oregano, and salt and process until well blended, about 10 seconds.

3. With the machine running, *very slowly drizzle* just enough of the remaining ¼ cup of warm water into the flour mixture so the dough forms a ball that cleans the sides of the bowl and rides the blade around. Process until the dough turns around the bowl 25 times.

4. Remove the dough and the steel blade from the processor bowl and form the dough into a ball. With your thumbs, punch a hole to form a doughnut shape and place it back in the processor bowl. Cover loosely with a damp tea towel or

microwavable plastic wrap. Place the processor bowl in the middle of the microwave.

5. Set an 8-ounce glass of water next to it. With the microwave power still set at the appropriate micro-rise setting, as in step 2, heat for 3 minutes. Rest for 3 minutes. Heat for 3 minutes. Rest for 45 minutes or until the dough has doubled in bulk. Meanwhile, lightly grease a 12 × 15-inch baking sheet.

6. Preheat the oven to 550°F. Remove the dough from the microwave to a well-floured surface. Divide the dough into 3 equal pieces. Lightly knead each piece to make a smooth ball (keep the remaining pieces covered with a damp tea towel or plastic wrap so they will not dry out). Roll each ball into a circle ⅛ inch thick and approximately 10 inches in diameter. Carefully transfer the dough to the prepared baking sheet (be careful not to tear or puncture the dough).

7. Bake, one at a time, on the bottom rack of the preheated oven until golden brown all over and puffed, approximately 4 to 6 minutes. While one bread bakes you can roll out another. Use the same baking sheet each time, greasing it only the first time. Transfer the hot breads to your serving platter, brush lightly with olive oil, and sprinkle with Parmesan. Serve hot or warm. Popping Pitas do not store well.

4. Scoop out the cooked flesh of the eggplant and add it to the pot, cooking 5 more minutes, adding olive oil if the mixture seems too dry. Now add diced tomatoes, parsley, olives, and capers and cook 3 to 4 more minutes.

5. Meanwhile, combine vinegar, brown sugar, and tomato paste and stir to dissolve the sugar. Pour over the cooking vegetables, cover, and continue to cook for about 15 minutes. Add water if mixture becomes thick enough to stick to the bottom of the pan. Don't overstir. Vegetables should not cook down to mush. Season to taste with salt and pepper.

6. Remove to a serving bowl, pour additional olive oil over the top, and refrigerate until serving time. Garnish with toasted pine nuts. Stick a spreading knife in the mix and pass the hot bread.

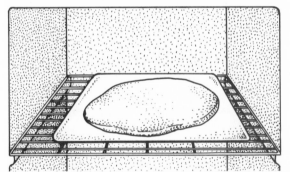

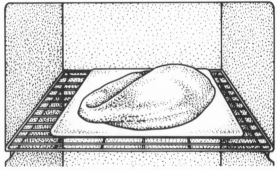

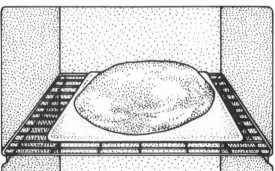

A good way to tell if your pears are "just ripe" is to give them one of two tests. Hold the pear in the palm of your hand and give a gentle squeeze; the pear should just give with pressure, and your fingers should not poke through the skin, as would be the case with a too-ripe pear.

The second test only works if your pear still has some of its stem. Hold the pear in your hand and pull on the stem to see if it gives and pops out. If it does, your pear is ready for eating or baking.

COUNTRY BREAD WITH PEARS, HAZELNUTS, AND GORGONZOLA

Makes 1 loaf in 2 hours and 30 minutes

Rustic and round describes this bread loaded with autumn's harvest of ripe pears and a new crop of hazelnuts. Serve the bread warm, spread with your favorite Gorgonzola or Camembert and a soft, buttery chardonnay.

½ C. hazelnuts	¾ C. rye flour
¾ C. water	¼ teas. ground ginger
½ C. dried pears, cut into ½-inch pieces	¾ teas. salt
	1 large egg
1 medium just ripe Bartlett pear, peeled, cored, and quartered	1 tbsp. unsalted butter or margarine
	2½ tbsp. honey
2 C. bread flour, divided	
	Glaze
2½ teas. 50% faster active dry yeast	1 egg, lightly beaten

1. Place the hazelnuts in a flat-bottomed saucer. Set them in the microwave, heat for 1 minute on high power, and stir. Heat for 1 more minute on high and remove the hazelnuts from the microwave and saucer to a clean tea towel or teacloth, enclosing them completely, and set them aside to steam.

2. Measure the water into a 4-cup liquid glass measure. Add the dried pears. Place the pears and water into the microwave and heat on high power for 90 seconds or just until the pears begin to simmer. Remove the dried pears from the microwave and add the quartered fresh pear. Set aside to cool. When the pears have cooled to warm (115° to 120°F), drain and reserve the pear liquid.

3. In the processor bowl fitted with the steel blade, add 1 cup of the bread flour, yeast, and cooled pears. Process for 15 seconds to blend. Remove the steel blade from the processor bowl. Cover it with a damp tea towel or plastic wrap, and place the bowl in the microwave.

4. Set an 8-ounce glass of water in the microwave. Lower the microwave power to the appropriate micro-rise setting (see page 35), and heat for 2 minutes. Rest for 3 minutes.

5. Meanwhile, rub the skins off the toasted hazelnuts in the cloth and chop coarsely; set aside.

6. Remove the processor bowl from the microwave, place back on the base, and fit with the steel blade. Add the remaining bread flour, rye flour, ginger, salt, egg, unsalted butter or margarine, and honey. Process for 15 seconds to see if the dough will form a ball on its own without the addition of any more liquid. If it does not, with the machine running, drizzle the reserved pear liquid very *slowly* through the feed tube until it does. It should not take more than a tablespoon or two. Process until the dough begins to leave the side of the bowl and forms a ball riding the blade around. Process for 1 minute to knead.

7. Remove the dough and the steel blade and prepare to micro-rise. On a lightly floured surface, knead the chopped hazelnuts into the dough. Form dough into a ball. With your thumbs, punch a hole to form a doughnut shape and replace in the processor bowl. Cover loosely with a damp tea towel or plastic wrap. Place the dough in the microwave.

8. Repeat step 4 except heat a second time for 3 minutes and then rest for 30 minutes or until the dough has doubled in bulk.

9. Meanwhile, lightly grease a glass baking sheet or 9-inch glass pie pan. Remove the dough to a lightly floured surface and knead by hand a few seconds. Form into an 8-inch-diameter ball and place on the prepared baking sheet or pie pan. Slash the top with a ticktacktoe pattern, holding the sharp knife or razor blade at a 45-degree angle.

10. Place the dough in the microwave. Repeat step 8. Meanwhile, preheat the oven to 350° F.

11. Brush the dough with the glaze. Bake on a rack in the bottom third of the preheated oven for 45 to 55 minutes until done, covering the last 10 minutes of baking time with aluminum foil if the loaf is getting too dark.

12. Remove the loaf from the pan to a rack to cool. Serve warm with Gorgonzola for an appetizer or toast for breakfast. Wrap in plastic wrap to store.

Now, good digestion wait on appetite,
And health on both!

—William Shakespeare
Macbeth

COUNTRY RAISIN-WALNUT BREAD

Makes 1 loaf in 2 hours and 15 minutes

Chewy and dark, this bread keeps well up to a week enclosed in a plastic bag.

2 C. bread flour, divided	½ C. rye flour
1½ C. water, divided	3 tbsp. soft seedless raisins (see page 231)
1 tbsp. 50% faster active dry yeast	
1 teas. sugar	⅓ C. coarsely chopped English or black walnuts
3 tbsp. gluten flour	
2 teas. salt	
1 C. whole wheat flour	Whole wheat flour, for dusting on top
¼ C. bran flakes	

1. In the processor bowl fitted with the steel blade, add ½ cup of the bread flour, ½ cup of the water, yeast, and sugar. Process for 10 seconds to blend. Remove the steel blade from the processor bowl. Cover the sponge with a damp tea towel or plastic wrap, and place the bowl in the microwave.

2. Set an 8-ounce glass of water in the back of the microwave. Lower the microwave power to the appropriate micro-rise setting (see page 35), and heat the sponge for 3 minutes. Rest for 3 minutes. Remove the processor bowl from the microwave. Place the processor bowl back on the base and fit with the steel blade. Add the remaining bread flour, gluten flour, salt, whole wheat flour, bran flakes, and rye flour and process until well blended, about 10 seconds.

3. Pour into a liquid measure the remaining 1 cup of water. With the machine running, *drizzle the liquid very slowly* into the dry ingredients, holding back the last portion of liquid to see if the dough will form a ball.

4. Process until the dough begins to leave the side of the bowl, forming a ball. Add the last portion of liquid only if necessary. Stop the machine and remove the dough to a lightly floured surface. Divide the dough in half, adding flour as necessary if it seems sticky; return half to the machine, and knead with the machine running for 1 minute. Remove that half of the dough and process the other half for 1 minute.

Remove the second half from the machine, and, by hand, knead the 2 halves together again. The dough should feel soft, tacky, smooth, elastic, and warm. Form the dough into a ball. With your thumbs, punch a hole to form a doughnut shape and replace in the processor bowl. Cover loosely with a damp tea towel or plastic wrap. Place the dough in the microwave.

5. With an 8-ounce glass of water in the back of the microwave and the power still set at the appropriate micro-rise setting, as in step 2, heat for 3 minutes. Rest for 3 minutes. Heat for 3 minutes. Rest for 30 minutes or until double in bulk.

6. Lightly grease a microwavable baking sheet. Remove the dough to a lightly floured surface and knead by hand a few seconds. Knead in the raisins and walnuts. Form into a 10-inch disk and place on the prepared baking sheet. Dust the top lightly with whole wheat flour and score the top in a ticktacktoe pattern. Cover loosely with a waxed paper tent.

7. Place the dough in the microwave. Repeat step 5 except rest for 25 minutes or until the dough has just about doubled in bulk. Meanwhile, preheat the oven to 475°F and make sure the rack for baking is placed as close to the bottom as possible.

8. Open the oven door and quickly spritz 5 or 6 sprays of water from a clean water bottle into the oven, creating a steamy interior. Quickly place the bread in the oven on the bottom rack. Bake for 8 minutes and turn the oven heat down to 375°F. Bake for 40 minutes or until the bottom of the bread sounds hollow when tapped.

9. Remove the bread from the pan to a rack to cool. Wrap in aluminum foil or a plastic bag to store.

Methods for ◇ Adding Fruit ◇

Most of our recipes direct you to add the fruit at the end of the kneading cycles. This is to keep the food processor from grinding the fruit into indistinguishable pieces.

If your food processor has a dough hook, like the Braun has, you can knead in fruits and nuts by machine.

Another way to use fruit in a basic bread recipe is to let it provide *both* the liquid and the sweetener, producing a flavorful loaf that keeps well. First, you must stew any sweet fruit—prunes, raisins, apricots, etc.—and purée them in the food processor with their cooking liquid. Let the purée cool. Use this mixture for up to half the total liquid in any basic recipe.

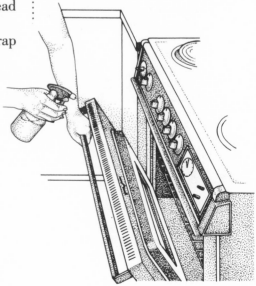

Crouton amounts needed to stuff turkeys:

For one 5- to 8-pound turkey, use 4½ cups croutons.

For one 12- to 16-pound turkey, use 9 cups croutons.

For one 18- to 22-pound turkey, use 13½ cups croutons.

....

CHICKEN STOCK	ONION, CHOPPED	CELERY, CHOPPED
1⅛ C.	½ C.	½ C.
2¼ C.	1 C.	1 C.
3½ C.	1½ C.	1½ C.

....

MARGARINE OR BUTTER	EGGS	CROUTONS
½ C.	1	4½ C.
1 C.	2	9 C.
1½ C.	3	13½ C.

....

Bring the rich chicken stock to a boil. Meanwhile, sauté the onion and celery with the margarine or butter until both are translucent. In a large bowl, lightly beat the eggs and add the croutons, the sautéed onion and celery, plus the margarine or butter, and the broth until all the croutons are moistened. Loosely pack the stuffing into the turkey, allowing room for the stuffing to expand during the cooking period.

Dressed-to-the-Nines ◇ Holiday Stuffing ◇

Makes 8 cups in 40 minutes

Stuffing takes on a new look for the holidays with the addition of colorful, tart cranberries and crisp, sweet apples.

SEASONED CROUTON BREAD

Makes 1 loaf or 12 cups of croutons in 2 hours

Well-seasoned croutons for stuffing your favorite game bird, turkey, or pork roast are now yours without all the preservatives or MSG or store-bought products. Take that electric knife out of the drawer and use it to slice the bread and make the croutons (you will now have reason to thank your aunt who gave it to you for a wedding gift).

3 teas. 50% faster active dry yeast
½ C. warm water
3½ C. bread flour, divided
1 tbsp. sugar
3 tbsp. oil
½ teas. salt
2 tbsp. soy flour or whole wheat flour
2 tbsp. instant potato flakes
2 strips crisp bacon, chopped
1 tbsp. minced onion
¼ teas. freshly ground black pepper

¼ teas. dried thyme or 1 tbsp. fresh
½ teas. dried savory or 2 tbsp. fresh
½ teas. dried sage or 2 tbsp. fresh sage leaves
¼ teas. celery seeds or 2 tbsp. celery leaves
¼ teas. dried marjoram or 1 tbsp. fresh
¼ teas. dried sweet basil or 1 tbsp. fresh basil leaves
½ C. plus 2 tbsp. warm milk

1. In the food processor bowl fitted with the steel blade, combine the yeast, water, ½ cup of the bread flour, and sugar. Process for 10 seconds to blend. Remove the steel blade from the processor bowl. Cover the bowl with a damp tea towel or plastic wrap and place the bowl in the microwave.

2. Set an 8-ounce glass of water in the microwave. Lower the microwave power to the appropriate micro-rise setting (see page 35). Heat the sponge for 3 minutes. Rest for 3 minutes. Remove the processor bowl from the microwave.

3. Place the processor bowl back on the base and fit with the steel blade. Add all of the remaining ingredients except for the milk and process until well blended and the herbs are chopped fine, about 10 seconds.

4. With the machine running, very slowly drizzle just enough of the warm milk into the flour mixture so the dough forms a ball that cleans the side of the bowl and rides the blade around. Process until the dough turns around the bowl 25 times.

5. Remove the dough and the steel blade from the processor bowl, and form the dough into a ball. With your thumbs, punch a hole to form a doughnut shape, and place it back in the processor bowl. Cover loosely with a damp tea towel or microwavable plastic wrap. Place the processor bowl in the middle of the microwave.

6. Set an 8-ounce glass of water in the microwave. With the microwave power still set at the appropriate micro-rise setting as in step 2, heat for 3 minutes. Rest for 3 minutes. Heat for 3 minutes. Rest for 15 to 20 minutes or until the dough has doubled in bulk. Meanwhile, lightly grease an 8½ × 4½-inch glass loaf pan.

7. Remove the dough from the microwave to a lightly floured surface and punch down. Shape into a loaf (see page 40) and place in the prepared pan. Cover loosely with a damp tea towel or microwavable plastic wrap; place the bread off-center in the microwave with an 8-ounce glass of water in the middle of the microwave.

8. Repeat step 6 except rest the dough for 5 to 10 minutes or until it has risen to 1 inch above the top of the pan. Meanwhile, preheat the oven to 375°F.

9. Remove the loaf from the microwave and bake on the middle rack of the preheated oven for 50 minutes or until golden brown.

10. Remove the bread from the pan to a wire rack to cool. After the loaf has cooled, slice and cut into 1-inch crouton cubes. Place the cubes on a baking sheet and bake in a preheated 350°F oven until browned lightly, approximately 25 minutes. Remove the croutons and let them cool thoroughly before storing in plastic bags. Use the croutons in your favorite dressing recipe, storing in the refrigerator until ready for use.

¼ pound sage bulk sausage, crumbled
2 tbsp. unsalted butter
½ C. finely chopped sweet onion
½ teas. minced garlic
½ C. chopped fresh cranberries
2 C. chopped unpeeled tart apples such as Granny Smith
½ teas. ground cinnamon
¼ teas. freshly grated nutmeg
2 C. Seasoned Crouton Bread croutons
¾ C. grated medium-sharp cheddar
1 C. rich chicken stock

1. In a large skillet over medium heat, fry the sausage until no longer pink. Drain off any excess fat and discard. Remove the sausage from the skillet and set aside. Wipe the skillet clean with a paper towel. Preheat the oven to 400°F.

2. Place the skillet over medium heat and melt the butter. Add the onion and sauté until almost soft, about 5 minutes. Stir in the garlic, cranberries, and apples and sauté until the apples are soft, about 6 minutes. Stir in the cinnamon and nutmeg.

3. In a large bowl, combine the sausage, apple-cranberry mixture, croutons, and cheese. Moisten with rich chicken stock until all the croutons are softened. Place the stuffing in a lightly greased 8-cup baking dish and bake on the middle rack of the oven for 20 minutes or until the cheese melts and the stuffing is heated through. (Of course if you *have* a bird handy, stuff the cavity loosely and truss closed. Roast as directed, according to weight of the bird and addition of stuffing.) Serve with turkey, roast pork, or any other white meat.

Pesto Torta
◇ with Tomatoes ◇

Makes 5 cups in 3 hours

¾ *C. minced sun-dried*
   tomatoes in olive oil
½ *C. freshly grated*
   Parmesan
¼ *C. freshly grated Romano*
½ *C. unsalted butter,*
   softened
1 *pound Neufchâtel (light*
   cream cheese)
½ *C. sour cream or light*
   sour cream
¾ *C. prepared pesto (see*
   page 170 for homemade)

1. Prepare a 6-cup mold or bowl by first lightly greasing it. Now line the entire surface with plastic wrap. Layer the minced sun-dried tomatoes on the bottom of the mold.

2. Place the cheeses, butter, and sour cream in the bowl of the food processor fitted with the steel blade. Blend until thoroughly mixed, about 60 seconds. Scrape down the sides of the bowl with a rubber spatula and pulse to mix again.

3. Spoon half the cheese mixture into the mold over the tomatoes. Spread half of the pesto atop the cheese. Then spoon remaining cheese mixture into the mold. Spread with the remaining pesto and cover loosely with plastic wrap. Chill for 3 hours or, if you wish, freeze it at this point. Keeps well frozen for up to a month.

4. To unmold, remove the plastic wrap from the top, turn the mold upside down on a flat serving tray, carefully pull the mold away, then remove the wrap. Serve with Tuscan Toasts.

TUSCAN TOASTS

Makes 30 toasts in 3 hours

Crunchy and tasty, Tuscan Toasts are a cross between toast and zwieback. They're made from an easy raised dough dappled with pine nuts, pesto, and anise seeds, each adding its own distinctive flavor. Try the toasts with your favorite Italian soup, such as white bean fagioli, or serve them as an appetizer bread with Pesto Torta with Tomatoes.

½–¾ *C. warm water*
      (110°F)
2¼ *C. bread flour*
3 *teas. 50% faster*
   active dry yeast
1 *tbsp. sugar*
½ *teas. anise seeds*
⅔ *C. pine nuts*
2 *tbsp. olive oil*

¼ *C. pesto, prepared*
   or homemade (see
   page 170)
1 *teas. salt*

Glaze
1 *egg, beaten*
Olive oil, for brushing on
   top

1. In the food processor bowl fitted with the steel blade combine ½ cup water, ¼ cup of the flour, yeast, sugar, and anise seeds. Process for 10 seconds to blend. Remove the steel blade from the processor bowl. Cover the bowl with a damp tea towel or plastic wrap and place the bowl in the microwave.

2. Set an 8-ounce glass of water in the microwave. Lower the microwave power to appropriate micro-rise setting (see page 35), and heat the sponge for 3 minutes. Rest for 3 minutes. Remove the processor bowl from the microwave. Place the processor bowl back on the base and fit with the steel blade. Add the remaining 2 cups flour, pine nuts, olive oil, pesto, and salt. Process until well blended and the nuts are chopped fine, about 20 seconds.

3. With the machine running, very slowly drizzle just enough of the remaining water into the flour mixture so the dough forms a ball that cleans the sides of the bowl. Process until the dough turns around the bowl 40 times.

4. Remove the dough and the steel blade from the processor bowl; form the dough into a ball. With your thumbs, punch a hole to form a doughnut shape and place it back in the processor bowl. Cover loosely with a damp tea towel or

microwavable plastic wrap. Place the processor bowl in the middle of the microwave.

5. Set an 8-ounce glass of water in the microwave. With the microwave power still set at the appropriate micro-rise setting, as in step 2, heat for 3 minutes. Rest for 3 minutes. Heat for 3 minutes. Rest for 20 minutes or until the dough has doubled in bulk.

6. Remove the dough from the microwave. Punch the dough down and divide it in half. Shape each half into a strand 12 inches long and about 3 inches wide. Place the strands about 2 inches apart on a microwavable baking sheet. Cover loosely with a damp tea towel or microwavable plastic wrap and return the baking sheet to the microwave. Keeping microwave power set as in steps 2 and 5, heat for 3 minutes. Rest for 3 minutes. Heat for 3 minutes. Meanwhile, preheat the oven to 375°F.

7. Remove the dough from the microwave and brush the tops liberally with the beaten-egg glaze.

8. Bake the dough on the middle shelf of the preheated oven for 35 minutes or until golden brown. Remove the breads from the baking sheet to a wire rack to cool.

9. Meanwhile, lower the oven temperature to 325°F. When the bread has cooled, cut the loaves into ½-inch-thick slices. Arrange the slices, leaving a little space between each, in a single layer on the baking sheet. Brush the tops lightly with the olive oil.

10. Bake on the middle rack of the oven for 30 minutes or until the toasts are dry all the way through and golden brown. Remove to a rack to cool and store in plastic bags.

Spinach-Cheese ◇ Torta ◇

Makes one 9-inch pie in 1 hour

Here's a crustless pie that gives you a bright green, firm addition to the appetizer board.

- *2 pounds fresh spinach, stemmed, washed, and dried*
- *1 tbsp. olive oil*
- *1 C. finely chopped green onions and tops*
- *5 large eggs*
- *2 C. grated Monterey Jack*
- *¼ C. grated cheddar*

Salt and freshly ground black pepper to taste

1. Parboil spinach leaves in a cauldron of boiling water for 10 seconds, then refresh under cold water to set the color. Drain and chop the spinach. Set aside. Meanwhile, preheat the oven to 350°F. Butter a 9-inch glass pie plate.

2. Heat olive oil in a 10-inch skillet over medium heat, then add green onions and sauté, stirring, until soft, about 10 minutes. Add spinach and cook until any remaining moisture has evaporated, no more than a minute. Remove to a bowl to cool.

3. In a large bowl, whisk eggs until frothy, then add cheeses and stir to mix. Stir in spinach mixture and season to taste with salt and pepper. Spoon mixture into prepared pie pan. Bake in the preheated oven until browned and until a toothpick inserted will come out clean, about 40 minutes. Cool to room temperature before slicing.

◇ Crete Crème ◇

Makes 3 cups in 5 minutes

Combine in the processor bowl a cup *each* of cream cheese, sour cream, and heavy cream. Add a pinch of salt, a whiff of cayenne, then purée until smooth. Spoon into a glass serving dish, garnish with raisins or caviar, and serve alongside thick slices of Crete Bread.

CRETE BREAD

Makes 1 round loaf in 1 hour and 30 minutes

Crete, known for the production of olive oil, raisins, wine, nuts, fruits, and vegetables, has also given us this rich, lovely free-form loaf glazed with walnuts, sesame and anise seeds, ginger, and Parmesan cheese. Try it with an eggplant entrée or lamb and pine nuts.

2½ teas. 50% faster active dry yeast
2½ C. bread flour
⅓ C. instant nonfat dry milk solids
1 teas. salt
¾ C. hot tap water (125°–130°F)
1 tbsp. mild honey
1 large egg
2 tbsp. unsalted butter or margarine, softened

Topping
¼ C. freshly grated Parmesan
¼ C. walnuts
2 tbsp. toasted sesame seeds (see page 72)
1 teas. anise seeds
¼ teas. ground ginger
1 egg, whisked until frothy

1. In the food processor bowl fitted with the steel blade, combine the yeast, flour, dry milk, and salt. Pulse to mix.

2. Combine in a glass measure the hot tap water, honey, egg, and butter or margarine and gradually pour liquids into the dry ingredients with the motor running.

3. Process until the dough begins to leave the side of the bowl. Knead 60 seconds, adding flour as necessary if the dough seems sticky.

4. Remove the dough and the steel blade and prepare to micro-rise. On a lightly floured surface, knead the dough by hand a few seconds, then form dough into a ball. With your thumbs, punch a hole to form into a doughnut shape and replace in the processor bowl. Cover loosely with a damp tea towel or plastic wrap.

5. Place an 8-ounce glass of water in the back of the microwave. Lower the microwave power to the appropriate micro-rise setting (see page 35). Place processor bowl in the microwave. Heat for 3 minutes. Rest for 3 minutes. Heat for 3 minutes. Rest for 6 minutes or until the dough has risen to about double in bulk.

6. Remove the dough to a lightly floured surface and knead by hand a few seconds. Form into an 8-inch-diameter ball and set the dough aside to rest.

7. Grease generously an 8-inch round glass pie plate. Preheat the oven to 350°F. Place the dough in the pie plate, press down slightly, then micro-rise, repeating step 5, or raise in a warm, draft-free place until nearly doubled in bulk.

8. Meanwhile, make the topping in the food processor. Use the grater for the cheese, then the steel blade for chopping the walnuts, then simply add the remaining ingredients and pulse to mix.

9. When the dough has nearly doubled in bulk, spoon the topping on, taking care not to allow any to run down the sides into the pie plate (it sticks like glue).

10. Bake on the middle rack in the preheated oven 25 to 30 minutes or until evenly browned.

11. Remove immediately from the pan to a rack to cool. Wrap in plastic to store. This bread keeps up to a week, properly stored.

FRENCH BREAD SALAD

Serves 2 in 15 minutes

Here's what you can do with the last half of a French baguette left over from yesterday. Makes a great addition to a dinner that's nothing more than grilled chicken breast garnished with Italian parsley.

6 thick slices day-old French-style bread (Pane al Olio, Sour Faux, Hands-off French Bread)
Olive oil
Garlic salt
2 Beefsteak tomatoes, quartered
1 C. large black olives
½ C. marinated artichoke hearts

1 tbsp. drained capers
½ C. freshly snipped Italian parsley
½ C. minced celery
½ C. finely chopped fresh broccoli
Salt and freshly ground black pepper to taste
Lettuce leaves

(continued)

If you wish, cook broccoli by placing uniformly cut small flowerets in a microwavable bowl. Sprinkle with water, cover tightly with microwave plastic wrap, then cook in the microwave on high power for 1 minute per cup of vegetables. Remove broccoli to a colander and refresh under cold water until cold. You have now set the color, cooked the broccoli just *al dente*, and learned a technique you can use with many vegetables: cauliflower, carrots, celery, beans, beets, and others. Notice how the taste develops with just a little cooking. Chez Panisse, in Berkeley, has made its reputation making salads that combine just-steamed vegetables and fresh-from-the-garden raw ones. Any starchy vegetable lends itself well to this technique. Add bread cubes to the salad, not as an afterthought in the form of croutons on the top, but as an integral part of the salad, and it's a wonderful new presentation.

1. Using the grill you're cooking meat over, or a preheated skillet, brush the bread with olive oil, season with garlic salt, then grill the bread on both sides until golden brown, about 2 minutes. Remove the bread to a cutting board, and cut into large crouton-sized cubes.

2. In a large salad bowl, combine the grilled bread cubes with the remaining ingredients except the salt and pepper and lettuce. Toss to mix. Season to taste with salt and pepper. Then arrange on dinner plates atop lettuce leaves.

3. Dress with either vinaigrette or yogurt dressing.

Plain Vinaigrette

Makes ½ cup in 5 minutes

1 tbsp. red wine vinegar or fresh lemon juice	Salt and freshly ground black pepper to taste
1 teas. Dijon-style mustard	½ C. fruity olive oil
1 large clove garlic, minced	

Whisk together vinegar or lemon juice with mustard, garlic, salt, and pepper. Whisk in olive oil to make an emulsion. Allow the dressing to stand a few minutes before tossing with salad.

Tomato Yogurt Dressing

Makes 1 cup in 5 minutes

1 large Beefsteak tomato	Shot of Tabasco
½ C. plain nonfat yogurt	1 teas. lime juice
1 teas. Worcestershire sauce	Salt and freshly ground black pepper to taste

Place the tomato in the food processor fitted with the steel blade. Purée. Add the remaining ingredients and pulse to mix. Allow this dressing to stand a few moments before tossing with salad.

5 ◆ BAGELS, BAGUETTES, BREADSTICKS, BUNS, AND ROLLS

Pumpernickel Baguette 139

Tomato-Basil Baguette 140

Water Bagels 142

Home-Style Soft Pretzels 144

Breadsticks Grande 146

Soft Parmesan Breadsticks 148

Grissini Anise 150

Brown and Serves 151

Rich Dinner Rolls in an Hour 153

Anadama Dinner Rolls 154

Divine Butterhorn Rolls 156

Hard Rolls 158

Parsley, Sage, Rosemary, and Thyme Pinwheel Loaf
  with Pine Nuts 160

Raleigh House Orange Rolls 162

If you haven't tried the Micro-Rise process yet, we encourage you to begin with small breads. Rolls, buns, baguettes simply jump when raised in the microwave.

Perhaps one of the easiest, most foolproof recipes in this book to begin making micro-rise breads is Rich Dinner Rolls in an Hour (see page 153). Only one micro-rise is needed to create a roll you'll want to make again and again. This is truly baking bread in half the time.

We also adore the Divine Butterhorn Rolls (see page 156), which remind us of long Sunday dinners in the South when people lingered around the dinner table, telling stories, punctuating them with "Just another roll, please, Mama."

Authentic bagels are one type of bread you can usually find only if you live in the neighborhood of a great bagel bakery. But by using the Micro-Rise process in concert with traditional bagel shaping, boiling, then baking on a stone, we find bagel making to be a joy. We admit ours never look as uniform and smooth as ones the bagel maker shapes, but we keep trying. Kids like to get in on the bagel shaping—even though they sometimes stop short and make long bagel ropes instead of rings.

You'll find another baguette recipe in the basic breads under Anita's Sour Faux (see page 58). Again, by using the Micro-Rise process combined with baking on a stone, you can have fine, traditional results using half-time kitchen methods.

Do try the hard rolls. Four rises give this bread an outstanding taste, and by cutting the proofing time down to size in the microwave, the process for making hard rolls seems much less daunting.

Breadsticks, both savory and sweet, are easy to do using the Micro-Rise process, although we're the first to admit that if there's one kind of bread that, made at home, seems to come out looking like a snake that swallowed lumpy things, this is it. If people make fun of your strange-looking breadsticks, you just tell them that they're *hand-crafted*, thank you very much.

Rolls are one of our favorite types of breads to micro-rise. We know you'll agree, once you've tried them a time or two.

PUMPERNICKEL BAGUETTE

Makes 1 loaf in 1 hour and 30 minutes

Here's the baguette you see in the deli, sliced thin and used as the base for hors d'oeuvres. Once you make it at home, you won't be satisfied with the store-bought version. Keep one in the freezer for impromptu parties.

1½ C. whole wheat flour
½ C. medium rye flour
½ C. unbleached white flour
1 tbsp. caraway seeds
1 tbsp. unsalted butter
1 teas. salt
3 teas. 50% faster active dry yeast

1 tbsp. cocoa
¾ C. milk

Glaze
1 tbsp. molasses
2 tbsp. cold water

1. Fit the processor bowl with the steel blade. Combine and pulse to mix the flours, caraway seeds, butter, salt, yeast, and cocoa.

2. Measure the milk into a 2-cup microwavable measure and heat on high power in the microwave for 1 minute or until it is the temperature of hot tap water, about 120° F. With the processor motor running, pour the milk into the flour mixture. When the dough leaves the side of the bowl and forms a ball, knead for 60 seconds.

3. Remove the dough and the steel blade from the bowl. Knead the dough by hand a few seconds on a floured surface and form into a doughnut shape. Replace the dough in the processor bowl. Cover the bowl loosely with a damp tea towel or microwavable plastic wrap. Place the processor bowl in the middle of the microwave.

4. Set an 8-ounce glass of water in the microwave. Lower the microwave power to the appropriate micro-rise setting (see page 35). Heat for 3 minutes. Rest for 3 minutes. Heat for 3 minutes. Rest for 6 minutes. The dough will not double in volume, but that's OK. If it raises by a third, that's enough. Lightly grease a microwavable baking sheet.

5. Remove the dough from the microwave and knead lightly on a floured surface for a few seconds. Shape the dough into a baguette (see page 42) about 15 inches long and place on the prepared baking sheet. *(continued)*

Let your imagination run wild when making toppings for this bread. Try a combination of chopped watercress, walnuts, and cream cheese. Or how about shrimp, chopped apple, mayonnaise, and a dash of curry powder? We tried a combination of cream cheese, horseradish, and lox that was divine. Also try a great ham, sliced thin or shaved with a good 4-grain mustard.

Watercress
◇ Cheese ◇

Makes 3 cups cheese in 10 minutes

2 *C. loosely packed watercress leaves, minced*
2 *green onions (white part only), minced*
2 *oz. cream cheese, room temperature*
½ *teas. salt*
⅛ *teas. freshly ground black pepper*
½ *C. whipping cream, whipped stiff*

Blend the watercress, onions, cream cheese, salt, and pepper in a bowl. Fold in the whipped cream. Cover and chill for 2 to 4 hours. Serve with the Pumpernickel Baguette.

6. Place the bread and an 8-ounce glass of water back in the microwave. Repeat step 4 except rest for 11 minutes, or until the baguette has just about doubled in bulk. Meanwhile, preheat the oven to 350°F and whisk together the molasses and water. Before baking, brush the loaf with the molasses mixture.

7. Bake the bread on the middle rack of the preheated oven for 35 to 40 minutes until a deep mahogany color. Remove the bread to a cooling rack. Let this bread cool completely before you try to slice it. Wrap in plastic to store.

TOMATO-BASIL BAGUETTE

Makes two 16-inch baguettes in 1 hour and 30 minutes

You can make the most divine sandwiches using this baguette for a base. Ricotta, fresh basil leaves, and thin slices of plum tomatoes. Or mozzarella and anchovy strips, run under the broiler until bubbly and browned. Turkey breast, sweet butter, and sprouts. You can also form this dough into a rosy 16-inch pizza crust.

2½ teas. 50% faster active dry yeast	¼ C. nonfat dry milk solids
1 tbsp. honey	12 fresh basil leaves, torn, or 1 tbsp. dried
¼ C. lukewarm water (110°F)	
⅓ C. tomato paste	
2 tbsp. olive oil	**Glaze**
⅔ C. lukewarm water (110°F)	1 egg plus 1 teas. water
3 C. bread flour	

1. Combine in a glass measure the yeast, honey, and ¼ cup warm water. Stir to mix. In a second container, combine tomato paste, olive oil, and ⅔ cup warm water. Stir to mix. Then combine both liquids.

2. In the food processor bowl fitted with the steel blade, combine bread flour and dry milk. Pulse to mix. With the motor running, drizzle in liquids slowly, holding back the last portion to see if the dough forms a ball. Add this liquid only if necessary.

You can make a wonderful sandwich by slicing the baguette in half lengthwise, drizzling with fruity olive oil, then layering on thinly sliced prosciutto, provolone cheese, fresh basil leaves, and roasted red pepper. Shake a little freshly grated Parmesan cheese, grate some pepper, and give the whole thing a few drops of balsamic vinegar.

3. Once the dough forms a ball, leaving the side of the processor bowl, process for 60 seconds.

4. Remove the dough from the bowl; remove the dough blade. Knead dough by hand a few seconds, kneading in the basil and adding flour if the dough seems sticky, then form dough into a ball. With your thumbs, punch a hole to form a doughnut shape and replace in the processor bowl. Cover loosely with a damp tea towel or with plastic wrap and prepare to micro-rise.

5. Place an 8-ounce glass of water in the back of the microwave. Lower the microwave power to the appropriate micro-rise setting (see page 35). Place the dough in the microwave. Heat for 3 minutes. Let rest for 3 minutes. Heat for 3 minutes. Let rest for 6 minutes or until the dough has doubled in bulk.

6. Remove the dough from the processor bowl to a lightly floured surface, punch down, and knead by hand a few seconds. Cover the dough with the processor bowl and allow it to rest for 10 minutes.

7. Sprinkle a glass cookie sheet with cornmeal and set aside. Preheat the oven to 400°F.

8. Roll out the dough to form a 14 × 7-inch rectangle. Cut in 2 pieces, so that you have two 14-inch pieces. Roll each up tightly, starting with the 14-inch side. Place on the prepared cookie sheet. Brush the tops with a mixture of 1 tablespoon egg plus 1 teaspoon water. Holding a razor blade at a 45-degree angle, gently cut slashes into the tops.

9. Place glass cookie sheet in the microwave and micro-rise, repeating step 5, except don't cover the bread.

10. Place the bread in the preheated oven, then immediately turn the oven down to 375°F. Bake 30 to 35 minutes or until golden brown.

11. Remove from the cookie sheet and cool on a rack. Don't slice until the loaf is cool enough to handle. Best eaten the day it's made.

Traditionally, bagels are split, covered with cream cheese, and topped with lox (smoked salmon). They're also delicious split and toasted with butter. Some New Yorkers like them split, buttered, and grilled. Californians make terrific sandwiches by splitting bagels, then piling them high with white cream cheese, black olives, purple onion, blood-red tomatoes, and green and white sprouts. We like them plain: as is, cold and whole, when they're no more than a couple of hours old.

◇

Bagels benefit from being cooked directly on a pizza stone or cooking tiles. The best crust and lift comes from direct contact with a hot rock.

◇

You can leave the sugar out of the boiling water if you wish. Actually, it barely sweetens the taste of the bagel, but helps to shine it.

WATER BAGELS

Makes 10 medium bagels or 20 miniature bagels in 1 hour and 30 minutes

Certain diehards say that only a bagel cooked in a coal-fired oven is the genuine article. Other old-timers remember when a real bagel required a good set of chops to bite into. What would they say about a bagel kneaded in a food processor and raised in a microwave? Oy vey.

We love these bagels cooked on a stone. In addition to the traditional toppings—coarse kosher salt, sesame or poppy seeds—try sprinkling the tops with red pepper flakes, or raw turbinado sugar, or fresh mixed herbs, including parsley and chives.

3 C. bread flour
1 tbsp. sugar
½ teas. salt
2½ teas. 50% faster active dry yeast
1⅛ C. hot tap water (120°F)

Water Bath
1 gallon water
1 tbsp. sugar

Glaze
1 egg, beaten with 1 teas. water
Poppy seeds, sesame seeds, red pepper flakes, turbinado sugar, mixed fresh herbs, onion, garlic, kosher salt, for sprinkling on top (optional)

1. In the food processor fitted with the steel blade, add flour, sugar, salt, and yeast. Pulse to mix.

2. With the motor running, *gradually drizzle in the water,* holding back the last tablespoon or so until the dough forms a ball.

3. Knead for 60 seconds, adding the last bit of water only if necessary. Pinch up a piece of the dough. It should feel soft, satiny, elastic, smooth, and warm.

4. Remove the dough and steel blade from the processor bowl and prepare to micro-rise. Knead the dough by hand a few seconds on a lightly floured surface, then form dough into a ball. With your thumbs, punch a hole to form a doughnut shape then replace in the processor bowl. Cover loosely with a damp tea towel or plastic wrap. Place in the microwave.

5. Position an 8-ounce glass of water in the back of the microwave. Lower the microwave power to the appropriate

micro-rise setting (see page 35). Heat for 3 minutes. Rest for 3 minutes. Heat for 3 minutes. Rest for 6 minutes or until the dough has doubled in bulk.

6. Remove the dough from the processor bowl to a lightly floured surface and punch down. Knead by hand a few seconds, then divide the dough into 10 equal pieces (20 for miniatures).

7. For 10 medium bagels, use the palms of both hands together, rolling each piece into a ball. With your fingers, punch a hole to form a doughnut shape. Alternately, roll or pat dough out into a 10-inch circle and cut with a large doughnut cutter.

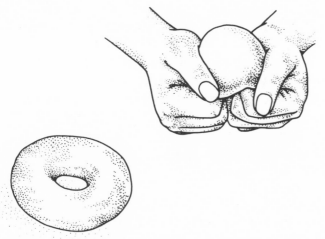

8. Place the bagels on a microwavable baking sheet sprinkled with cornmeal. Spritz the tops with water. Micro-rise, repeating step 5, or raise the bagels in a warm, draft-free space until almost double in bulk.

9. In a large soup pot, bring a gallon of water to a boil. Add a tablespoon of sugar to the water. Reduce to a simmer. Slip bagels into simmering water—don't crowd them, no more than can comfortably rest in water without touching—and cook for 7 minutes, turning once. Drain well on a rack.

10. Meanwhile, preheat the oven to 400°F. If you're baking on a stone (see pages 21–25), be sure to allow a minimum of 30 minutes for preheating the oven with the stone inside. Brush the tops of bagels with the egg mixture, then sprinkle with desired topping (if any).

11. Bake on the middle rack in the preheated oven 20 to 25 minutes or until golden brown. Remove to a rack to store. Bagels are best if eaten within a few hours of baking.

Fresh Berry
◇ Jam ◇

Makes 2 cups in 35 minutes

This is the easiest jam to make that we know of, and the fresh, uncooked flavor is the best. Try it with your favorite berry.

> 2 C. berries, your favorite kind
> 1/3 C. sugar (depending on the sweetness of the berries, you may need more or less)
> Juice of 1 lemon (optional—if the berries are not the ripest)
> 1/4 teas. finely ground black pepper

1. Place the berries, sugar, lemon juice (if using), and the black pepper in the bowl of the food processor fitted with the steel blade. Using several on and off turns, process the fruit just until it is the desired consistency.

2. Remove the metal blade. Cover and let the berries sit until the sugar dissolves, about 30 minutes. The jam is now ready to serve and will keep in the refrigerator anywhere from 3 days to 1 week, depending on the kind of berries used.

HOME-STYLE SOFT PRETZELS

Makes 2 dozen small pretzels or 1 dozen large pretzels in 1 hour and 30 minutes

Pretzels date back to ancient Rome. Later, a Northern Italian monk is said to have twisted the ropes of dough into the characteristic shape we know now to suggest arms in an attitude of prayer.

German and Alsatian children were given pretzels as rewards for memorizing their prayers. The bread twists were also considered good luck and were sometimes baked in large enough twists to wear around the neck.

A pretzel is really just a bagel with a twist, being cooked first in simmering water, then baked. You'll notice that this recipe has a large proportion of gluten flour. The gluten is what gives the pretzel its exceptional lift, even crumb, and shiny crust. Also note that this is a fat-free bread. Ideal for a diet. Good chewy bite and all complex carbohydrates.

3 C. bread flour	**Water Bath**
¾ C. gluten flour	**1 quart water**
1 teas. salt	**3 tbsp. baking soda**
1 teas. sugar	**1 tbsp. sugar**
2½ teas. 50% faster active dry yeast	**Kosher salt, for sprinkling on top**
1½ C. hot tap water (120°F)	

1. In the processor bowl fitted with the steel blade, add flours, salt, sugar, and yeast. Pulse to mix.

2. Pour hot tap water into a glass measure, then with the processor motor running, *drizzle the water very slowly* into the dry ingredients, holding back the last portion of liquid to see if the dough will form a ball.

3. Process until dough begins to leave the sides of the bowl, forming a ball. Add the last liquid only if necessary. Knead 60 seconds, adding flour as necessary if the dough seems sticky. Pinch up a piece of the dough. It should feel soft, tacky, smooth, elastic, and warm.

4. Remove the dough and the steel blade and prepare to micro-rise. On a lightly floured surface, knead dough by hand a few seconds, then form dough into a ball. With your thumbs,

punch a hole to form a doughnut shape and replace in the processor bowl. Cover loosely with a damp tea towel or plastic wrap. Place the dough in the microwave.

5. Place an 8-ounce glass of water in the back of the microwave. Lower the microwave power to the appropriate micro-rise setting (see page 35). Heat for 3 minutes. Rest for 3 minutes. Heat for 3 minutes. Rest for 6 minutes or until the dough has risen to about double in bulk.

6. Remove the dough to a lightly floured surface and knead by hand a few seconds. Form into a ball, cover the dough with the processor bowl, and allow it to rest for 5 minutes or so.

7. Preheat the oven to 425°F. Punch down the dough and cut it into 12 or 24 equal pieces. Roll each of the 12 pieces into a 16-inch-long rope with tapered ends, then knot each into a pretzel shape. Alternately, roll each of the 24 pieces into pencil-thin strands and don't twist. Place the pretzels on a cornmeal-sprinkled glass cookie sheet, then micro-rise, repeating step 5, or raise in a warm, draft-free place until nearly doubled in bulk.

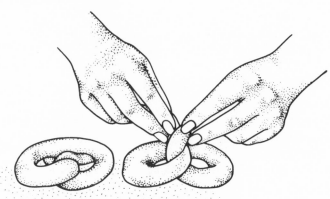

8. Meanwhile, combine the quart of water with the baking soda and sugar in a large saucepan and heat to a simmer.

9. When the pretzels have nearly doubled in bulk, slide them into the simmering water, 3 at a time, and cook for 20 seconds per side, turning them once gently with a slotted spoon. Lift from the water with the slotted spoon to the cookie sheet. Sprinkle the tops with coarse salt.

10. Bake on the center rack in the preheated oven 15 minutes or until evenly browned. Remove immediately to a rack to cool. Wrap in plastic to store. Pretzels taste best if eaten the day they're made.

BREADSTICKS GRANDE

Makes 16 large breadsticks or 40 salad-size breadsticks in 1 hour and 10 minutes

We first started making these breadsticks when catering the Sons of Italy yearly reunion. Bunched together and tied with raffia, they looked sensational. When everyone started nibbling on the centerpieces and telling us how wonderful they were, we started serving them. Salute!

3 C. bread flour
1 tbsp. sugar
3 tbsp. fresh herbs of your choice, basil, oregano, Italian parsley (optional)
5 teas. 50% faster active dry yeast
¼ C. olive oil
1 C. hot tap water (120°–130°F)

Glaze
1 large egg white, beaten until frothy with 1 tbsp. water
Toasted sesame seeds (see pages 72 and 191) or poppy seeds or Kosher salt, for sprinkling on top (optional)

1. In the processor bowl fitted with the steel blade, add the flour, sugar, herbs, yeast, and oil. Process until the herbs are finely chopped, or for 10 seconds to blend if you're not using herbs.

2. Pour the hot water into a liquid measure. With the motor running, *drizzle the liquid very slowly* into the dry ingredients, holding back the last portion of liquid to see if the dough will form a ball.

3. Process until the dough begins to leave the side of the bowl, forming a ball. Add the last of the liquid only if necessary. When the dough forms a ball, stop. *Do not knead.*

4. Remove the dough to a lightly floured board (the rough texture of a breadboard or a pizza peel will keep the slippery dough from sliding under your hands) and form into a ball. Set aside to rest, covered with a damp tea towel or plastic wrap, while preparing the baking sheets. Heavily oil 2 large baking sheets. For grande breadsticks, cut the dough into 16 equal-sized pieces. For salad breadsticks, cut the dough into 40 equal-sized pieces.

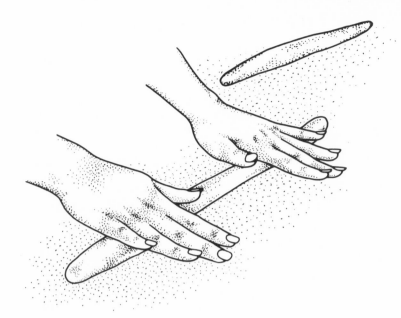

Breadsticks can become striking focal points in a centerpiece. For a beautiful rustic red stick, after brushing with the egg-white wash, heavily coat the sticks with dried red pepper flakes (caution your guests about nibbling on these, as they are *hot*). Bake as directed. When completely cool, tie together in large bunches with raffia and tuck into a country basket along with fresh red, yellow, and green peppers and purple eggplants.

5. For grande sticks, roll each piece into a 20-inch-long rope. For salad breadsticks, roll each piece into a 12-inch-long rope. Place the sticks on the prepared baking sheets (sides not touching). With a light brush or feather, brush the sticks with the excess oil in the pans. Set aside in a warm place and allow to rise until puffy, about 15 minutes. (You may micro-rise here if you have used microwavable baking sheets and the breadsticks will fit in the microwave. Heat on the appropriate micro-rise power [see page 35] for 3 minutes. Rest for 3 minutes. Heat for 3 minutes.) Meanwhile, preheat the oven to 350°F.

6. When the breadsticks are puffy, lightly brush with the frothy egg white and water. Sprinkle with the desired seed, salt, or leave plain.

7. Bake on the middle rack of the preheated oven for 30 to 35 minutes or until light brown. Let cool on the baking sheet for 5 minutes before removing. Serve warm or at room temperature. Store in airtight containers or plastic bags.

These breadsticks make flavorful croutons for salad. We let them dry overnight, brush with additional butter, then sprinkle lightly with red pepper flakes before cutting into croutons.

SOFT PARMESAN BREADSTICKS

Makes 20 breadsticks in 1 hour

Better than the soft breadsticks served as an appetizer in the neighborhood pizzeria. Offer these with your favorite marinara sauce for dipping.

2½ C. bread flour
3 teas. 50% faster active dry yeast
½ teas. garlic salt
¾ teas. Italian seasoning or dried oregano
1 tbsp. sugar
¼ C. freshly grated Parmesan
1 tbsp. unsalted butter

¼ C. hot tap water
½ C. milk
1 large egg, room temperature
¼ C. (4 tbsp) unsalted butter, melted, for brushing on top
½ C. freshly grated Parmesan, for sprinkling on top

1. Fit the processor bowl with the steel blade. Combine and pulse to mix the flour, yeast, garlic salt, Italian seasoning or oregano, sugar, ¼ cup Parmesan, and 1 tablespoon butter.

2. In a 2-cup microwavable glass measure, combine the hot water, milk, and egg.

3. With the motor running, add all but 1 tablespoon of the liquid ingredients to the dry ingredients. The dough should leave the side of the bowl and form a ball. If it doesn't, add the remaining 1 tablespoon of liquid ingredients, and the dough will form a ball. Knead with the machine running for 30 seconds. (Discard the 1 tablespoon of liquid if not used.)

4. Remove the dough and the steel blade from the bowl. Knead the dough by hand a few seconds, adding flour if the dough seems too sticky. Form the dough into a doughnut shape and replace it in the processor bowl. Cover the bowl loosely with a damp tea towel or microwavable plastic wrap. Place the processor bowl in the middle of the microwave and an 8-ounce glass of water next to it.

5. To micro-rise, set the microwave power at the appropriate micro-rise setting (see page 35). Heat for 3 minutes. Rest for 3 minutes. Heat for 3 minutes. Rest for 21 minutes or until about doubled in bulk.

6. Remove the dough from the microwave and processor bowl. Punch down and knead the dough for a few seconds on a floured surface.

7. Lightly grease a 13 × 9-inch microwavable pan. Roll the dough into a 13 × 9-inch rectangle; place in the prepared pan. Cut the dough into 10 13-inch strips. Then, cut the strips in half forming 20 strips.

8. Brush the sticks with 2 tablespoons of the melted butter and sprinkle with ¼ cup of the Parmesan.

9. Place the breadsticks back in the microwave beside the glass of water. Repeat step 5, but rest for 6 minutes. Meanwhile, preheat the oven to 375°F.

10. Bake the breadsticks on the middle rack in the preheated oven for 18 to 22 minutes or until golden brown. Remove the breadsticks from the oven. Set the oven control to broil. Brush the hot breadsticks with the remaining 2 tablespoons of butter and sprinkle with the remaining ¼ cup Parmesan. Place the breadsticks under the broiler and broil for 2 to 3 minutes or just until the cheese starts to sizzle and turn light brown. Watch carefully—they burn. Remove from the oven and serve warm.

◇ Café Brûlot ◇

Drip a pot of good espresso-style coffee, heat rich milk in a separate pan, then pour equal parts of hot milk and coffee into coffee cups for a bracing coffee drink that's great for dunking sweet breadsticks.

If you're in the mood for even more punched-up flavor, you can make café brûlot. Begin by brewing a pot of fine espresso-style coffee. While the coffee is dripping, combine in a 10-inch skillet a couple of sticks of cinnamon, zest from half an orange and half a lemon, 3 or 4 allspice berries, and ¼ cup sugar. Pour in 1 cup cognac, brandy, or bourbon, and heat to just under simmering. Now flame the liquor and stir with a long-handled spoon until the flame dies out. Pour in 5 cups of espresso coffee, stir, then strain into a coffeepot. Serve in demitasse cups alongside rich cream, more sugar, and a plateful of breadsticks.

If you want to be utterly decadent, combine coffee with whipped cream and dip grissini into the coffee infused whipped cream for a dessert that's to die for.

Makes ¾ cup in 10 minutes

½ C. whipping cream
2 tbsp. cold strong
   espresso-style coffee
2 tbsp. Dutch process cocoa
4 tbsp. confectioners' sugar
1 tbsp. dark rum

Beat cream in a bowl until it forms soft peaks, then add cold coffee and cocoa and stir to mix. Now whip in sugar a bit at a time until it is perfectly blended. Fold in rum. Spoon into 2 footed glass dishes and refrigerate until serving time.

GRISSINI ANISE

Makes 2 dozen breadsticks in under 2 hours

Licorice-scented anise finds its way into baked goods from Greek Easter bread to German springerle. Rolled into breadsticks glistening with a raw sugar topping, the result is a sweet Italian-style breadstick ideal for dipping into espresso, *latte*, or mocha. Stored in an airtight tin, these breadsticks keep well enough to ship for a pleasant surprise gift.

3½ C. bread flour
  2 tbsp. granulated
     sugar
 ¾ teas. salt
2½ teas. active dry yeast
1⅛ C. hot tap water
  1 tbsp. fruity olive oil

1 tbsp. brandy
½ teas. vanilla extract
1 tbsp. plus 1 teas.
   anise seeds
2 tbsp. turbinado
   sugar

1. Combine in a large processor bowl fitted with the steel blade the flour, sugar, salt, and yeast. Pulse to mix.

2. With the motor running, pour hot water, olive oil, brandy, and vanilla extract through the feed tube, then process until the dough leaves the side of the bowl and forms a ball. Knead with the machine running for 60 seconds.

3. Remove the blade and dough from the bowl. Knead the dough by hand a few seconds, kneading in anise seeds, adding flour as necessary if the dough seems sticky. Then form the dough into a doughnut shape and replace in the processor bowl.

4. Cover the bowl loosely with a damp tea towel or microwavable plastic wrap and prepare to micro-rise.

5. Place the processor bowl in the middle of the microwave and place an 8-ounce glass of water beside it.

6. Lower the microwave power to the appropriate micro-rise setting (see page 35). Heat for 3 minutes. Rest for 3 minutes. Heat for 3 minutes. Rest for 6 minutes or until the dough has just about doubled in bulk.

7. Remove the dough from the processor bowl, punch down, and knead by hand a few seconds. On a lightly floured surface, roll the dough into a 16 × 6-inch rectangle, then set it aside to rest 5 minutes or so. Meanwhile, preheat the

oven to 400°F. Coat 2 microwavable baking sheets lightly with olive oil.

8. Cut dough into twenty-four 6-inch strips. Stretch each strip to about 15 inches, then place the strips on the prepared baking sheets, about an inch apart. Cover the strips with waxed paper.

9. Raise the dough a second time, until puffy, either by placing the microwavable baking sheet of breadsticks in the microwave and repeating step 6, or by placing in a warm, draft-free place.

10. Just before baking, spritz breadsticks with water, then sprinkle with turbinado sugar. Bake on the middle rack in the preheated oven for 10 minutes, then rotate baking sheets. Spray again with water and continue baking for 5 minutes or until sticks are golden. Cool on a rack. Store in airtight tins.

BROWN AND SERVES

Makes 18 rolls in 2 hours

Old-fashioned Brown and Serves are truly bread in half the time. The dough is made on a day when you have a spare 2 hours, partially baked, then stored. Brown and serve on a day when time is precious. These rolls will keep up to 2 weeks stored in your refrigerator.

To freshen stale rolls, you can wrap the rolls in a damp paper towel and place in a plastic bag. Refrigerate the rolls for 12 hours. To reheat, remove the rolls from the bag, place on a baking sheet, and heat in a preheated 375° F oven for 5 minutes.

3 C. bread flour	**⅛ C. water**
¼ C. sugar	**¼ C. (½ stick)**
½ teas. salt	**unsalted butter,**
3 teas. 50% faster	**melted and cooled**
active dry yeast	**1 large egg**
¾ C. milk	

1. Fit the processor bowl with the steel blade. Combine and pulse to mix the flour, sugar, salt, and yeast.

2. Measure the milk and water into a 2-cup microwavable measure and heat on high power in the microwave for 30 seconds or until warm, about 110°F. Add the butter and egg to the warm milk and water. Whisk lightly to break and blend the egg.

(continued)

3. With the processor motor running, add all of the milk-water mixture to the flour mixture. The dough will leave the side of the bowl and form a ball. If not, gradually add an additional tablespoon of water and the dough will form a ball. Knead for 60 seconds.

4. Remove the dough and the steel blade from the bowl. Knead the dough by hand a few seconds on a floured surface and form into a ball. With your thumbs, punch a hole to form a doughnut shape. Place the dough in the processor bowl. Cover loosely with a damp tea towel or microwavable plastic wrap. Place the processor bowl in the middle of the microwave.

5. Set an 8-ounce glass of water in the microwave and prepare to micro-rise. Lower the microwave power to the appropriate micro-rise setting (see page 35). Heat for 3 minutes. Rest for 3 minutes. Heat for 3 minutes. Rest for 30 minutes or until the dough has doubled in bulk.

6. Grease well a glass baking sheet. Remove the dough from the microwave and processor bowl. Punch the dough down and knead by hand a few seconds on a lightly floured surface. Shape the dough into 18 equal-sized balls. Place the rolls on the prepared baking sheet. Preheat the oven to 350°F.

7. Place the rolls in the microwave and the glass of water next to it. Repeat step 5 except rest for 3 minutes or until the rolls have doubled in bulk.

8. Bake the rolls on the middle rack of the preheated oven until the rolls are baked thoroughly but not browned, about 10 minutes. You can tell when they are done by pressing the tops and sides; they will feel firm and not doughy.

9. Remove the rolls from the oven and the baking sheet to a rack to cool for 5 minutes. Place the warm rolls in a single layer in 2 plastic bags to cool completely. After the rolls have cooled completely, remove them from the bag and wipe the condensation from the bag with a paper towel. Return the rolls to the bag and store in the refrigerator.

10. To brown the rolls, place the number of rolls you want on a baking sheet and bake in a preheated 400°F oven for 5 to 8 minutes or until the rolls are golden on top and light brown on the bottom.

RICH DINNER ROLLS IN AN HOUR

Makes 16 rolls in under 1 hour

Rich, tender, flaky, and flavorful dinner rolls made with only one micro-rise go from flour to finished product in less than an hour, filling your house with the marvelous aroma of yeast bread.

3 C. bread flour
2 tbsp. sugar
1½ teas. salt
5 teas. 50% faster
    active dry yeast
2 tbsp. unsalted butter
    or margarine

2 large eggs
¾ C. hot tap water
Sesame or poppy seeds,
    for sprinkling on top

1. In the processor bowl fitted with the steel blade, add the flour, sugar, salt, yeast. Pulse to mix. Now, cut in butter or margarine finely, and pulse to blend so that it almost disappears.

2. Separate 1 egg; set the white aside. Combine in a glass measure the hot tap water, remaining egg and egg yolk. Whisk together, then with the processor motor running, *drizzle the liquid very slowly* into the dry ingredients, holding back the last portion of liquid to see if the dough will form a ball.

3. Process until the dough begins to leave the side of the bowl, forming a ball. Add the last liquid only if necessary. Knead 60 seconds, adding flour as needed if the dough seems sticky. Pinch up a piece of the dough ball. It should feel soft, tacky, smooth, elastic, and warm.

4. Remove the dough from the processor bowl to a lightly floured surface, and knead dough by hand a few seconds. Cover the dough with the processor bowl and let it rest 5 minutes. Meanwhile, generously butter a 9-inch round glass cake pan.

5. Divide the dough into 16 equal-sized pieces. Form into balls (see pan rolls, page 44) and arrange in the prepared pan, sides touching. Beat the reserved egg white until foamy and brush over the rolls, taking care that none runs down the sides (it sticks). Sprinkle the rolls with sesame or poppy seeds. Place the rolls in the microwave. *(continued)*

I saw an aged, aged man,
    A-sitting on a gate.
"Who are you, aged man?" I said.
    "And how is it you live?"
. . . "I sometimes dig for buttered
    rolls,
    Or set limed twigs for crabs;
I sometimes search the grassy
    knolls
    For wheels of hansom-cabs."

—Lewis Carroll
Through the Looking Glass

◇

6. Prepare to micro-rise. Place an 8-ounce glass of water in the back of the microwave. Lower the microwave power to the appropriate micro-rise setting (see page 35). Heat for 3 minutes. Rest for 3 minutes. Heat for 3 minutes. Rest for 6 minutes or until the rolls have risen to about double in bulk.

7. Meanwhile, preheat the oven to 425°F. When the dough has nearly doubled in bulk, bake on the middle rack in the preheated oven about 20 minutes or until the rolls are a deep golden brown.

8. Remove immediately to a rack to cool. Serve hot with butter and honey. Wrap in plastic to store. Heat leftovers the next day a few moments in the oven or toaster oven for best results.

ANADAMA DINNER ROLLS

Makes 16 rolls in 1 hour and 30 minutes

No telling what they would have said about that poor Ana, damn her, if she'd had a microwave. Then not only would Ana have made such damn good rolls, she'd have done it in an hour and a half.

A sweet, light, pumpkin-colored roll, this is a winter bread with a crunch to it from the cornmeal and a dark sweetness from the addition of molasses. Begs for a smear of salty Stilton, and a glass of red wine.

A heavy, sticky dough, you may have to turn your food processor off, take an extra minute, scoop out half the dough, and knead it in 2 parts. Then knead the dough together by hand before micro-rising.

2 C. milk
½ C. yellow cornmeal
⅓ C. unsulfured
   molasses
3 C. bread flour
1 C. whole wheat flour
2 teas. salt
2½ teas. 50% faster
   active dry yeast

2 tbsp. unsalted butter
   or margarine

Glaze
1 large egg, beaten
   with 1 teas. water

1. In a quart-sized microwavable bowl, stir together the milk and cornmeal. Cook in the microwave set on 100%

power for 5 minutes. Remove and stir to eliminate any lumps. Stir in the molasses. Cool this porridge to about 120°F. (The easiest way is to place the bowl in a cold-water bath while you're measuring out the other ingredients).

2. In the processor bowl fitted with the steel blade, add flours, salt, and yeast. Pulse to mix. Now cut in butter or margarine finely, and pulse to blend so that it almost disappears.

3. With the motor running, *drizzle the cornmeal porridge very slowly* into the dry ingredients, holding back the last portion of it to see if the dough will form a ball.

4. Process until the dough begins to leave the side of the bowl, forming a ball. Add the last bit of porridge only if needed. Knead 60 seconds, adding flour as necessary if the dough seems sticky. If your food processor complains, divide the dough in 2 parts to knead. Pinch up a piece of the dough. It should feel soft, tacky, smooth, elastic, and warm.

5. Remove the dough and the steel blade and prepare to micro-rise. On a lightly floured surface, knead the dough by hand a few seconds, then form dough into a ball. With your thumbs, punch a hole to form a doughnut shape and replace in the processor bowl. Cover loosely with a damp tea towel or plastic wrap. Set the dough in the microwave.

6. Place an 8-ounce glass of water in the back of the microwave. Lower the microwave power to the appropriate micro-rise setting (see page 35). Heat for 3 minutes. Rest for 3 minutes. Heat for 3 minutes. Rest for 6 minutes or until the dough has risen to about double in bulk.

7. Remove the dough to a lightly floured surface and knead by hand a few seconds. Re-form into a doughnut shape, place in the food processor bowl, and micro-rise again, repeating step 6.

8. Sprinkle a microwavable baking sheet with cornmeal. Punch dough down, and cut into 16 equal pieces. Form into balls (see pan rolls, page 44) and transfer to the prepared sheet, spacing balls about 1½ inches apart. Cover rolls with a damp tea towel or plastic wrap and micro-rise, repeating step 6. Meanwhile, preheat the oven to 375°F. Brush the tops of the rolls with the egg glaze.

9. Bake on the middle rack in the preheated oven 20 to 25 minutes or until browned and crisp.

10. Remove immediately to a rack to cool. Serve these rolls warm with butter or cheese. Wrap in plastic to store. These rolls keep 3 or 4 days, properly stored.

Zesty Orange ◇ Butter ◇

Makes ½ cup in 5 minutes

½ C. (1 stick) unsalted
    butter
1 tbsp. orange zest

Blend butter and zest in the processor until smooth. Pack into a crock. Refrigerate at least an hour before serving.

Good

DIVINE BUTTERHORN ROLLS

Makes 16 rolls in 2 hours

These lovely rolls are typical of the fine hot breads made in the South. The velvety dough is rich in eggs and does not need to be kneaded as heavily as lean doughs. The rolls age better than most and freeze well.

2½ C. bread flour
  2 large eggs, room temperature
¼ C. vegetable oil
½ teas. salt
¼ C. sugar
2½ teas. 50% faster active dry yeast

¼ C. warm milk (110°–120°F)
  2 tbsp. unsalted butter, melted, for brushing on top

1. In the food processor bowl, combine the flour, eggs, oil, salt, sugar, and yeast. Process for 10 seconds to blend.

2. With the machine running, very slowly drizzle just enough of the warm milk into the flour mixture so the dough forms a ball that cleans the sides of the bowl. Process until the dough ball turns around the bowl 10 times.

3. Remove the dough and the steel blade from the processor to a lightly floured surface, adding a little flour as necessary if the dough seems sticky. Form the dough into a ball. With your thumbs, punch a hole to form a doughnut shape and place it back in the processor bowl. Cover loosely with a damp tea towel or microwavable plastic wrap. Place the processor bowl in the middle of the microwave.

4. Set an 8-ounce glass of water in the microwave. Lower the microwave power to the appropriate micro-rise setting (see page 35). Heat for 3 minutes. Rest for 3 minutes. Heat for 3 minutes. Rest for 45 minutes or until the dough has doubled in bulk. Meanwhile, lightly grease 2 glass microwavable baking sheets. (A metal baking sheet may be used, in which case the rolls must be raised in a warm, draft-free place before baking.)

5. Remove the dough from the microwave to a lightly floured surface and punch down. Divide the dough into 2 equal parts. Roll each part into a ball. Working with 1 ball at a time and keeping the other ball covered with a damp tea

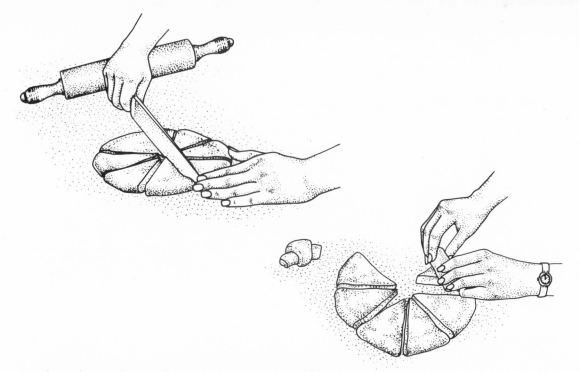

towel or plastic wrap, roll the ball on the floured surface into an 8-inch-diameter circle. Cut each circle into 8 wedges. Beginning with the wide end, roll up the wedges jelly-roll fashion.

6. Arrange the butterhorns on the prepared baking sheets about 2 inches apart. Cover the rolls loosely with a damp tea towel or microwavable plastic wrap and prepare for the final rising.

7. Set 1 baking sheet of rolls aside to rest while you micro-rise the other. (The resting rolls will micro-rise faster when they are placed in the microwave, so watch them carefully and micro-rise them just until doubled in bulk.) Place 1 baking sheet back in the microwave. Set an 8-ounce glass of water next to it.

8. Repeat step 4 except rest for 20 minutes or until the rolls have doubled in bulk. Repeat with the second baking sheet. Alternately, raise the rolls in a warm draft-free place. Meanwhile, preheat the oven to 375°F. When the rolls have doubled in bulk, remove them from the microwave and brush lightly with the melted butter.

9. Bake the rolls on the middle rack of the preheated oven for 12 to 15 minutes or until they are a nice pale gold. Remove the rolls from the oven to racks to cool. To store, place the rolls in plastic bags.

Now for the tea of our host,

Now for the rollicking bun,

Now for the muffin and toast,

Now for the gay Sally Lunn!

—Sir William Schwenck Gilbert

The Sorcerer

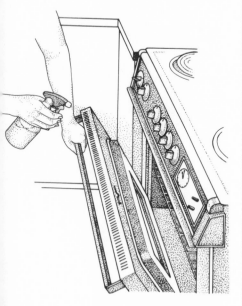

HARD ROLLS

Makes 6 large rolls or 1 dozen small rolls in 2 hours

Give yourself 2 hours and you can make hard rolls that compare favorably with those from a good bakery. These wonderful hard-on-the-outside, soft-on-the-inside rolls make the best deli sandwiches. If your food processor complains about 4 cups of flour, take an extra minute and knead the dough in 2 parts, then knead the dough balls together by hand. If you don't have gluten flour on hand, use all bread flour, but don't expect the lift you'd get with the addition of gluten flour.

With this 4-rise process, you'll save time by micro-rising but won't sacrifice taste development or texture. Cook these rolls on a pizza stone or tiles (see pages 21–25) at 425°F for the best crust. Mist the oven with water several times during the first 10 minutes of the baking process for ultimate crispness.

3 C. bread flour
1 C. gluten flour
1 teas. sugar
1½ teas. salt
5 teas. 50% faster active dry yeast
1½ C. hot tap water (120°F)

Glaze
1 egg white, whisked with 1 teaspoon water

1. In the processor bowl fitted with the steel blade, add flours, sugar, salt, and yeast. Pulse to mix.

2. Pour into a glass measure the hot tap water, then with the motor running, *drizzle the water very slowly* into the dry ingredients, holding back the last portion of liquid to see if the dough will form a ball.

3. Process until the dough begins to leave the side of the bowl, forming a ball. Add the last liquid only if necessary. Knead 60 seconds, adding flour as necessary if the dough seems sticky. Pinch up a piece of the dough. It should feel soft, tacky, smooth, elastic, and warm.

4. Remove the dough and the steel blade and prepare to micro-rise. On a lightly floured surface, knead the dough by hand a few seconds, then form dough into a ball. With your

thumbs, punch a hole to form a doughnut shape and replace in the processor bowl. Cover loosely with a damp tea towel or plastic wrap. Position the dough in the microwave.

5. Place an 8-ounce glass of water in the back of the microwave. Lower the microwave power to the appropriate micro-rise setting (see page 35). Heat for 3 minutes. Rest for 3 minutes. Heat for 3 minutes. Rest for 6 minutes or until the dough has risen to about double in bulk.

6. Remove the dough to a lightly floured surface and knead by hand a few seconds. Cover the dough with the processor bowl and let it rest on the counter for 15 minutes.

7. Now cut the dough into 6 equal pieces. Roll into balls. Place the dough balls on a microwavable cookie sheet and micro-rise again, repeating step 5 except don't cover the dough.

8. Note that the tops are now crusty and dry. Flatten each ball and fold it in half, the crusty side in. Roll between the palms of your hands, forming a torpedo-shaped *petit pain*, about 5½ × 1½ inches, tapering the ends. Arrange rolls on a pizza peel (see page 24) or other flat surface that you've sprinkled generously with cornmeal. Micro-rise again, repeating step 5, or allow to raise in a warm draft-free place until doubled in bulk. Remember to keep the rolls *uncovered*.

9. Meanwhile, preheat a pizza stone or tiles in the oven at 425°F for at least 30 minutes. Once the rolls have risen, make a deep slash about 4 inches long down the center of each. Brush gently with the egg-white glaze, then shake onto the pizza stone or tiles in the oven.

10. Bake in the preheated oven 20 minutes or until the rolls have turned a golden brown. Mist the oven with water several times during the first 10 minutes of the baking process for the best possible crust.

11. Transfer the rolls immediately to a rack to cool. Wrap in a paper bag to store. Hard rolls freeze well if properly wrapped in plastic freezer bags and will keep up to 3 months.

Broiled Brie and ◇ Roasted Garlic ◇

Serves 6 in 2 hours

For an hors d'oeuvre worth remembering—delicious with a robust red wine and best friends—roast some garlic, broil some Brie, and hunt up your best spreading knives so that your guests can smear hot, runny, aromatic Brie and soft, sweet roasted garlic onto pieces of hard rolls.

3 large heads garlic (at least 2½ inches in diameter)
¼ C. olive oil
Salt
Three 4-ounce wheels Brie
Hard rolls, heated

1. Preheat the oven to 350°F. Remove all but one layer of the papery skin from the heads of garlic, taking care not to expose the flesh. Pack the garlic into a small baking dish, sides touching. Drizzle with olive oil and sprinkle with salt. Cover and bake until garlic is tender, 75 to 90 minutes.

2. Preheat the broiler. Score a large X in the top of each cheese wheel. Set each wheel inside a small baking dish. Broil until browned and bubbly, about 5 minutes. Serve immediately with garlic and hot, hard rolls.

Use fresh herbs for the most intense flavors; use dried only if you have no choice. Don't keep dried herbs longer than a year or so. They lose all their aroma. One tip we learned was to date the container the day you bring it into the kitchen. Then when the herb is out-of-date, throw it away.

◇

The Value of Parsley, Sage, Rosemary, and Thyme: In Pinwheels and ◇ Beyond ◇

According to Waverly Root, in his fine book *Food* (Simon and Schuster, 1980), the Druids believed sage to be so curative that it could raise the dead. Mme. de Sevigne wrote in the 1600s that she always kept rosemary in her pocket because it "is excellent against sadness." The Romans thought thyme would "dispel melancholy." And English gardeners wrote in 1548 that parsley "seeds help those who are light-headed to resist drink better."

Good grief. No wonder we keep combining these herbs and folding them into everything from omelets to rolls.

PARSLEY, SAGE, ROSEMARY, AND THYME PINWHEEL LOAF WITH PINE NUTS

Makes 1 large loaf in under 2 hours

Herbs release their flavors best in the presence of oil, so sauté them a moment or two in butter before you add the herbs to the dough, and you'll get the most intense flavor and aroma.

This herb-infused oil can be made in a skillet on the stove or in a glass dish in the microwave. Either way, it produces a loaf of bread that makes people take deep, deep breaths of sheer pleasure before the first bite.

Cook together (handwritten)

1/3 C. unsalted butter or margarine	2 1/2 C. bread flour
3/4 C. minced fresh parsley, divided into 1/4 C. for dough and 1/2 C. for rolling into the pinwheel	1 C. whole wheat flour
	1 teas. salt
	2 tbsp. sugar
	2 tbsp. nonfat dry milk solids
1 tbsp. fresh thyme leaves or 1 teas. dried	2 1/2 teas. 50% faster active dry yeast
1 teas. fresh sage leaves or 1/4 teas. dried	1 1/4 C. hot tap water (120°–130°F)
1/4 teas. rosemary needles	2 tbsp. unsalted butter or margarine, softened, for rubbing on loaf
1 tbsp. fresh grated onion	1/4 C. pine nuts, for sprinkling on top
1/4 teas. ground white pepper	

For top (handwritten)

Mix into the dough. (handwritten)

1. In a small sauté pan (or microwavable bowl) combine 1/3 cup butter or margarine with 1/4 cup of the parsley, the thyme, sage, rosemary, onion, and white pepper. Cook and stir over medium heat for 1 minute, then set aside. (You may do this on the range top or in the microwave set on 50 percent power.)

2. In the food processor bowl fitted with the steel blade combine flours, salt, sugar, dry milk, and yeast. Pulse to mix.

3. With the motor running, add herb-infused butter and hot tap water. When the dough forms a ball, knead for 60 seconds.

4. Remove the dough and the steel blade from the bowl. Knead the dough by hand a few seconds on a floured surface, adding a little flour if the dough seems sticky. It will be quite soft. Form the dough into a ball. With your thumbs, punch a hole to form a doughnut shape and replace it in the processor bowl. Cover the bowl with a damp tea towel or plastic wrap. Place the bowl in the microwave oven and prepare to micro-rise.

5. Put an 8-ounce glass of water in the back of the microwave. Lower the microwave power to the appropriate micro-rise setting (see page 35). Heat for 3 minutes. Rest for 3 minutes. Heat for 3 minutes. Rest for 6 minutes or until the dough has risen to about double in bulk.

6. Remove the dough to a lightly floured breadboard and knead by hand a few seconds. Form into a 15 × 9-inch rectangle.

7. Rub the additional 2 tablespoons soft butter or margarine over the surface, then sprinkle with pine nuts and the remaining ½ cup parsley.

8. Roll up the dough, jelly-roll fashion, starting at the narrow end, so that you have a 9-inch roll.

9. Place the roll, seam side down, in a buttered 8½ × 4½ × 2½-inch glass loaf pan. Cover lightly with a damp tea towel and micro-rise until almost doubled in bulk, repeating step 5. Meanwhile, preheat the oven to 400°F.

10. Brush the top of the risen dough with water, and bake on the middle rack in the preheated oven about 45 minutes, until golden brown and it taps hollow.

11. Remove the bread from the pan to a wire rack to cool. Wrap in plastic to store.

Fresh Flavored
◇ Butters ◇

You can experiment with herbs you find or grow and make wonderful flavor-infused butters that are delicious not only on rolls and breads, but also on just-grilled chicken breasts and fish steaks.

Using fruits or spices, you can also make sweet butters that go wonderfully with breakfast breads.

The technique is simple. Mince the fresh additives in the food processor, then add unsalted butter, and process. You may have to open the processor top and stir down the butter with a rubber spatula a time or two.

Finally, pack the flavored butter into small crocks, cover, and refrigerate until ready to serve. Remove from the refrigerator 20 minutes or so before serving to let the butter warm up and the flavor arise.

Alternately, chill the flavored butter, roll into a log, pack into aluminum foil, and hold until serving time. Slice and serve disks of flavored butter along with fresh, hot breads. Make 2 or 3, choosing alternate colors and textures of the additives, and you can make a trio of punched-up flavors to serve with home-baked bread.

Or pack into a mold. To unmold, dip the edges of the mold in warm water, or place a hot wet towel on the bottom of the mold until enough of the butter melts so that it will fall out onto the serving plate.

For best results, make the butter in small quantities, and use promptly. The best flavors are as evanescent as a dream. These butters will keep from 2 or 3 days up to a week, properly covered and refrigerated. You can freeze them for up to a month.

RALEIGH HOUSE ORANGE ROLLS

Makes 3 dozen rolls in under 1 hour and 30 minutes

You can bake these rolls in a muffin tin, or for brunch use a half-size muffin tin, in which case in 90 minutes, you'll get 6 dozen of the best bites for breakfast that you can imagine. The restaurant in Texas where the rolls originated has probably served a million of these fabulous rolls to people who come back summer after summer on the strength of their memory of heavenly rolls. We were practically prone with delight and began imagining all kinds of alternate suave toppings besides Martha Johnson's Orange Butter. Try it with a purée of sun-dried tomatoes, olive oil, and pine nuts. Umm.

4 C. bread flour	1/3 C. sugar
1 teas. salt	1 C. hot tap water
2 tbsp. 50% faster active dry yeast	2 large eggs
	1/3 C. vegetable oil

1. Combine the flour, salt, yeast, and sugar in the processor bowl fitted with the steel blade. Pulse to mix.

2. Combine in a glass measure the water, eggs, and oil. Whisk with a fork. With the machine running, very slowly add liquids to the flour, holding back the last portion of the liquid to see if the dough forms a ball. Add last portion of liquid only if necessary.

3. When the dough leaves the side and forms a ball, knead with the machine running for 60 seconds, adding flour as necessary to maintain a soft, nonsticky dough.

4. Remove the dough and steel blade from the bowl. Knead the dough by hand a few seconds. If the dough seems sticky, knead in a little flour, then form the dough into ball. With your thumbs, punch a hole to form a doughnut shape and place in the processor bowl. Cover loosely with a damp tea towel or microwavable plastic wrap and prepare to micro-rise.

5. Place an 8-ounce glass of water in the back of the microwave. Lower the microwave power to the appropriate micro-rise setting (see page 35). Place the dough in the microwave. Heat for 3 minutes. Let rest 3 minutes. Heat 3 minutes. Let rest 6 minutes or until doubled in bulk.

6. Remove the dough from the processor bowl to a lightly floured surface, punch down, and knead by hand a few seconds. Then cover the dough with the processor bowl and allow the dough to rest for 10 minutes. Grease well muffin tins or cookie sheets. Preheat the oven to 375°F.

7. Form the dough into 36 equal golf-ball-sized balls and place in tins or on cookie sheets. Allow to rise again in a warm, draft-free place until nearly doubled in bulk, or, if using microwavable baking pans, micro-rise, repeating step 5.

8. Bake on the middle rack in the preheated oven about 25 minutes or until golden brown (less time for smaller rolls). Cool on a rack and top with Orange Butter. Best if eaten the day they are made.

◇ Orange Butter ◇

Makes 3 cups in 5 minutes

- 1/4 C. fresh orange juice
- 3/4 C. butter
- 2 C. confectioners' sugar

1. Combine orange juice, butter, and sugar in the processor bowl and mix until smooth.
2. Spread over warm rolls, then stand back.

Parsley-Dill ◇ Butter ◇

- 1/4 C. minced fresh parsley
- 1 tbsp. minced fresh dill
- 1/2 C. (1 stick) unsalted butter

◇ Pesto Butter ◇

- 1/4 C. fresh basil
- 2 tbsp. minced fresh Italian parsley
- 2 large cloves garlic, minced
- 1 tbsp. fruity olive oil
- 1 tbsp. pine nuts
- 1/2 C. (1 stick) unsalted butter

Herbes de Jardine ◇ Butter ◇

- 1 tbsp. minced fresh tarragon leaves
- 1 1/2 teas. minced fresh thyme leaves
- 1 1/2 teas. minced fresh oregano
- 1/4 teas. cracked black pepper
- 2 tbsp. minced fresh parsley
- 1/2 C. (1 stick) unsalted butter

Rosemary ◇ Butter ◇

- 6-inch sprig fresh rosemary, needles stripped and chopped, stem discarded
- 1/2 C. (1 stick) unsalted butter

Los Angeles ◇ Butter ◇

- 2 green onions and tops, chopped
- 1/2 teas. ground cumin
- 1 teas. minced fresh oregano leaves
- Salt and freshly ground black pepper to taste
- 1/2 C. (1 stick) unsalted butter

◇ El Paso Butter ◇

- 2 tbsp. chili powder
- 1/2 C. (1 stick) unsalted butter

◇ Garlic Butter ◇

- 4 cloves garlic, minced
- 1/2 C. (1 stick) unsalted butter

Cinnamon-Sugar ◇ Butter ◇

- 1 tbsp. freshly ground cinnamon
- 1 tbsp. turbinado sugar
- 1/2 C. (1 stick) unsalted butter

◇ Apricot Butter ◇

- 4 rehydrated dried apricots, chopped (see step 2, page 126)
- Sugar to taste
- 1/2 C. (1 stick) unsalted butter

◇ Avocado Butter ◇

- 1 dead-ripe avocado, peeled, seeded, and mashed
- 1 tbsp. minced onion
- Salt to taste
- 1/2 C. (1 stick) unsalted butter

Cracked-Pepper ◇ Butter ◇

- 2 tbsp. cracked black pepper
- 1/2 C. (1 stick) unsalted butter

◇ Chili Butter ◇

1 teas. fresh lime juice
¼ teas. cayenne pepper
¼ teas. ground cumin
½ C. (1 stick) unsalted
butter

Saffron-Leek ◇ Butter ◇

¼ teas. saffron threads
1 tbsp. dry vermouth
¼ C. minced leek bulb
1 teas. fresh lemon juice
½ cup (1 stick) unsalted
butter

Roasted Red Pepper ◇ Butter ◇

1 red bell pepper, roasted
(see page 123) and
chopped
½ teas. fresh lime juice
½ C. (1 stick) unsalted
butter

Shallot-Garlic ◇ Butter ◇

3 large cloves garlic
¼ C. thinly sliced shallot
¼ tbsp. cooking oil
½ C. (1 stick) unsalted
butter

Sauté garlic and shallot in cooking
oil, then mince and mix with soft
butter.

Strawberry-Honey ◇ Butter ◇

1 C. fresh strawberries,
hulled and pureed
1 tbsp. mild honey
½ teas. fresh lime juice
½ C. (1 stick) unsalted
butter

Four Pepper ◇ Butter ◇

1 tbsp. paprika
¼ teas. cayenne pepper
¼ teas. white pepper
½ C. (1 stick) unsalted
butter

Mustard-Tarragon ◇ Butter ◇

1 teas. Dijon mustard
1 teas. minced fresh
tarragon leaves
1 tbsp. minced fresh chives
1 tbsp. minced fresh parsley
½ C. (1 stick) unsalted
butter

Chocolate-Almond ◇ Butter ◇

½ C. semisweet chocolate
morsels, melted
½ teas. sugar
1 teas. Amaretto
2 tbsp. toasted almonds (see
page 220), minced
½ C. (1 stick) unsalted
butter

Horseradish-Chive ◇ Butter ◇

1 tbsp. prepared horseradish
1 tbsp. fresh minced chives
½ C. (1 stick) unsalted
butter

◇ Anchovy Butter ◇

2 teas. drained capers,
minced
2 anchovy fillets, mashed to
a paste
1 clove garlic, pressed
1 teas. fresh lime juice
½ C. (1 stick) unsalted
butter

Red Pepper ◇ Butter ◇

½ jar (3½ oz.) roasted red
peppers, drained
1 tbsp. brandy
1 teas. fresh chives
2 tbsp. freshly snipped
parsley
Salt and freshly ground
black pepper to taste
½ C. (1 stick) unsalted
butter

Herbes de Provence ◇ Butter ◇

1 tbsp. herbes de Provence
½ C. (1 stick) unsalted
butter

Quatres Épices ◇ Butter ◇

5 cloves
1 teas. white peppercorns
½ stick cinnamon
⅓ teas. ground ginger
¼ teas. freshly grated
nutmeg
½ C. (1 stick) unsalted
butter

◇ Sonoma Butter ◇

2 tbsp. minced sun-dried
tomatoes
1 tbsp. minced fresh basil
1 minced shallot
½ C. (1 stick) unsalted
butter

◇ Caper Butter ◇

2 tbsp. drained capers
1 shallot
1 clove garlic
½ C. (1 stick) unsalted
butter

6 ◆ PIZZA, FOCACCIA, FLATBREADS, AND FILLED BREADS

Plain Ole Pizza Dough 167

Chicago-Style Two-Crust Pizza 168

Summer Pizza in an Hour 170

Italian Loaf Rustica 172

All-Star Calzone 174

Green Onion Market Bread with Italian Filling 176

Filled Swiss-Cheddar Bread 178

Sedona Bread 180

Green Olive Fougasse 182

Plain Ole Focaccia 184

Rosemary-Raisin Focaccia with Pine Nuts 185

Cracked Pepper–Parmesan Bread 187

Pita Bread 188

The earliest breads known to man were flat, cooked on a heated stone, or—in torrid climates—perhaps on a rock heated by the sun alone.

From unleavened breads to leavened flatbreads, the form has evolved. The original pizza was sold on the streets of Italy from a board held high overhead by a vendor who wended his way through town. Americans have taken this simple bread and practically raised it to an art form. Some Los Angeles pizzas are so aesthetically pleasing, you hate to bite into them. But then the aroma gets you. You'll bite.

If you want to get into a real argument, try to get some agreement between an easterner and a Californian on what a pizza even is. To the easterner, it may mean a thin, crisp crust, a dark, rich red sauce, and simple cheese. To the Californian, pizza may conjure up artful, irregular shapes, goat cheese, sun-dried tomatoes, black olives, fresh green basil leaves. We've tried to present a balance of pizzas from around the country. We especially have been taken with the stuffed Chicago-style pizza (see page 168), which is a direct descendant of the Italian *torta rustica*. For a robust, full meal on a cold night, we highly recommend it.

We have also included filled breads here, such as calzone (see page 174), an Italian-style filled and baked pizza that must be the Mediterranean answer to the sandwich. Since sandwiches are only as good as their breads, we agree that these special filled breads make splendid entrées for those who eat on the run.

These types of breads lend themselves well to the Micro-Rise process and are a good place to try out this new craft for baking bread. Good grief. You can make a plain ole pizza using the Micro-Rise process in the same amount of time it takes us to get to the neighborhood pizzeria and fight our way through the teenagers to get to the tables.

For the most authentic pizzas, focaccias, and calzones, you'll want to use a pizza stone or quarry tiles and a pizza peel. You'll find a detailed discussion of these invaluable tools on pages 21–25.

PLAIN OLE PIZZA DOUGH

Makes 1 large 14-inch pizza dough in under 1 hour

Here's an easy pizza with the added crunch of cornmeal. Roll it out so thin you can nearly read a newspaper through it, bake it on a pizza stone (see pages 21–25), and you'll be close to the genuine Neapolitan style that started this whole pizza craze.

Anchovies, capers, pepperoni, very thinly sliced onions, green and red bell peppers, and mushrooms are toppings you may also like. Californians like fresh tomatoes. Some fools like pineapple. We say, you want pineapple? Put it in an upside-down cake. Leave it offa da pizza.

2 C. bread flour	1½ –2 teas. 50% faster
½ C. cornmeal	active dry yeast
1 teas. salt	2 tbsp. olive oil
1 tbsp. nonfat dry milk	¾ C. hot tap water
1½ teas. sugar	(120°–130°F)

1. Place the pizza stone in the upper third of the oven and preheat to 500°F for at least 30 minutes before baking.

2. Combine all the ingredients in the processor bowl fitted with the steel blade. With the motor running, process until the dough begins to leave the side of the bowl. Knead 60 seconds, adding flour as necessary if the dough seems sticky.

3. Remove the dough and the steel blade and prepare to micro-rise. Knead the dough by hand a few seconds, then form dough into a ball. With your thumbs, punch a hole to form a doughnut shape and replace in the processor bowl. Cover loosely with a damp tea towel or plastic wrap.

4. Place an 8-ounce glass of water in the back of the microwave. Lower the microwave power to the appropriate micro-rise setting (see page 35). Place the dough in the microwave. Heat for 3 minutes. Rest for 3 minutes. Heat for 3 minutes. Rest for 6 minutes or until the dough has risen to about double in bulk.

5. Remove the dough to a lightly floured surface and knead by hand a few seconds. Then roll out into a 14-inch circle. Place this disk on a pizza peel (see page 24) or a cookie sheet with no sides that has been heavily sprinkled with cornmeal.

(continued)

Everyday Pizza ◇ Sauce ◇

Makes 1½ cups sauce in 30 minutes

For a no-fuss pizza, simply combine these ingredients and simmer while the pizza is rising the first time. Try to find tomato paste in those toothpaste-style tubes the Italians use. Then squeeze out just what you need and save the rest in the refrigerator. Why can't American manufacturers be so considerate?

Use the processor to slice the mozzarella thin. Add anchovies if you've got them. Other toppings of your choice. This is getting better all the time.

- 1 medium onion, sliced thin
- 2 or 3 large cloves garlic, sliced thin
- 1 tbsp. fruity olive oil
- 1 8-oz. can tomato sauce
- 2 tbsp. tomato paste
- 1 teas. sugar
- Salt and freshly ground black pepper to taste
- ¼ C. fresh parsley, cut fine with scissors
- 8 oz. mozzarella

1. In a 10-inch skillet over medium heat, sauté the onion and garlic in olive oil until the onion begins to turn clear. Then stir in the tomato sauce, paste, sugar, salt, and black pepper to taste. Thin with a little water and simmer over low heat while the pizza dough rises, stirring and tasting the sauce from time to time. Keep the consistency about like that of catsup, adding water by the tablespoon to maintain this thickness. Just before placing on the prepared pizza, stir in parsley. If you have access to other fresh herbs, such as oregano or basil, toss in a bit of those if you like.

(continued)

2. For a 14-inch pizza, we like to add about 8 ounces finely sliced mozzarella. Lightly oil the pizza dough with fruity olive oil, add a layer of cheese, then tomato topping, then a final layer of cheese.

Cook pizza immediately after adding the toppings so that the crust doesn't get soggy.

6. Top with your favorite topping, then slide the pizza off the peel or cookie sheet onto the hot pizza stone and bake. Reduce oven temperature to 425°F immediately after you close the oven door. Pizza will be cooked and golden in 15 to 20 minutes. You will see the topping bubbling, the cheese melting, and the lovely bread edges golden with brown specks.

7. Lift pizza back onto the peel or cookie sheet and allow to cool 3 or 4 minutes before cutting, so that the topping will settle back.

CHICAGO-STYLE TWO-CRUST PIZZA

Serves 4 in 1 hour and 30 minutes

For tailgate parties, a deep-dish two-crust pizza makes a terrific centerpiece. A plate and fork is required, however, to best enjoy this savory pie.

Use the food processor to good advantage here for shredding and grating cheeses and thin slicing vegetables.

1 recipe Plain Ole Pizza Dough (see page 167)
4 links sweet Italian sausage (or hot if you like it)
2 C. shredded mozzarella
½ C. thinly sliced mushrooms
½ C. thinly sliced red onion

½ C. of your favorite tomato pizza sauce (could be prepared pasta sauce out of a jar)
¾ C. mixed freshly grated Parmesan and/or Romano
Cracked black pepper to taste

1. Follow instructions for making Plain Ole Pizza Dough up through the micro-rise (step 5), then divide the dough in 2 balls. On a lightly floured surface, roll and stretch out each ball into a thin 12-inch circle.

2. Grill the sausages until done. Meanwhile, preheat the oven to 400°F.

3. Place one circle of dough in a 9-inch glass cake pan that's sprinkled with cornmeal. Allow the edges to overlap the pan.

4. Add a generous layer of shredded mozzarella, saving a quarter of it for the top. Now add the cooked sausages. Arrange mushrooms, onion, or any other favorite pizza filling you like atop the sausages. The filling should *not* come up to the top of the pan.

5. Add the second layer of dough, pinching both layers of dough together and packing the excess dough down inside the pan. Press the filling and dough down so that you have a concave top.

6. Spread a thin layer of your favorite tomato pizza sauce over the dough. Sprinkle grated Parmesan and/or Romano and season to taste with cracked black pepper.

7. Place pizza on the middle rack of the preheated oven and bake 25 to 30 minutes or until the crust is golden brown.

8. To serve, allow the pizza to stand a few minutes so that the filling will settle down. Delicious either warm or at room temperature. *Buon appetito*, Chicago.

Homemade
◇ Pesto ◇

Makes about 1 pint in 5 minutes

1 large bunch fresh basil
  leaves
½ C. pine nuts
¾ C. freshly grated
  Parmesan
½ C. fruity olive oil

Place the basil leaves in the bowl of the processor fitted with the steel blade. Pulse to chop finely. With the motor running, add pine nuts, cheese, and olive oil in turn. Shut off the processor. You will have a coarse purée. If you don't use all of the pesto on your pizza, freeze what's left over and use a table-spoon or so in the next vegetable soup you make.

Sadie Kendall's Provençal Pizza with Goat Cheese ◇ and Tapenade ◇

Makes one 14-inch pizza in 45 minutes

Here's an alternative topping for the Sun-dried Tomato Pizza Dough that makes a great hors d'oeuvre, served room temperature and cut into bite-sized squares.

1 recipe Sun-dried Tomato
  Pizza Dough
1 recipe homemade
  Tapenade or from a jar
6 oz. fresh goat cheese
3 tbsp. olive oil
2 tbsp. fresh oregano leaves
1 dozen or so sun-dried
  tomatoes in olive oil
½ C. Niçoise (Mediterranean
  style) black olives, pitted
3 tbsp. drained capers
½ C. Parmesan

SUMMER PIZZA IN AN HOUR

Makes one 14-inch pizza in 1 hour

The taste of California, evanescent as a movie image, this brightly flavored pizza works only when the summer tomato harvest is at its peak. As far as the onions, you can find the same sweet ones going by different names in different parts of the country. Georgia's Vidalia, Washington's Walla Walla, the Maui onion, and the Texas Sweet are all variations on the theme of a hybrid known to farmers as the granex type F sweet yellow onion. Available only a few weeks a year in the beginning of the summer, buy them when you find them. Besides using it for pizza, you can eat this onion like an apple, as Errol Flynn—playing Custer—did in the 1941 film *They Died with Their Boots On.*

Sun-Dried Tomato Pizza Dough

2¼ C. bread flour
  2 tbsp. sugar
  1 tbsp. nonfat dry milk
  1 teas. salt
  1 tbsp. fruity olive oil
  1 tbsp. 50% faster
    active dry yeast
  2 tbsp. minced
    sun-dried tomatoes
    in olive oil
⅔ C. tepid tap water
  5 medium Roma
    tomatoes, dead-ripe
½ medium sweet onion
  2 tbsp. fruity olive oil
½ teas. (2 large cloves)
    minced fresh garlic

Salt and freshly ground
  black pepper to taste
  6 oz. mozzarella or
    regular Monterey
    Jack
 20 Niçoise olives
    (Mediterranean or
    plain black), pitted
½ C. pesto (homemade
    or a store-bought
    jar)
  1 tbsp. chopped fresh
    oregano or ½ teas.
    dried, crushed
¼ C. pine nuts

Garnish
Fresh basil leaves

1. Place rack in upper third of the oven and preheat to 450°F. If you're using a stone (see pages 21–25), preheat for at least 30 minutes.

2. Attach the steel blade to the food processor. Add the flour, sugar, dry milk, salt, olive oil, yeast, and sun-dried tomatoes to processor and pulse to blend.

3. With the machine running, add the water through the feed tube, holding back the last portion to see if the dough will form a ball. Process until the dough forms a ball and cleans the sides of the bowl. Use the last bit of water only if necessary. Process 60 seconds to knead.

4. Remove the dough from the processor. If the dough seems sticky, knead in a little flour. Form into a doughnut shape. If you have 2 bowls for your processor, replace dough in the processor. Otherwise, place in a second greased glass bowl of equal size. Cover with a damp tea towel or plastic wrap and set aside.

5. Place an 8-ounce glass of water in the back corner of the microwave. Lower the microwave power to the appropriate micro-rise setting (see page 35). Place the dough in the microwave and heat for 3 minutes. Let the dough rest in the microwave for 3 minutes. Heat 3 minutes, and rest 6 minutes or until the dough has doubled in bulk.

6. Meanwhile, while the dough is micro-rising, prepare the topping. Place the processor bowl in the food processor and add the slicing disk. Slice the tomatoes, remove from the bowl, then slice the onion. Season the tomatoes with olive oil, garlic, salt, and pepper, and set aside along with the onions.

7. Wipe out the processor bowl, add the shredding disk, and shred the cheese. Remove and set aside.

8. If the olives are large, slice. Set aside.

9. Remove the dough from the microwave to a lightly floured surface, punch down, then pull and flatten into an irregular 14-inch circle. Place on a lightly greased pizza screen or peel (see page 24), prepared with cornmeal, or pan. Turn under a 1-inch lip. Set aside to rise in a warm draft-free place for 10 minutes.

10. Spread the pizza dough with the pesto. Sprinkle with half the cheese. Layer sliced onion and tomatoes, then sprinkle with oregano leaves or crushed, dried oregano. Add remaining cheese, olives, and pine nuts. If the pizza's on a peel, give it a trial shake before opening the oven door.

11. Bake in the upper third of the preheated oven until the edges and bottom are well browned and the topping bubbles and browns, 12 to 15 minutes. Remove to a cutting board and slice into wedges. Garnish with basil leaves. Serve hot or at room temperature.

1. Make the dough and tapenade according to recipe instructions. Preheat the oven to 450°F. If using a stone (see page 22), preheat for at least 30 minutes in the upper third of the oven.

2. Using a fork, break up the goat cheese, then mix together with olive oil.

3. Wipe out the processor bowl, then add the grating disk. Grate the Parmesan. Set aside.

4. Remove the raised dough from the microwave, punch down, pull and press into a rough 14-inch circle. Place on a lightly greased pizza screen (see page 294) or pan or, if using a stone, on a pizza peel (see page 24) sprinkled with cornmeal. Turn under a 1-inch lip. Set aside to rise for 10 minutes.

5. Spread pizza dough with a thin layer of tapenade. Add the goat cheese mixture. Arrange oregano, sun-dried tomatoes, olives, and capers, then sprinkle with Parmesan.

6. Bake on a stone in the upper third of the preheated oven until edges and bottom are well browned and topping bubbles and browns, 12–15 minutes. Remove to a board and slice into wedges. Serve warm.

Homemade ◇ Tapenade ◇

Makes ½ cup in 10 minutes

12 Niçoise black olives, pitted
2-oz. tin rolled anchovies
with capers in olive oil
2 tbsp. capers, drained
¼ C. olive oil
½ teas. minced garlic
Juice of half a lemon
Grating of fresh black pepper

In the processor bowl, fitted with the steel blade, combine ingredients and pulse to mix to a grainy purée. Store covered in the refrigerator up to a week.

ITALIAN LOAF RUSTICA

Makes 1 large loaf in 1 hour and 30 minutes

A meal in a loaf could be the translation for Italian Loaf Rustica. A hearty filling, closely related to that found in a pizza, is packed inside this crusty brown round loaf. The meal travels well because the filling is dense and dripless. Add Columbus Circle salad and a robust zinfandel and you're ready to go!

1 pound sweet Italian sausage
½ C. chopped onion
2 cloves garlic, finely chopped
1½ C. bread flour
1 tbsp. sugar
1 C. hot tap water
1 tbsp. 50% faster active dry yeast
½ C. whole wheat flour
½ C. yellow cornmeal
½ teas. salt
1 tbsp. unsalted butter or margarine
½ pound mozzarella, cubed
¼ C. (about 1 oz.) freshly grated Parmesan

14-oz. can Italian plum tomatoes, drained well and chopped coarsely
½ C. sliced black olives
1 tbsp. minced fresh basil or oregano or 1 teas. dried

Glaze
1 small egg, beaten

Garnish
2–3 teas. finely chopped fresh herbs, your choice

1. Remove and discard the sausage casing from the sausage. In a large skillet, crumble the sausage and add the onion and garlic. Sauté, stirring occasionally, until the sausage is browned and the onion is translucent. Drain off the accumulated fat and set the sausage aside to cool.

2. In the food processor bowl fitted with the steel blade, combine ½ cup of the bread flour, sugar, ½ cup of the hot water, and the yeast. Process for 10 seconds to blend. Remove the steel blade from the processor bowl and place the bowl in the microwave. Set an 8-ounce glass of water next to it.

3. Lower the microwave power to the appropriate micro-rise setting (see page 35), and heat the sponge for 3 minutes. Rest for 3 minutes. Remove the processor bowl from the microwave. Place the processor bowl back on the base and fit with the steel blade. Add the remaining 1 cup bread flour, whole wheat flour, ½ cup cornmeal, salt, and butter or margarine. Process until well blended, about 10 seconds.

4. With the machine running, very slowly drizzle the remaining ½ cup hot water into the flour mixture so the dough forms a ball that cleans the side of the bowl. Process until the dough turns around the bowl 10 times. The dough will be very soft and sticky.

5. Remove the dough and the steel blade from the processor bowl and form the dough into a ball. With your thumbs, punch a hole to form a doughnut shape, and place it back in the processor bowl. Cover loosely with a damp tea towel or microwavable plastic wrap. Place the processor bowl in the middle of the microwave. Set an 8-ounce glass of water next to it. With the microwave power set as in step 3, heat for 3 minutes. Rest for 3 minutes. Heat for 3 minutes. Meanwhile, lightly grease a 9-inch springform pan and lightly sprinkle the bottom with cornmeal.

6. To the cooled sausage mixture, add the mozzarella, Parmesan, tomatoes, black olives, and basil or oregano. Stir to mix.

7. Remove the dough from the microwave. With buttered fingers, punch the dough down and remove ⅔ of the dough from the processor bowl and place in the prepared pan. Carefully press the dough onto the bottom of the pan and 2 inches up the side. Spoon the sausage mixture into the pan, spreading evenly. Remove the remaining third of the dough and spread and press it evenly over the filling. Carefully press the top edge of the dough that is attached to the pan down onto the top crust to seal. Cover the loaf loosely with a damp tea towel or plastic wrap and place in a warm place, away from drafts, to rise until doubled—about 30 minutes. Meanwhile, preheat the oven to 400°F.

8. When the loaf has risen, brush the top with the beaten egg. Bake the loaf on the middle shelf of the oven for 25 to 30 minutes or until the loaf is golden brown. Cool for 5 minutes in the pan and then loosen the edges and remove the side of the pan. Sprinkle with the fresh herbs. Serve warm.

Columbus Circle Salad with Garlic ◇ Vinaigrette ◇

Serves 8 in 15 minutes

In the food processor bowl fitted with the steel blade, combine 2 large cloves garlic, 1 tablespoon mayonnaise, ¼ teaspoon freshly ground black pepper, ½ cup vegetable oil or olive oil, and ⅓ cup red wine vinegar. Process for 10 seconds or until the garlic is finely chopped. Toss the dressing with 2 small heads of romaine torn into bite-sized pieces and ¾ cup freshly grated Parmesan.

Cheddar and Clam
◇ Calzone ◇

*Serves 2 to 4 in 1 hour
and 30 minutes*

Clams and calzone are a wonderful marriage, because the crust on the top of the clams keeps them from drying out in the intense heat. Serve with your favorite chardonnay and fresh green salad.

- 1 recipe All-Star Calzone
- 1 C. (3 oz.) grated high-quality white cheddar
- 1½ C. freshly shucked or canned and drained small clams
- 2 cloves garlic, pressed
- Salt and freshly ground black pepper to taste
- 2 tbsp. freshly grated Parmesan
- ⅛ teas. red pepper flakes

Layer the ingredients on the calzone in the order given and bake according to the All-Star Calzone basic recipe.

ALL-STAR CALZONE

Makes 1 calzone in 1 hour and 15 minutes, serves 4

The half-moon calzone, stuffed with oozing cheese, popping olives, and sweet tomatoes (see Crusty Calzone, page 299, for additional fillings) is a portable feast for gatherings large and small. Just remember to drain excess liquid from your filling ingredients. Also, whatever is inside must be able to cook in 10 to 15 minutes, or should have been partially cooked previously.

- 2 C. bread flour
- ¼ C. medium rye flour
- ¾ C. water
- 2 teas. 50% faster active dry yeast
- 1 teas. sugar
- 1 tbsp. nonfat dry milk solids

- 2 tbsp. olive oil
- 1 teas. salt
- Filling of your choice
- Olive oil, for brushing on calzone

1. Preheat baking tiles or stone* (see pages 21–25) to 500°F. In the food processor bowl fitted with the steel blade, combine ½ cup of the bread flour, rye flour, ½ cup of the water, yeast, and sugar. Process for 10 seconds to blend. Remove the steel blade from the processor bowl and place the bowl in the microwave. Set an 8-ounce glass of water next to it.

2. Lower the microwave power to the appropriate microrise setting (see page 35) and heat the sponge for 3 minutes. Rest for 10 minutes. Remove the processor bowl from the microwave. Place the processor bowl back on the base and fit with the steel blade. Add the remaining 1½ cups bread flour, dry milk solids, olive oil, and salt and process until well blended, about 10 seconds.

3. With the machine running, *very slowly drizzle* just enough of the remaining ¼ cup water into the flour mixture so the dough forms a ball that cleans the sides of the bowl and rides the blade around. Process until the dough turns around the bowl 25 times.

* Calzones can be baked on the middle rack of a preheated 450°F oven on a heavy baking sheet, lightly sprinkled with cornmeal, in lieu of baking tiles or a stone. The calzones are done when they are browned nicely and the bottom crust is fairly thick and lightly browned, about 20 minutes.

4. Remove the dough and the steel blade from the processor bowl, and form the dough into a ball. With your thumbs, punch a hole to form a doughnut shape, and place it back in the processor bowl. Cover loosely with a damp tea towel or microwavable plastic wrap. Place the processor bowl in the middle of the microwave. Set an 8-ounce glass of water next to it.

5. With the microwave power set as in step 2, heat for 2 minutes. Rest for 3 minutes. Heat for 2 minutes. Rest for 20 to 30 minutes or until the dough has doubled in bulk. Meanwhile, prepare your ingredients for the chosen filling and sprinkle a pizza peel (see page 24) generously with cornmeal.

6. Remove the dough to a lightly floured surface and knead for a few seconds. Shape into a ball and cover with the processor bowl. Let rest for 10 minutes.

7. On a lightly floured surface, roll the dough into a circle 14 inches in diameter. Place the dough circle on the pizza peel. Arrange the filling ingredients on half of the circle, leaving a 1-inch rim around the edge. Fold the unfilled half of the dough over the filled half and pinch the rims together to seal. Brush lightly with olive oil. Give the calzone a few quick jerks on the peel to make sure it is not sticking. Open the oven door and with 1 or 2 quick movements, and slide the calzone onto the preheated tiles or stone.

8. Bake the calzone for 10 to 15 minutes or until nicely browned all over. Carefully remove the calzone from the oven to a serving platter and let it rest for 5 minutes before slicing. Calzone may be served hot or at room temperature. Wrap in a plastic bag to store.

Fresh Tomato, Chicken, and ◇ Cheese Calzone ◇

Serves 2 to 4 in 2 hours

Try this combination for a light entrée in the summer, when the tomatoes are sun ripened and the emerald basil is at its peak.

- 1 recipe All-Star Calzone
- 1 C. shredded mozzarella
- 1 C. ricotta
- 1/4 C. freshly grated Parmesan
- 1 C. seeded and sliced vine-ripened Roma tomatoes
- 4-oz. chicken breast, skin and bones removed, grilled, cooled, and shredded
- 1/8 C. fresh basil leaves, torn
- 2 cloves garlic, pressed

In a medium bowl, combine the cheeses and mix well. Starting with the cheese mixture, layer the ingredients on half of the crust in the order given and bake according to the directions in the All-Star Calzone recipe.

GREEN ONION MARKET BREAD WITH ITALIAN FILLING

Makes 1 loaf in 2 hours, to serve 4

It was love at first bite when we chomped into this sandwich. The allspice and cloves are surprisingly compatible with Italian olives. Make sure the selection of meats and cheeses are sliced paper thin.

Olive Filling
- ½ C. coarsely chopped pimiento-stuffed green olives
- ½ C. coarsely chopped Kalamata olives
- ½ C. olive oil
- ¼ C. thinly sliced celery
- 2 tbsp. minced fresh parsley
- 1 tbsp. red wine vinegar
- 1 medium clove garlic, minced
- 1 teas. dried oregano
- ½ teas. dried thyme
- ¼ teas. sugar
- Freshly ground black pepper to taste

Dough
- 1½ tbsp. olive oil
- 1 C. thinly sliced green onions and tops
- 1 clove garlic, minced
- ⅛ teas. ground cloves
- ¼ teas. ground allspice
- 1 teaspoon dried thyme
- 1 tbsp. 50% faster active dry yeast
- 1½ teas. sugar
- 1 C. warm water (105°–115°F)
- 2 C. bread flour
- 1 teas. salt

Glaze
- 1 small egg beaten with 1 teas. water
- 1 tbsp. sesame seeds, for sprinkling on top

Cheese and Meat Filling
- 4 thin slices mozzarella
- 4 thin slices provolone
- 4 thin slices mortadella
- 4 thin slices cotto salami with peppercorns
- 8 thin slices imported dry cured salami

1. Thoroughly combine all of the olive-filling ingredients in a glass bowl. Cover and refrigerate for 12 hours. Bring to room temperature before filling the sandwich.

2. To make the bread, heat the olive oil in a medium skillet over medium-high heat. Add the green onions and garlic and stir until the onions are limp, about 1 minute. Reduce the heat to low. Add the cloves, allspice, and thyme. Cook 2 minutes, stirring occasionally. Set aside.

3. In the food processor bowl, combine the yeast, sugar, ¾ cup of the warm water and ¾ cup of the bread flour. Process for 10 seconds to blend. Remove the metal blade from the processor bowl and place the bowl in the microwave. Set an 8-ounce glass of water next to it.

4. Lower the microwave power to the appropriate micro-rise setting (see page 35). Heat the sponge for 3 minutes. Rest for 3 minutes. Remove the processor bowl from the microwave. Place the processor bowl back on the base and fit with the steel blade. Add the remaining 1¼ cups bread flour and salt and process until well blended, about 5 seconds.

5. With the machine running, very slowly drizzle just enough of the remaining ¼ cup warm water into the flour mixture so the dough forms a ball that cleans the sides of the bowl. Process until the dough turns around the bowl 10 times. Remove the dough from the processor bowl to a lightly floured surface and knead the onion-spice mixture into the dough.

6. Remove the steel blade from the processor bowl. Form the dough into a ball. With your thumbs, punch a hole to form a doughnut shape, adding a little flour as necessary if the dough seems sticky, and place it back in the processor bowl. Cover loosely with a damp tea towel or microwavable plastic wrap. Place the processor bowl in the middle of the microwave. Set an 8-ounce glass of water next to it.

7. With the microwave power set as in step 4, heat for 2 minutes, then rest for 3 minutes. Heat for 2 minutes. Rest for 20 minutes or until the dough has doubled in bulk. Meanwhile, preheat your pizza stone or tiles (see pages 21–25) on the middle rack to 375°F for 30 minutes and sprinkle a pizza peel (see page 24) with cornmeal.

8. Remove the dough from the microwave to a lightly floured surface and punch down. Form the dough into a ball and then roll into a 12-inch diameter circle and place on the peel. Cover loosely with a damp tea towel or plastic wrap and set aside in a warm place to double in bulk, about 25 minutes. When the dough has doubled in bulk, remove the plastic and brush lightly with the egg glaze and sprinkle with the

(continued)

Just because I starch and iron the tablecloth, people think I can cook.

—Elizabeth Collingwood

◊

sesame seeds. Discard any remaining egg glaze. Giving the peel a fast, quick jerk, place the dough on the stone.

9. Bake until golden brown, 25 to 35 minutes. Remove from the stone to a rack to cool.

10. When the bread has completely cooled, slice the loaf horizontally. Strain the olive filling through a sieve, reserving the marinade. Brush the cut surfaces of the bread with the marinade. Spread half of the olive filling on the bottom of the bread; layer with the meats and cheeses. Top the meats and cheeses with the remaining olive filling. Place the top half of the bread on the olive filling and enjoy!

FILLED SWISS-CHEDDAR BREAD

Makes 1 large loaf in 2 hours

Terrific for picnics, simply add a bottle of wine, fresh fruit, and a friend.

⅔ C. milk	*1 teas. salt*
2 tbsp. sugar	*½ pound Swiss cheese*
3 tbsp. unsalted butter	*½ pound white cheddar*
1 large egg	
2½ teas. 50% faster active dry yeast	**Glaze**
	1 egg, lightly beaten
3 C. bread flour	*with water*

1. In a 2-cup glass measure, combine the milk, sugar, and butter. Heat to about 120°F in the microwave set on high power, about 1 minute. Whisk in egg.

2. In the processor bowl fitted with the steel blade, combine the yeast, flour, and salt. Pulse to mix. Then with the motor running, *drizzle the liquid very slowly* into the dry ingredients, holding back the last portion of the liquid to see if the dough will form a ball.

3. Process until the dough begins to leave the side of the bowl, forming a ball. Add the last of the liquid only if necessary. Knead 60 seconds with the motor running, adding flour as necessary through the feed tube if the dough seems sticky. Pinch up a piece of the dough. It should feel soft, tacky, smooth, elastic, and warm.

4. Remove the dough and the steel blade and prepare to micro-rise. On a lightly floured surface, knead dough by hand a few seconds, then form dough into a ball. With your thumbs, punch a hole to form a doughnut shape; coat with additional butter, and replace in the processor bowl. Cover loosely with a damp tea towel or plastic wrap. Place the dough in the microwave.

5. Set an 8-ounce glass of water in the back of the microwave. Lower the microwave power to the appropriate micro-rise setting (see page 35). Heat for 3 minutes. Rest for 3 minutes. Heat for 3 minutes. Rest for 6 minutes or until the dough has risen to about double in bulk.

6. Remove the dough to a lightly floured surface and knead by hand a few seconds. Form into a ball, coat with additional butter, cover with the processor bowl, and allow the dough to rest for 15 minutes.

7. Punch the dough down, roll into a ball, coat with butter, place in a glass bowl, cover with a damp tea towel or plastic wrap, and repeat step 5. Meanwhile, preheat the oven with a pizza stone (see pages 21–25) in place to 400°F for at least 30 minutes.

8. Attach the grater and coarsely grate the cheeses in the food processor. Mix the two and set aside.

9. On a lightly floured work surface, roll the dough out into an oval about 16 × 13 inches. Coat with an even layer of the cheeses, leaving a ½-inch margin around the edge. Fold the dough over, making a 16-inch-long loaf, then wet the edges and pinch to seal. Be sure you've completely sealed this bread so that the cheese won't run out during the baking process.

10. Generously sprinkle a pizza peel (see page 24) with cornmeal and roll the cheese-filled bread onto it so that the pinched edges are now on the bottom, and the loaf is shaped like a fat French bread. Prick the top of the bread all over with a fork, then brush lightly with a wash made from beaten egg and a little water. Allow the bread to raise about 10 minutes before baking. Give the bread a trial shake to make sure it will slide freely from the peel.

11. Shovel the bread onto the hot stone and bake in the preheated oven 20 to 25 minutes or until golden brown. With the peel lift off the bread onto a rack to cool. Let the bread cool at least an hour before cutting. Wrap in plastic to store. This bread is best served in thick, warm slices, and keeps 2 or 3 days properly wrapped.

Mushroom ◇ Pickles ◇

Makes 1 quart in 3 days

Forget those old-fashioned methods. Make these a couple of days before you wish to serve, refrigerate, and you have on hand a wonderful fresh bite to add to the antipasti.

2 pounds fresh button or
  brown mushrooms

Vinaigrette
¾ C. olive oil
½ C. white wine vinegar
3 cloves garlic, pressed
1 bay leaf
10 whole peppercorns
2 teas. salt
½ teas. dry mustard
½ teas. brown sugar
¼ C. mixed fresh herbs of
  your choice: parsley,
  basil, oregano

1. Clean and trim the mushrooms. Place in a soup kettle with water to cover. Add a pinch of salt and raise to a boil. Cook until the mushrooms sink to the bottom. Remove from the heat and drain.

2. Meanwhile, in a saucepan, combine the remaining ingredients *except* the fresh herbs and raise to a boil. Reduce the heat and simmer 10 minutes.

3. Pack the mushrooms into hot, sterilized jars with fresh herbs. Pour boiling vinaigrette over and seal. Cool, then refrigerate for up to 3 days.

Corn and Roast
◇ Pepper Gazpacho ◇

*Serves 4–6 in 20 minutes;
marinates overnight*

4 C. tomato juice
½ C. dry vermouth
2 tbsp. fresh lime juice
2 tbsp. fruity olive oil
1 pound Roma tomatoes
½ C. roasted red peppers
   (see page 123)
½ medium red bell pepper
1 medium yellow onion
½ rib celery
1 C. fresh, frozen, or
   canned corn, cooked and
   chilled
1 teas. chili powder
Salt and freshly ground black
   pepper to taste
Tabasco to taste
Avocado slices
Sour cream

1. Combine the tomato juice,
vermouth, lime juice, and olive oil
in a large bowl. Stir and set aside.

2. In the food processor fitted
with the steel blade, chop, one at a
time, and in order, the fresh tomatoes, roasted red peppers, fresh
bell pepper, yellow onion, and celery. After you finely chop each vegetable, add it to the tomato juice
mixture. Now add whole cooked
corn kernels. Season with chili
powder, salt, black pepper, and
Tabasco. Adjust this to suit yourself. (You might wish a shot of lime
juice or a little more hot stuff.
We've seen the time when people
dosed this soup with tequila. Border mania. Comes over us all. It's
the sun.) Now refrigerate at least 4
hours or overnight.

3. To serve, pour the gazpacho
in tall clear glasses; garnish with a
thin sliver of avocado and a dollop
of sour cream.

SEDONA BREAD

Makes 1 loaf in 2 hours

When a professional baker falls in love, she doesn't write
a sonnet or symphony. She invents a recipe. Here's one
from a baker at Manna From Heaven after a trip to Arizona.

Notice how this professional mixed hard and soft wheat
flours. The bread flour gives the final product lift; the soft
wheat makes for a fine texture.

2 C. bread flour
1 C. cake flour
2 tbsp. sugar
1 teas. salt
2½ teas. 50% faster
   active dry yeast
¼ C. (½ stick)
   unsalted butter
1 C. less about 2 tbsp.
   milk
1 large egg

Filling and Topping
3 tbsp. cold unsalted
   butter, cut into bits
1 large egg, whisked
2 tbsp. diced green
   chilies
⅔ C. grated cheddar
1 tbsp. crushed dried
   red chilies

1. In the processor bowl fitted with the steel blade, add
flours, sugar, salt, and yeast. Pulse to mix. Now, cut butter
in finely, and pulse to blend so that it almost disappears.

2. In a glass measure, heat the milk in the microwave to
about 120°F (about 45 seconds on high power), then add the
egg. Whisk together with a fork, then with the motor running,
gradually pour the liquid into dry ingredients, holding back
the last couple of tablespoons of liquid to see if the dough will
form a ball.

3. Process until the dough begins to leave the side of the
bowl, using the last of the liquid only if necessary. Knead 60
seconds, adding flour as necessary if the dough seems sticky.
Pinch up a piece of the dough. It should feel tacky, smooth,
elastic, and warm.

4. Remove the dough and the steel blade and prepare to
micro-rise. On a lightly floured surface, knead the dough by
hand a few seconds, then form the dough into a ball. With
your thumbs, punch a hole to form a doughnut shape and
place in the processor bowl. Cover loosely with a damp tea
towel or plastic wrap.

5. Place an 8-ounce glass of water in the back of the

microwave. Place the dough in the microwave and lower the microwave power to the appropriate micro-rise setting (see page 35). Heat for 3 minutes. Rest for 3 minutes. Heat for 3 minutes. Rest for 6 minutes or until the dough has risen to about double in bulk.

6. Remove the dough to a lightly floured surface and knead by hand a few seconds. Form into a doughnut shape again, place in the processor bowl, and raise again in the microwave, repeating step 5, or in a warm, draft-free place until doubled in bulk.

7. Grease generously a standard 8½ × 4½ × 2½-inch glass loaf pan. Preheat the oven to 375°F.

8. Once the dough has risen a second time, punch down, and roll into a rectangular shape about 10 × 12 inches. Spot with pieces of cold butter, then chop the butter in, using a pastry scraper. Paint the dough with all but 2 tablespoons of the whisked egg and chop that in. Spread green chilies and cheese and chop these in, holding back a hefty pinch of each for the top. Now roll up, jelly-roll fashion, beginning at the 10-inch side. Gently place the dough into the prepared loaf pan, seam side down, and let it rise a final time, either in the microwave, repeating step 5, or in a warm, draft-free place until the dough is nearly doubled in bulk.

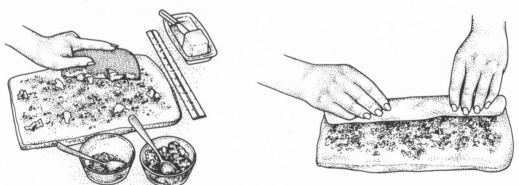

9. When the dough has risen, brush with reserved 2 tablespoons egg to make a glaze, taking care not to allow any to run down the sides of the pan (it sticks). Make 3 deep, diagonal slashes in the top with a sharp knife or razor blade. Sprinkle the top with reserved green chilies, cheddar, and the crushed dried red chilies.

10. Bake in the preheated oven 25 to 30 minutes or until evenly browned. Remove immediately to a rack to cool. Wrap in plastic to store. This bread keeps up to a week, properly stored.

The only difference between the French fougasse and the Italian focaccia is that while the Italians content themselves with a dimpled flatbread, the French slash and shape these breads into interesting designs. You can use any focaccia recipe to create a fougasse. Simply shape and cut the flatbread into an intriguing pattern. The sun, a sunflower, a moon, an octopus with dangling legs: these are some of the more popular shapes found in French bakeries. You could even make a gingerless-bread man if you are so inclined. We love to use these breads in centerpieces with raffia bows and edible accoutrements, including olives, walnuts, and carrot and celery sticks.

Serve with Composed Salad of Italian Roasted Red and Green Peppers (see page 123). Looks good. Tastes good. Sets a festive mood for a party.

GREEN OLIVE FOUGASSE

Makes 2 flatbreads in under 1 hour and 30 minutes, serving at least 12

The fougasse comes from Provence and is traditionally served alongside *salade Niçoise*. This flatbread is a rectangle with diagonal slashes forming a pattern that looks like the negative of a tree branch. Other traditional shapes for the fougasse include a sunburst, a sunflower, a moon. Whatever shape you choose, serve warm, then simply break off a piece of this rich olive bread. So good you won't even want butter.

2½ C. bread flour	½ C. water
1 tbsp. 50% faster active dry yeast	¼ C. fruity olive oil
2 teas. sugar	⅓ C. chopped green olives
¼ teas. salt	Olive oil, for coating dough
½ C. milk	

1. Combine the flour, yeast, sugar, and salt in the processor bowl fitted with the steel blade and pulse to mix.

2. In a glass measure, warm milk and water to lukewarm in the microwave (set on high power for about 30 seconds), then combine with the olive oil.

3. With the processor motor running, pour the liquids into the flour, holding back the last portion of liquid to see if the dough will form a ball.

4. Process until the dough forms a ball and leaves the sides of the bowl, adding last bit of liquid only if necessary. Knead in the processor 60 seconds.

5. Remove the dough and blade from the processor bowl. Add flour if the dough seems sticky, and knead by hand a few seconds. Then knead olives in by hand.

6. Form the dough into a ball. With your thumbs, punch a hole to form a doughnut shape and place in the processor bowl. Cover loosely with a damp tea towel or microwavable plastic wrap and prepare to micro-rise.

7. Place an 8-ounce glass of water in the back of the microwave. Lower the microwave power to the appropriate micro-rise setting (see page 35). Place the dough in microwave. Heat for 3 minutes. Rest for 3 minutes. Heat 3 minutes. Rest 6 minutes or until about doubled in bulk.

8. Remove the dough from the processor bowl, punch down, and knead by hand a few seconds. Then set the dough aside to rest.

9. Divide the dough into 2 equal portions. Roll and stretch each portion into an oval about 8 × 10 inches. Place on a greased glass baking sheet, and with a sharp knife, make 6 to 8 evenly spaced diagonal slashes in 2 rows, cutting all the way through the dough. Open these slits by pulling them well apart with your hands.

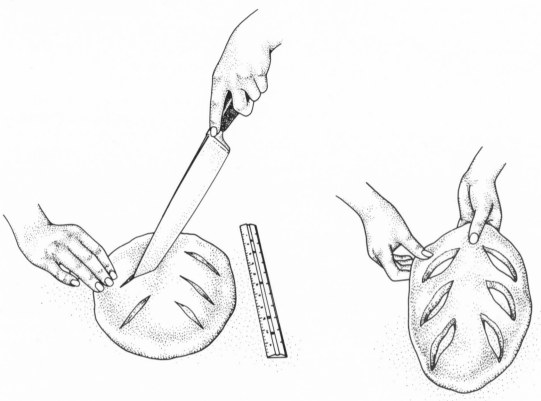

10. Coat flatbreads with olive oil and set aside. Preheat the oven to 375°F.

11. Place each piece of the dough in the microwave separately and repeat step 7, or raise in a warm, draft-free place until about doubled in bulk.

12. Bake in the preheated oven 15 to 20 minutes or until golden brown.

13. Turn out on a rack to cool. Store in plastic wrap. Best if eaten the same day they're made.

- To make an onion focaccia, simply follow the Plain Ole Focaccia recipe and top the bread with about ½ cup thinly sliced onions just before baking.
- To make a sage focaccia, top the bread with a dozen fresh sage leaves, or 2 teaspoons dried sage, just before baking.
- To make a bacon focaccia, cook 6 slices of bacon in the microwave until crisp (about 5 minutes on high power), then drain the bacon and crumble it finely atop the dough just before baking.
- To make a potato focaccia, cook 4 red potatoes in boiling water until soft, then cut into thin slices and arrange atop the focaccia dough. Sprinkle with red pepper flakes and rosemary needles, season to taste with salt and freshly ground black pepper, and bake as directed.
- To make anchovy focaccia, open a 2-ounce tin of anchovy fillets and arrange them atop the dough. Drizzle the anchovy oil over all, then dimple the top with capers. Bake as directed.
- To make sun-dried tomato focaccia, arrange sun-dried tomatoes in oil over the dough, drizzle this oil over all, sprinkle with basil, then bake as directed.

PLAIN OLE FOCACCIA

Makes one 14-inch round flatbread in 1 hour

3 C. bread flour
2 teas. salt
2½ teas. 50% faster active dry yeast
¾ C. hot tap water (120°F)

¼ C. olive oil
3 tbsp olive oil, for the top
Coarse sea salt or kosher salt, for sprinkling on top

1. Place a pizza stone in the upper third of the oven and preheat to 500°F for at least 30 minutes before baking (see pages 21–25).

2. Combine in the processor bowl fitted with the steel blade 1 cup of the flour, salt, yeast, and water. Process for 30 seconds.

3. Remove the blade and bowl from the processor. Cover the bowl loosely with a damp tea towel or microwavable plastic wrap and prepare to micro-rise the sponge.

4. Place an 8-ounce glass of water in the back of the microwave. Lower the microwave power to the appropriate micro-rise setting (see page 35). Place the sponge in the microwave. Heat for 3 minutes. Rest for 3 minutes.

5. Place the steel blade back in the bowl, and the bowl back on the base of the processor. Add the remaining ingredients except 3 tablespoons of the olive oil and the coarse salt. With the motor running, process until the dough begins to leave the side of the bowl. Knead for 60 seconds, adding flour as necessary, if the dough seems sticky.

6. Remove the dough and the steel blade and prepare to micro-rise. Knead dough by hand a few seconds, and form dough into a ball. With your thumbs, punch a hole to form a doughnut shape and place the dough in the processor bowl. Cover loosely with a damp tea towel or plastic wrap.

7. Micro-rise the dough, repeating step 4. Then add an additional cycle, heating for 3 minutes and resting for 6 minutes or until the dough has about doubled in bulk.

8. Place the dough on a lightly floured surface and roll and stretch into a 14-inch circle. It should be about ¼ inch thick. If you prefer a thicker, chewier bread, you can roll it smaller and thicker, say 12 inches and ⅜ inch thick.

9. Sprinkle a pizza peel generously with cornmeal (see page 24), place the dough disk on it, and set aside to raise until puffy, about 10 minutes. Then rub the surface with the remaining 3 tablespoons of olive oil and sprinkle generously with coarse or kosher salt. Poke the surface of the focaccia with your fingertips to dimple the bread. Give the peel a sample shake to make sure the bread will slide off.

10. Pop the focaccia off the peel onto the preheated stone, turn the oven down to 400°F, and bake 15 minutes. After 15 minutes check to see if it is evenly golden brown. If not, cook it 5 minutes or so longer.

ROSEMARY-RAISIN FOCACCIA WITH PINE NUTS

Makes two 8-inch flatbreads in 1 hour and 30 minutes

The traditional flatbread of Northern Italy stands alone, to be eaten as a snack along with a glass of wine or to be a centerpiece to a more elaborate hors d'oeuvre offering. This particular version is sweeter than most and marries well with a cup of steaming *caffe con latte* on a cold winter's day.

2 tbsp. fruity olive oil	*2 teas. 50% faster*
3-inch sprig fresh	*active dry yeast*
rosemary	*¾ C. hot tap water*
¼ C. raisins	*⅓ C. pine nuts, toasted*
2 C. bread flour	*2 teas. chopped fresh*
½ C. whole wheat flour	*rosemary needles*
¾ teas. salt	*Olive oil, for coating*
1 teas. sugar	*dough*

1. Combine the olive oil and rosemary sprig in a small glass bowl and heat at full power in the microwave while the oil bubbles, about 1 minute. Add raisins; heat an additional 20 seconds, then set the mixture aside.

2. In the processor bowl fitted with the steel blade combine the flours, salt, sugar, and yeast. Pulse to mix.

3. With the motor running, add the hot water, holding back the last portion to see if the dough will form a ball.

(continued)

To toast pine nuts: Place the nuts on a flat baking sheet in a 350°F oven and bake 3 to 5 minutes, watching like a hawk. Boy will they burn. Or you can place them in a dry skillet and shake them over medium-high heat until they begin to color up. Immediately pour them into a cool container.

◇

To vary this sweet focaccia, delete the rosemary, substitute dried Michigan cherries for the pine nuts, use golden raisins, and sprinkle the top with turbinado sugar. Now you have a breakfast bread that's fragrant with fruit, sweet enough to satisfy, and infinitely more wholesome than fat-laden croissants. A high-fiber, low-fat, super-satisfaction breakfast for life in the half-time kitchen.

Process until the dough leaves the side of the bowl and forms a ball, adding the last bit of water only if necessary. Knead with the machine running for 60 seconds, adding flour by the teaspoonful as necessary to eliminate stickiness.

4. Remove the steel blade and dough from the processor. Knead the dough on a lightly floured surface, then form a well in the middle of the dough ball. Discard the sprig of rosemary from the oil, then pour the oil and raisins into the well. Add toasted pine nuts and fresh chopped rosemary needles, and knead the dough by hand to incorporate the fruit, nuts, and herb.

5. Form the dough into a ball. With your thumbs, punch a hole to form a doughnut shape and place in the processor bowl. Cover loosely with a damp tea towel or plastic wrap and prepare to micro-rise.

6. Place an 8-ounce glass of water in the back of the microwave. Place the processor bowl of dough in the middle. Lower the microwave power to the appropriate micro-rise setting (see page 35). Heat for 3 minutes. Rest for 3 minutes. Heat for 3 minutes. Rest for 6 minutes or until the dough has nearly doubled in bulk.

7. Remove the dough from the processor bowl, punch down, and knead by hand a few seconds. Cover the dough with the processor bowl and let it rest for 10 minutes.

8. Preheat the oven to 400°F. Coat two 8-inch cake pans with olive oil. Cut the dough into 2 pieces. Pat each portion into a pan, coat the dough with additional olive oil, then cover and raise a second time. In the microwave, repeat step 6, or place the dough in a warm, draft-free place until puffy.

9. Using the tips of your fingers, dimple the top of the focaccia, then place in the top half of the preheated oven and bake. Immediately upon placing the bread in the oven, spritz the inside of the oven with water. After 10 minutes, spritz the bread with water. Bake an additional 15 minutes or until the bread is browned. Remove immediately to a rack to cool. Best served the same day it's cooked.

CRACKED PEPPER–PARMESAN BREAD

Makes 1 loaf in 3 hours

It's so delicious even butter gilds the lily; try this bread with a big tossed salad for a memorable lunch. Add a glass of cabernet, spread the whole thing on a checkered cloth in the park, and it's a picnic.

You'll like this free-form loaf best if you can cook it on a pizza stone (see pages 21–25) or quarry tiles. A crisp crust, an even, tender crumb, and an aromatic bite. This is bread.

2½ C. bread flour
1 teas. fresh basil leaves, chopped, or ¼ teas. dried
1 teas. fresh oregano leaves or ¼ teas. dried
¼ C. freshly grated Parmesan
½ teas. salt
1 tbsp. sugar
2½ teas. 50% faster active dry yeast
1 tbsp. unsalted butter or margarine
1 large egg
½ teas. Tabasco
½ teas. cracked black pepper
¾ C. hot tap water (120°–130°F)

1. Combine in the processor bowl fitted with the steel blade the flour, basil, oregano, Parmesan, salt, sugar, and yeast. Pulse to mix.

2. With the motor running, add the butter, egg, Tabasco sauce, cracked black pepper, and hot water. When the dough leaves the side of the bowl and forms a ball, knead for 60 seconds.

3. Remove the blade and dough from the bowl to a lightly floured work surface and knead by hand a few seconds, adding flour as necessary if the dough seems sticky. It will be soft. Form the dough into a ball. With your thumbs, punch a hole to form a doughnut shape and place in the processor bowl. Prepare to micro-rise. Cover loosely with a damp tea towel or plastic wrap and place the dough in the microwave.

4. Place an 8-ounce glass of water in the back of the microwave. Lower the microwave power to the appropriate micro-rise setting (see page 35). Heat for 3 minutes. Rest for

(continued)

3 minutes. Heat for 3 minutes. Rest for 6 minutes or until the dough has risen to about double in bulk.

5. Remove the dough to a lightly floured breadboard and knead by hand a few seconds. Form into an 8-inch-diameter ball and place on a pizza peel (see page 24) or cookie sheet with no sides that has been well dusted with cornmeal. Press dough down slightly, then micro-rise, repeating step 4, or raise in a warm, draft-free place until nearly doubled in bulk.

6. Meanwhile, preheat the oven to 400°F. If using a stone, preheat in the oven for at least 30 minutes. When the dough has risen, make four 1-inch-deep slashes in the top with a sharp knife in a herringbone pattern. Brush the loaf with water, then slip onto the hot pizza stone or the prepared cookie sheet and bake in preheated oven 30 minutes until golden.

7. Remove to a metal rack to cool. Wrap in plastic to store.

PITA BREAD

Makes 1 dozen pitas in 1 hour and 30 minutes

Another bread best cooked on tiles or a pizza stone (see pages 21–25), pita is elegant in its simplicity, much the same as the ancients must have made it.

3 C. bread flour	*1 teas. salt*
1 teas. sugar	*1 tbsp. shortening*
2½ teas. 50% faster active dry yeast	*1 C. hot tap water*

1. In the processor bowl fitted with the steel blade, combine the flour, sugar, yeast, and salt. Pulse to mix. Add shortening and mix until fat disappears. (Count to 10. Whoa.)

2. With the motor running, add hot tap water, holding back the last portion to see if the dough will form a ball and adding only if necessary. When the dough cleans the sides of the bowl, forming a ball, knead with the motor running for 60 seconds.

3. Remove the blade and dough from the processor bowl. On a lightly floured surface, knead dough by hand a moment, adding flour if the dough seems sticky. Form dough into a

ball. With your thumbs, punch a hole to form a doughnut shape and place in the processor bowl. Cover loosely with a damp tea towel or microwavable plastic wrap. Prepare to micro-rise.

4. Place an 8-ounce glass of water in the back of the microwave. Lower the microwave power to the appropriate micro-rise setting (see page 35). Place the dough in the center of the microwave and heat for 3 minutes. Rest for 3 minutes. Heat for 3 minutes, and rest for 6 minutes or until the dough has about doubled in bulk. Meanwhile, preheat the oven to 475°F. If you wish to cook the pitas on a stone, preheat the oven for at least 30 minutes with the stone in place.

5. Remove the dough to a lightly floured surface and punch down. Oil your hands with shortening, and divide the dough into 12 equal-sized pieces. Shape them into balls; spritz them with plain water; then cover with a damp tea towel or plastic wrap and let them rest for 15 minutes.

6. After the dough has rested, carefully flatten each ball of dough with your fingers. Take care not to stretch, wrinkle, or puncture the dough. With a rolling pin, roll each flattened ball into a 6-inch diameter round. Without stretching the dough, transfer each round to a pizza peel (see page 24) or ungreased cookie sheet sprinkled with cornmeal.

7. Bake 2 or 3 pitas at a time in the preheated oven, preferably on the stone. The pitas will bake in 4 or 5 minutes on the first side, and 2 minutes on the second. Turn with tongs. The rounds should be puffy and slightly browned on both sides. Cool on a rack. Stack and store in plastic bags.

Cut an edge off the pita, forming a pocket, and fill with cooked meats, tomatoes, lettuce, chopped cucumber; even plain old tuna fish tastes better in a pita.

Here's one of our favorites.

Cottage Cheese Sun-Dried Tomato ◇ Filling ◇

Makes 2 cups in 10 minutes; 2 hours for marinate

- 16 oz. small-curd low-fat cottage cheese
- 1/3 C. thinly sliced green onions and tops
- 1/3 C. finely chopped red or yellow bell pepper
- 2 tbsp. minced fresh basil leaves
- 2 tbsp. peas, fresh or frozen
- 1/2 teas. capers, drained
- 3 tbsp. drained and minced sun-dried tomatoes packed in olive oil

Juice of half a lime
Salt and freshly ground black pepper to taste
Whiff of cayenne

1. Combine all the ingredients in a medium bowl. If you're using frozen peas, just shake them in, as is. If you're using fresh, parboil them 3 minutes before adding. Refrigerate the filling 2 hours to allow the flavors to marry.

2. To serve, stuff pita pockets with heaping tablespoons of filling and dust with cayenne.

7 ◆ SOUP AND SANDWICH BREADS

Bettie Henry's Three-Seeded Cottage Bread 191

Lager Bread 193

Spiked-with-Ale Rye and Kraut Loaf 194

Swiss Cheese–Potato Savarin 195

Sour Rye Bread with Dillweed 197

Swedish Rye Bread 198

Nuevo York Corn Rye 200

Dampfnudeln 202

Garden Batter Bread 204

One-Rise Sauerkraut Rye 205

Home-baked bread plays a leading role in soup and sandwiches. In this chapter you'll find breads that have the character to stand on their own as well as the strength to enfold the most delicious sandwiches.

We've also included some of our favorite soups and sandwiches here. These are meals we make again and again, when time is precious, and satisfaction a must.

You'll also find sandwich breads in other places in this book. In fact, in every chapter are breads that you could use to make sandwiches. (For example, see Gloria's Whole Meal Bread, page 81.) Even in the chapter on sweet breads, you'll find a panettone sandwich that we adore.

We have also learned to make giant sandwiches to take on picnics, to tailgate parties, and for potlucks. The sight of a big, generous sandwich, with the fillings layered and peeking out from the middle of a whole loaf cut in half, is mouth-watering. We especially recommend the onion-walnut bagel sandwich. It looks as good as it tastes.

BETTIE HENRY'S THREE-SEEDED COTTAGE BREAD

Makes 1 loaf in 1 hour and 30 minutes

From time to time, we run across a bread that makes us say, "Now this is the best one yet." Bettie clipped a recipe out of the paper thirty years ago—a prize-winning batter bread that incorporated cottage cheese and dillweed. Like all good cooks, she started fiddling with the recipe, and it evolved to a three-seeded bread. Now we've adapted the recipe to micro-rising, and we like it so much, we want it every day.

Aromatic with the scent of dill, onion, poppy, and sesame seeds, the texture is light, and the calcium level is boosted by the addition of cottage cheese. A robust bread that will stand up to the heartiest meal, we suggest it for buffets that may include everything from hot casseroles to deli meats, muscular cheeses, and potato salads.

¼ C. fresh minced yellow onion or 1 tbsp. dried	1 teas. sugar
1 tbsp. 50% faster active dry yeast	1 tbsp. unsalted butter or margarine, softened
2½ C. bread flour	1 cup small-curd low-fat cottage cheese
1 teas. salt	1 egg
¼ teas. baking soda	¼ C. hot tap water
2 teas. dill seed	Seeds of your choice, for sprinkling on top
½ teas. poppy seed	
2 tbsp. toasted sesame seeds	

1. In the processor bowl fitted with the steel blade combine the minced onion, yeast, flour, salt, soda, seeds, and sugar. Pulse to mix. (The onion may be minced in the bowl before adding the other ingredients.)

2. With the motor running, add the remaining ingredients except the seeds for the top and process until the dough begins to leave the side of the bowl. Knead 60 seconds, adding flour as necessary if the dough seems too sticky. At

(continued)

One quick way to toast sesame seeds is to place them in a dry skillet and, over high heat, toss and turn them until they begin to pop like corn. No more than 2 or 3 minutes. Transfer to another bowl immediately, or they may burn. (See page 72 also.)

◊

When using the food processor to mince onions or other soft, watery fruits or vegetables, pulse the machine off and on, watching the progress so that you don't just make onion juice by accident.

the end of the kneading period, the dough will be very heavy, more like batter than dough. Don't worry.

3. Remove the steel blade and prepare to micro-rise. Cover the dough loosely with a damp tea towel or microwavable plastic wrap. Place an 8-ounce glass of water in the back of the microwave.

4. Lower the microwave power to the appropriate micro-rise setting (see page 35). Heat for 3 minutes. Rest for 3 minutes. Heat for 3 minutes. Rest for 6 minutes or until the dough has risen to half again its original size. (This may take up to 15 minutes.)

5. Using a rubber spatula, remove the dough to a lightly floured breadboard and knead by hand a few seconds. Form into a ball, then cover with the processor bowl and allow the dough to rest 5 or 10 minutes. Meanwhile, grease generously an 8-inch round glass casserole dish.

6. Place the dough in the prepared dish and spritz the top with water. Sprinkle it with additional seeds of your choice. Place in the microwave and repeat step 4. It takes this bread longer to rise than most. Be patient. Let the rising bread rest in the microwave until it has nearly doubled in bulk, up to 45 minutes. Preheat the oven to 350°F.

7. Bake in the preheated oven 40 to 50 minutes, or until golden brown on top, and until it taps hollow.

8. Turn out immediately onto a rack to cool. Wrap in foil to store.

LAGER BREAD

Makes 1 loaf in 1 hour and 30 minutes

Now that we have such choices in beers, you'll find the taste of this bread can vary depending on the kind of brew you choose. We've made it with Heinekens, Beck's, even Tsingtao and Anchor Steam. No matter what you choose, you'll find the addition of beer makes the dough almost leap out of the bowl. This bread is practically salt free and makes a marvelous close-grained home for fine cheeses.

1 C. lager-style beer	1½ C. whole wheat flour
1 tbsp. 50% faster active dry yeast	½ teas. salt
½ C. brown sugar	4 tbsp. (½ stick) unsalted butter or margarine
2 C. unbleached white flour	

1. In a 2-cup glass measure, heat beer to lukewarm in the microwave (about 10 seconds at high power).

2. Stir the yeast and brown sugar into the warm beer.

3. Combine the flours and salt in the processor bowl, then pulse to mix.

4. Melt the butter or margarine in the microwave, then stir 2 tablespoons of it into the yeast mixture.

5. With the processor motor running, add the yeasty liquid to the flours. When dough leaves the side and forms a ball, knead with the machine running for 60 seconds.

6. Remove the dough and blade from the bowl. Knead the dough by hand a few seconds, adding flour if the dough seems sticky, then form into a ball. With your thumbs, punch a hole to form a doughnut shape and replace in the processor bowl. Cover loosely with a damp tea towel or plastic wrap and prepare to micro-rise.

7. Place an 8-ounce glass of water in the back of the microwave. Lower the microwave power to the appropriate micro-rise setting (see page 35). Place the dough in the microwave. Heat for 3 minutes. Let rest for 3 minutes. Heat for 3 minutes. Let rest for 6 minutes or until doubled in bulk.

8. Remove the dough from the processor bowl to a lightly floured surface, punch down, and knead by hand a few seconds. Cover the dough with the processor bowl, then allow it

(continued)

Combine in the food processor a stick of sweet butter with 4 or 5 anchovy fillets, a sprig of parsley, and a clove of garlic. Pulse to make a rough puree. Then pile onto thin slices of toasted Lager Bread. Pop a beer. Here's lunch.

Aromatic Egg ◇ Salad ◇

Makes 2 cups in 20 minutes

Combine 6 chopped hard-cooked eggs in a big bowl with ⅓ cup mayonnaise, juice of half a lemon, ¾ teaspoon chili powder, ¼ cup each finely chopped celery, green onion and tops. Add minced fresh jalapeño, salt, and freshly ground black pepper to taste. Layer with thick slices of Beefsteak tomato on Lager Bread for a lovely lunch with a beer.

Waldorf ◇ Sandwich ◇

Makes 2 cups in 10 minutes

Combine 8 ounces softened cream cheese with 1 tablespoon milk and the juice of half a lemon. Add a finely chopped apple, ½ cup chopped dates, and ¼ cup finely chopped walnuts. Butter a couple of slices of Lager Bread, add lettuce, then top with this filling.

to rest for 10 minutes. Meanwhile, grease a glass bread pan and set aside. Preheat the oven to 350°F.

9. Form the dough into a loaf shape (see page 40) and place in the prepared pan. Drizzle the remaining melted butter or margarine atop, coating thoroughly.

10. Set the dough in the microwave and repeat step 7, watching carefully that you don't overrise this one. You may find it's ready after only 6 minutes.

11. Bake the bread in the preheated oven 50 minutes or until it sounds hollow when tapped. Immediately turn out on a rack to cool. Wrap in aluminum foil to store.

SPIKED-WITH-ALE RYE AND KRAUT LOAF

Makes 1 loaf in 1 hour and 30 minutes

This bread makes excellent company for winter dinners of smoked meats. We tried it once with smoked pork chops and again with marinated venison roast. We served kraut, mashed potatoes with butter and cream, and a bowl of steaming homemade applesauce.

1½ C. bread flour
1½ C. rye flour
3 teas. 50% faster active dry yeast
¼ C. nonfat dry milk solids
1 tbsp. sugar
1 tbsp. caraway seeds

1 teas. salt
½ C. drained and chopped sauerkraut
1 tbsp. vegetable oil
¾ C. ale, Henry Weinhard's or your favorite

1. Fit the processor bowl with the steel blade. Combine and process for 30 seconds the flours, yeast, nonfat dry milk, sugar, caraway seeds, salt, sauerkraut, and oil.

2. Measure the ale into a 2-cup microwavable measure and heat on high power in the microwave for 45 seconds or until it is the temperature of hot tap water, about 120°F.

3. With the motor running, pour the ale through the feed tube. When the dough leaves the side of the bowl and forms a ball, knead with the machine running for 30 seconds.

We know of no ale that compares with Irish-style ales in terms of smoothness and flavor. The ale chosen for this bread will give it character and moistness.

Thick slices of rye and kraut bread make a great beginning to a grilled cheddar and turkey sandwich with sweet pickles and tomato. Don't forget the mustard. We like 4-seeded mustard with this bread.

4. Remove the dough from the bowl. Knead the dough by hand a few seconds on a lightly floured surface, adding flour as necessary if the dough seems too sticky.

5. Grease well one 8½ × 4½ × 2½-inch glass loaf pan. Shape the dough into a loaf (see page 40) and place it into the prepared pan. Cover the pan loosely with a damp tea towel or microwavable plastic wrap. Place the bread off-center in the microwave.

6. Set an 8-ounce glass of water in the microwave. To micro-rise, lower the microwave power to the appropriate micro-rise setting (see page 35). Heat for 3 minutes. Rest for 3 minutes. Heat for 3 minutes. Rest until doubled in bulk, about 30 minutes. Meanwhile, preheat your oven to 375°F.

7. Place the loaf on the middle rack of the preheated oven and bake for 35 to 40 minutes or until the loaf is light brown and sounds hollow when tapped.

8. Remove the bread from the pan to a rack to cool. Wrap in aluminum foil to store.

SWISS CHEESE–POTATO SAVARIN

Makes 1 large ring loaf in under 1 hour and 30 minutes

This cheese tube bread makes the ultimate grilled cheese sandwich. Add a Comice pear and a fruity white wine and you'll have an Oregon harvest lunch. The bread is close grained and tangy. The addition of potato gives it wonderful keeping qualities.

1½ C. hot tap water (120°F)
¼ C. instant potato flakes
1 teas. sugar
4 oz. Swiss cheese
4 C. bread flour
1 teas. salt

1 tbsp. 50% faster active dry yeast
¼ C. (½ stick) butter or margarine, melted
2 large eggs

1. Mix the hot tap water, potato flakes, and sugar in a 2-cup glass measure.

(continued)

Oregon Harvest ◇ Sandwich ◇

Makes 1 sandwich in 10 minutes

Our best grilled cheese sandwich tastes best in the fall when the pear crop is just in. We cook these in an electric sandwich grill to get that crisp melding of flavors and interesting textures: golden crust outside, smooth runny cheeses inside, sharp with spiced butter and sweet with hot pear slices for a surprise.

Cream a half stick softened butter with a whiff of ground nutmeg, ground cinnamon, ground coriander, and ground ginger. Spread bread slices with this spiced butter, then add thick slices of peeled, cored pear. Add thick slices of Gruyère and Fontina. Cover with second bread slice and press down so sandwiches will hold their shape.

Brush the bread lightly with butter and grill, either in a sandwich grill or in a skillet over medium heat. Weight tops with a pan lid and flip them once if you're cooking in a skillet. Takes about 4 minutes to the side.

2. In the processor bowl fitted with the grating disk, grate the cheese and set aside.

3. Without washing the processor bowl, fit it with the steel blade, then pulse to mix the flour, salt, and yeast.

4. With the motor running, add in order, allowing each ingredient time to mix, the melted butter, eggs, hot water–potato flakes mixture, and grated cheese. When the dough leaves the side of the bowl and forms a ball, knead for 60 seconds.

5. Remove the blade and dough from the bowl. On a lightly floured surface, knead the dough by hand a few seconds, adding flour as necessary if the dough seems sticky. Then form the dough into a ball. With your thumbs, punch a hole to form a doughnut shape and replace in the processor bowl. Cover loosely with a damp tea towel or microwavable plastic wrap and prepare to micro-rise.

6. Place an 8-ounce glass of water in the center of the microwave. Lower the microwave power to the appropriate micro-rise setting (see page 35). Place the dough beside it. Heat for 3 minutes. Rest for 3 minutes. Heat 3 minutes. Rest 6 minutes or until the dough has about doubled in bulk.

7. Remove to a lightly floured breadboard. Punch down and knead by hand a few seconds. Then cover the dough with the processor bowl and let it rest for 10 minutes.

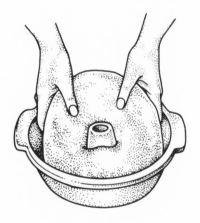

8. Grease one 8-inch microwavable tube pan. Form the dough into a ball, and with your fingers, punch a hole in the center and widen this to slip over the tube in the pan. Push the dough to the bottom of the pan. Cover the pan loosely with a damp tea towel or plastic wrap, replace in the microwave, and repeat step 6.

9. Place the bread in a cold conventional oven on the middle rack. Set the oven at 375°F, and bake until golden brown, about 50 minutes.

10. Slide the loaf from the pan onto a rack to cool before slicing. Wrap in aluminum foil to store.

SOUR RYE BREAD WITH DILLWEED

Makes 1 round loaf in 90 minutes

Try this chewy rye for a turkey sandwich; serve a big kosher dill on the side and the deli's best potato salad.

3 C. bread flour
2 tbsp. 50% faster active dry yeast
1 C. sour dill pickle brine
¾ C. hot tap water (120°F)
2 tbsp. vegetable shortening
2 tbsp. sugar
1 large egg, room temperature

2 teas. salt
1 tbsp. dried dillweed
1½ C. medium rye flour
1½ teas. caraway seeds
1 egg, lightly beaten with 1 tbsp. milk

1 tbsp. dried dillweed or 3 tbsp. fresh, for sprinkling on top

1. Combine the bread flour and yeast in the processor bowl fitted with the steel blade, and pulse to mix.

2. With the motor running, add the sour dill pickle brine and hot tap water.

3. Open the top and add the shortening, sugar, egg, salt, dried dillweed, and rye flour.

4. Close the lid and process, adding additional bread flour if needed so that the dough will form a ball that leaves the side of the processor bowl. Knead the dough 45 seconds.

5. Remove the blade and dough from the bowl. On a lightly floured surface, knead the dough by hand a few seconds, adding flour as necessary if the dough seems sticky, then form into a ball. With your thumbs, punch a hole to form a doughnut shape and replace in the processor bowl. Cover loosely with a damp tea towel or microwavable plastic wrap and prepare to micro-rise.

6. Place an 8-ounce glass of water in the back of the microwave. Lower the microwave power to the appropriate micro-rise setting (see page 35). Place the dough in the microwave. Heat for 3 minutes. Rest for 3 minutes. Heat 3 minutes. Rest 6 minutes or until the dough is about doubled in bulk. *(continued)*

To quickly warm an egg to room temperature, lower the cold egg *still in the shell* into a bowl of hot tap water and let it stand 5 minutes or so. Now feel the shell. See? Warm.

Turkey-Swiss on Rye Open-Faced ◇ Sandwiches ◇

Makes 6 sandwiches in 20 minutes

Combine equal parts chopped cooked turkey breast and shredded Swiss cheese, about a cup of each. Now add equal parts mayonnaise and plain yogurt, about ¼ cup each. Add a little chopped dill pickle, Dijon mustard, and salt and freshly ground black pepper to taste. Stir to combine, then spread on thin slices of rye. Dust with paprika. Run these sandwiches under the broiler, 4 inches away from the heat, and cook until cheese melts and sandwiches are bubbly and brown.

7. Remove the dough to a lightly floured surface, punch down, and knead by hand a few seconds. Knead in caraway seeds by hand. Cover the dough with the processor bowl and let it rest for 10 minutes. Meanwhile, lightly grease a glass baking sheet. Preheat the oven to 375°F.

8. Form the dough into a ball and place on the prepared baking sheet. With a sharp knife and quick, sure slashes, make several parallel cuts in the top. Brush with the egg-milk mixture, and sprinkle with the dillweed. Place in the microwave and repeat step 6, or raise in a warm, draft-free place.

9. Bake in the preheated oven about 50 minutes or until it sounds hollow when tapped.

10. Remove from the pan and cool on a rack. If you wish a chewier crust, brush with water once you've taken it out of the oven, while still hot. Wrap in aluminum foil to store.

SWEDISH RYE BREAD

Makes 1 loaf or 2 baguettes in under 2 hours

These dark-as-death baguettes are an absolutely perfect beginning for a sandwich of Forestier ham, Dijon mustard, and butter lettuce. The hint of orange and fennel in the loaf gives the bread a faint anise flavor that plays well against ham. And does this bread keep. Wow.

1 C. stout or dark beer (we like Guinness)
⅓ C. molasses
1 tbsp. 50% faster active dry yeast
Zest of an orange
2 C. rye flour
1 C. bread flour

½ teas. salt
2 tbsp. unsalted butter, softened
2 teas. fennel seeds

Glaze
1 tbsp. molasses plus 1 tbsp. water

1. Heat beer to lukewarm (110°F) in a 2-cup glass measure in the microwave set on high power (up to 45 seconds).

2. Add the molasses and yeast to the beer and set aside.

3. Place the zest in the processor bowl fitted with the steel blade. Add the flours and salt to the processor bowl and pulse to mix. With the motor running add the butter, then the beer

and yeast mixture to the bowl. When the dough leaves the side and forms a ball, knead with the machine running for 60 seconds.

4. Remove the dough from the bowl, then remove the blade. Knead the dough by hand a few seconds. Knead in the fennel seeds by hand and add flour as necessary if the dough seems sticky. Form the dough into a ball. With your thumbs, punch a hole to form a doughnut shape and replace in the processor bowl. Cover loosely with a damp tea towel or plastic wrap and prepare to micro-rise.

5. Place an 8-ounce glass of water in the back of the microwave. Lower the microwave power to the appropriate micro-rise setting (see page 35). Place the dough in the microwave. Heat for 3 minutes. Let rest for 3 minutes. Heat 3 minutes. Rest for 6 minutes or until doubled in bulk.

6. Remove the dough to a lightly floured surface, punch down, and knead by hand a few seconds. Cover the dough with the processor bowl, and let it rest for 10 minutes. Meanwhile, butter a 13 × 9-inch oblong glass baking dish.

7. Shape the dough into a long thin loaf, or 2 thin baguettes (see page 42), and place in a glass baking dish. Place in the microwave and repeat step 5, or raise in a warm, draft-free place until doubled in bulk. Meanwhile, preheat the oven to 300°F.

8. Prick the loaf all over with a toothpick and bake in the preheated oven 30 to 40 minutes. After 15 minutes, brush with water to which a little molasses has been added.

9. Turn out on a rack to cool. While the loaf is still hot, brush it again with molasses glaze. Wrap in foil to keep the crust soft.

You can make colorful, brightly flavored cocktail sandwiches open-faced and easy by buttering thin slices of rye baguette, then sprinkling with dillweed and topping with paper-thin slices of radish, cucumber, and cold, boiled, shelled cocktail shrimp.

Here's a sandwich that proves East can meet West. California tops New York. At least in a sandwich. And chased by Russian vodka.

One World
◇ Sandwich ◇

Onto thick slices of corn rye bread, add a smooth layer of soft cream cheese, dot with red salmon caviar, nasturtium blossoms, and snipped chives. Serve cold with icy shot glasses of vodka.

NUEVO YORK CORN RYE

Makes 1 large loaf in under 2 hours

The traditional New York corn rye is a dense, small loaf that's sold by the pound, in pieces, in kosher dairy delis. Originally it was "corned" rye, cousin to "corned" beef, in that the dough was made from a sour-dough rye. We rarely take the time for souring now, but we still love the many permutations of rye bread. The original corned rye along with our own nuevo version are a part of a tradition that goes back to early times in Eastern Europe, where rye grew more readily than wheat in the cold climate.

For Germans, Poles, Scandinavians, Jews, Russians, and others, dark, dense rye-based breads were—in fact—the staff of life. The more costly white flour and eggs were saved for challah and special dinners.

We can thank the Eastern Europeans for bringing to the United States the tradition of rich, dark, chewy breads. This Nuevo York Corn Rye makes a glorious round loaf to use with a pastrami sandwich or alongside corned beef and cabbage. Don't forget the kosher pickles or the cole slaw.

2 C. bread flour	Glaze
1 C. medium rye flour	1 egg white, beaten
2 tbsp. yellow cornmeal	with 1 teas. tepid water
1 tbsp. 50% faster active dry yeast	1 tbsp. cornmeal for sprinkling on top
1 teas. salt	
1½ tbsp. sugar	
1 C. hot tap water	
¼ C. milk	
1 tbsp. salad oil	
1½ teas. caraway seeds	

1. Combine flours, 2 tablespoons cornmeal, yeast, salt, and sugar in the processor bowl fitted with the steel blade and pulse to mix.

2. Combine in a 2-cup glass measure the water, milk, and oil. Heat to lukewarm in the microwave set on high power (30 seconds).

3. With the motor running, pour liquids into the flour mixture, holding back the last portion to see if the dough will form a ball. When the dough leaves the sides of the bowl and forms a ball, knead for 60 seconds. Add the last bit of liquid only if needed.

4. Remove the dough and blade from the bowl to a lightly floured surface. Knead the dough by hand a few seconds, kneading in the caraway seeds by hand and adding bread flour as necessary if the dough seems sticky. Then form into a ball. With your thumbs, punch a hole to form a doughnut shape and replace in the processor bowl. Cover loosely with a damp tea towel or microwavable plastic wrap and prepare to micro-rise.

5. Place an 8-ounce glass of water in the back of the microwave. Lower the microwave power to the appropriate micro-rise setting (see page 35). Place the dough in the microwave. Heat for 3 minutes. Rest for 3 minutes. Heat 3 minutes. Rest 6 minutes or until the dough has about doubled in bulk.

6. Remove the dough to a lightly floured surface, punch down, and knead by hand a few seconds. Then cover the dough with the processor bowl and allow it to rest for 10 minutes.

7. Meanwhile, dust a glass 8-inch plate with yellow cornmeal. Preheat the oven to 350°F.

8. Form the dough into a round loaf and place in the pie plate. Brush generously on all sides with egg-white mixture, then sprinkle with cornmeal.

9. Place in the microwave and repeat step 5, or raise in a warm, draft-free place until doubled in bulk.

10. Bake in the preheated oven about 45 to 50 minutes or until the loaf is golden brown and it sounds hollow when tapped.

11. Remove to a rack to cool. Wrap in foil to store.

DAMPFNUDELN

Old-Fashioned Newfangled Raised Dumplings

Makes 1 dozen dumplings in 1 hour and 30 minutes

It's possible you've never met a dumpling that you could like. The ones that stick in our memory stuck to the roof of the mouth and the teeth, mostly. But adapting this German yeast version of a raised dumpling cooked in chicken stock has revised our attitudes toward breads cooked in stock. Now we can't wait to serve them to company.

Naturally, the first thing you must do is poach a chicken. While the bird is cooking, you can begin to make these succulent bites, then simmer them in the stock that remains after the bird is cooked. What's surprising about this bread is that it is light and fluffy, not soggy but rather shiny on top, raised and dry as any roll in the middle, and the bottom tastes like you just mopped it in the best-tasting soup. The next day, serve leftover dumplings like any other bread, slathered with butter and with chicken salad.

½ C. milk	½ tbsp. 50% faster active dry yeast
1 large egg	
1 tbsp. unsalted butter	2 tbsp. chopped fresh parsley or ½ tbsp. dried
1½ tbsp. sugar	
½ teas. salt	
1¾ C. bread flour	

1. In a 2-cup glass measure heat the milk to lukewarm in the microwave (about 45 seconds on high power), then whisk together with the egg, butter, and sugar.

2. In the processor bowl fitted with the steel blade, pulse to mix the salt, flour, yeast, and parsley.

3. With the processor motor running, pour the liquids through the feed tube, holding back the last portion to see if the dough will form a ball. When the dough leaves the sides of the bowl and forms a ball, knead for 60 seconds with the machine running.

4. Remove the dough and blade from the bowl. On a lightly floured board, knead the dough by hand a few seconds, adding flour as needed if the dough seems sticky. Then form into

a ball. With your thumbs, punch a hole to form a doughnut shape and replace in the processor bowl. Cover the bowl loosely with a damp tea towel or microwavable plastic wrap and prepare to micro-rise.

5. Place an 8-ounce glass of water in the back of the microwave and place the processor bowl beside it. Lower the microwave power to the appropriate micro-rise setting (see page 35). Heat for 3 minutes. Rest for 3 minutes. Heat 3 minutes. Rest for 6 minutes or until the dough has doubled in bulk.

6. Remove the dough from the processor bowl, punch down, and knead by hand a few seconds. Pat out ½ inch thick on a lightly floured board and, using a biscuit cutter, cut into a dozen pieces.

7. Lightly grease a glass pie plate and arrange the dumplings, leaving space around each one. Cover loosely, then place in the microwave and repeat step 5, or raise in a warm, draft-free place until doubled in bulk.

8. While the dumplings are rising, lift the cooked chicken from the stock and adjust seasonings of the stock by adding salt or pepper as needed. Lower the temperature of the stock until it is just barely simmering. Make sure that it doesn't come up higher than the halfway mark in a 10-inch-wide soup pot, so there's plenty of room for the dumplings.

9. Carefully slip the dumplings into the simmering stock. To get light, fluffy dumplings, it's important not to peek at these while they are cooking but to keep the temperature at just below boiling. Too much heat will toughen them. Use a glass cover, or simply use a glass pie plate for a cover, so that you can monitor the temperature and adjust as necessary to maintain a simmer. Cook about 25 minutes or until done. The dumplings will puff up even farther in the hot liquid. To test for doneness, remove one from the stock. Break it open with a fork. Inside it should look about like any other roll just cooked. Although steamy, it should not be doughy. The top will be shiny and dry and the bottom will be soaked with delicious stock.

10. Remove the dumplings from the stock and drain. To serve, ladle some stock into a soup bowl, add some chicken pieces, then float a couple of dumplings on top. Dumplings are also delicious served with chicken fricassee or even slathered with butter and eaten out of hand like any other roll. Store covered in the refrigerator.

Mom's Poached Chicken and ◇ Dumplings ◇

Serves 8 in 4 hours

Let the winter wind howl. Let the snow pile up. Let your troubles drift away. Here's comfort. Primal comfort.

1 chicken (3–4 pounds)
1 large onion, peeled and quartered
1 large carrot, scraped and cut into large pieces
1 rib celery with leaves, broken into pieces
1 leek, rinsed well and cut into 1-inch pieces
Salt and freshly ground black pepper to taste
1 recipe Old-Fashioned Newfangled Raised Dumplings

1. **Pull the visible fat away from the chicken and rinse thoroughly. In a large, 10-inch-wide soup pot combine chicken with onion, carrot, celery, and leek, season to taste with salt and pepper, then cover with cold water. Raise to a boil, then turn the heat down to simmer and poach the chicken until tender, a little under 2 hours. Turn the chicken a time or two.**

2. **Lift the chicken and vegetables from the stock using a slotted spoon. Discard vegetables. Debone and skin the chicken. Discard skin and bones. Tear remaining chicken meat into bite-sized pieces and set aside.**

3. **Heat the stock to a bare simmer, adjust seasonings, and cook dumplings in the stock. Serve in soup bowls with stock, chicken, and dumplings.**

Helen Corbitt's Canadian Cheese ◇ Soup ◇

Makes 2 quarts in 30 minutes

Helen Corbitt made this soup famous in Texas forty years ago. Combined with our Garden Batter Bread it makes a hearty winter dinner.

- ½ C. each finely diced yellow onion, carrots, and celery
- ¼ C. (½ stick) unsalted butter
- ¼ C. flour
- 1 quart rich chicken stock
- 1 quart milk
- ⅛ teas. baking soda
- 1 C. grated sharp cheddar
- 2 tbsp. finely minced fresh parsley

Salt and freshly ground black pepper to taste

1. In a soup pot, over medium heat sauté the vegetables in butter until clear. Sprinkle with flour and cook to a golden roux. Add stock and simmer for 15 minutes, stirring to make a smooth sauce. Add milk and raise to a boil.

2. Remove from heat and stir in soda, cheddar, and parsley. Season to taste with salt and pepper. Serve hot. *Don't* boil this soup after you've added the cheese. It curdles.

GARDEN BATTER BREAD

Makes 1 round loaf in under 1 hour and 30 minutes

Batter breads are appealing because they're quick, usually require only one rise, and keep well. Speckle the batter with sautéed vegetables and you'll have a round loaf that mellows and tastes better the third day than it did the first.

Feel free to vary the vegetables depending on the contents of your larder and your own personal taste. Prepare to enjoy the pleasure of a kitchen redolent with the aromas of onion, other vegetables, and yeast. Ummmm.

½ medium onion	2 teas. salt
1 medium carrot	¼ C. light molasses
1 rib celery with leaves	2 tbsp. olive oil
¼ C. mushrooms	1 large egg
2 tbsp. unsalted butter	1¼ C. warm water
3 C. bread flour	¼ C. fresh parsley, cut fine with scissors
2½ teas. 50% faster active dry yeast	¼ C. rolled oats

1. Fit the processor with the steel blade and finely chop the vegetables one at a time—onion, carrot, celery, and mushrooms—measuring after chopping, until you have a total of 1 cup finely chopped fresh vegetables.

2. Place the butter in a 2-cup microwavable dish, then heat on high power in the microwave for 30 seconds. Add the vegetables, stir to coat, then replace, uncovered, in the microwave and sauté 3 minutes on high. Remove from the microwave and set aside.

3. Fit the processor bowl with the steel blade and add flour, yeast, and salt. Pulse to mix.

4. In a 2-cup glass measure combine molasses, olive oil, egg, and warm water. Stir to mix. With the processor motor running, gradually pour in liquids. Mix for 60 seconds. Note that the batter is heavy but never really forms a ball.

5. Stir parsley and rolled oats into the reserved vegetables, then add this mixture to the processor bowl. Pulse to mix.

6. Generously grease a 2-quart round glass casserole dish, then turn vegetable batter into it, smoothing the top. Cover

loosely with a damp tea towel or plastic wrap. Prepare to micro-rise.

7. Place an 8-ounce glass of water in the back of the microwave. Lower the microwave power to the appropriate micro-rise setting (see page 35). Place the dough in the microwave. Heat for 3 minutes. Let rest for 3 minutes. Heat 3 minutes. Rest for 6 minutes or until the batter has risen to about double in bulk. Meanwhile, preheat the oven to 350°F.

8. When the batter has risen, place in the preheated oven and bake 40 to 50 minutes, until the top is a dappled golden brown. Remove baked bread from the dish immediately to a rack to cool. Store in plastic wrap. Makes wonderful toast to go with soup.

ONE-RISE SAUERKRAUT RYE

Makes one loaf in 1 hour and 30 minutes

Although this loaf only rises once, it takes a while—up to a half hour—because the dough is laden with sauerkraut. The resulting loaf is moist with a big hole crumb and a remarkable sour, tart taste that makes it a natural for a Reuben sandwich. Because of the addition of sauerkraut, the bread is a good keeper.

1½ C. bread flour
  1 C. medium rye flour
2½ teas. 50% faster
    active dry yeast
 ¼ C. nonfat dry milk
    solids
  1 tbsp. sugar
  1 teas. salt
 ⅛ teas. ground ginger
  1 tbsp. canola oil
 ½ C. chopped
    sauerkraut with juice
    plus up to 2 tbsp.
    additional juice

 ½ C. hot tap water
1½ teas. caraway or
    fennel seeds

Glaze
  1 teas. molasses plus 1
    teas. water
Caraway or fennel seeds
    for sprinkling on top

(continued)

Real Reuben
◇ Sandwiches ◇

Butter thin slices of rye, then top with thinly sliced corned beef, sauerkraut, and slices of Swiss cheese. Spread generously with Russian dressing, top with second slice of bread, and grill in a skillet or in a sandwich grill until bread is golden and Swiss cheese is runny and hot.

Russian Dressing
◇ for Sandwiches ◇

To mayonnaise, add a dollop of horseradish, a dash of catsup, some grated onion, and a little caviar if you've got it. Season to taste with salt and freshly ground black pepper.

A tip about adding whole seeds to any recipe being mixed in the food processor: If you add the seeds at the beginning, the seeds will be ground by the metal blade and blend completely into the mixture, giving the most pungent taste. If you'd rather get tiny explosions of taste, add the seeds by hand at the end of the mixing process so that they remain whole during the baking period. If your food processor has a dough hook, use it. The seeds will remain whole and you will have saved yourself a step.

1. Fit the processor bowl with the steel blade and add flours, yeast, dry milk, sugar, salt, and ground ginger. Pulse to mix.

2. Combine in a glass measure the oil, sauerkraut, and water, then heat in the microwave (about 45 seconds set on high power) until about 120°F to 130°F. Open the top of the processor bowl, and add the sauerkraut and liquids to the flours all at once.

3. Process until the dough begins to leave the side of the bowl. Knead 60 seconds, adding extra sauerkraut juice only if the dough seems too stiff.

4. Remove the dough and the steel blade and prepare to micro-rise. Dust your hands with flour to prevent sticky fingers. Add the seeds to the dough, knead the dough by hand a few seconds, then form into a loaf shape (see page 40). The dough will be sticky and heavy. Lightly grease and coat the inside of an 8½ × 4½ × 2½-inch glass loaf pan with cornmeal. Place the loaf in the pan and cover loosely with a damp tea towel or plastic wrap.

5. Place an 8-ounce glass of water in the back of the microwave. Lower the microwave power to the appropriate micro-rise setting (see page 35). Heat for 3 minutes. Let rest for 3 minutes. Heat 3 minutes. Rest until the dough has risen to about double in bulk, which may exceed 30 minutes. Meanwhile, preheat the oven to 375°F.

6. When the dough has nearly doubled in bulk, brush lightly with the glaze made from molasses and water, taking care not to allow any to run down the sides of the pan (it sticks). Make 4 slashes in the top of the loaf in a herringbone pattern, about an inch deep. Sprinkle with seeds.

7. Bake in the preheated oven 35 to 40 minutes or until evenly browned. Remove immediately to a rack to cool. Wrap in plastic to store. This bread keeps up to a week, properly stored.

8 ◆ FESTIVE SWEET, HOLIDAY, DESSERT, AND HIGH-TEA BREADS

Babas au Rhum 209

Sugar-Crusted Galette 210

Chocolate-Cherry Kugelhupf 212

Amber Waves of Grain 214

Saffron Challah 216

Orange Danish from the Danes 218

Hazelnut Coffee Ring 220

Panettone 222

Pecan Praline Sugar Loaf 224

Kolacky 226

Orange Grove Bread 230

Portuguese Sweet Bread 231

Brioche Bread Pudding with Bourbon Sauce 233

Bing Hasty Pudding with Raspberry Sauce 234

Erica's Favorite Butterscotch Bread Pudding 235

Sweet breads, holiday breads, breads for dessert and high teas: these are the specialty breads we love to make when we want to turn an occasion into an event. However, truth be told, holidays and special times for us always mean a shortage of time.

Never is the Micro-Rise method more appreciated than at such times. Whether you're making Babas au Rhum (see page 209), Panettone (see page 222), or Portuguese Sweet Bread (see page 231), we know you'll find it's easier and more fun to employ the Micro-Rise technique.

It will make your special occasions memorable not only for the quality of the bread you turn out, but also for the time you save.

One thing we like to do at such events is make the holiday bread the centerpiece. Amber Waves of Grain (see page 214), in particular, made to look like a gorgeous sheaf of wheat, can be tied with raffia and used for a centerpiece on the sideboard before you break it into crunchy, delicious servings.

You'll also find here some fabulous bread puddings that are made with breads from other chapters. Erica's Favorite Butterscotch Bread Pudding (see page 235) has become our favorite too. Sometimes we make it using Gloria's Whole-Meal Bread (page 81). Other times, we just use day-old store-brought bread. Either way, it makes a fine finish to a festive dinner. In fact, make Erica's bread pudding and the dinner *is* festive.

BABAS AU RHUM

Makes 2 dozen babas in 2 hours plus soaking time 2 hours to overnight

Rum-drenched sweet buns make a fine choice for a teatime treat.

3½ C. bread flour
¼ teas. salt
¼ C. sugar
5 teas. 50% faster active dry yeast
½ C. (1 stick) unsalted butter or margarine
½ C. hot tap water
4 eggs
1 C. currants (optional)

Rum Sauce
2 C. water
1 C. sugar

6 thin orange slices with rind
6 thin lemon slices with rind
1½ C. light Jamaican rum

Topping
⅓ C. apricot jam
1 tbsp. lemon juice
24 glacé cherries (optional)

1. In the processor bowl fitted with the steel blade, add the flour, salt, sugar, and yeast. Pulse to mix. Now cut butter or margarine in finely, and pulse to blend so that it almost disappears.

2. Combine in a glass measure the hot tap water and eggs. Whisk together with a fork, then with the motor running, *drizzle the liquids very slowly* into the dry ingredients.

3. Process 60 seconds. You will have a thick batter, not a dough (what French bakers call "paste"). Add the currants, if using, and pulse to mix. The paste should have the texture of taffy.

4. Remove the steel blade, cover the bowl loosely with a damp tea towel or plastic wrap, and prepare to micro-rise.

5. Lower the microwave power to the appropriate micro-rise setting (see page 35) and place an 8-ounce glass of water in the back of the microwave. Place the dough in the microwave, and heat for 3 minutes, rest for 3 minutes, heat for 3 minutes, then rest for 6 minutes or until the dough is about doubled in bulk.

(continued)

If you're making babas in the summer, you can create a luscious teatime centerpiece by arranging babas in a flat white serving dish, then surrounding them with a quart of just-picked raspberries, blueberries, blackberries, or strawberries. Pour baba syrup over the berries and allow this to stand a few moments so the syrup will soak into the berries. Whip some cream and flavor it with a spot of rum and a spoonful of confectioners' sugar to taste. Serve the cream in a bowl alongside the babas and berries and let people help themselves, spooning rum-drenched babas, berries, and whipped cream into clear fruit bowls. The last time we served this we were practically dazed, it was so delicious.

6. Remove from the microwave and turn out on a lightly floured surface. Punch down and knead by hand a moment. Divide into 24 equal pieces and cover with a damp tea towel or plastic wrap. Leave them to rest 5 minutes or so.

7. Generously butter twenty-four 2-inch-deep, 2-inch-diameter baba molds, or 3-inch muffin cups, or popover pans. If you wish to micro-rise, use microwavable muffin cups. Place a heaping tablespoon of batter into each prepared cup. Cover loosely with a damp tea towel or plastic wrap. Raise until the center of the dough is slightly above the tops of the molds, either micro-rising, repeating step 5, or in a warm, draft-free place. *Don't* allow these to overrise, or they may collapse. Meanwhile, preheat the oven to 375°F.

8. Bake in the preheated oven 15 to 20 minutes or until golden brown. Remove immediately to a rack to cool slightly before soaking in rum sauce.

9. While babas are baking, combine the sauce ingredients *except* rum in a 2-quart microwavable bowl and cook 5 minutes in the microwave set on high. Set aside to cool. Discard orange and lemon slices. Stir in rum.

10. Arrange babas in a shallow baking dish and spoon warm sauce over them. Cover, and let the babas stand at least 2 hours, turning several times to absorb the sauce.

11. To serve, combine the apricot jam and lemon juice. Brush atop each baba, then top each one with a glacéed cherry, if desired, and serve in a frilly paper cup with a freshly made pot of tea.

SUGAR-CRUSTED GALETTE

Makes one 16-inch flat cake in under 1 hour and 30 minutes

A French flatbread, buttery and crunchy, topped with granulated sugar, this simple-to-make dessert or high-tea bread originated in Pérouges, a medieval city near Lyon.

1¾ C. bread flour
2½ teas. 50% faster active dry yeast
½ C. (8 tbsp.) sugar
⅛ teas. salt

¾ C. (1½ sticks) unsalted butter or margarine
¼ C. hot tap water
1 large egg
Zest of half a lemon

1. In the processor bowl fitted with the steel blade, add flour, yeast, 3 tablespoons of the sugar, and salt. Pulse to mix. Now cut ½ cup of the butter in finely, and pulse to blend so that it almost disappears.

2. Combine the hot tap water and egg in a glass measure. Whisk together with a fork, then with the motor running, *drizzle the liquid very slowly* into the dry ingredients, holding back the last portion of liquid to see if the dough will form a ball.

3. Process until the dough begins to leave the side of the bowl, forming a ball. Add the last liquid only if necessary. Knead 60 seconds, adding flour as necessary if the dough seems sticky. Pinch up a piece of the dough. It should feel soft, tacky, smooth, elastic, and warm. Add the lemon zest and pulse to mix.

4. Remove the dough and the steel blade and prepare to micro-rise. On a lightly floured surface, knead the dough by hand a few seconds, then form dough into a ball. With your thumbs, punch a hole to form a doughnut shape and replace in the processor bowl. Cover loosely with a damp tea towel or plastic wrap. Place the dough in the microwave.

5. Place an 8-ounce glass of water in the back of the microwave. Lower the microwave power to the appropriate micro-rise setting (see page 35). Place the dough in the microwave. Heat for 3 minutes. Rest for 3 minutes. Heat for 3 minutes. Rest for 6 minutes or until the dough has risen to about double in bulk.

6. Remove the dough to a lightly floured surface and knead by hand a few seconds. Roll out into a circle about 12 inches in diameter, cover with a damp tea towel or plastic wrap, and let it rest for 10 minutes.

7. Grease generously a 16-inch pizza pan. Preheat the over to 425°F. Place the dough in the pizza pan, and pat and stretch the dough to fill the pan. Pinch up the edge to make a slight lip. Dot the top of the galette with the reserved ¼ cup butter, first by cutting butter into 24 pieces, then distributing it evenly over the surface. Sprinkle the top of the galette with the reserved 5 tablespoons of sugar.

8. Bake in the preheated oven 12 to 15 minutes or until evenly browned. Cut into wedges while warm. Wrap in plastic to store. This bread is best eaten the day it's baked.

Create your own high tea by serving cucumber sandwiches made from your favorite bread cut into thin slices, crusts removed, spread with sweet butter and cream cheese, layered with fresh thin slices of cucumber, topped with another slice of crustless bread, then cut into bite-sized triangles. Snip some chives over all and serve alongside the warm galette and a pot of tea.

Chocolate
◇ Butter ◇

Makes ¾ cup in 5 minutes

½ C. (1 stick) unsalted
butter, room temperature
½ teas. vanilla extract
⅓ C. confectioners' sugar
2 tbsp. unsweetened cocoa
powder, preferably Dutch
process

In the processor bowl fitted with the
steel blade, process the butter and
vanilla extract until creamy. Add
the sugar and cocoa to the butter-
vanilla mixture and process until
smooth, about 1 minute. Serve at
room temperature. To store, cover
and refrigerate.

CHOCOLATE-CHERRY
KUGELHUPF

*Makes 1 large loaf in 2 hours and 30 minutes, serving
8 to 10*

It is almost impossible to resist this wonderful yeast bread.
A light chocolate-cherry-nut mixture fills the rich buttery
bread. Serve the bread warm as a dessert for brunch or teatime, smothered with Chocolate Butter.

If you have a microwavable tube pan, micro-rise the
kugelhupf both times. If you use a metal tube pan, simply
raise the dough the second time in a warm, draft-free place.

¾ C. warm milk
(110°F)
1 teas. sugar
3½ teas. 50% faster
active dry yeast
4¾ C. bread flour,
divided
½ C. light brown sugar,
packed
2 large eggs
2 large egg yolks
½ C. (1 stick) unsalted
butter, room
temperature
2 teas. vanilla extract

1½ teas. salt
2 teas. finely grated
orange zest
8 oz. semisweet
chocolate, finely
chopped
¾ C. dried tart cherries
or dried cranberries
1¼ C. coarsely chopped
pecans
½ teas. ground
cinnamon
2 tbsp. confectioners'
sugar, for sprinkling
on top

1. In the food processor bowl fitted with the steel blade,
combine the warm milk, sugar, yeast, and 1 cup of the bread
flour. Process for 10 seconds to blend. Remove the steel
blade from the processor bowl and place the bowl in the
microwave.

2. Set an 8-ounce glass of water in the microwave. Lower
the microwave power to the appropriate micro-rise setting
(see page 35) and heat the sponge for 3 minutes. Rest for 6
minutes. Remove the processor bowl from the microwave.

3. Place the processor bowl back on the base and fit again
with the steel blade. Add the remaining 3¾ cups bread flour,
brown sugar, eggs and egg yolks, unsalted butter, vanilla
extract, salt, and grated orange zest. Process for 30 to 45

seconds or until the dough begins to form a ball. The dough will be soft and slightly sticky.

4. Turn the dough out onto a lightly floured surface and form the dough into a ball. With your thumbs, punch a hole to form a doughnut shape. Remove the steel blade from the processor bowl and place the dough back in the processor bowl. Cover loosely with microwavable plastic wrap or a damp tea towel. Place the processor bowl in the middle of the microwave.

5. Repeat step 2, except heat for 3 minutes, then rest for 3 minutes. Heat for 3 minutes. Rest the dough for 30 minutes or until doubled in bulk. Meanwhile, in a medium bowl combine the chocolate, cherries or cranberries, pecans, and cinnamon; set aside. Lightly grease a tube or bundt pan, microwavable preferred.

6. Remove the dough from the microwave to a lightly floured surface and punch down. Roll the dough into a 12-inch circle. Sprinkle the dough with half of the chocolate-cherry mixture and press the mixture into the dough with the palm of your hand. Fold the outside edge of the circle to the middle of the circle, forming another 6- to 8-inch circle. Pinch the seams together in the middle and turn the circle over. With a heavy rolling pin, roll the dough into a 12-inch circle again. Sprinkle with the remaining chocolate-cherry mixture and repeat the folding process. Poke a hole in the middle of the circle with your thumbs and place the dough into the prepared tube or bundt pan. Cover loosely with a damp tea towel or microwavable plastic wrap and prepare to raise again.

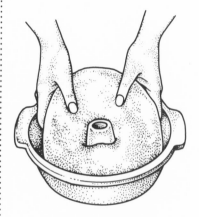

7. Micro-rise, repeating step 5, or allow to raise in a warm, draft-free place until doubled in bulk. It will raise several inches above the top of the pan. Meanwhile, preheat the oven to 375°F.

8. When the dough has doubled in bulk, bake on the middle shelf of the preheated oven for 50 minutes or until the top is dark brown.

9. Carefully loosen the sides of the kugelhupf from the mold with a sharp knife and turn out onto a rack to cool completely. Sprinkle lightly with the confectioners' sugar and wrap in aluminum foil to store. Serve warm with Chocolate Butter.

AMBER WAVES OF GRAIN

A Thanksgiving Festive Bread

Makes 1 loaf in 1 hour and 30 minutes

When the holidays roll around, we love to participate in all of the festivities and have found that the microwave makes this easier by cutting back the time required for certain dishes. Bread is no exception, and this one is a real showstopper. Use this bread as a centerpiece, or pass around in the breadbasket for everyone to see, and then serve.

1½ *C. whole wheat flour*
2½ *C. bread flour*
¼ *C. bran flakes*
1 *large shredded-wheat biscuit or ½ C. small biscuits*
1½ *teas. salt*
1 *tbsp. molasses*
2 *tbsp. honey*
3 *tbsp. unsalted butter, cut into tablespoon-sized pieces*

1 *tbsp. plus 1 teas. 50% faster active dry yeast*
1½ *C. warm tap water*

Glaze
1 *egg white lightly beaten with 1 teas. water*
1 *tbsp. sunflower seeds, for sprinkling on top (optional)*

1. Fit the processor bowl with the steel blade. Combine and pulse to mix the flours, bran flakes, shredded-wheat biscuit(s), salt, molasses, honey, butter, and yeast.

2. With the motor running, *very slowly drizzle* the warm water through the feed tube, holding back the last small portion of water to see if the dough will form a ball. If it does not, continue to slowly drizzle the remaining water until it does. When the dough leaves the side of the bowl and forms a ball, turn the machine off.

3. Remove the dough from the bowl, return half of it to the processor bowl, and knead with the machine running for 60 seconds. Remove the kneaded portion and add the unkneaded portion. Knead for 60 seconds.

4. On a lightly floured surface, knead the 2 halves together by hand, form into a doughnut shape, and place back

in the processor bowl. Cover the bowl loosely with a damp tea towel or microwavable plastic wrap. Place the processor bowl in the middle of the microwave.

5. Set an 8-ounce glass of water in the microwave. To micro-rise, set the microwave power at the appropriate micro-rise setting (see page 35). Heat for 3 minutes. Rest for 3 minutes. Heat for 3 minutes. Rest for 30 minutes or until doubled in bulk. Meanwhile, lightly grease a baking sheet (glass if you plan to micro-rise).

6. Remove the dough from the microwave and the processor bowl. Punch down and knead by hand a few seconds on a lightly floured surface. Divide the dough into 16 equal pieces, and roll 7 pieces into ropes about 16 inches long, 8 pieces into ropes 12 to 14 inches long, and 1 piece into a rope 10 inches long that you twist lightly. Place the 16-inch ropes close together on the baking sheet and lay the 12- to 14-inch pieces on the top and sides, bending the tops at varying angles to form a "wheat sheaf" shape as illustrated. Lay the twisted rope across the middle, tucking the ends under on the sides.

7. Place the dough in a warm, draft-free place to raise until double (about 40 minutes), or to micro-rise, repeat step 5 except remove the dough from the microwave after the first 9 minutes; do not let it raise for the last 30 minutes. Meanwhile, preheat the oven to 350°F.

8. Clip the tops of the wheat stalks with scissors to resemble wheat grains and brush lightly with the egg glaze. Lightly sprinkle the wheat "tops" with sunflower seeds for extra flavor if desired.

9. Bake the bread on the middle rack of the preheated oven for 25 minutes or until the bread is lightly browned. Remove the bread from the baking sheet to a rack and serve warm.

The rich, bitter taste of Saffron Challah is offset beautifully by smoked turkey, fresh parsley, and Swiss. Simply butter a piece of the challah, then top with a thin slice of smoked turkey breast, chopped parsley, and grated Swiss. Run the whole thing under the broiler until just bubbly, no more than 3 minutes.

SAFFRON CHALLAH

Makes 1 braided loaf in under 2 hours

Adding saffron to a classic challah intensifies the rich gold color and adds a pleasant bitter bite to the smooth egg bread. This bread's dazzling to look at. A natural centerpiece.

1 teas. sugar
¼ C. hot tap water
1 tbsp. 50% faster active dry yeast
⅛ teas. saffron threads
⅓ C. water
2½ C. bread flour
½ teas. salt
1 large egg
2 tbsp. unsalted butter or margarine, softened

Glaze
1 egg yolk plus 2 tbsp. water
Sesame or poppy seeds, for sprinkling on top

1. Combine in a glass bowl the sugar, ¼ cup water, and yeast.

2. Combine in another glass bowl and heat to boiling in the microwave at full power (under a minute) the saffron threads and ⅓ cup water.

3. In the processor bowl fitted with the steel blade, pulse to mix the flour and salt.

4. With the processor motor running, add egg, butter, yeast then saffron liquids, holding back the last portion of the saffron liquid to see if the dough will form a ball.

5. When the dough leaves the side of the bowl and forms a ball, knead for 60 seconds. Use the last of the liquid only if necessary. Pinch up a piece of the dough. It should feel smooth, elastic, supple, and warm.

6. Remove the dough and blade from the bowl. Knead the dough by hand a few seconds, adding flour as necessary if dough seems sticky, then form into a ball. With your thumbs, punch a hole to form a doughnut shape and replace in the processor bowl. Cover loosely with a damp tea towel or microwavable plastic wrap and prepare to micro-rise.

7. Place an 8-ounce glass of water in the back of the microwave. Lower the microwave power to the appropriate micro-rise setting (see page 35). Place the dough in the microwave. Heat for 3 minutes. Rest for 3 minutes. Heat 3 minutes. Rest 6 minutes or until the dough is about doubled in bulk.

8. Remove the dough from the processor bowl, punch down, and knead by hand a few seconds. Cover the dough with the processor bowl and allow it to rest for 10 minutes.

9. Oil a glass baking sheet. Preheat the oven to 350°F.

10. Form the dough into a braid by dividing into 3 equal pieces, then rolling each into a long strip about 1 inch in diameter. Lay the strips out beside one another, then begin braiding from the middle to the end, forming a fat braid, pinching top and bottom ends under neatly. Place on the prepared baking sheet.

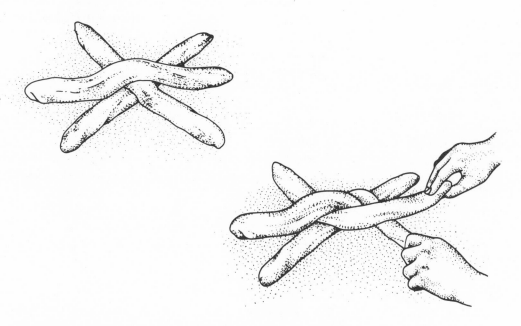

11. Place in the microwave and repeat step 7, or place in a warm, draft-free place to rise until nearly doubled in bulk.

12. Just before baking, brush the top with the glaze mixture. Sprinkle generously with sesame or poppy seeds and bake in the preheated oven about 40 to 50 minutes or until a luscious golden color.

13. Remove to a rack to cool. Store in plastic wrap.

Christmas Swiss ◇ Cheese Fondue ◇

Serves 6 in 20 minutes

For a holiday sideboard, offer a savory counterpart to sweet Danish with this colorful vegetable-cheese dish. You'll need to dredge up great bread crumbs from leftovers: rye bread, potato, Grandmother's white. Your choice. A mixture looks best and offers wonderful taste surprises.

- ¾ *pound small whole new potatoes, scrubbed*
- 1 *C. broccoli flowerets*
- 2 *C. shredded Swiss cheese*
- 2 *tbsp. unbleached white flour*
- ¼ *teas. dry mustard*
- ¼ *teas. caraway seeds*

Garlic salt to taste
- ½ *C. dry vermouth*
- ¼ *teas. Worcestershire sauce*
- 2 *C. hot buttered bread cubes of your choice: rye, potato, white, or a mixture of dark and white breads*
- 1 *large red bell pepper, cut into julienne strips*

1. Cut potatoes into bite-sized pieces, then place in a 1½-quart microwavable casserole dish. Add a tablespoon of water, cover, and cook on high power in the microwave until almost tender, about 5 minutes. Add the broccoli flowerets, and bell pepper strips, cover, and cook another minute. Drain, and set aside.

2. In a 1-quart microwavable dish, combine cheese, flour, mustard, caraway seeds, and garlic salt to taste. Stir in vermouth and Worcestershire sauce. Cook, uncovered, on high for 3 to 4 minutes or until the mixture is heated through. Stir every minute.

ORANGE DANISH FROM THE DANES

Makes 20 rolls in 2 hours

We were a little bit skeptical when we were given this recipe by a Danish family in Midlothian, Texas. How could a country that far north know anything about citrus? We forgot that even though they couldn't grow citrus, they had those long cold winters to bake all those wonderful Danish pastries and breads. And who knows? Maybe the citrus was added after they moved to Texas where local south Texas orange groves provide citrus products that are a part of every Texas child's Christmas celebration.

- 3½ *C. bread flour*
- ¼ *C. sugar*
- 1 *teas. salt*
- 3 *teas. 50% faster active dry yeast*
- ¼ *C. (½ stick) unsalted butter or margarine*
- ½ *C. milk*
- ½ *C. water*
- 1 *large egg, room temperature*

Pecan Filling
- 2 *C. pecans*
- ½ *C. firmly packed light brown sugar*

- ¼ *C. (½ stick) unsalted butter or margarine*
- 1 *large egg*
- 2 *tbsp. milk*
- 1 *teas. orange extract*

Marmalade Glaze
- 2 *C. sifted confectioners' sugar*
- 1 *tbsp. unsalted butter or margarine*
- ½ *C. orange marmalade*
- 1½ *teas. orange extract*

1. Fit the processor bowl with the steel blade. Combine and pulse to mix the flour, sugar, salt, yeast, and butter or margarine.

2. Measure the milk and water into a 2-cup microwavable measure and heat on high power in the microwave for 1 minute or until it is the temperature of hot tap water, about 120°F.

3. Using a fork, whisk the egg into the milk-and-water mixture. With the processor motor running, pour the liquids through the feed tube, holding back the last portion to see if

the dough will form a ball. When the dough leaves the side of the bowl and forms a ball, knead with the machine running for 60 seconds.

4. Remove the dough from the bowl. Knead the dough by hand a few seconds, adding flour as necessary if the dough seems sticky. Then place the dough in a large microwavable bowl, lightly greased.

5. Cover the bowl loosely with a damp tea towel or microwavable plastic wrap. Place the bowl off-center in the microwave.

6. Set an 8-ounce glass of water in the microwave and prepare to micro-rise. Lower the microwave power to the appropriate micro-rise setting (see page 35). Heat for 3 minutes. Rest for 3 minutes. Heat for 3 minutes. Rest for 30 minutes or until the dough has doubled in bulk.

7. Meanwhile, wash the processor bowl and prepare the pecan filling. Fit the processor bowl with the steel blade. Add the pecans to the bowl and pulse until they are chopped coarsely. Add all of the other ingredients and pulse until the pecans are chopped fine, no more than 8 to 10 seconds.

8. Grease lightly a large baking sheet or 2 smaller ones, preferably microwavable. Remove the dough from the processor bowl and roll out on a lightly floured surface to a 20 × 15-inch rectangle. Spread with the pecan filling. Starting at the wide side of the dough, roll up as for a jelly roll. Seal the edges by pinching them closed. Gently pull the

(continued)

3. Meanwhile, butter the bread of your choice and cut into bite-sized cubes. Arrange 1 layer deep on a cookie sheet and heat in a 350°F oven until toasty, about 5 minutes.

4. To serve, arrange bread cubes in a flat serving dish, arrange cooked potatoes, broccoli, and red pepper strips atop, then spoon cheese sauce over all.

dough to make a 20-inch-long roll. Slice the dough all the way through at 1-inch intervals, forming 20 rolls. Place cut side down on the prepared baking sheet. Cover with waxed paper.

9. If baking sheet is microwavable, repeat step 6 and rest for 21 minutes, or raise in a warm, draft-free place until doubled in bulk. Meanwhile, preheat your oven to 325°F.

10. Bake the rolls on the middle rack of the preheated oven for 40 to 45 minutes or until light brown. Remove the rolls from the oven to cool.

11. Meanwhile, make the marmalade glaze. Combine all glaze ingredients in the processor bowl fitted with the steel blade and process until smooth, about 1 minute. Glaze the rolls when they have cooled. Store up to a week in plastic wrap.

HAZELNUT COFFEE RING

Makes 1 large ring in under 2 hours

Use the nuts of your choice for this crunchy brunch wreath. Glaze the wreath with citrus-sugar shine, then decorate with candied red and green cherries, and it makes a lovely Christmas morning breakfast bread. Decorate with whole toasted nuts, and it's Thanksgiving.

Toast the nuts by arranging 1 layer deep on a cookie sheet and placing in a 350°F oven until they begin to brown and give off a pungent, toasty smell. Careful you don't burn them. They'll toast in about 5 minutes. We use a toaster oven because it's handy and because we can keep an eye on it at the same time we're making the dough.

3–3½ C. bread flour	**Filling**
¾ teas. salt	*1½ C. hazelnuts*
1½ teas. ground	*¼ C. sugar*
cardamom	*¼ C. (½ stick)*
⅓ C. sugar	*unsalted butter*
2½ teas. 50% faster	
active dry yeast	**Glaze**
6 tbsp. (¾ stick)	*½ C. confectioners'*
unsalted butter	*sugar*
1 C. half-and-half	*1½ tbsp. lemon juice*

1. Combine in a processor bowl fitted with the steel blade the flour, salt cardamom, sugar, and yeast. Pulse to mix.

2. Combine in a glass measure the butter and half-and-half. Heat in the microwave to lukewarm (95°F), about 30 seconds set on high power. With the processor motor running, gradually pour warm liquid into the flour mixture.

3. Process until the dough begins to leave the side of the bowl. Knead 60 seconds, adding flour as necessary if the dough seems sticky.

4. Remove the dough and the steel blade and prepare to micro-rise. Knead dough by hand a few seconds, then form into a ball. With your thumbs, punch a hole to form a dough-nut shape and replace in the processor bowl. Cover loosely with a damp tea towel or plastic wrap.

5. Place an 8-ounce glass of water in the back of the microwave. Lower the microwave power to the appropriate micro-rise setting (see page 35). Heat for 3 minutes. Rest for 3 minutes. Heat for 3 minutes. Rest for 6 minutes or until the dough has risen to about double in bulk.

6. Meanwhile toast the nuts in the oven set at 350°F for 2 to 3 minutes or until brown, then chop coarsely, reserving about 2 tablespoons whole nuts to decorate the top of the ring (fruits may be used if you prefer). Combine chopped nuts in a small bowl with sugar and butter. Set aside. Oil a 12-inch springform pan or glass dish.

7. Remove the dough to a lightly floured surface and knead by hand a few seconds. Roll out into a 12 × 15-inch rect-angle, then spread with the toasted-nut mixture. Roll the dough up, jelly-roll fashion, beginning with the long side.

8. Place the roll in the prepared pan, press down slightly, then cover with a damp tea towel or plastic wrap and micro-rise, repeating step 5, or raise in a warm, draft-free place until nearly doubled in bulk. Meanwhile preheat the oven to 375°F.

9. Decorate the top of the ring with the reserved nuts or fruits. Whisk together powdered sugar and lemon juice for glaze.

10. Bake in the preheated oven 45 to 50 minutes or until evenly browned. Remove immediately to a rack to cool. While the ring is still warm, glaze with the sugar and lemon juice. Serve warm. Great cut into thin pinwheels and toasted. Store in plastic wrap up to a week.

At Christmas play and make good cheer,
For Christmas comes but once a year.

—Thomas Tusser
A Hundred Points of Good Husbandry, The Farmer's Daily Diet

Grill panettone with a slice of sweet Gorgonzola cheese and sliced purple figs, then garnish with mint leaves for an astonishing open-faced sandwich.

PANETTONE

Makes 1 large coffee cake in under 2 hours

No Italian Christmas is complete without a tall, sweet, fruit-studded panettone. One myth credits its invention to a Milanese baker called Antonio, who named the bread for himself—Tony's bread.

Tony was improving on an Italian brioche known as cherub's bread when he began tossing in fruits and nuts. Now, Italian children leave a bowl of panettone soaked in water on the windowsill at New Year's Eve for the camels bearing the three wise men, much as American children leave cookies and milk for Santa on Christmas Eve.

The bread makes a batter rather than a dough, so don't be surprised when you see it lying in the bottom of the processor bowl instead of forming a ball. Stir the fruits and nuts in by hand.

If you don't have a charlotte mold, substitute two 1-pound coffee cans or 1 medium ovenproof saucepan that you've greased and floured. The idea is to create a tall cylinder of sweet bread with a rounded top. Italians are reminded of a cathedral dome when they see that top.

We don't like candied fruits as much as the Italians do, so we sometimes make this bread using all raisins. Now that is raisin bread!

2 C. bread flour	2 large eggs plus 2 egg
1¾ C. cake flour	yolks
⅓ C. sugar	Zest of half an orange
½ teas. salt	½ C. golden raisins
5 teas. 50% faster	¼ C. Marsala
active dry yeast	⅓ C. each slivered
¼ teas. ground nutmeg	candied cherries and
⅔ C. unsalted butter or	diced mixed candied
margarine, softened	fruits
¼ C. milk	¼ C. pine nuts
½ C. water	Confectioners' sugar, for
1 teas. vanilla extract	dusting on top

1. In the processor bowl fitted with the steel blade, combine flours, sugar, salt, yeast, and nutmeg. Pulse to mix. Now

cut butter in finely, and pulse to blend so that it almost disappears.

2. Combine the milk and water in a glass measure. Heat to 120°F in the microwave set on high power, about 40 seconds, then with a fork whisk in the vanilla, eggs, and egg yolks. With the processor motor running, *drizzle the liquids very slowly* into the dry ingredients.

3. Process for 60 seconds. Add the orange zest and pulse to mix. Remove the blade from the processor bowl and prepare to micro-rise. Cover loosely with a damp tea towel or plastic wrap. Place the batter in the microwave.

4. Place an 8-ounce glass of water in the back of the microwave. Lower the microwave power to the appropriate micro-rise setting (see page 35). Place the dough in the microwave. Heat for 3 minutes. Rest for 3 minutes. Heat for 3 minutes. Rest for 6 minutes or until the batter has risen to about double in bulk. It will look bubbly and light.

5. Meanwhile, soak the raisins in Marsala.

6. Stir the batter down, then stir in the raisin mixture, cherries, candied fruits, and pine nuts until well distributed.

7. Grease generously and lightly flour a 9½- to 10-cup charlotte mold (about 7½ inches in diameter and 4 inches deep). Preheat the oven to 325°F. Spoon the batter into the mold, press down slightly, then raise in a warm, draft-free place until nearly doubled in bulk, about 30 minutes.

8. Bake in the preheated oven 1 hour or until evenly browned and a skewer stuck in the center comes out clean.

9. Remove immediately to a rack to cool, with the rounded side up. Dust with confectioners' sugar while warm. Wrap in plastic to store. Makes a great gift when packed in a tin. This bread keeps a week, properly stored.

Chocolate Café au ◇ Lait ◇

Makes 4 cups in 15 minutes

Make this dark, rich drink and serve with the Pecan Praline Sugar Loaf on a cold winter's day. Notice the recipe calls for German chocolate. Mr. German was a fellow who worked for a chocolate factory in Pennsylvania, by the way, and he invented this sweet chocolate. The cake that bears his name doesn't come from Europe but from Texas and Oklahoma where they took to Mr. German's chocolate like the proverbial duck to . . . We learned to make this Texas-style Café au Lait while visiting the Lone Star State at a time when the north wind blew so hard it knocked all the pecans off the tree into the backyard. What a lucky break.

2 C. freshly brewed French roast coffee
½ C. whipping cream
2 tbsp. confectioners' sugar
1 teas. vanilla extract
¼ C. German sweet chocolate, grated

1. While the coffee's dripping, whip cream in a small bowl, adding sugar a bit at a time, vanilla last, until you have soft peaks. Stir in the grated chocolate.
2. Pour clear glass coffee cups half full of hot coffee, then top with chocolate cream. Serve at once.

PECAN PRALINE SUGAR LOAF

Makes 1 loaf in 1 hour and 30 minutes

For those times when nothing but sugar will do.

1 tbsp. 50% faster active dry yeast
2¼ C. bread flour
2 tbsp. sugar
1¼ teas. ground cinnamon
2 teas. baking powder
½ teas. salt
¼ C. (½ stick) unsalted butter or margarine, cut into chunks
¼ C. hot tap water (120°F)
⅓ C. milk, microwaved until warm (110°F 30 sec.)
1 egg, slightly beaten

¾ C. brown sugar
1 teas. ground cinnamon
1 C. pecan halves (you can toast them if you wish)
2 tbsp. honey
2 tbsp. water

Streusel
½ C. chopped pecans
3 tbsp. butter or margarine, melted
½ C. unbleached white flour
½ C. packed light brown sugar
½ teas. ground cinnamon

Topping
2 tbsp. unsalted butter or margarine

1. Combine in the processor bowl fitted with the steel blade the yeast, flour, sugar, cinnamon, baking powder, and salt, and pulse to mix.
2. Open the top. Place butter or margarine in chunks atop the flour mixture, then pulse to mix.
3. Combine in a 2-cup measure the hot tap water, milk, and the slightly beaten egg. Warm in the microwave set on high for 1 minute.
4. With the processor motor running, pour the liquids into the flour mixture, holding back the last portion to see if the dough will form a ball. When the dough leaves the side of the bowl and forms a ball, knead with the motor running for 60 seconds. Add last of the liquid only if necessary.
5. Remove the dough from the bowl, then remove the

dough blade. Knead the dough by hand a few seconds, adding flour as necessary if dough seems sticky. Form into a doughnut shape and replace in the processor bowl. Cover loosely with a damp tea towel or plastic wrap and prepare to micro-rise.

6. Lower the microwave power to the appropriate micro-rise setting (see page 35). Place an 8-ounce glass of water in the center of the microwave, then place the dough beside it. Heat for 3 minutes. Rest for 3 minutes. Heat 3 minutes. Rest 6 minutes or until doubled in bulk.

7. Meanwhile, prepare the pan, topping, and streusel mixture. Melt 2 tablespoons of butter or margarine and spread on the bottom of a 9 × 5 × 3-inch glass loaf pan. In a small bowl combine the brown sugar, cinnamon, pecan halves, honey, and water, then sprinkle over the butter. Set aside. In a small bowl, mix the streusel topping until crumbly and set aside.

8. Preheat the oven to 350°F. Remove the dough from the processor bowl, punch down, and knead by hand a few seconds until it is no longer sticky. Roll out to a 15 × 10-inch rectangle. Sprinkle with the streusel mixture, then roll up from the short side (like a jelly roll). Cut into 3 equal pieces and place in the prepared glass loaf pan, cut sides up. Press lightly with your fingers.

9. Cover with oiled plastic wrap and micro-rise again, repeating step 6, or raise the dough in a warm, draft-free place. The dough should rise just to the top of the pan.

10. Place in a preheated oven and bake until golden brown, about 45 to 50 minutes.

11. Remove to a rack to cool. Wrap in plastic to store.

Makes 1 turtle in 90 minutes

Prepare a recipe of kolacky dough, micro-rise once, then form into a turtle shape:

1. Twist off a ½-cup piece of dough and set aside.

2. Shape the remaining piece into a 5-inch oval ball, the same shape as a turtle's shell. Place on a greased cookie sheet.

3. Roll the reserved piece into a 7-inch rope. From the rope, cut a 2-inch piece for the head, and four 1-inch legs. Make a pointed tail with the remainder. Using scissors, snip toes in the feet, and eyes and a mouth into the head.

4. Press the legs, tail, and head up under the "shell," then finish by snipping a shell design into the body with scissors and completing the shaping by hand. Let the turtle rise until almost doubled in bulk. Brush with an egg wash made from egg whisked with water, then sprinkle with colored sugar. Press raisins or currants into eyes. Bake in a pre-heated 375°F oven until browned, about 20 minutes.

K O L A C K Y

Makes 8 buns in 2 hours

The Czech word *kolac* means "wheel-shaped cake" and is made up of a sweet bun topped with fruit, cheese, or poppy-seed filling.

This same sweet egg dough can be used to make raisin bread, turtle bread, or hot cross buns. The great thing about using machines to do the kneading and raising is that it leaves you time to do the creative, fun part of forming and filling these fine sweet breads: choose from among the nine fillings that follow.

2¼ C. bread flour
¼ teas. ground cardamom
½ teas. salt
¼ C. sugar
2½ teas. 50% faster active dry yeast

¼ C. (½ stick) unsalted butter
½ C. milk
1 large egg

1. Fit the processor bowl with the steel blade, then add the flour, cardamom, salt, sugar, and yeast. Pulse to mix.

2. Place the butter and milk in a 2-cup glass measure and, in the microwave set on high power, heat to lukewarm to begin melting the butter (about 40 seconds). Now, with a fork, whisk in egg. With the processor motor running, pour liquid through the feed tube, holding back the last portion to see if it will form a ball.

3. When the dough leaves the side of the bowl and forms a ball, knead with the machine running for 60 seconds. Use the last of the liquid only if necessary.

4. Remove the dough from the bowl and remove the steel blade. Knead the dough by hand a few seconds, adding flour as necessary if the dough seems sticky. Then form the dough into a ball. With your thumbs, punch a hole to form a dough-nut shape and replace in the processor bowl. Cover the bowl loosely with a damp tea towel or microwavable plastic wrap and prepare to micro-rise.

5. Place an 8-ounce glass of water in the microwave and place the processor bowl of dough beside it. Lower the microwave power to the appropriate micro-rise setting (see page

35). Heat for 3 minutes. Rest for 3 minutes. Heat for 3 minutes. Rest for 6 minutes or until doubled in bulk.

6. Remove the dough from the processor bowl, punch down, and knead by hand a few seconds. Cover the dough with the processor bowl and allow it to rest for 10 minutes.

7. Preheat the oven to 375°F. Lightly grease a cookie sheet. Divide the dough into 8 equal pieces and roll into balls. Place the balls on the cookie sheet, 3 inches apart. Cover lightly, then let rise either in the microwave, repeating step 5, or in a warm, draft-free place until doubled in bulk, 30 to 40 minutes.

8. Meanwhile prepare the filling (see recipes below).

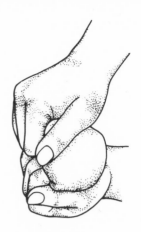

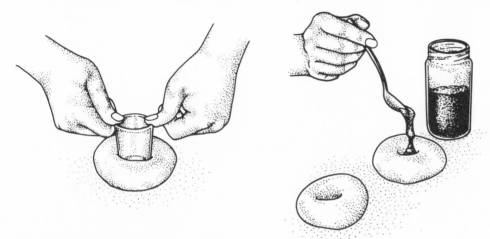

When the dough has risen, dip the bottom of a small glass (like a shot glass, about 1½ inches in diameter) in a little melted butter and press an indentation in the middle of each bun. Drop about 1 tablespoon of filling into the center. Finish one of three ways:

a) Make streusel.
b) Sprinkle with turbinado sugar.
c) Make a glazed finish by beating an egg with a tablespoon of milk, then paint the buns with this mixture before baking.

9. Bake in the preheated oven about 20 minutes until golden and bubbly. Remove to a rack to cool. Store in a plastic bag. Serve the kolacky warm. Best if eaten the day it's made. Reheat in the oven or toaster oven, not the microwave.

Cottage Cheese
◇ Filling ◇

Fills 8 rolls in 10 minutes

½ C. small-curd cottage
   cheese
¼ C. sugar
1 egg yolk
½ teas. vanilla extract
Grating of fresh nutmeg
Turbinado sugar, slivered
   blanched almonds, or
   confectioners' sugar, for
   sprinkling and dusting
   (optional)

In a small bowl combine all ingredients to mix, then drop by tablespoonful onto the center of each kolacky before baking. If you wish, sprinkle with turbinado (raw) sugar and/or slivered blanched almonds before baking. Or when the kolacky has finished baking, you can dust with confectioners' sugar.

Cream Cheese
◇ Filling ◇

Fills 8 rolls in 5 minutes

½ C. cream cheese
1 egg yolk
1½ tbsp. sugar
1 teas. vanilla extract
¼ teas. lemon extract
Pinch ground cardamom
1 recipe Apricot Glaze

In a 2-cup glass measure, soften cream cheese in the microwave set on high power, about 15 seconds, then combine with the remaining ingredients except the glaze into a smooth paste. Drop by tablespoonful onto prepared kolacky, then bake as directed. Brush while hot with Apricot Glaze.

◇ Prune Filling ◇

Fills 8 rolls in 15 minutes

20 large pitted prunes
1 tbsp. fresh lemon juice
4 tbsp. currant jelly
1 teas. unsalted butter
¼ teas. ground cinnamon

1. In a 2-cup glass measure cover prunes with water and simmer until soft in the microwave set on medium power, stirring and testing from time to time, about 5 minutes. Set aside 5 minutes.

2. Drain water from the prunes, then combine the prunes with the remaining ingredients in the processor bowl fitted with the steel blade. Pulse to make a rough puree. Drop by the tablespoonful onto each kolacky, then bake as directed.

◇ Apricot Filling ◇

Fills 8 rolls in 10 minutes

20 large apricot halves
¼ C. apricot jam
1 tbsp. fresh lemon juice
1 teas. butter
Confectioners' sugar and
   chopped walnuts, for
   sprinkling on top

1. Place the apricots in a 2-cup glass measure and barely cover with water. Simmer in the microwave set on medium power until fruit is soft, stirring and testing every minute or so, for about 5 minutes. Remove from the microwave and drain.

2. Combine in the processor bowl fitted with the steel blade the fruit, jam, lemon juice, and butter. Pulse to mix into a rough puree. Drop by the tablespoonful onto prepared kolacky, sprinkle with confectioners' sugar and nuts, then bake as directed.

◇ Cherry Filling ◇

Fills 8 rolls in 10 minutes

- 1/2 pound pitted sweet cherries (Bing or Queen Anne are great)
- 2 tbsp. sugar
- 1 tbsp. fresh lemon juice
- 1 1/2 teas. cornstarch
- 1 recipe Almond Crumb Streusel (optional)

Mix all the ingredients, then drop by tablespoonful onto the center of each kolacky before baking. If you wish, top with Almond Crumb Streusel before baking as well.

◇ Apricot Glaze ◇

Fills 8 rolls in 5 minutes

- 3 tbsp. apricot preserves
- 1/2 C. water
- 1/2 C. sugar

1. Combine ingredients in a 2-cup glass measure and raise to a boil in the microwave set on high power, about 2 minutes.
2. Brush hot glaze on kolacky just as they come out of the oven.

◇ Nut Filling ◇

Fills 8 rolls in 5 minutes

- 1/2 C. (1 stick) butter, softened
- 1/2 C. chopped nuts (almonds, hazelnuts, walnuts, or pecans)
- 1/2 C. confectioners' sugar
- 1/2 teas. ground cinnamon

Combine the ingredients and mix with a fork, then drop by the tablespoonful onto prepared kolacky. Bake as directed.

Poppy-Seed ◇ Filling ◇

Fills 8 rolls in 15 minutes

- 1 C. poppy seeds
- 1/2 C. milk
- 2 tbsp. unsalted butter or margarine
- 2 tbsp. mild honey
- 1 tbsp. sugar
- Pinch of salt
- 1 egg

1. Grind poppy seeds in a blender or coffee grinder.
2. Combine with remaining ingredients *except the egg* in a 2-cup glass measure. Cook in the microwave on high power until thick, stirring and turning every minute for about 5 minutes. Remove from the microwave and whisk in the egg thoroughly. Cool, then drop by tablespoonful onto each kolacky. Bake as directed.

Almond Crumb ◇ Streusel ◇

Tops 8 rolls in 5 minutes

- 1/4 C. ground toasted almonds (see page 220)
- 1/4 C. sugar
- 1/4 C. unbleached white flour
- 1/4 C. (1/2 stick) butter

In the processor bowl fitted with the steel blade combine almonds, sugar, and flour, then add butter and process until mixture resembles coarse crumbs, about 10 seconds. sprinkle on kolacky *and* filling.

Almond-and-Spice
◇ Honey ◇

Makes 1⅓ cups in 10 minutes

In the processor bowl fitted with the steel blade, add ⅓ cup blanched almonds; process until the almonds are chopped fine. Remove the almonds to a small bowl and add 1 cup honey, ½ teaspoon ground cinnamon, ¼ teaspoon ground nutmeg, and ½ teaspoon dried orange peel. Stir to blend thoroughly. Store covered and allow the honey to sit 24 hours for the flavor to develop.

Orange Bread
Pudding with
◇ Chocolate Sauce ◇

Serves 6 in 30 minutes

- ¾ C. milk
- ¾ C. half-and-half
- 2 eggs
- ¾ C. sugar
- 1 teas. vanilla extract
- Zest of half an orange
- ¼ C. (½ stick) unsalted butter, softened
- 2 C. cubed Orange Grove Bread or Challah (see page 63) or other white bread cut into 1-inch cubes

Syrup
- ½ C. semisweet chocolate morsels
- ½ C. whipping cream
- 2 teas. Triple Sec or other orange liqueur

1. Combine the milk and cream in a 1-quart microwavable measure and cook in the microwave on high power for 2 minutes or until hot but not boiling.

2. In a small bowl, whisk together the eggs, sugar, vanilla, and

ORANGE GROVE BREAD

Makes 1 loaf in 2 hours, serving 6–8

Most orange breads are of the quick-bread variety; however, this yeast bread flavored with orange juice and orange zest has a tender and slightly sweet crumb. Fresh or frozen orange juice may be used. Toast and serve with Almond-and-Spice Honey for breakfast.

- 3½ C. bread flour
- 1 tbsp. 50% faster active dry yeast
- 1½ tbsp. shortening
- 1 teas. salt
- ¼ C. sugar
- ⅛ C. grated orange zest
- 1 large egg
- ¾ C. hot water (125°–130°F)
- ⅛ C. fresh or frozen orange juice

1. In the processor bowl fitted with the steel blade, add the flour, yeast, shortening, salt, sugar, orange zest, and egg. Process for 10 seconds or until the ingredients are well blended.

2. Combine in a glass measure the hot water and orange juice. With the motor running, *drizzle the liquids very slowly* into the dry ingredients, holding back the last portion of liquid to see if the dough will form a ball.

3. Process until the dough begins to leave the side of the bowl, forming a ball. Add the last of the liquid only if necessary. Knead with the machine running for 60 seconds, adding flour as necessary if the dough seems sticky. Pinch up a piece of the dough. It should feel soft, tacky, smooth, elastic, and warm.

4. Remove the dough and the steel blade and prepare to micro-rise. On a lightly floured surface, knead the dough by hand a few seconds, then form into a ball. With your thumbs, punch a hole to form a doughnut shape and replace in the processor bowl. Cover loosely with a damp tea towel or plastic wrap. Place the dough in the microwave.

5. Place an 8-ounce glass of water in the back of the microwave. Lower the microwave power to the appropriate micro-rise setting (see page 35). Heat for 3 minutes. Rest for 3 minutes. Heat for 3 minutes. Rest for 20 minutes or until

the dough has risen to double in bulk. Meanwhile, lightly grease an 8½ × 4½-inch glass loaf pan.

6. Remove the dough to a lightly floured surface and knead by hand a few seconds. Form into a loaf (see page 40) and place in the prepared pan. Cover the loaf with a damp tea towel or microwavable plastic wrap and place the loaf off-center in the microwave with an 8-ounce glass of water in the middle of the microwave.

7. With the microwave power set as in step 5, heat for 3 minutes, then rest for 3 minutes. Heat for 3 minutes. Rest for 10 minutes or until the dough has risen 1 inch above the top of the pan. Meanwhile, preheat the oven to 375°F.

8. Bake the loaf on the middle rack of the preheated oven for 45 minutes or until the loaf is golden brown and sounds hollow when tapped on the bottom.

9. Remove from the pan to a rack to cool. Wrap in aluminum foil or a plastic bag to store.

orange zest. Then whisk into the hot milk. Now cook the custard in the microwave set on high until thickened, up to 6 minutes, turning and stirring every minute or so. Meanwhile, butter an 8-inch microwavable baking dish.

3. Melt the butter, then toss with the bread cubes and place in the prepared baking dish. Pour hot custard over the bread cubes, then place in the microwave and cook on medium for about 10 minutes or until a knife inserted into the center comes out clean. Remove the pudding from the microwave, cover with waxed paper, and let it stand 10 minutes before serving.

4. In a 2-cup microwavable measure, combine chocolate chips and cream. Microwave on high for 30 seconds or until the chips melt. Whisk together, then add orange liqueur and whisk that in. Drizzle the hot chocolate syrup over the pudding, cut into squares, and serve.

PORTUGUESE SWEET BREAD

Makes 1 loaf in 2 hours and 30 minutes

Below a golden, tanned crust lies a sinfully rich bread made of eggs and butter. The crumb is fine textured and slightly sweet. Folklore says this bread originated in the Azores and was the traditional Easter bread.

3 C. bread flour
1 tbsp. 50% faster active dry yeast
¼ C. sugar
1 teas. salt
Dash of vanilla extract
¼ C. (½ stick) unsalted butter, cut into tablespoon-sized pieces

½ C. tepid milk
2 large eggs, lightly beaten
⅛ C. raisins
1 tbsp. sugar, for decorating

There is nothing worse than biting into a piece of bread containing raisins and hitting something more akin to a rock than a piece of fruit.

The raisins should have about the same moisture content as the dough. If your raisins are hard, place them in a glass measure, cover with water, and bring to a simmer in the microwave. Cook for 1 minute, drain immediately, and set aside to cool before using.

(continued)

Christmas Citrus-Avocado ◇ Salad ◇

Serves 10–12 in 20 minutes

3 *large oranges*
2 *large grapefruit*
2 *medium Haas avocados,*
peeled, seeded, and cut
into slivers
⅓ *C. pomegranate seeds*
Red-tipped lettuce leaves
Belgian endive leaves
¾ *C. walnut halves*

Dressing
½ *C. rice wine vinegar*
⅓ *C. canola oil*
1 *tbsp. brown sugar*
½ *teas. soy sauce*
Salt and freshly ground black
pepper to taste

1. Peel, seed, and section fruits over a bowl to catch the juices, then arrange fruit segments, avocado, and pomegranate seeds over lettuce leaves. Reserve juices.

2. Combine dressing ingredients in a small bowl, pouring reserved citrus juices back in, then whisk to mix and drizzle over the fruits. Top with walnut halves and serve.

1. In the processor bowl fitted with the steel blade, add the flour, yeast, sugar, salt, vanilla extract, and butter. Process for 10 seconds or until the butter disappears into the flour mixture.

2. Pour the milk into a glass measure and add the beaten eggs, reserving 2 tablespoons of the eggs for the glaze. With the motor running, drizzle the liquids very slowly into the dry ingredients, holding back the last portion of liquid to see if the dough will form a ball.

3. Process until the dough begins to leave the side of the bowl, forming a ball. Add the last of the milk-egg mixture only if necessary. Knead with the machine running for 45 seconds, adding flour as necessary if the dough seems sticky. Pinch up a piece of the dough. It should feel soft, tacky, smooth, elastic, and warm.

4. Remove the dough and the steel blade and prepare to micro-rise. On a lightly floured surface, add raisins and knead the dough by hand a few seconds, then form dough into a ball. With your thumbs, punch a hole to form a doughnut shape and replace in the processor bowl. Cover loosely with a damp tea towel or plastic wrap. Place the dough in the microwave.

5. Position an 8-ounce glass of water in the back of the microwave. Lower the microwave power to the appropriate micro-rise setting (see page 35). Heat for 3 minutes. Rest for 3 minutes. Heat for 3 minutes. Rest for 30 minutes or until the dough has risen to double in bulk.

6. Lightly grease a 9-inch glass pie plate. Remove the dough to a lightly floured surface and knead by hand a few seconds. Pat the dough into a round, flat disk about 8 inches across. Place in the prepared pan.

7. Cover the loaf with a waxed-paper tent or plastic wrap and place the loaf off-center in the microwave with an 8-ounce glass of water in the middle of the microwave.

8. Repeat step 5. Alternately, you may raise the dough in a warm, draft-free place until doubled in bulk, about 40 minutes. Meanwhile, preheat the oven to 350°F. When the loaf has sufficiently risen, brush it lightly with the reserved beaten egg.

9. Bake the loaf on the middle rack of the preheated oven for 1 hour or until it is golden brown on the outside and a wooden skewer inserted into the loaf comes out clean. Remove from the pan to a rack to cool. When cool, wrap in a plastic bag or airtight container to store.

BRIOCHE BREAD PUDDING WITH BOURBON SAUCE

Makes 6–8 servings in 1 hour

The idea of leftover brioche may seem laughable, but if you can hide a half-dozen brioches to make this dessert, it's worth it. Otherwise, substitute Challah (see page 63) or other egg-rich breads. Although most bread pudding recipes suggest cutting away the crust, who are we kidding? The crust is too delicious to sacrifice.

6–8 day-old brioches	2 large eggs
Unsalted butter	2 egg yolks
1/3 C. golden raisins	1/4 C. bourbon
1/3 C. pecan halves	1/3 C. sugar
1 1/2 C. milk	1 teas. vanilla extract

1. Preheat the oven to 350°F. Heat a quart of water in the microwave set on 100% power, about 5 minutes.

2. Slice off the brioche tops (the hats) and set aside. Slice the brioches into ½-inch-thick slices. Lightly butter the slices, then fit into a buttered 8½ × 5-inch loaf pan, layering the buttered bread with strewn raisins and pecans.

3. In a large mixing bowl, whisk together milk, eggs, egg yolks, bourbon, sugar, and vanilla. Slowly pour this mixture over the layered brioche, allowing the bread time to absorb all the milk. When the milk reaches 1 inch below the top of the loaf pan, stop adding. Butter the underside of the brioche "hats" and artfully arrange them atop the pudding.

4. Place the loaf pan in the middle of a deep ovenproof pan. Pour boiling water into the large pan until it reaches halfway up the sides of the loaf pan. Place the pans in the center of the preheated oven and bake until the pudding is set, about 45 minutes. Lift the loaf pan from its water bath and cool on a rack.

5. Cut in thick slices and serve warm with a dollop of Bourbon Sauce atop. Good cold, leftover, for breakfast the next morning too.

◇ Bourbon Sauce ◇

Makes 1 1/2 cups in 5 minutes

Try this over curried fruit as well as bread pudding and you'll swear you remember it from Mardi Gras.

4 egg yolks
1/3 C. sugar
1/3 C. bourbon

1. Combine the egg yolks, sugar, and bourbon in a microwavable batter bowl with deep sides. Beat until light with a balloon (wire) whisk.

2. Place in the microwave. At 100% power, cook for 30 seconds. Remove from the microwave and whisk thoroughly, then repeat for 30 seconds more. Keep repeating, cooking and whisking until the sauce is thick and creamy. Serve hot or cold.

Makes 1 cup in 10 minutes

**10-oz. package frozen
  raspberries in light syrup,
  thawed**
1 teas. cornstarch
1 teas. water
**2 teas. kirsh or framboise
  liqueur**

1. Into a medium microwavable bowl, press the raspberries and syrup through a fine sieve or strainer to remove pulp and seeds.

2. In a small bowl, stir together the cornstarch and water until smooth. Stir the cornstarch mixture into the raspberry mixture and cook in the microwave set on medium power, stirring every 30 seconds until the mixture comes to a boil. Boil for 1 minute. Remove from the microwave and stir in the kirsch *or* framboise. *Cool to room temperature and chill thoroughly before serving.*

BING HASTY PUDDING WITH RASPBERRY SAUCE

Makes 1 pudding in 2 hours to serve 6

Two of our favorite flavor combinations come together in this tasty hasty: sweet, port-colored Bing cherries and ruby-red raspberries. Fresh or frozen cherries will do and you can skip the raspberry sauce if you're really in a hurry. Bing Hasty Pudding looks beautiful served in a pool of raspberry sauce on a white or green dessert plate with a dollop of whipped cream and another ribbon of ruby red sauce flowing over the whipped cream.

**¾ pound good-quality
  French, Italian, or
  white bread,
  trimmed of crust and
  cut into
  ½-inch-thick slices**
**½ C. (1 stick) unsalted
  butter, melted**
2 C. milk
½ C. heavy cream
1½ C. sugar
2 large egg yolks
**1¼ C. fresh or frozen
  pitted dark sweet
  Bing cherries,
  thawed and drained**

**2 tbsp. kirsch or
  framboise liqueur**

Whipped Topping
1 C. heavy cream
**2 tbsp. confectioners'
  sugar**

**Raspberry Sauce
  (optional)**

1. Cut the bread slices into rectangles or triangles (whichever best suits the shape of the 8-cup, 3-inch-deep casserole dish that you have chosen). Brush the slices with the butter on both sides. Set aside.

2. In a quart-sized microwavable bowl or measure, combine the milk, cream, and ½ cup of the sugar. Place in the microwave and cook on medium-high power for 5 minutes, stirring occasionally until the sugar dissolves. Remove from the microwave and set aside.

3. Preheat the oven to 350°F. In a large mixing bowl, lightly beat the egg yolks. Stir in the hot cream mixture.

Arrange half of the bread over the bottom of the casserole dish. Pour half of the custard mixture evenly over the bread.

4. Combine the cherries, 1 cup remaining sugar, and kirsch or framboise in a small bowl, mixing thoroughly. Spoon this mixture over the bread in the casserole, reserving 5 cherries for garnish on the top.

5. Layer the remaining half of the bread in the dish and pour the remaining custard mixture over the top. Lightly press the top bread slices down with the back of a spoon to make sure that all bread slices are moistened. Place the remaining cherries on top.

6. Bake on the middle rack of the preheated oven for 45 minutes or until the pudding is lightly browned.

7. Meanwhile, prepare the whipped topping. Place the cream and the beaters to your mixer in a medium mixing bowl and place in the freezer for 10 minutes to chill. Remove the bowl from the freezer and beat the cream with the sugar until stiff peaks form.

8. Serve the pudding warm or at room temperature in a pool of raspberry sauce, if desired, with a dollop of whipped cream.

ERICA'S FAVORITE BUTTERSCOTCH BREAD PUDDING

Serves 8 in 90 minutes

It's delicious for dinner, better for breakfast—you'll find yourself licking the spoon when you make this heavenly butterscotch pudding. The bread pudding squares are delicate. Take care when transferring them to dessert plates not to break them.

4 *large eggs*	1 *tbsp. turbinado*
½ *C. sugar*	*sugar*
4 *C. whipping cream*	1 *recipe Butterscotch*
1½ *tbsp. vanilla extract*	*Sauce*
8 *C. whole wheat*	
bread, cut into	
1-inch cubes	*(continued)*

The lion and the unicorn
Were fighting for the crown;
The lion beat the unicorn
All round about the town.
Some gave them white bread,
And some gave them brown;
And some gave them plum cake,
And sent them out of town.

—Nursery rhyme

◇

1. Preheat the oven to 325°F, and butter a 9 × 13-inch baking pan.

2. In a large mixing bowl, whisk the eggs thoroughly with ½ cup sugar, then whisk in cream and vanilla.

3. Arrange the bread cubes in the prepared baking pan, then slowly pour the egg-and-cream mixture over, allowing the liquid to soak into the bread. Sprinkle the top evenly with the tablespoon of turbinado sugar.

4. Bake 40 to 50 minutes, until evenly puffed and the edges of the bread cubes are golden brown. Jiggle the pan. The center should be just set.

5. Cool on a rack to room temperature before cutting. Carefully transfer squares to dessert plates and top with warmed Butterscotch Sauce.

Butterscotch Sauce

Makes 2 cups in 10 minutes

½ C. (1 stick) unsalted butter	*1½ C. heavy cream*
1 C. packed light brown sugar	*1 tbsp. vanilla extract*
⅓ C. corn syrup	*1 teas. strained fresh lemon juice*
	1 tbsp. lemon zest

6. In a quart glass measure, combine the butter and sugar, then melt in the microwave set on high power for 1 minute. Stir in the corn syrup. Whisk in the heavy cream, return to the microwave, and cook set on high, turning and stirring every minute, until the sauce is thickened, about 5 minutes.

7. Remove from the microwave, stir in vanilla, lemon juice, and zest, then cover and cool. Store in the refrigerator until time to serve.

8. To use, stir and reheat in the microwave set on medium, stirring every 30 seconds until hot, about 2 minutes.

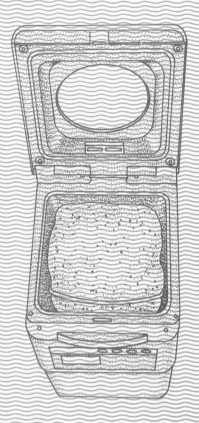

PART TWO

Home-Baked
Bread in the
Bread Machine

◆ BREAD MACHINE BASICS

It would be naive to suggest that our busy lives can return to simpler times. But with a bread machine, one quality of times past that we don't have to lose is home-baked bread. Nothing tastes quite as good as bread you bake yourself—fresh and soft with an aroma that greets you when you open the door. A family time of breaking bread, the flaky golden brown crust with just the right amount of snap, a light, creamy interior full of flavor. Peace, home, family: this is it. Using a bread machine, all you do is combine the ingredients in the baking pan, close the lid, press a button, and go about your business. Some three or more hours later, your kitchen is filled with the tantalizing fragrance of home-baked bread, and you have been offered by the bread machine the most precious gift of all: time.

The bread machine, a new kitchen tool, gift for the 1990s, gives back more than it costs, loaf after loaf after lovely loaf. Bread machines are especially welcome by people wanting to control the contents of their diet to avoid salt, fat, sugar, or chemical additives in their bread. For those who haven't the time to bake, the bread machine makes home baking possible.

But we didn't think the bread machine was so great when we first got it. Why? The hardware is ahead of the software. The recipes that come in the recipe booklets with the machines make variations on commercial white bread. We wanted *real* bread, made *easy*, in a machine. In fact, we began this whole project by tinkering with our favorite recipes to make them work in the bread machine. After a lot of trial and error, we began to be able to make great bread in the machine.

We have been working with bread machines for more than a year and have found them to be a blessing for the complete kitchen. Bread machines are ushering in an age of computer-driven kitchen appliances. Buy one and you can peek into the future. With computer chips programming kitchen appliances, we can now have a warm, steaming loaf of bread, freshly brewed coffee, or cold, frozen ice cream just by adding the ingredients and flipping a switch.

Now that a bread machine has become a fixture on the counter in each of our kitchens for more than a year, we've evolved methods for baking bread that we couldn't have envisioned a year ago.

One of the most satisfactory ways for making bread we've learned is to use the bread machine to do the work of mixing, kneading, and raising the dough for the first time, using the *dough* setting. Then we like to pull the dough out of the machine, knead it by hand a few seconds—ahh, that lovely aroma, the feel of warm satiny dough in your hands, the yielding responsive mass that takes any shape you want—form the loaf, and change gears and use the Micro-Rise method for the second rise. Fifteen minutes later the bread dough is ready for the oven. Pop it in. Can you beat it?

What we've developed here is a new baking technique that combines the bread machine *and* the Micro-Rise method. This way we get everything. A bread machine to do the dirty work. A chance to play with warm bread dough. A microwave to raise the loaf up real quick. And the oven to bake bread. Good grief. It's practically a symphony.

Men in particular seem to be intrigued by these newfangled toys and are turning to machine baking as a hobby. When we do baking demonstrations in stores, men show the greatest interest in these machines. Fascinated by the mechanics, men turn out creative, innovative breads and rolls. One has turned his kitchen into a veritable herring factory and runs up and down the street giving bread to all his neighbors.

Features of Different Brands of Bread Machines

Bread machines are so new that the engineering on them is far from standard. We were surprised at the differences. There are about ten models on the market at the time of this writing. We tested six different ones. Basically, each machine is roughly the size of a bread box, 14 inches by 9 inches by 12 inches. The machine contains a removable bread pan with a kneading blade on the bottom. A motor turns the kneading blade, mixing and kneading the ingredients into a dough. In the bottom of the machine is a heating coil that bakes the bread. A microcomputer tells the machine when to start each successive cycle. All models we tested baked a tasty, crusty loaf of bread. Although all have the features that are necessities, some have features that seem mere frill.

The shape of the loaf produced varies from brand to brand. A vertical rectangle, a horizontal rectangle, and a cylinder are the basic shapes. The vertical rectangle seems to be the one used by most manufacturers. The bread from this shape slices almost into a perfect square and fits most toasters nicely. However, we had problems with the top caving in on this loaf shape. It seems as if the dough can only raise straight up so far before collapsing a little under its own weight. It still tastes great; it's just not as pretty.

The horizontal rectangle is used in only one machine we tested, the Panasonic, but looks like the one your grandmother used to make in her tried-but-true, weary-looking bread pans. It slices well, and we experienced very few sunken tops.

Round bread. No, not baked in a coffee can like a Boston brown bread, but in a machine by Welbilt similar in appearance to R2D2. The bread slices well with a nice rounded top; however most slices must be sliced in half again to fit into the toaster, though they can be toasted whole in most toaster ovens.

The bread-baking time settings vary widely from machine to machine, even from the same manufacturer. The *basic bread setting* range for the machines is between 3 hours and 10 minutes in the Sanyo Home Bakery up to 4 hours and 15 minutes in the 1½-pound capacity Panasonic/National. Yet, we found little difference in the quality of the bread despite the time variation.

The dough setting, standard on all machines, mixes the ingredients and lets the dough raise in the machine the first time. Then you remove the dough from the machine, shape it into various rolls, coffee cakes, or sweet breads, raise it a second time outside the bread machine then bake it in the conventional oven. The time required for the dough setting ranges between 1 hour and 20 minutes in the MK Seiko Home Bakery up to 1 hour 55 minutes in the Panasonic/National machines. The 1½-pound capacity Panasonic/National allows the dough cycle to be used in conjunction with the timer—a wonderful idea because it permits the cook to walk in the door from work and have pizza, calzone, or roll dough ready to be filled or shaped and baked. This is also a great way to have a coffee cake or sweet dough waiting for you in the morning for breakfast or brunch. Just fill, shape, micro-rise, and bake. In fact, we agree that combining the bread machine with the micro-rise method is our favorite way to bake.

On those days when time is of the essence, the *rapid bake setting* is a wonderful feature, allowing you to have bread in as little as 2 hours and 45 minutes. Here again, we found little or no difference in the quality of the bread baked on the *basic bread setting* and that baked on the *rapid bake setting.* Panasonic/National, Seiko, and Zojirushi offer this setting on their machines.

The *raisin bread setting* can be used for all kinds of chopped fruits and nuts, and is usually the basic bread cycle, plus an alarm that sounds approximately 5 minutes before the end of the first kneading cycle to allow you to add the raisins, fruit, or nuts.

The fruit will then receive the minimum kneading and not "disappear" into the dough. At the time of this writing, only the Zojirushi, Sanyo, and Welbilt have this cycle.

The French bread setting allows hands-off baking of a usually difficult bread. The crusts are cracking and crunchy and the interior tears just like bread from the best *boulangerie,* even though the shape is odd looking. The cycle times range from 3 hours and 30 minutes in the MK Seiko Home Bakery to 7 hours in the 1½-pound capacity Panasonic/National baker. Panasonic/National's newest model offers a *whole wheat cycle* to help home bakers with heavier doughs turn out superior whole grain breads.

The Zojirushi features a manual setting allowing you to convert your personal bread recipes to the cycles of the machine. If you want to do Auntie Em's Cream Bread from Kansas and the dough raises to the top of the pan and is ready to bake after 40 minutes, but the machine says that it still has 20 minutes to go before baking, you can manually advance to the bake cycle and bypass the computer's memory. Wonderful feature. We think all bread machines should have it.

If you want to bake bread while you're away at the office, look for a cool-down cycle. It is found on some models from Welbilt, Panasonic/National, Sanyo, and Zojirushi. This cycle starts a fan after the machine is finished baking and cools the bread while it is still in the pan. This allows the baker to be gone when the machine finishes baking and still come home to a house filled with the aroma of baked bread and a nice loaf with a crisp crust. Bread left in the pan without this cycle becomes soggy crusted and develops a wetter than normal interior with an off-flavor.

Panasonic and Zojirushi *quick bread settings* designed for yeast-free breads seem to be a frill and need more time on the engineer's drawing board and in the test kitchen. On the Zojirushi bread machine that mixes and bakes quick bread, the quality of the finished product is inferior. The 1½-pound capacity Panasonic bread machine that only bakes quick bread, requiring you to mix the bread manually, then pour the batter into the machine to bake, offers no real time or energy saved. It would, however, free up a conventional oven for other use at the same time the bread is baking.

The cake setting available on the Zojirushi machine is still rather primitive and needs improvement. When we tried it, the outer crust was hard and overcooked, causing chocolate in the cake to taste burnt.

The standard crust on a machine loaf is a little thicker, a slightly deeper tan, and much crisper than that of store-bought bread. The light crust selection found on some models is closer to that of store-bought breads. The crisp crust selection is darker than the standard crust, but crisper, more akin to a French bread crust.

The Zojirushi, Sanyo, and Welbilt have viewing windows. A viewing window eliminates the need to open the lid to see what's going on. However, we found, when developing recipes, that it was essential to be able to see and follow the progress of the dough. We learned we could open the machine in the mixing phase to see if the dough was too wet or too dry and no harm was done. Once the rising and baking cycles begin, though, opening the lid allows heat to escape and alters the moisture content, reducing the chances for an ideal loaf of bread.

How to Bake Perfect Machine Loaves

Before using the bread machine recipes in this book, you need to know what capacity machine you have purchased. If it is not clearly stated in the owner's manual as being a one pound or a one-and-a-half pound machine, look in the recipe booklet that came with the machine. If the manufacturer's recipes call for about two cups of flour, the machine can easily make our recipes for the one pound machine. If the manufacturer's recipes call for three cups or more of flour, use our recipes for the one-and-one-half pound machine.

In our book, the ingredients list and directions for the main recipe are for the one pound machine; the ingredients listed in the margin are for the one-and-one-half pound machine. The directions are the same for both, though the cycles for the basic settings require different times from manufacturer to manufacturer. Check the owner's manual to see how much time will be required in your machine for the different cycles.

After the ingredients have been added to the bread pan and the desired setting chosen for preparation, check your ingredients by lifting the lid to check on progress about 5 minutes after the machine has been started.

What to look for. On all settings, the machine will be mixing fairly fast and the ingredients will be mixing together to make a dough. If you have any dry chunks, you will need to add a tablespoon or so of the main liquid called for in the recipe (see illustration). Check again after a few moments to see if the dough is massing around the blade into a soft, pliable ball. If not, add an additional liquid, tablespoon or so until it does. Sometimes all it takes is just a dribble of liquid to bring the dough to the proper consistency.

The ball that is now formed should be soft and pliable. If it feels dry and stiff add additional liquid, tablespoon by tablespoon until the dough feels soft, smooth, and elastic. A dough that is too dry will remain in a dense ball—what we call a cannonball—

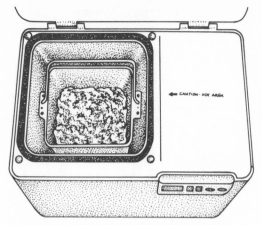

Dry chunks of dough

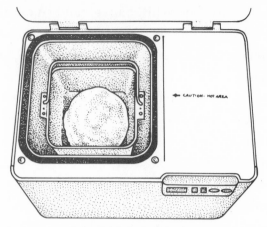

Soft pliable ball of dough

hugging the blade (see illustration). A too-dry dough will crack when baked, not form to the shape of the pan, and not raise sufficiently. The resulting loaf will be dense, close-grained, and heavy. A too-dry dough rarely rises to the top of the pan.

With the *bake* setting, the dough should be soft enough that it relaxes and *very slowly* edges its way to the corners of the pan (see illustration). When the dough begins to rise, it will totally fill the corners of the pan.

The dough produced in the *dough* cycle can be a little drier than that produced on the *bake* setting because it will be removed and shaped by hand and needs to be manageable, not sticky.

If your ingredients have too much liquid, they will not form a ball and will look like a batter instead of dough. Sometimes a too wet dough will raise extremely high then collapse on itself, or it may blow out of the pan in a mushroom shape (see illustrations).

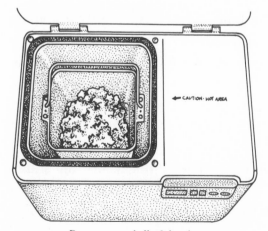

Dense cannonball of dough

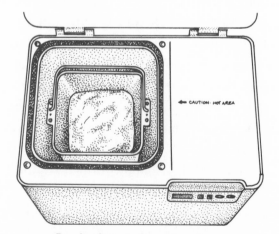

Dough relaxes to the pan's corners

These are also the characteristics of a dough that is too hot. In the summer in a hot kitchen, or in a warm, humid climate save time and trouble by using ice water in the recipe and a little less yeast. If the dough is too wet and sticky, try adding additional flour tablespoon by tablespoon to see if a dough will begin to mass around the blade. If you've added up to four tablespoons of flour and the dough still is too wet, we suggest you remove it from the pan, add enough flour by hand to achieve the proper consistency, then hand knead and bake in the conventional oven as if it were a traditional loaf.

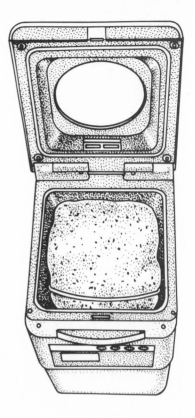

Flours absorb moisture from the air. When we tested recipes in humid regions, we found we had to add an additional 2 tablespoons of flour to several recipes to counterbalance the extra moisture absorbed by the flours and alleviate the sticky dough problem. When using the living organism of yeast and the many different strains and varieties of flour available, remember that no recipe is *ever* set in stone. The humidity, room temperature, ingredient quality, and temperature affect the finished product. With that in mind, please use our recipes as guidelines; experiment with them and make them *your* recipes.

Remember that science and technology can provide guidance only up to a point. You can add the word *about* to the measurements given for yeast in these recipes, because in a hot kitchen you may need less yeast than in a cold kitchen. If your loaf rises insufficiently, you may need to add more yeast. If the loaf overrises, you may need to use less next time. Machine or no machine, computer or no computer, bread making is still more art than science.

Try not to become discouraged with these machines if you have a failure or so in the beginning. With a little patience and practice, your bread machine will become as indispensable as your coffee pot.

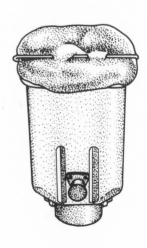

The result of dough that is too wet

BREAD MACHINE BASIC FEATURES COMPARISON CHART

	Panasonic/National 1 pound	Panasonic-National 1½ pound	Sanyo Home Bakery	Seiko MK Home Bakery	Welbilt The Bread Machine	Zojirushi
SIZE						
Bread pan capacity ½ pound (*about 4 servings*)	✔	✔	✔	✔	✔	✔
Bread pan capacity 1 pound (*about 6–8 servings*)	✔	✔	✔	✔	✔	✔
Bread pan capacity 1½ pounds (*about 8–10 servings*)		✔			✔	✔
SHAPE						
Vertical rectangular loaf	✔		✔	✔		✔
Horizontal rectangular loaf		✔				
Cylindrical loaf					✔	
BREAD, DOUGH, AND MISCELLANEOUS SETTINGS						
Basic bread mode	✔	✔	✔	✔	✔	✔
Whole grain mode		✔				
Dough mode	✔	✔	✔	✔	✔	✔
Rapid bake basic bread mode	✔	✔		✔		✔
Raisin bread mode (*permits addition of raisins and other dried fruits and nuts at end of first kneading period*)			✔		✔	✔
French bread mode		✔		✔	✔	✔
Variety bread mode (*yeast breads formed and/or filled after first mixing/raising period and placed back in pan for machine to bake; examples: Raisin Swirl Bread, Monkey Bread, Chinese Steamed Buns*)		✔				
Quick bread mode–totally automatic (*mixes and bakes breads leavened with baking powder or baking soda*)						✔
Quick bread mode—combination (*bakes only; breads leavened with baking soda or baking powder mixed manually and batter poured into baking pan*)		✔				
Manual mode (*allows conversion of personal bread recipes to machine's cycles*)						✔
Cool-down cycle (*enables bread to remain in machine and not become soggy and wet after finished baking*)		✔	✔		✔	✔
Cakes						✔
Jam (*about 2 cups*)						✔

	Panasonic/National 1 pound	Panasonic-National 1½ pound	Sanyo Home Bakery	Seiko MK Home Bakery	Welbilt The Bread Machine	Zojirushi
CRUST SELECTIONS						
Standard	✔	✔	✔	✔	✔	✔
Light	✔	✔				
Crisp	✔	✔				
OTHER FEATURES						
Separate kneading blade (*produces crisp crust*)		✔				
Clear glass viewing window (*allows whole process to be viewed without lifting lid*)			✔		✔	✔
Solid, one-piece bread pan (*can be removed for ease in filling*)	✔	✔	✔	✔		✔
Separate yeast dispenser (*yeast added separately to dispenser instead of mixed in with other ingredients*)	✔	✔				
Kneading pin (*All machines have mixing blades pressing dough; kneading pin pulls it also.*)				✔	✔	✔
Power-outage override (*If power outage or interruption is less than 10 minutes, machine will continue when power is resumed.*)	✔	✔			✔	✔
Measuring cup and spoon	✔	✔	✔	✔		✔
PROGRAMMABLE MEMORY TIMER						
Timer can be set for delayed baking of breads (*up to 13 hours*)	✔	✔	✔	✔	✔	✔
Timer can be set for delayed mixing and first raising of dough (*up to 13 hours*)		✔				
24-hour digital clock						✔
COLOR SELECTION						
White	✔	✔	✔	✔	✔	✔
Other						

Tips for Getting the Most from Your Bread Machine

All of our recipes were tested using active dry yeast. In the beginning, we tried testing with the 50-percent-faster yeast; however, we found that some of the machine cycles did not coincide with the rising rate of the 50-percent-faster active dry yeast. The finished loaves were concave or overrisen and blown out of the bread pan, making the kitchen help extremely cranky when they had to clean the machines! Some manufacturers give directions for using the faster-type yeasts. Their recommendations and directions should be followed when using faster yeasts.

A separate yeast dispenser located on the top of the Panasonic/National machines calls for the yeast to be added after the ingredients have been mixed, heated, and partially kneaded. We could find no advantage to this feature. There is a human tendency to slam the lid and start the machine after the ingredients are added to the pan and then forget to add yeast to the dispenser. We bypassed the dispenser and added the yeast with the other ingredients and found no difference in the final loaf.

When using the delayed timer, however, the dispenser is a plus, because it prevents the liquids from coming into contact with the yeast prematurely, possibly causing an underinflated loaf. When using the timer without the separate yeast dispenser, there is little chance of error if the instructions for layering the ingredients are followed precisely. Always place the yeast into the pan first, then the dry ingredients, and all liquids last.

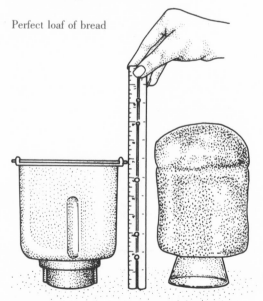

Perfect loaf of bread

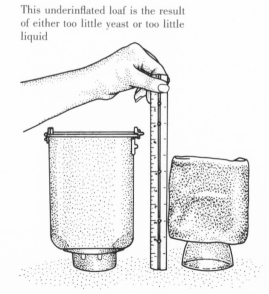

This underinflated loaf is the result of either too little yeast or too little liquid

Several models, Zojirushi, Welbilt, and Sanyo, use a kneading pin in conjunction with the mixing blade. The blade pushes and slaps the dough ball around the pan while the kneading pin pulls it, maximizing the production of gluten. We think this produces a slightly better kneading process, the only drawback being that the removable pin is easy to lose (and the resultant bread has a small hole in its side).

The mixing blade in any bread machine leaves an indentation on the bottom of each loaf baked, and occasionally the blade comes loose and embeds itself in the bottom of the loaf when the bread is removed from the pan. The blade must then be carefully removed from the bottom of the loaf, taking care not to scratch the blade's nonstick surface. The round loaves have a larger indentation in the bottom than the rectangular loaves because their mixing blade is larger and has a slightly different design. We found the easiest way to disengage a stuck blade is to let the bread cool completely and then use your fingers to pull the blade out.

The power-outage override will never be missed until you've been elected to bring the bread to Aunt Grace's surprise birthday dinner party. The bread is in the final 15 minutes of the bake cycle and the kids have been told to get their shoes on and go get in the van, we're just waiting on the bread to finish. *Surprise!* The electricity goes off for just a second and the machine stops dead in its tracks. What to do? Pull the bread out of the machine and try to finish baking it in the conventional oven? Not recommended, but without an override this could happen and did happen to Diana. A machine with the override feature gives you 10 minutes to get some juice to it before it finally gives up. For just a few cents more this feature could be added to all machines and should be. The override feature is found on Welbilt, Zojirushi, and 1½-pound Panasonic/National machines.

If the dough is in the bake cycle when this mishap occurs, you may be able to salvage the bread by baking it in a 375°F conventional oven for the remaining baking time plus an additional 10 minutes. If the machine is in the mixing, kneading, or raising cycle, remove the pan from the machine, cover, and refrigerate. When the power returns, remove the dough from the refrigerator and allow it to return to room temperature, reset the machine, and start over.

The programmable memory timer found in all tested machines is a desirable feature. With it you can delay starting the bread up to about 9 hours and see the finished product in about 13 hours. The machine can be set the night before for delay baking, and you can sleep until your nose tells you it's time to get up. Remember to actually set the machine to be finished about 1 hour before you want to eat it because hot bread is hard to slice. One machine, the 1½-pound Panasonic/National, has this cycle available for the dough setting also, which is extremely handy for dinner. Dough ready to be shaped into rolls or rolled into a pizza crust can be willing and waiting at 5:15 P.M. Just add the ingredients before leaving for work, and it will be ready when you are. Micro-rise for the second rise, and you're out of there!

Outfitting the Kitchen for the Bread Machine

An electric knife is wonderful for slicing fresh bread; however, any knife with a long serrated blade will do. Choose half-moon serrations. Use a gently back and forth sawing motion for a nice even slice. A cooling rack, accurate liquid and dry measuring cups (a liquid measuring cup is included with most machines), and accurate measuring spoons are just about all of the special equipment needed to turn out the perfect loaf.

We believe bread machines will get smarter each year. Our wish list for the machines includes more choice for appliance color, a cycle for doing whole-grain breads (now available on some Panasonic/National models), and perhaps a pasta cycle. We would also like to see a larger optional bread pan with the capacity and power for mixing and kneading 6 to 9 cups of flour. This would allow the baker to use the dough cycle to make large free-form loaves, two loaves baked in a conventional oven, or 3 to 4 dozen rolls.

For us, the bread machine has become as essential as a food processor. We admit it. We're spoiled. We love the smell of home-baked bread. We love the fact that we can have fresh bread every day without too much work. We are hooked on bread machines. We believe you will be too, given software as good as the hardware. We hope you enjoy using the recipes we've devised for the bread machines.

9 ◆ BASIC BREADS

Half-Time Granny's White Bread   252

Sally Lunn   253

Dr. Michael's Yeast Corn Bread   253

Country White Potato Bread   254

Machine Pain de Mie   254

Hands-Off French Bread   255

100% Whole Wheat Bread   256

Narsai David's Light Rye   256

Free-Form French Baguettes   257

Simple Sourdough Bread   258

Simple Sour English Muffins   259

Half-Time Granny's
◇ White Bread ◇

Makes 1 large 1½-pound loaf,
basic bread setting

1¼ C. milk
  2 tbsp. unsalted butter or
     margarine
  2 tbsp. sugar
  1 teas. salt
  3 C. bread flour
2½ teas. active dry yeast

HALF-TIME GRANNY'S WHITE BREAD

Makes one 1-pound loaf, basic bread setting

We wish our grandmothers could see these gleaming white machines in our kitchens that turn out bread as good as many grannies used to make. A crisp golden crust, a white, even crumb, this bread is that slightly sweet, soft bread so prized by hopeful pioneers who thought that dark, whole-grain breads represented a darker, grainier time.

One of the reasons bread machines make such fine, grandmotherly bread is that the long, slow rising periods of the machines give the bread time to develop that aromatic yeasty aroma and taste we've almost forgotten.

Reminds Linda of hot summer afternoons in her grandmother's Kansas ranch kitchen, when the only machines around were the giant red combines out in the golden fields, cutting another crop of wheat. For a grandmother more attuned to feeding a threshing crew than entertaining a child, refreshments for the day were nothing more than a cold drink made from fresh white bread crumbled into an iced-tea glass with sugar sprinkles and brimming with cold milk.

⅞ C. (1 cup minus 2 tbsp.) milk
1½ tbsp. unsalted butter or margarine
1½ tbsp. sugar
¾ teas. salt
2 C. bread flour
1½ teas. active dry yeast

Bake according to manufacturer's instructions for basic white bread with a medium crust. Remove from machine and cool on a rack before slicing. Wrap in aluminum foil to store.

SALLY LUNN

Makes one 1-pound loaf, basic bread setting

Sally Lunn is a sweet yeast batter bread, full of eggs and butter. This loaf is not to be kneaded, but beaten only. It was made for the bread machine because the paddle in the bottom of the pan does a terrific job. History states that Sally lived in England in the eighteenth century, where she baked this bread for all of the townsfolk. Too bad Sally never had a bread machine.

2⅓ C. bread flour	¼ C. (½ stick)
½ teas. salt	unsalted butter
3 tbsp. sugar	¼ C. milk
1½ teas. active dry yeast	¼ C. water
2 large eggs	

1. Process the ingredients according to the manufacturer's instructions for a basic bread setting or a light crust bread setting if your machine has one.
2. Remove the bread from the bread pan to a rack to cool. Wrap in aluminum foil to store.

DR. MICHAEL'S YEAST CORN BREAD

Makes one 1-pound loaf, basic bread setting

Dr. Michael makes this bread every year as a Christmas gift. Lucky we're on his list. Thanks, Dr. Michael.

2½ C. sifted bread flour	⅔ C. milk
⅓ C. cornmeal	2 tbsp. water
½ teas. salt	1 large egg
2 tbsp. sugar	2 teas. active dry yeast
2 tbsp. shortening	

1. Process the ingredients according to the manufacturer's instructions for a basic bread setting.
2. Remove the bread from the bread pan to a rack to cool. Wrap in aluminum foil to store.

◇ Sally Lunn ◇

Makes one 1½-pound loaf, basic bread setting

3¾ C. bread flour
1 teas. salt
⅓ C. sugar
1½–2 teas. active dry yeast
3 large eggs
½ C. (1 stick) butter
½ C. milk
½ C. water

Dr. Michael's Yeast
◇ Corn Bread ◇

Makes one 1½-pound loaf, basic bread setting

3½ C. sifted bread flour
½ C. cornmeal
1 teas. salt
3 tbsp. sugar
3 tbsp. shortening
1 C. milk
⅛ C. water
1 large egg
2½ teas. active dry yeast

Country White
◇ Potato Bread ◇

Makes one 1½-pound loaf, basic bread setting

3 C. bread flour
½ C. potato flour (potato starch) or ½ C. bread flour
¾ C. mashed potato, room temperature (microwave a large potato, cool, peel, and mash)
1 C. water
1½ tbsp. honey
1½ teas. salt
3 tbsp. unsalted butter, room temperature and cut into bits
⅓ C. instant nonfat dry milk solids
1½ teas. active dry yeast

COUNTRY WHITE POTATO BREAD

Makes one 1-pound loaf, basic bread setting

High rising with a crisp crust, this loaf gets its wonderful flavor from mashed potatoes and potato starch.

2 C. bread flour
⅓ C. potato flour (potato starch) or ⅓ C. bread flour
⅓ C. mashed potatoes, room temperature (microwave a medium potato, cool, peel, and mash)
⅞ C. (1 cup minus 2 tbsp.) water
1½ tbsp. honey
1 teas. salt
2 tbsp. unsalted butter, room temperature and cut into bits
⅓ C. instant nonfat dry milk solids
¾–1 teas. active dry yeast

1. Process the ingredients according to the manufacturer's instructions for a basic bread setting.
2. Remove the bread from the bread pan to a rack to cool. Wrap in aluminum foil to store.

Machine Pain de
◇ Mie ◇

Makes one 1½-pound loaf, basic bread setting

3¼ C. bread flour
¾ C. semolina flour
2¼ tbsp. sugar
1½ teas. salt
⅔ C. instant dry milk solids
2 tbsp. unsalted butter
1¼ C. plus 3 tbsp. water
1½–2 teas. active dry yeast

MACHINE PAIN DE MIE

Makes one 1-pound loaf, basic bread setting

The soft, white sandwich bread of France, noted for its thin, crisp crust and tender, white crumb can be nearly duplicated in a bread machine. The addition of semolina flour seems to give the bread that close, even grain required for this type of bread. If the pan of your bread machine is a vertical rectangle, all you have to do is cut off the "hat," or top of the bread, and you'll have that splendid shape so favored by the French. You can slice this bread as thin as you like; you can use it for canapés or fancy sandwiches; you can make melbas or croutons from it once it's 2 or 3 days old.

2 C. bread flour
½ C. semolina flour
1½ tbsp. sugar
1 teas. salt
⅓ C. instant nonfat
    dry milk solids

1 tbsp. unsalted butter
⅞ C. (1 cup minus 2
    tablespoons) water
1–1½ teas. active dry yeast

1. Place all the ingredients in the bread pan and process on the standard bread setting.

2. Remove bread from the pan and cool on a rack. Wrap in a plastic bag or foil to store.

HANDS-OFF FRENCH BREAD

Makes one 1-pound loaf, French bread or basic bread setting

Who would have believed we would see the day when we could have French bread and never touch the dough until we were ready to taste the finished product? Abracadabra, now we can. We admit this doesn't look like traditional French bread, but it has a definite Gallic taste and texture. If your machine has a French bread setting, or a crisp crust setting, use it. It takes a little longer, but it's definitely worth it. If you don't have the crisper settings, don't worry; you will still love the bread and all the time the machine saved while it worked and you played.

3 C. bread flour
1 C. water
1 teas. salt

1 teas. sugar
2 teas. active dry yeast

1. Process the ingredients according to manufacturer's instructions for basic bread or a French bread or crisper crust setting.

2. Remove the bread from the bread pan to a rack to cool. Wrap in a paper bag to store.

Hands-Off French ◇ Bread ◇

Makes one 1½-pound loaf, French bread or basic bread setting

4 C. bread flour
1⅓ C. water
1 teas. salt
1 teas. sugar
2½ teas. active dry yeast

Tomato-Basil ◇ Bruschetta ◇

Serves 4 in 10 minutes

Make this bruschetta with summer's sun-ripened tomatoes and fresh basil.

4 large Roma tomatoes,
    seeded and diced
¼ C. fresh basil leaves,
    chopped
⅓ C. olive oil
½ fennel bulb, trimmed and
    diced
Salt and freshly ground black
    pepper to taste
Four 1-inch-thick slices
    Hands-Off French Bread
4 small cloves garlic,
    flattened

Combine first 4 ingredients in a medium bowl. Season to taste with salt and pepper. Toast bread slices. Rub each bread slice on both sides with one garlic clove. Transfer bread slices to serving plates. Spread each bread slice with ¼ of the tomato mixture. Cut each bread slice into 4 triangles and serve.

100% Whole Wheat ◇ Bread ◇

Makes one 1½-pound loaf, whole wheat or basic bread setting

    3 C. plus 3 tbsp. whole
       wheat flour
    ⅓ C. plus 3 tbsp. instant
       nonfat dry milk solids
    3 tbsp. honey
    1¼ teas. salt
    4½ tbsp. unsalted butter,
       room temperature and
       cut into bits
    1⅓ C. water
    2½–3 teas. active dry yeast

We recommend 2½ teaspoons of yeast if your bread pan is a horizontal shape and 3 teaspoons of yeast if your bread pan is shaped vertically.

Narsai David's ◇ Light Rye ◇

Makes one 1½-pound loaf, basic bread setting

    ¾ C. medium rye flour
    2 C. bread flour
    1 teas. salt
    2 tbsp. caraway seeds
    1 tbsp. vegetable oil
    1 tbsp. molasses
    1 C. water
    2½–3 teas. active dry yeast

100% WHOLE WHEAT BREAD

Makes one 1-pound loaf, whole wheat or basic bread setting

Our variation of whole wheat bread never fails to please. Its texture is tender and light due to the long raising period.

2⅓ C. whole wheat flour
  ⅓ C. instant nonfat
     dry milk solids
  2 tbsp. honey
  1 teas. salt
  3 tbsp. unsalted
     butter, room
     temperature and cut
     into bits
  ⅞ C. (1 cup minus 2
     tablespoons) water
  1½–2 teas. active dry
     yeast

1. Process the ingredients according to manufacturer's instructions for a whole wheat or basic bread setting.

2. Remove the bread from the bread pan to a rack to cool. Wrap in aluminum foil to store.

NARSAI DAVID'S LIGHT RYE

Makes one 1-pound loaf, basic bread setting

Narsai David featured this excellent rye bread recipe in his *San Francisco Chronicle* column, "California Cuisine."

  ½ C. medium rye
     flour
  1½ C. bread flour
  ¾ teas. salt
  1 tbsp. caraway
     seeds
  2 teas. vegetable oil
  2 teas. molasses
  ¾ C. water
  2–2½ teas. active dry
     yeast

1. Process the ingredients according to the manufacturer's instructions for a basic bread setting.

2. Remove the bread from the bread pan to a rack to cool. Wrap in aluminum foil or a paper bag to store.

FREE-FORM FRENCH BAGUETTES

Makes 1 large baguette or 2 small baguettes, dough setting

An all-purpose baguette is made easily when combining the mixing and kneading capabilities of the machine and the baking qualities of a stone (see pages 21–25).

2½ C. bread flour
½ C. medium rye flour
2 teas. salt

1 cup plus 2 tbsp. water
1½ teas. active dry yeast

1. Process the ingredients according to your manufacturer's instructions for a dough setting.

2. Remove the dough to a lightly floured surface and knead for a few seconds to remove any remaining air bubbles. Cover the dough with an inverted bowl and set aside to rest for 10 minutes. Meanwhile, lightly sprinkle a pizza peel (see page 24) with cornmeal and preheat the oven to 450°F with the stone or baking tiles in place on the bottom rack.

3. When the bread has rested for 10 minutes, remove the bowl and form the dough into 1 large or 2 small baguettes (see page 42). Place the baguettes on the prepared peel and cover with a damp tea towel, plastic wrap, or waxed paper. Set the dough in a warm, draft-free place to raise until doubled in bulk, about 40 to 50 minutes.

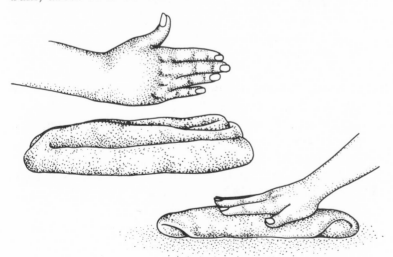

(continued)

Herb's Herbed Croutons with ◇ Cheese ◇

Makes 3½ cups in 20 minutes

When the herb garden and bread box are overflowing, make these croutons for serving on your favorite mixed green salad (we love the greens in a Mesclun mix, fresh greens plucked and packed with edible flowers). Serve with a salad dressing composed of 3 parts olive oil, 1 part balsamic vinegar, and a sprinkling of sesame seeds.

1 small Free-Form French Baguette
¼ C. olive oil
1 large clove garlic, crushed
2 teas. fresh thyme, minced
2 teas. fresh basil, minced
2 teas. fresh oregano, minced
¼ teas. salt
½ teas. freshly ground black pepper
2 tbsp. freshly grated Parmesan or Romano

1. Preheat the oven to 350°F. Cube the baguette, crust and all, into 1-inch cubes (about 3½ cups) and place in a large bowl.

2. In a small skillet pour in the olive oil and heat over a medium flame for 1 minute. Add the garlic, herbs, salt, and pepper. Sauté for 5 minutes. Remove from heat. Add the oil mixture to the bread cubes and toss.

3. Spread the croutons in a single layer on a large baking sheet. Bake on the middle rack of the preheated oven for 10 minutes. Sprinkle the croutons with the cheese and bake for an additional 5 minutes or until golden brown. Bring to room temperature before serving on salad. The croutons will keep in a plastic bag in the refrigerator for up to 1 week.

The cowboy cook who made his starter in a 5-gallon nail keg might have added a little vinegar or maybe a po-tat-er, if he could lay hands on one. He stirred his mixture, put his hat over it, and set it out in the sun to ferment. If it got too cold at night, he took the danged thing to bed with him so it wouldn't quit working. Once the starter was bubbling good, he'd start in making bread for the boys, a durn sight better—he wuz quick to tell you—than "bacon" powder biskits.

Simple Sourdough ◇ Bread ◇

Makes one 1½-pound loaf, basic bread setting

- 3 C. bread flour
- 1 teas. salt
- 1 teas. sugar
- ½ C. Easy Sourdough Starter for Bread and Biscuits (see page 259)
- 1 C. water
- 1 tbsp. active dry yeast

4. When the baguettes have doubled in bulk, remove the covering and cut 3 diagonal slashes across the tops with a razor blade or sharp knife. Spray the baguettes lightly with water and, with a quick jerking motion, place the baguettes on the hot stone. Bake the baguettes at 450°F for 10 minutes and then reduce the temperature to 375°F and bake for an additional 30 minutes.

5. Carefully remove the baguettes from the stone to a rack to cool. Serve warm or room temperature. These are best served the same day as made.

SIMPLE SOURDOUGH BREAD

Makes one 1-pound loaf, basic bread setting

Some of the machine manufacturers say, "Hey, we can't make sourdough, there isn't a long enough rising period on our machine." We didn't have any problem with the standard 4-hour bread cycle when we eliminated the sponge process called for in some sourdough methods and used our favorite cowboy starter instead.

- 2 C. bread flour
- ¾ teas. salt
- ¾ teas. sugar
- ⅓ C. Easy Sourdough Starter for Bread and Biscuits (see page 259)
- ⅔ C. water
- 2–2½ teas. active dry yeast

1. Add all of the ingredients to the bread pan, including the yeast.

2. Process the ingredients according to your manufacturer's instructions for a basic bread setting or a French bread setting if your machine has one.

3. Remove the bread from the bread pan to a rack to cool. Wrap in aluminum foil or a paper bag to store.

SIMPLE SOUR ENGLISH MUFFINS

Makes 1 dozen muffins in the 1-pound machine, dough setting

Baking with sourdough becomes addictive. We found these muffins, creamy on the inside, golden brown on the outside, to be main-line satisfaction. Do try them with our version of Eggs Sardou.

3¾ **C. bread flour**
½ **C. Easy Sourdough Starter for Bread and Biscuits**
1 **C. warm milk (about 100°F)**
¼ **C. water**
2½ **teas. active dry yeast**
1 **tbsp. sugar**
¾ **teas. salt**
Cornmeal, for sprinkling on top

1. Process the ingredients according to your manufacturer's instructions for a dough setting.

2. Lightly coat a large microwavable baking sheet with cornmeal. Turn the dough out onto a lightly floured surface and knead for a few seconds, adding flour if necessary to prevent the dough from sticking. Roll out or pat the dough until it is about ½ inch thick.

3. Cut the dough into rounds with a 3-inch cookie cutter. Place the rounds on the baking sheet about 2 inches apart. (Make sure the muffins will not touch after rising or they will deflate when you try to pull them apart.) Sprinkle the tops lightly with cornmeal. Place the muffins in the microwave. Prepare to micro-rise.

4. Lower the microwave power to the appropriate micro-rise setting (see page 35). Place an 8-ounce glass of water in the microwave. Heat for 3 minutes. Rest for 3 minutes.

5. Meanwhile, preheat a lightly greased griddle to medium or a lightly greased large skillet to low. Very carefully transfer the muffins to the griddle or skillet and cook until golden brown, about 10 to 12 minutes on each side.

6. Cool on a metal rack. Split muffins in half, toast, and serve with your favorite toppings. Wrap in aluminum foil to store.

Easy Sourdough Starter for Bread, Muffins, and ◇ Biscuits ◇

OUR VERSION

Makes 1½ cups in 18–24 hours

1 **C. skim milk or low-fat milk**
3 **tbsp. plain yogurt**
1 **C. unbleached white flour**

1. In the microwave, heat the milk to 90°F to 100°F. Remove from the microwave and stir in the yogurt. Pour the mixture into a 1½-quart glass or plastic container. Cover tightly and let stand in a warm place. Temperatures of 80°F to 100°F are ideal (we use the top of the water heater). An oven with the light turned on also works. After about 18 to 24 hours, the starter should be about the consistency of yogurt (a curd forms and the mixture takes on the appearance of yogurt).

2. After a curd has formed, stir in the flour and blend well. Cover loosely with cheesecloth or plastic wrap and let stand in the warm place until the mixture is full of bubbles and has a good sour smell; usually 2 to 4 days.

3. Stir the clear mixture you see forming back down into the starter and refrigerate, tightly covered. *However*, if your sponge turns pink, throw it out, and start over.

4. When you use some of the sponge, replace what you've taken out with equal parts flour and water; let it stand overnight in a warm place again before you refrigerate.

10 ◆ FITNESS, HEALTH, AND HIGH-FIBER BREADS

Light White Bread   261

Salt-Free Potato Bread   261

Seven-Grain Wheat Bread   262

Whole Wheat Cottage Bread   263

Scotland Oat Bread   264

Whole Wheat Beer Bread   264

Birdseed Bread   265

LIGHT WHITE BREAD

Makes one 1-pound loaf, basic bread setting

We make this bread after New Year's to help trim the waistline. It makes an excellent base for all of those diet sandwiches and toasts beautifully. Slice the bread thin to keep the calorie count low.

2 C. bread flour
1 tbsp. sugar
1 teas. salt
1 tbsp. instant nonfat dry milk solids

⅞ C. (1 cup minus 2 tbsp.) water
½ tbsp. unsalted butter or margarine
1½ teas. active dry yeast

1. Process the ingredients according to your manufacturer's instructions for a basic bread setting.
2. Remove the bread from the bread pan to a rack to cool. Wrap in aluminum foil to store.

Light White ◇ Bread ◇

Makes one 1½-pound loaf, basic bread setting

3 C. bread flour
1½ tbsp. sugar
1½ teas. salt
2 tbsp. instant nonfat dry milk solids
1⅓ C. water
1 tbsp. unsalted butter or margarine
2 teas. active dry yeast

SALT-FREE POTATO BREAD

Makes one 1-pound loaf, basic bread setting

The sodium is missing in this bread so the mellow taste of the potato shines through. Chopped, fresh herbs or the minced zest of lemons, limes, or grapefruits may be added if you like a little more punch.

2 teas. active dry yeast
1½ teas. sugar
2 C. bread flour
½ C. plus 1 tbsp. water
1 tbsp. vegetable oil

¼ C. potato, baked, peeled, and cooled
1 tbsp. instant nonfat dry milk solids

1. Process the ingredients according to your manufacturer's instructions for a basic bread setting. This bread may also be used on a light crust setting if your machine has one.
2. Remove the bread from the bread pan to a rack to cool. Wrap in aluminum foil or a paper bag to store.

Salt-Free Potato ◇ Bread ◇

Makes one 1½-pound loaf, basic bread setting

2½ teas. active dry yeast
1 tbsp. sugar
3½ C. bread flour
1 C. plus 1 tbsp. water
2 tbsp. vegetable oil
⅓ C. potato, baked, peeled, and cooled
2 tbsp. instant nonfat dry milk solids

Makes one 1½-pound loaf, whole wheat or basic bread setting

2½–3 teas. active dry yeast
   3 tbsp. gluten flour
1½ C. bread flour
1½ C. whole wheat flour
 ½ C. 7-grain or 5-grain cereal
 ⅓ C. instant nonfat dry milk solids
 ¼ C. wheat germ
  1 teas. salt
 ⅛ C. (2 tbsp.) vegetable oil
1½ C. water

SEVEN-GRAIN WHEAT BREAD

Makes one 1-pound loaf, whole wheat or basic bread setting

This wheat bread is made with seven-grain hot cereal available in supermarkets, health food stores, and specialty food stores. The cereal consists of stone-ground wheat, rye, triticale, oats, rice, flaxseeds, and barley. Using a blend of the different grains gives a much better flavor than using just one of the grains.

2–2½ teas. active dry yeast	¼ C. instant nonfat dry milk solids
2 tbsp. gluten flour	2 tbsp. wheat germ
1 C. bread flour	¾ teas. salt
1 C. whole wheat flour	1½ tbsp. vegetable oil
⅓ C. 7-grain or 5-grain cereal	1 C. water

1. Add all of the ingredients to the bread pan, including the yeast. Process the ingredients according to the manufacturer's instructions for whole wheat or basic bread setting.

2. Remove the bread from the bread pan to a rack to cool. Wrap in aluminum foil or a paper bag to store.

WHOLE WHEAT COTTAGE BREAD

Makes one 1-pound loaf, whole wheat or basic bread setting

Using low-fat cottage cheese and canola oil along with whole wheat flour will give you a healthy, whole-meal bread that serves well for sandwiches or, toasted, for breakfast. Low in cholesterol, high in complex carbohydrates, it even tastes good. Delete the salt if you wish. Vary the flavor by exchanging the onion and poppy seeds for the mixed fresh herbs of your choice.

¼ C. hot tap water	1½ tbsp. honey
1 large egg	1 tbsp. poppy seeds
1 tbsp. canola oil	¾ teas. salt, optional
¾ C. low-fat cottage cheese	⅓ teas. baking soda
2 tbsp. minced fresh onion	2 C. whole wheat flour
	2 tbsp. gluten flour
	1½ teas. active dry yeast

1. Process the ingredients according to manufacturer's instructions for whole wheat or basic bread setting.

2. Remove the bread from the pan to a rack immediately after the beeper sounds to cool. Wrap in foil to store.

Whole Wheat
◇ Cottage Bread ◇

Makes one 1½-pound loaf, whole wheat or basic bread setting

½ C. hot tap water
1 large egg
2 tbsp. canola oil
1 C. low-fat cottage cheese
¼ C. minced fresh onion
2 tbsp. honey
1½ tbsp. poppy seeds
1½ teas. salt, optional
½ teas. baking soda
3 C. whole wheat flour
3 tbsp. gluten flour
2 teas. active dry yeast

Scotland Oat
◇ Bread ◇

Makes one 1½-pound loaf, whole wheat or basic bread setting

2½ C. bread flour or 1 C.
  bread flour plus 1½ C.
  oat flour
1½ C. whole wheat flour
 ¾ C. oat bran (oat-bran hot
  cereal)
 3 tbsp. gluten flour
 2 teas. salt
 3 tbsp. canola oil or
  safflower oil or any
  100%-vegetable oil
 ¼ C. water
1½ C. milk
 3 tbsp. honey
 3 teas. active dry yeast

SCOTLAND OAT BREAD

Makes one 1-pound loaf, whole wheat or basic bread setting

If you are a disciple of oat bran, then this bread is for you. Skip the commercial oat-bran breads with eggs and saturated fats. Fight cholesterol with this great-tasting loaf of oats.

1¼ C. bread flour or	2 tbsp. canola oil or
¾ C. bread flour	safflower oil or any
plus ½ C. oat flour	100%-vegetable
1 C. whole wheat	oil
flour	⅛ C. (2 tbsp.) water
¾ C. oat bran	1 C. milk
(oat-bran hot cereal)	3 tbsp. honey
2 tbsp. gluten flour	1¾–2 teas. active dry
1½ teas. salt	yeast

1. Add all of the ingredients to the bread pan, including the yeast. Process the ingredients according to manufacturer's instructions for whole wheat or basic bread setting.
2. Remove the bread from the bread pan to a rack to cool. Wrap in aluminum foil or a paper bag to store.

Whole Wheat
◇ Beer Bread ◇

Makes one large 1½-pound loaf, whole wheat or basic bread setting

 ⅞ C. (1 C. minus 2 tbsp.)
  beer
 1 large egg
 2 tbsp. canola oil
 2 tbsp. sugar
 1 teas. salt
 2 C. bread flour
 1 C. whole wheat flour
 3 tbsp. sunflower seeds
2½ teas. active dry yeast

WHOLE WHEAT BEER BREAD

Makes one 1-pound loaf, whole wheat or basic bread setting

A great bread for sandwiches or toast, this close-grained whole wheat bread owes its crunch and its nutrition to a generous sprinkling of sunflower seeds.

⅝ C. (½ C. plus 1	¾ teas. salt
tbsp.) beer	1¼ C. bread flour
1 large egg	¾ C. whole wheat flour
1½ tbsp. canola oil	2 tbsp. sunflower seeds
1½ tbsp. sugar	1½ teas. active dry yeast

Bake according to manufacturer's instructions for basic bread. Cool on a rack before slicing. Wrap in plastic to store.

BIRDSEED BREAD

Makes one 1-pound free-form loaf, dough setting

Keith, one precocious 4-year-old, calls this birdseed bread. It is a twin brother to Gold-Dust Loaf (see page 92). We think it is one of the best go-with-soup breads. We give directions for the dough setting; it can be made and baked in either the 1 or 1½-pound machine with no changes, however, the flavor will not be the same. Serve warm.

2½ teas. active dry yeast	⅓ C. millet
¾ C. water	⅓ C. yellow cornmeal
3 tbsp. honey	2 tbsp. vegetable oil
1½ C. bread flour	1 teas. salt
½ C. whole wheat flour	

1. Process the ingredients according to your manufacturer's instructions for a dough setting. Meanwhile, lightly grease a baking sheet (microwavable if you are micro-rising).

2. Remove the dough to a lightly floured surface and knead for a few seconds to remove any remaining air bubbles. Shape into a ball and flatten slightly with the palm of your hand. Place on the prepared baking sheet. Cover loosely with a damp tea towel or plastic wrap and set aside to rise in a warm, draft-free area until doubled in bulk, about 1 hour, or you may micro-rise (see page 35). Meanwhile preheat the oven to 375°F.

3. When the dough has doubled in bulk, score the top with a sharp knife or razor blade being held at a 45-degree angle to the bread. Bake the bread on the middle rack of the preheated oven for 30 minutes or until the loaf sounds hollow when tapped.

4. Transfer from the baking sheet to a rack to cool. Wrap in a plastic bag to store.

11 ◆ BREAKFAST AND BRUNCH BREADS

Beginner's Brioche 267

Sweet Sunday Honey Buns 268

Pecan-Date Swirl Loaf 269

Blueberry Granola Breakfast Bread 270

Black Walnut–Banana Bread 271

Apricot–Cream Cheese Braid 272

Pain Perdu 274

BEGINNER'S BRIOCHE

Makes 1 dozen brioche rolls, dough setting

Brioche Bread Pudding with Bourbon Sauce (see page 233) is a heavenly way to use up leftover brioche.

Classic brioche is hard to handle: sticky, greasy, a dough that's best left to experts. A natural for the bread machine, it leaves nothing for the cook but shaping the dough—the fun part. This brioche can be made into the classic topknotted French breakfast roll or can be rolled flat to form the basis for Provence-style pizza, Pissaladière (see page 296).

*¼ C. hot tap water
(120°F)*
3 large eggs
2¼ tbsp. sugar
½ teas. salt
3 C. bread flour
*1 C. (2 sticks) unsalted
butter, cut into small
pieces*

*1½–2 teas. active dry
yeast*

Glaze
*1 egg yolk, whisked
with 1 tbsp. cold
water*

1. Use the dough setting of the bread machine and process as directed.

2. Butter generously a dozen brioche molds or custard or muffin cups. Pinch off about ¾ cup of the dough and set aside. Divide the remaining dough into 12 equal-sized pieces.

3. To shape brioches, butter your hands generously, then shape each piece of dough into a golf-ball-sized ball. Place each golf ball of dough into the mold. Then roll the reserved dough into a dozen marble-sized balls. Using your thumb, make a deep indentation in the top of each larger dough ball and firmly press the smaller ball atop.

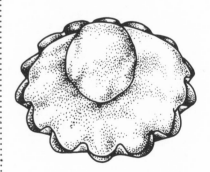

4. Cover the molds lightly with waxed paper and raise rolls until doubled in bulk in a warm, draft-free place, under an hour. If using microwavable molds, micro-rise (see page 35). Meanwhile, preheat the oven to 425°F.

5. When the rolls have risen, brush lightly with the egg-yolk glaze, taking care that the glaze doesn't slip into the mold (it sticks).

6. Bake brioches for 12 to 15 minutes, until puffed and browned, then reduce the oven temperature to 350°F and cook 10 minutes more.

7. Remove the brioches from the oven and let them cool in the pans about 5 minutes before removing to a rack. Wrap in foil to store.

Bread and
◇ Chocolate ◇

This same sweet, soft dough makes an excellent bread to fold around chocolate for breakfast or for tea. If you wish, you can even spread a few tablespoons of raspberry jam or orange marmalade onto the dough before sprinkling with chocolate. This is just too decadent and delicious. Kids of all ages love it. Make the bread in mini-loaf pans if you have them, otherwise try a Texas (large) muffin tin, or a standard loaf pan, adjusting time upward to 35 minutes for a big loaf.

> 1 recipe sweet dough (see Sweet Sunday Honey Buns)
> 4 tbsp. raspberry jam or orange marmalade (optional)
> ½ C. semisweet chocolate morsels

Glaze
> 1 egg, whisked with 1 tbsp. milk
> Turbinado sugar or brown sugar, for sprinkling on top

1. Prepare the dough using the dough setting as instructed in step 1 for Sweet Sunday Honey Buns.

2. Meanwhile, preheat the oven to 350°F. Then grease four 2½ × 4-inch miniature loaf pans. Set aside.

3. When the dough has completed the first rise, turn out onto a well-floured breadboard. The dough will be quite soft and may be sticky. Knead a few seconds, then roll out onto a rectangle about 10 × 8 × ¾ inches. Cut into 4 equal pieces about 2½ × 8 × ¾ inches. Spread with jam or marmalade if desired, then scatter chocolate morsels evenly over the surface of each rectangle and roll up the loaves, jelly-roll fashion.

SWEET SUNDAY HONEY BUNS

Makes 1 dozen buns, dough setting

Acousin to the sticky bun, these sweet, rich pinwheels are best if served the day they are made. Use the delayed start and the dough setting on the bread machine before you go to bed on Saturday night, then you can shape the final buns, raise, and bake them within an hour come Sunday morning.

Sweet Dough
> 1 C. minus 1 tbsp. warm water
> 2 tbsp. sugar
> 1 large egg
> 3 tbsp. nonfat dry milk solids
> ¼ C. (1 stick) unsalted butter
> ½ tbsp. lemon zest
> ½ teas. salt
> 2½ C. plus 2 tbsp. bread flour
> 2½ teas. 50% faster active dry yeast

Filling
> ½ C. firmly packed light brown sugar
> 1 teas. ground cinnamon
> ½ C. currants or raisins

Topping
> ½ C. (1 stick) butter
> ½ C. firmly packed brown sugar
> ⅓ C. mild honey
> ½ C. pecans

1. Use the dough setting on the bread machine and combine the first nine ingredients for the sweet dough. Process according to manufacturer's instructions for the dough setting.

2. Meanwhile combine in a small bowl the filling ingredients of brown sugar, cinnamon, and currants or raisins and set aside.

3. In a microwavable glass bowl, make the topping. Melt the ½ cup butter (15 seconds on high power in the microwave), then combine about half (¼ cup) of it with the brown sugar and honey. Stir to mix thoroughly. Prepare a 12-muffin tin by buttering each cup generously with some of the reserved melted butter. Set aside remaining butter for brushing over tops of the buns.

4. Place a heaping teaspoon of the brown sugar–honey butter in the bottom of each muffin cup. Top with a teaspoon of pecans. Set aside. Preheat the oven to 350°F.

5. When the dough cycle is complete, turn the dough out onto a well-floured surface. The dough will be quite soft and perhaps a little sticky. Flour your hands, then knead the dough a few seconds. With a floured rolling pin, roll the dough into about an 8 × 12-inch rectangle.

6. Sprinkle the filling mixture onto the dough. Then, from the long side, roll the dough into a jelly roll, pinching ends shut. Now cut dough into 12 equal pieces and place each piece, cut side down, into a prepared muffin cup. Pat down to seat firmly in the muffin tin.

7. Brush the tops with the remaining reserved melted butter, then place in a warm, draft-free place and raise until doubled in bulk, about 25 minutes. If you're using a microwavable muffin pan, you can micro-rise (see page 35).

8. Bake buns in the preheated oven until browned and bubbly, about 25 minutes.

9. Immediately invert the muffin pan onto a sheet of plastic wrap. Scoop any remaining hot pecan-honey butter onto the rolls. Serve warm. Store in plastic wrap.

4. Place each miniature loaf of bread, seam side down, into a small loaf pan and set aside to raise until doubled in bulk in a warm, draft-free place, about 25 minutes.

5. Brush egg-milk glaze gently on raised loaves. Discard any remaining egg-milk mixture. Sprinkle the tops of the loaves with turbinado or brown sugar. Bake in the preheated oven about 25 minutes or until golden brown.

6. Carefully turn out onto a rack to cool for about 10 minutes before serving. Slice each miniature loaf into several pieces.

PECAN-DATE SWIRL LOAF

Makes 1 large loaf, dough setting

Reminiscent of the popular quick bread, this bread has a filling chock-full of pecans and dates. A food processor makes chopping the filling a breeze. The tender wheat dough is so delicious it would be wonderful just by itself.

2 C. bread flour
1 C. whole wheat flour
2 tbsp. sugar
2 teas. salt
3 tbsp. unsalted butter
or margarine
2 teas. grated lemon
zest
⅓ C. milk
½ C. plus 2 tbsp. water
2½ teas. active dry yeast

Pecan-Date Filling
⅔ C. coarsely chopped
pecans
1 C. coarsely chopped
dates
⅓ C. firmly packed
light brown sugar
⅔ C. water
4 teas. fresh lemon
juice

Softened cream cheese is the spread of choice for this bread. We serve the bread for afternoon tea in the garden with several different spreads, crème fraîche, and candied cranberry conserve. If you can find prepared Nesselrode sauce in your area, try mixing ½ cup of the sauce with 8 ounces of softened cream cheese. Toast the pecan-date bread and use the Nesselrode cream cheese for a true English tea spread.

(continued)

1. Add the flours, sugar, salt, butter or margarine, lemon zest, milk, water, and yeast to the bread pan. Process the ingredients according to the manufacturer's instructions for a dough setting.

2. For the filling, combine all the filling ingredients in a medium saucepan; bring to a boil over medium heat, stirring constantly so that the filling does not burn. Continue boiling, about 3 minutes or until the mixture is thick enough to spread. Set aside to cool. Grease well a 9 × 5 × 3-inch loaf plan (use a microwavable pan if you are micro-rising).

3. When the dough cycle is finished, turn the dough out onto a lightly floured surface. Knead the dough for a few seconds to remove any remaining air bubbles.

4. Roll the dough into a 12 × 9-inch rectangle; spread with the pecan-date filling. Roll the dough into a roll 9 inches long; pinch the edges to seal.

5. Place the roll in the prepared pan, seam side down. Cover with a piece of waxed paper and set aside in a warm, draft-free place to rise until 1 inch above the top of the pan, about 1 hour, or micro-rise (see page 35). Meanwhile, preheat the oven to 400°F.

6. Bake the loaf on the middle rack of the preheated oven for 25 minutes or until the bread taps hollow.

7. Very carefully turn the bread out onto a rack to cool. Wrap in aluminum foil to store.

BLUEBERRY GRANOLA BREAKFAST BREAD

Makes one 1-pound loaf, basic bread setting

Here's a good choice for the delay timer on a bread machine. Set the machine to begin about 4½ hours before you want breakfast, and you're nearly there for fresh, hot breakfast bread. Serve with a bowl of fresh blueberries, maple sugar, and cream. Cup of hot coffee.

We made this using blueberry granola. Vary the granola according to what's available or what you like. If you wish to add fresh or canned blueberries to the bread, use the raisin bread setting on your machine and brace yourself for a bread the color of shirt-boards dotted with deep purple flecks. We prefer using dried blueberries in the granola. Then we get a golden loaf with blue flecks.

Blueberry Granola Breakfast ◇ Bread ◇

Makes one 1½-pound loaf, basic bread setting

1⅛ C. (1 C. plus 2 tbsp.) water
1½ tbsp. unsalted butter or margarine
2 tbsp. dark brown sugar
1 teas. salt
2⅔ C. bread flour
1 tbsp. whole wheat flour
1 tbsp. wheat germ
½ C. dry milk
½ C. blueberry granola or granola of your choice
1 tbsp. active dry yeast

¾ C. plus 1 tbsp. water
1 tbsp. unsalted butter or margarine
1 tbsp. dark brown sugar
¾ teas. salt
2 C. bread flour
1 tbsp. whole wheat flour
1 tbsp. wheat germ
⅓ C. instant nonfat dry milk solids
⅓ C. blueberry granola or granola of your choice
1½ teas. active dry yeast

1. Make according to the manufacturer's instructions for basic bread, or follow instructions for delayed timing.

2. Remove the bread from the bread pan to a rack to cool. Wrap in aluminum foil.

BLACK WALNUT–BANANA BREAD

Makes one 1-pound loaf, basic bread setting

Black Walnut–Banana Bread is for those mornings when there's no time for cornflakes. Just grab a big slice and go. Slice the bananas right into the pan as if you were slicing them onto breakfast cereal.

2¼ C. bread flour
2 tbsp. unsalted butter or margarine
1 small ripe banana, sliced
¼ C. sugar
½ teas. salt
2½ teas. active dry yeast
⅛ C. (2 tbsp.) water
⅛ C. (2 tbsp.) milk
1 large egg
½ C. chopped black walnuts or pecans

1. Add the flour, butter or margarine, banana, sugar, salt, yeast, water, milk, and egg to the bread pan. Process the ingredients according to your manufacturer's instructions for a basic bread setting or a raisin bread setting.

2. Add the nuts to the dough at the beginning of the second kneading cycle of your machine. This keeps them from being pulverized; or if your machine has a raisin bread cycle, add the nuts when you are supposed to add the raisins.

3. Remove the bread from the bread pan to a rack to cool. Wrap in aluminum foil or a paper bag to store.

Black Walnut–
◇ Banana Bread ◇

Makes one 1½-pound loaf, basic bread setting

3 C. bread flour
3 tbsp. unsalted butter or margarine
1 small ripe banana, sliced
⅓ C. sugar
1 teas. salt
2½–3 teas. active dry yeast
¼ C. water
¼ C. milk
1 large egg
⅓ C. chopped black walnuts or pecans

APRICOT–CREAM CHEESE BRAID

Makes 1 coffee cake, dough setting

This braid is made from a very moist and soft dough with a combination of 2 fillings, a cream cheese filling and an apricot filling. The dough can be made the night before and refrigerated and then filled, raised, and baked the next morning.

The filling in this bread can be changed to suit your whim. We tried dried sour cherries from Michigan and dried blueberries. Prunes would be another good candidate, or perhaps dried peaches. You will have to adjust the sugar accordingly. Some of these fruits have more natural sugar than others.

Dough
- 1/2 C. sour cream
- 1/4 C. sugar
- 1/4 C. (1/2 stick) unsalted butter, melted
- 1/2 teas. salt
- 2 1/2 teas. active dry yeast
- 1/4 C. water
- 1 egg
- 2 C. bread flour

Cream Cheese Filling
- 4 oz. cream cheese, room temperature
- 3 tbsp. sugar
- 1 large egg
- 1/2 teas. vanilla extract

Apricot Filling
- 8-ounce package dried apricots
- 3/4 C. water
- 1/3 C. sugar
- 1/4 teas. ground cinnamon

Glaze
- 1 C. confectioners' sugar
- 2 tbsp. sour cream
- 1/2 teas. vanilla extract

1. Process the dough ingredients according to your manufacturer's instructions for a dough setting. Meanwhile, prepare the fillings and glaze.

2. Process all of the cream cheese filling ingredients in a food processor or electric mixer until smooth. Set aside.

3. Prepare the apricot filling. In a 4-cup glass measure, bring the apricots and water to a low boil in the microwave set on high power (about 4 minutes). Reduce the power to medium-low; cover; simmer for 10 minutes. Remove from the microwave and let stand for 15 minutes or until almost all of the water has been absorbed by the apricots. In a food processor or blender, process the apricots with the sugar and cinnamon until smooth. Set aside.

4. Process the glaze ingredients until smooth in a food processor or blender. Set aside.

5. Lightly grease a 10 × 15-inch cookie sheet or jelly-roll pan. When the dough has finished the dough setting, remove it from the bread pan to a lightly floured surface. Knead lightly a few times to remove any remaining air bubbles. The dough will be very soft. Roll the dough into a 10 × 15-inch rectangle and place it on the cookie sheet or in the pan.

6. Spread the cream cheese filling in a 4-inch-wide strip lengthwise down the middle of the dough rectangle.

7. Spread all of the apricot mixture on top of the cream cheese filling.

8. With a knife, cut the dough on the sides of the mixtures crosswise into 1-inch-wide strips. Fold the strips across the fillings alternately, resembling crossed arms.

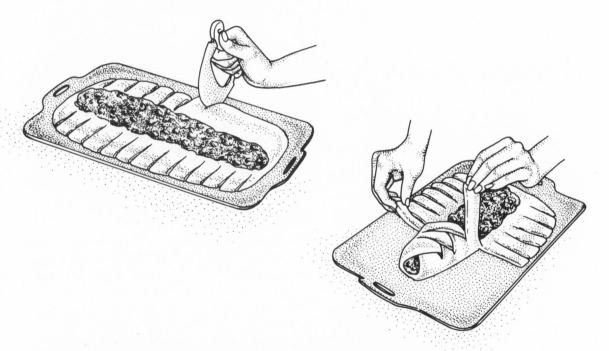

9. Cover with a damp tea towel or plastic wrap and let rise in a warm, draft-free place for approximately 40 minutes or until doubled in bulk. Meanwhile, preheat the oven to 375°F.

10. Bake the bread for 20 minutes or until golden brown. Cool on the cookie sheet, or in the jelly roll pan, then drizzle the glaze over the cake when cool. Best eaten the day it's made.

We sometimes sift confectioners' sugar through a small tea strainer using a spoon to urge the sugar through so that we get just a dusting of confectioners' sugar on the toast. No clods of sugar on this delicate bread.

◇

Another great topping for Pain Perdu is made by whisking together ½ cup plain yogurt, a tablespoon or so of orange juice, and orange zest. Place a dollop of this flavored yogurt atop the slices, then—if you wish—sprinkle with confectioners' sugar.

◇

Fill 2 slices of this toast with ham and Swiss cheese, and you have *croque monsieur*. Replace the ham with poached chicken breast, and you've made *croque madame*.

PAIN PERDU

Serve 4 in 20 minutes

Mme. Elizabeth Begue, a late-nineteenth-century innkeeper in New Orleans, made her reputation with great breakfasts. She was also renowned for her frugality. Waste not, want not, was Mme. Begue's philosophy. One of her leftover successes was yesterday's stale French bread made into a skillet bread that has metamorphosed into today's French toast. But Madame demanded real French bread to begin. If you want to experience this pure breakfast pleasure, make no substitutions. Not even California brandy.

4 large eggs, beaten until frothy
2 C. milk
¼ C. sugar
¼ C. French brandy
Twelve 1-inch-thick slices day-old Hands-Off French bread (see page 255)

¼ C. cooking oil
Confectioners' sugar, for sprinkling on top

1. Combine beaten eggs with milk, sugar, and brandy. Stir to dissolve sugar.

2. Preheat a 10-inch skillet over medium heat, then heat oil until water flicked onto the surface will leap back up, screaming.

3. Using tongs, dip bread into egg mixture, soaking each piece about 30 seconds. Then hold bread up and allow excess to drip back into the bowl.

4. Cook bread in hot oil over medium heat until brown on both sides. Turn once with a spatula when golden brown. Cook no more than 3 pieces at a time. Drain on paper towels.

5. Place 3 slices of browned bread on a warmed breakfast plate and sprinkle with confectioners' sugar before serving.

12 ◆ HORS D'OEUVRES, TOASTS, CROUTONS, AND SALAD BREADS

Khachapuri 276

Petit Prosciutto Bread 278

French Filbert Bread 279

Walnut-Butter Loaf 280

Khachapuri cheese bread may be frozen for later use. Place in freezer bags and use within 2 months. To use, let the bread thaw at room temperature for about 4 hours and heat in a 350°F preheated oven for 20 to 25 minutes for the large bread and 15 minutes for the small breads.

KHACHAPURI

Georgian Cheese Bread

Makes 1 large entrée or 6 hors d'oeuvres, dough setting

This Russian-inspired bread can be shaped different ways. As an entrée or for hors d'oeuvres for a large gathering (15 to 20 people), we make the larger golden, cheese-filled 10-inch round version. Chilled white wine and tossed greens or a beet borscht make nice accompaniments. For gift giving or for "as needed" hors d'oeuvres, we like the smaller breads (4-inch), which can be frozen and reheated as necessary. Each of the smaller breads serves 4 to 6 people.

Use different cheeses in the filling if you wish. Try 1 pound grated Tilsit and 1 pound grated Havarti plus ⅛ pound crumbled Oregon or Maytag blue instead of the Jack and Muenster.

2½ teas. active dry yeast
⅔ C. milk
1 tbsp. honey
¼ C. (½ stick) unsalted butter, room temperature
1 large egg
½ teas. salt
2½ C. bread flour

Cheese Filling
1 pound Monterey Jack, grated
1 pound Muenster, grated
¼ C. minced fresh parsley
2 eggs, lightly beaten

1 egg yolk, lightly beaten
2 tbsp. (¼ stick) unsalted butter or margarine, room temperature
1½ teas. ground coriander or 2 tbsp. finely chopped fresh cilantro leaves
¼ teas. freshly ground black pepper

Glaze
1 large egg, lightly beaten with 1 tbsp. milk

1. Add the yeast, milk, honey, butter, egg, salt, and flour to the bread pan.

2. Process the ingredients according to your manufacturer's instructions for a dough setting.

3. For the filling, combine in a bowl all of the ingredients; stir to mix thoroughly. Set aside.

4. For the large bread, grease a 10-inch round cake pan on the bottom and sides. Cut a piece of parchment or waxed paper to fit the bottom and place it in the bottom of the pan. Grease the paper. Generously sprinkle the bottom of the pan with cornmeal. For smaller breads we use a Texas muffin tin (each muffin cup being approximately 2 inches deep and 4 inches in diameter). Place muffin papers in the tin. Spray the papers lightly with nonstick cooking spray. Sprinkle the bottoms generously with cornmeal.

5. Turn the dough out onto a lightly floured surface. The dough will be very soft and slightly sticky. Knead for a few seconds to remove any remaining air bubbles.

6. For the large bread, roll the dough out into a circle with a 15-inch diameter. For the 6 small breads, divide the dough into 6 equal portions and roll each portion into an 8-inch-diameter circle. Dust the dough lightly with flour. Fold into quarters and transfer to the prepared pan. Unfold the dough and gently press into the bottom of the pan or each muffin cup.

7. Spoon the filling into the dough. Gather the overhanging dough into even folds over the filling, gather the ends together, and twist slightly to form a topknot. Brush the bread with the glaze. Set the bread aside to rise in a warm, draft-free area for 20 minutes. Meanwhile, preheat your oven to 350°F.

8. Bake the bread on the middle rack of the preheated oven for approximately 50 minutes for the large loaf and 30 minutes for the small loaves.

9. Cool in the pan for 15 minutes. Carefully remove them from the pan and cool another 15 minutes before serving.

To form 1 large baguette, roll the dough into a rectangle about 10 × 16 inches. Add prosciutto evenly over the surface, leaving a 1-inch rim. Wet the rim, fold the baguette in half, lengthwise, and pinch the seam shut. Roll the loaf onto a cornmeal-dusted cookie sheet so that the seam is on the bottom. Make diagonal slashes with a razor blade, at a 45-degree angle. Raise until doubled in bulk. Then bake 25 to 30 minutes or until golden brown.

PETIT PROSCIUTTO BREAD

Makes 1 dozen rolls, dough setting

A winner for cocktail parties. If you'd like, you can also form this into 1 regular baguette with equally good results. Don't cheat on the ham. Use genuine prosciutto for best results. Remember how divine this taste is with melon. Whether for breakfast or for cocktails, that burst of salty, rosy ham played against the yeasty richness of bread just begs for thin slices of melon to accompany. Once, for a party, we fanned alternate layers of melon: green, orange, and red varieties. The prosciutto rolls and melon new moons were mouth-watering.

2 C. bread flour
2 tbsp. sugar
1 tbsp. instant nonfat
dry milk solids
1 teas. salt
1 tbsp. unsalted butter
⅞ C. water

1½ teas. active dry yeast
1½ C. chopped
prosciutto ham

Glaze
1 egg, beaten

1. Add flour, sugar, dry milk, salt, butter, water, and yeast to the pan of the machine and process on the dough setting. Meanwhile, dust a microwavable cookie sheet generously with cornmeal.

2. Remove the dough from the machine, divide into 12 balls, and let rest for 10 minutes.

3. Flatten each ball into a 4- to 5-inch circle. Place 2 tablespoons chopped prosciutto on one side of each circle. Roll up the circle from the ham side to make a miniature baguette; seal well by wetting the edges, then pinching shut. Roll the baguettes so that the seam is on the bottom.

4. With a sharp knife, make 3 shallow diagonal cuts in the dough. Place on the prepared cookie sheet. Raise until doubled in a warm draft-free place or micro-rise (see page 35). Meanwhile, preheat oven to 350°F.

5. Brush the rolls with the beaten egg. Place the rolls in preheated oven, and bake for 15 to 20 minutes or until golden brown.

6. Remove rolls to a rack to cool. Wrap in plastic wrap to store. Can be frozen for up to a month, then reheated in a toaster oven 10 to 15 minutes.

FRENCH FILBERT BREAD

Makes one 1-pound loaf, basic bread setting

The traditional French dinner offers a cheese course following the salad. This nut-laden bread makes an admirable mother for soft cheeses: Brie, carambazola, Saga blue, Neufchâtel, even ordinary cream cheese. Add a smattering of fresh fruit of the season and a cup of tea and it's lunch. If your bread machine doesn't have a raisin bread setting, choose the basic bread setting, then add the nuts at the end of the second kneading period, or else the nuts will simply pulverize in the dough.

2¼ **C. bread flour**	⅞ **C. (1 cup minus 2**
¾ **teas. sugar**	**tbsp.) water**
⅓ **teas. salt**	1–1½ **teas. active dry**
1½ **teas. butter**	**yeast**
½ **C. chopped filberts**	
(hazelnuts)	

1. Add all ingredients to the bread pan and place in the machine. Process the ingredients according to the manufacturer's instructions for a raisin bread setting.

2. Remove the loaf from the pan to a rack to cool. Wrap in a plastic bag or foil to store.

French ◇ Filbert Bread ◇

Makes one 1½-pound loaf, basic bread setting

3¼ **C. bread flour**
1 **teas. sugar**
¾ **teas. salt**
1 **tbsp. butter**
¾ **C. chopped filberts**
(hazelnuts)
1¼ **C. water**
1½–2 **teas. active dry yeast**

Walnut-Butter
◇ Loaf ◇

*Makes one 1½-pound loaf, basic
bread setting*

3½ C. bread flour
½ C. whole wheat flour
1½ teas. salt
1 C. milk
⅓ C. water
1 C. coarsely chopped
  walnuts
½ C. (1 stick) unsalted
  butter, room temperature
  and cut into
  tablespoon-sized pieces
3 teas. active dry yeast

WALNUT-BUTTER LOAF

Makes one 1-pound loaf, basic bread setting

This bread is at its best still warm from the oven or toasted. The chewy crust conceals a slightly coarse-textured walnut-studded center. The subtle, nutty flavor of this bread is wonderful with sweet butter, salty cheeses, and wine.

2 C. bread flour
¼ C. whole wheat flour
1 teas. salt
½ C. milk
¼ C. water
½ C. coarsely chopped
  walnuts

¼ C. (½ stick)
  unsalted butter,
  room temperature
  and cut into
  tablespoon-sized
  pieces
2½ teas. active dry yeast

1. Process the ingredients according to your manufacturer's instructions for a basic bread setting.
2. Remove the bread from the bread pan to a rack to cool. Wrap in aluminum foil or a paper bag to store.

◇ Summer's Bread Salad ◇

Serves 4–6 in 30 minutes

When we tried this bread salad we knew it was a must with our Walnut-Butter Loaf. The riper the tomatoes, the better.

Vinaigrette
3 tbsp. walnut oil
5 tbsp. extra virgin olive oil
4 cloves garlic, minced
2 tbsp. fresh lemon juice
2 tbsp. sherry or white wine
  vinegar
½ teas. salt
1 teas. freshly ground black
  pepper
3 tbsp. olive oil
3 tbsp. walnut oil

1 clove garlic, minced
6 C. 1-inch bread cubes
  using Walnut Butter Loaf
  with the crust on
4 tbsp. chopped fresh
  Italian parsley
2 tbsp. chopped fresh
  cilantro
2 C. diced, seeded Roma
  tomatoes
1 C. toasted walnuts (see
  page 185)
¾ C. marinated artichoke
  hearts
1 bunch arugula, washed
  and dried

1. Combine the ingredients for the vinaigrette in a small bowl, whisk, and allow to stand for 1 hour.
2. Preheat the oven to 300°F. Heat the oils in a large skillet and add the garlic. Toss in the bread cubes; stir until lightly browned. Place in the preheated oven on a baking sheet for 20 minutes to crisp. Remove and let cool.
3. Toss 2 tablespoons of parsley, cilantro, tomatoes, walnuts, artichoke hearts, arugula, bread cubes, and vinaigrette in a large bowl. Sprinkle with the rest of the parsley; serve immediately.

13 ◆ BAGELS, BAGUETTES, BREADSTICKS, BUNS, AND ROLLS

Bread Machine Bagels 282

Parker House Rolls 284

Holiday Dinner Rolls 285

Alpine Kaiser Rolls 286

McCully House Inn Fresh Dill Rolls 287

Dried Cherry Butterfly Rolls 288

Hot Cross Buns with Orange 290

After Church Angel Biscuits 291

Onion-Cream-Cheddar Rolls 292

See page 142 for suggestions for serving bagels.

BREAD MACHINE BAGELS

Makes 10 medium 3-inch bagels or 1 large 8-inch-diameter bagel or 20 miniature 1½-inch bagels, dough setting

If you're having a party, try making 1 giant bagel, then stuffing it with cream cheese, lox, red onion, ripe red tomato. Give it a grating of freshly milled black pepper. Cut the bagel into individual pie wedges and serve.

2 C. bread flour	**Poppy seeds, sesame**
1 tbsp. sugar	**seeds, red pepper**
½ teas. salt	**flakes, turbinado sugar,**
¾ C. water	**mixed fresh herbs,**
1 teas. active dry yeast	**minced onion, minced**
	garlic, kosher salt, for
Water Bath	**sprinkling (optional)**
1 gallon water	
1 tbsp. sugar	

Glaze
  **1 egg beaten with 1
  teas. water**

1. Using the dough setting on the bread machine, prepare the dough using flour, sugar, salt, water, and yeast. When the beeper sounds, remove the dough and divide into equal-sized pieces, depending on the number of bagels you're making.

2. For 10 medium bagels, use the palms of both hands together and form each piece on a lightly floured board into a ball. Punch a hole in the middle with your fingers. For 20 miniature bagels, repeat except form smaller balls of dough, 4 to 5 inches long. For a giant bagel, roll the dough into a large ball, then form it into a circle as directed. Alternately, you can cut bagels with a doughnut cutter.

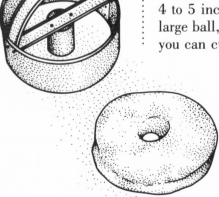

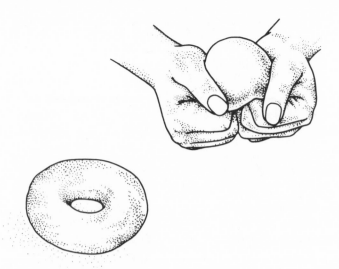

3. Place the bagels on a microwavable baking sheet sprinkled with cornmeal. Spritz the tops with water. Set an 8-ounce glass of water in the back of the microwave. Put the bagels in the microwave.

4. Lower the microwave power to the appropriate microrise setting (see page 35). Heat 3 minutes. Rest 3 minutes. Heat 6 minutes or until doubled in bulk. Alternately, raise bagels in a warm, draft-free place until almost doubled in bulk.

5. In a large soup pot, bring a gallon of water to a boil. Add a tablespoon of sugar to the water. Reduce to a simmer. Slip the bagels into the simmering water—don't crowd them, no more than can comfortably rest in water without touching—and cook for 7 minutes, turning once. Drain well.

6. Meanwhile, preheat the oven to 400°F. Brush the tops of the bagels with the egg mixture, then sprinkle with the desired topping (if any).

7. Bake on the middle rack in the preheated oven 20 to 25 minutes or until golden brown. Remove to a rack to cool. Bagels are best if eaten within a few hours of baking.

In the past, these rolls were served for the holidays and large gatherings. This may have been because they reheat well. To reheat, wrap the rolls in aluminum foil and place in a preheated 350°F oven for 10 minutes.

PARKER HOUSE ROLLS

Makes 18 rolls, dough setting

Parker House Rolls are the half-moon American dinner roll classic. For a flavored version, try adding 1 teaspoon dill-weed or leaf oregano.

2¾ C. bread flour
3 tbsp. instant nonfat dry milk solids
3 tbsp. unsalted butter, room temperature and cut into 3 pieces
3 tbsp. sugar

1 large egg, lightly beaten
1 teas. salt
¾ C. water
2½ teas. active dry yeast
Approximately 2 tbsp. unsalted butter, melted, for brushing on tops

1. Process the ingredients except the melted butter according to your manufacturer's instructions for a dough setting.

2. Lightly grease a large baking sheet. Remove the dough from the bread pan. Roll the dough to a thickness of approximately ¼ inch. Brush the dough lightly with the melted butter.

3. Cut the rolls out with a round cookie cutter or glass somewhere between 2½ to 3 inches in diameter. Crease the middle of each roll with a table knife and fold the halves together. Reroll and cut any leftover dough. Lightly brush the rolls again with butter. Place the rolls on the baking sheet and set in a warm, draft-free place to rise. This will take approximately 20 to 30 minutes. Meanwhile, preheat your oven to 375°F.

4. Bake the rolls on the middle rack of the preheated oven for 12 to 15 minutes. Remove the rolls from the baking sheet and serve warm. Place in plastic bag to store.

HOLIDAY DINNER ROLLS

Makes 18 rolls, dough setting

We hate to admit it, but these gems seem to be saved for company or the holidays. The wonderful aroma and taste is the result of a long, cool rise. You may want to kiss your bread machine after you receive such rave reviews for your homemade bread. You won't save these for the relatives anymore.

3½ C. bread flour
4½ tbsp. sugar
3 tbsp. instant nonfat dry milk solids
1½ teas. salt
6 tbsp. unsalted butter, room temperature
2 large eggs
¾ C. water
1½ teas. active dry yeast

1. Process the ingredients according to your manufacturer's instructions for a dough setting.

2. When the dough setting is finished, remove the bread pan from the machine and let the dough rest in the pan for about 20 minutes. Lightly grease a large baking sheet.

3. Remove the dough from the bread pan, punch down, and knead briefly on a lightly floured surface. Divide the dough into 18 equal-sized balls, and place on the prepared baking sheet.

4. Cover the rolls with plastic wrap and let rise in a warm, draft-free place until almost doubled (30 to 50 minutes). Meanwhile, preheat your oven to 350°F.

5. Bake the rolls on the middle rack of the preheated oven for 10 to 15 minutes or until golden brown. Remove from the baking sheet and serve warm. Wrap in aluminum foil or place in a plastic bag to store.

These rolls are wonderful served with herb butters (see pages 163–164), fresh fruit spreads, and different cheeses. We served them with the traditional holiday ham and honey mustard instead of biscuits. Divine!

Honey-Lemon ◇ Holiday Butter ◇

Makes ⅔ cup in 5 minutes

½ C. (1 stick) unsalted butter, room temperature
¼ C. honey (your favorite)
1 teas. grated lemon zest
2 tbsp. fresh lemon juice

Combine all of the ingredients; blend well. Serve at room temperature.

We tried several methods to achieve the traditional 5-petal-blossom look of the kaiser roll. The German bakers have a metal stamp with which they stamp each roll to create the pattern. We could not find one of the stamps and substituted an apple corer/slicer and stamped our rolls with it. We then pinched up a small piece of dough in the middle and twisted slightly. This gives the curved indentations seen in authentic kaiser rolls. A knife with a very dull blade can also be used by pressing the 5 lines on the rolls lightly. Make sure you do not cut through the dough, because this will allow gases to escape and the rolls will not raise as they should. Authentically formed or not, the rolls are tender, light, and delicious.

Alpine Kaiser ◇ Rolls ◇

Makes 8 large rolls, dough setting

4²/₃ C. bread flour
   3 teas. active dry yeast
   3 tbsp. sugar
   1 teas. salt
1½ C. milk
   2 large eggs
   1 tbsp. shortening or
      unsalted butter
   4 tbsp. unsalted butter,
      melted, for a soft crust
      (optional)
Poppy seeds and/or sesame
   seeds, for sprinkling on top

ALPINE KAISER ROLLS

Makes 4 large rolls, dough setting

There seems to be a difference of opinion about the true characteristics of an authentic kaiser, or emperor, roll. Americans prefer a soft crust, while Germans prefer a thicker, crunchier crust. We like them both. Try the rolls both ways and see which you prefer.

2⅓ C. bread flour
1½ teas. active dry yeast
1½ tbsp. sugar
   ½ teas. salt
   ¾ C. milk
   1 large egg
   ½ tbsp. shortening or
      unsalted butter

   2 tbsp. unsalted
      butter, melted, for a
      soft crust (optional)
Poppy seeds and/or
   sesame seeds, for
   sprinkling on top

1. Process the ingredients, except for the melted butter and seeds, according to your manufacturer's instructions for a dough setting.

2. When the dough setting is finished, remove the dough from the machine and the bread pan. Lightly grease a baking sheet (microwavable if you are micro-rising).

3. On a lightly floured surface, punch the dough down to remove any air bubbles. Divide the dough into 4 equal pieces. Roll each piece into a ball and flatten with the palm of your hand until the dough is approximately ½ inch thick. If you want the traditional 5-petal-blossom pattern on the rolls, try stamping them with an apple corer/slicer. Place on the prepared baking sheet.

4. *For a soft crust:* Brush the tops of the rolls with the melted butter and sprinkle with your selection of seeds.

5. *For a hard crust:* Brush the tops of the rolls with water and sprinkle with your selection of seeds.

6. The rolls may rise the second time in a warm, draft-free place for about 40 minutes, or you may micro-rise them. To micro-rise, set the power to the appropriate micro-rise setting (see page 35). Heat for 3 minutes. Rest for 3 minutes. Heat for 3 minutes. Rest for 12 minutes or until the rolls have doubled in bulk. Preheat the oven for your desired crust.

7. *For a soft crust:* Preheat your oven to 350°F. Bake the rolls on the middle rack of the preheated oven for 20 to 25

minutes or until they are lightly browned. Remove from the oven to a rack to cool.

8. *For a hard crust:* Preheat your oven to 450°F. Spray the rolls lightly with water and place on the middle rack of the preheated oven. Steam must be created in the oven during the first 10 minutes of baking. Open the oven door at least 2 more times during these 10 minutes and lightly spray the rolls with water again. Bake the rolls for 25 minutes or until crispy and brown. Wrap in aluminum foil or plastic wrap to store.

McCULLY HOUSE INN FRESH DILL ROLLS

Makes 9 rolls, dough setting

The McCully House Inn is an Oregon bed-and-breakfast becoming famous for delectable food. St. Patrick's Day is a splendid time for these rolls. Serve them in a breadbasket lined with a green napkin and garnish them with fresh dill. Serve with plenty of sweet butter.

2⅓ C. bread flour
1 tbsp. chopped fresh dillweed or ½ teas. dried dillweed
½ teas. salt
⅛ C. vegetable oil
1 large egg
2 tbsp. sugar
½ C. water
1½ teas. active dry yeast

1. Process the ingredients according to your manufacturer's instructions for a dough setting. Meanwhile, lightly grease 9 muffin cups.

2. When the dough setting is complete, remove the dough and divide into 9 equal-sized balls. Place them in the prepared muffin tins. Cover the pan with a damp tea towel or plastic wrap and let rise until doubled in bulk in a warm place (approximately 25 minutes). Meanwhile, preheat your oven to 350°F.

3. When the rolls have risen to nearly double in bulk, bake on the middle rack of the preheated oven for 15 minutes or until lightly browned. Turn the rolls out onto a rack to cool. Serve immediately. Begorra, that's good!

McCully House Inn
◇Fresh Dill Rolls◇

Makes 18 rolls, dough setting

4 C. bread flour
1 tbsp. chopped fresh dillweed or 1 teas. dried dillweed
¾ teas. salt
¼ C. vegetable oil
1 large egg
¼ C. sugar
1 C. water
1 tbsp. active dry yeast

DRIED CHERRY BUTTERFLY ROLLS

Makes 10 rolls, dough setting

Tart, dried sour cherries are the newest fruit to hit the market. A little larger than raisins, they have all that wonderful cherry flavor condensed in one bite. Be sure to purchase dried sour cherries, not Bing or black cherries. Dried red sour cherries are available by mail order from American Spoon Foods, 411 E. Lake St., Petoskey, Michigan 49770 (1-800-222-5886).

2¼ C. bread flour
¼ C. sugar
½ teas. salt
½ C. milk
¼ C. (½ stick) unsalted butter or margarine
1 large egg
1 teas. almond extract
2 teas. active dry yeast

½ C. water
⅓ C. sugar
1 tbsp. unsalted butter or margarine, melted

Glaze
1 large egg, lightly beaten
Confectioners' sugar, for sprinkling on top

Dried Cherry Filling
4 ounce package dried red tart cherries, minced

1. Process the flour, sugar, salt, milk, ¼ cup butter or margarine, egg, almond extract, and yeast according to your manufacturer's instructions for a dough setting. Meanwhile, prepare the cherry filling and let it cool.

2. For the filling, in a 1-quart saucepan over high heat, heat the cherries and the water to boiling. Reduce the heat to low; cover and simmer for 15 minutes or until the cherries are tender; drain. With a fork or whisk, combine the sugar and cherries until the cherries are mashed; allow the cherry filling to cool before using.

3. Lightly grease a 12 × 17-inch cookie sheet (a microwavable cookie sheet if you plan to micro-rise). When the dough has finished the dough setting, remove it from the bread pan to a lightly floured surface. Knead lightly a few

times to remove any remaining air bubbles. Roll the dough into a 20 × 14-inch rectangle. Brush generously with the melted butter or margarine. Spread the filling to within ½ inch of the edge. From the long side, tightly roll the dough jelly-roll fashion; pinch the edges to seal. Turn the roll seam side down and cut into 10 wedges, each about 2½ inches at the wide side and about 1 inch at the short side.

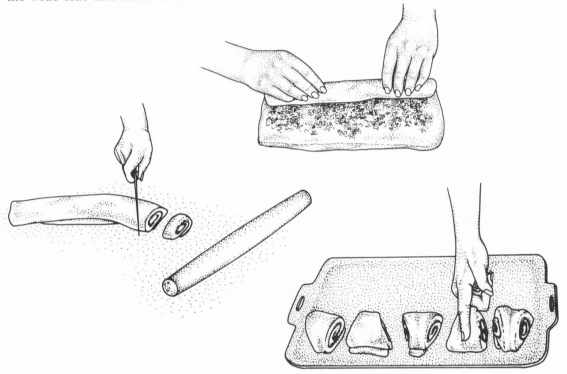

4. Place on the prepared cookie sheet seam side down and about 2 inches apart. With your fingers, press down lightly on the tops to form butterflylike wings. Let the rolls rise in a warm, draft-free place until doubled in bulk, about 30 minutes or you may micro-rise them (see page 35). Meanwhile, preheat your oven to 350°F.

5. When the rolls have doubled, brush the tops lightly with the beaten egg. Discard any remaining egg. Bake the rolls on the middle rack in the preheated oven for 20 minutes or until lightly browned.

6. Remove the rolls to a rack to cool. When the rolls have cooled, sprinkle the tops with sifted confectioners' sugar. Wrap in plastic bags to store and serve warm or at room temperature.

Hot Cross Buns ◇ With Orange ◇

Makes 18 rolls, dough setting

- 1 C. golden raisins
- 1½ C. orange juice (with 1 cup reserved for dough)
- 4 C. bread flour
- 2 teas. grated orange zest or 1½ teas. dried orange peel
- 3 large eggs
- ½ teas. salt
- ½ teas. ground cinnamon
- ½ C. sugar
- ½ C. (1 stick) unsalted butter or margarine
- 3 teas. active dry yeast

Glaze
- 1 C. confectioners' sugar
- 1 tbsp. orange juice
- ½ teas. vanilla extract

HOT CROSS BUNS WITH ORANGE

Makes 9–10 rolls, dough setting

An old English recipe for Lent, these buns are based on an ancient Greek recipe, spiced and baked with plumped raisins, then iced with a traditional cross of frosting. Substitute water for the orange juice if you want to be completely true to the historic recipe.

- ½ C. golden raisins
- ¾ C. orange juice
- 2 C. bread flour
- 1½ teas. grated orange zest or 1 teas. dried orange peel
- 1 large egg
- ¼ teas. salt
- ¼ teas. ground cinnamon
- ¼ C. sugar
- ¼ C. (½ stick) unsalted butter or margarine
- 2½ teas. active dry yeast

Glaze
- 1 C. confectioners' sugar
- 1 tbsp. orange juice
- ½ teas. vanilla extract

1. Place the raisins in a 2-cup microwavable measure and add the ¾ cup orange juice. Place the raisins and juice in the microwave and heat on high power for 70 seconds. Remove the raisins and juice from the microwave and let rest 10 minutes or until the raisins are slightly plumped. Drain the raisins, reserving ½ cup orange juice.

2. Process the raisins, ½ cup reserved orange juice, flour, orange zest or peel, egg, salt, cinnamon, sugar, butter or margarine, and yeast according to the manufacturer's instructions for a dough setting.

3. Lightly grease a large baking sheet, microwavable if you intend to micro-rise. When the dough cycle is finished, turn the dough out onto a lightly floured surface. Knead the dough for a few seconds to remove any remaining air bubbles. Form the dough into 9 or 10 equal balls and place on the prepared baking sheet. Cover the buns with waxed paper or plastic wrap and set aside in a warm, draft-free place to double in bulk, about 1 hour, or you may micro-rise (see page 35). Meanwhile, preheat the oven to 350°F.

4. Just before baking, clip or cut a cross on the top of each bun with scissors or a sharp knife. Bake the buns on the middle rack in the preheated oven for 20 minutes or until golden brown. Remove to a rack to cool slightly.

5. Meanwhile, blend well the confectioners' sugar, 1 tablespoon orange juice, and vanilla for the glaze. Drizzle the glaze over the cross on the top of each bun. Serve warm. Place in plastic bags to store.

One a penny, two a penny, hot
    cross buns;
If you have no daughters, give
    them to your sons.

—Nursery rhyme

◇

AFTER CHURCH ANGEL BISCUITS

Makes a baker's dozen biscuits, dough setting

Start these before you leave the house on Sunday and they're ready for shaping when you get home.

3½ **C. bread flour (try**
    substituting half
    whole wheat for a
    healthy variation)
 2 **large eggs**
⅔ **C. milk**

1 **teas. salt**
⅓ **C. unsalted butter,**
    softened
1 **tbsp. honey**
1 **tbsp. active dry**
    yeast

1. Add to the machine pan and process on the dough setting the flour, eggs, milk, salt, butter, honey, and yeast.

2. When the dough is ready, turn it onto a lightly floured surface, roll out to a thickness of ½ inch, and cut 13 biscuits with a floured biscuit cutter. Place each biscuit on a buttered glass cookie sheet, about an inch apart, then cover lightly with a damp tea towel or plastic wrap and prepare to micro-rise.

3. Place an 8-ounce glass of water in the back of the microwave. Lower the microwave power to the appropriate micro-rise setting (see page 35). Place the biscuits inside and heat for 3 minutes. Rest for 3 minutes. Heat again for 3 minutes. Rest for 6 minutes or until almost doubled in bulk.

4. Place the biscuits on the middle rack in a cold conventional oven, set at 425°F, and bake 15 to 20 minutes or until golden brown. Serve warm.

Cream of Cheese
◇ Soup ◇

Makes 8 cups in 30 minutes

For a nice pick-me-up on a cold day, try Cream of Cheese Soup with Onion-Cream-Cheddar Rolls.

¼ C. (½ stick) unsalted butter
¼ c. flour
2 C. homemade or purchased chicken stock
1 C. classic ale (we use Henry Weinhard's)
2 C. half-and-half
2 C. grated sharp cheddar
Salt and freshly ground black pepper to taste

1. Over low heat in a medium stockpot, melt the butter and add the flour, stirring constantly and being careful so the roux does not burn. Cook 5 minutes.
2. Add the chicken stock and ale and simmer for 10 to 15 minutes. Add the half-and-half and cheese, whisking constantly so the cheese will melt evenly and not settle on the bottom. Don't boil, it curdles. Season to taste with salt and pepper and serve.

ONION-CREAM-CHEDDAR ROLLS

Makes 15–18 rolls, dough setting

Light as a feather with just a hint of onion, these lovelies lend a nice counterbalance to the spiciness of meats off the grill. Try them at the next barbecue.

2½ C. bread flour
⅓ C. grated cheddar
2 oz. cream cheese, softened
1 tbsp. unsalted butter, at room temperature
3 large egg yolks
¾ teas. salt
¼ C. minced onion
2 tbsp. instant potato flakes

¼ C. sugar
1 tbsp. instant nonfat dry milk solids
½ C. water
2 teas. active dry yeast

Glaze
1 egg, lightly beaten with 1 tbsp. water

1. Process the ingredients except those for the glaze according to the manufacturer's instructions for a dough setting.
2. Lightly grease a large baking sheet, microwavable if you plan to micro-rise. When the dough cycle is finished, turn the dough out onto a lightly floured surface. Knead the dough for a few seconds to remove any remaining air bubbles. Form the dough into 15 to 18 balls of equal size and place on the prepared baking sheet. Cover the rolls with waxed paper or plastic wrap and set aside in a warm, draft-free place to double in bulk, about 40 to 50 minutes, or you may micro-rise (see page 35). Meanwhile, preheat the oven to 350°F.
3. Lightly brush the tops of the rolls with the egg glaze; discard any remaining glaze. Bake the rolls on the middle rack of the preheated oven for 8 to 10 minutes or until golden brown.
4. Remove from the baking sheet to a rack to cool. Serve warm or at room temperature. Place in a plastic bag to store.

14 ◆ PIZZA, FOCACCIA, FLATBREADS, AND FILLED BREADS

West Coast New Wave Pizza 294

Pissaladière 296

Garlic-Pepper Bread 297

Finally Focaccia 298

Crusty Calzone 299

Calzone Niçoise 301

Eggplant, Pepper, and Artichoke Torta 302

Chinese Steamed Buns with Barbecued
  Pork Filling 304

Beef and Potato Knishes in Half the Time 305

You may use a pizza screen or pizza pan to bake this pie, but it will not have the crusty brown bottom characteristic of being baked on the stone or tiles. Bake the pizza on a screen or in a pan for 20 to 25 minutes or until bubbly and the toppings are lightly browned.

WEST COAST NEW WAVE PIZZA

Makes one 15-inch pizza, dough setting

Here on the West Coast we incorporate ethnic influences and raw ingredients from all over the world. The smokiness of the Fontina and the saltiness of the chèvre and prosciutto are in robust contrast to the acid sweetness of fresh tomatoes and the silky blandness of mozzarella. For best results, this pizza should be made on a pizza peel and baked on a pizza stone or baking tiles (see pages 21–25). Remember to preheat the stones or tiles at least 30 minutes before baking.

Dough

   3 C. bread flour
 ¼ C. plus 2 tbsp. semolina flour
   1 C. plus 2 tbsp. water
   1 tbsp. sugar
   2 teas. salt
   2 tbsp. plus 1 teas. olive oil
 2½ teas. active dry yeast

Topping

 ½ pound fresh mozzarella, sliced thin
 ½ pound Fontina or Edam, sliced thin
   5 ripe plum tomatoes, sliced thin

   4 large cloves garlic, minced
   1 tbsp. dried sweet basil
   4 oz. thinly sliced prosciutto, chopped coarse
   1 medium sweet onion, sliced thin
   1 red or green bell pepper, seeded and diced
   6 oz. feta, crumbled, or fresh chèvre goat cheese, crumbled
   2 tbsp. olive oil, for brushing on the dough

1. Combine all of the ingredients for the dough in the bread pan and process according to the manufacturer's instructions for a dough setting. Meanwhile, preheat the pizza stone or tiles (see page 21) to 500°F for 30 minutes, prepare your topping ingredients, and line them up in the order listed. (To avoid having cornmeal all over the floor, hold your pizza peel over the sink and generously sprinkle cornmeal—approximately 3 tablespoons—on it to prevent the pizza from sticking.)

2. When the machine has completed the dough cycle, remove the dough from the bread pan to a lightly floured surface. Knead the dough several times. Roll and stretch the dough into a 15-inch circle. Place the dough on the prepared peel (see page 24).

3. Brush the dough with the 2 tablespoons olive oil. Layer the dough with the mozzarella and Fontina or Edam first, which forms a nonskid surface for the rest of the ingredients. Finish layering the pizza with the tomatoes, garlic, sweet basil, prosciutto, onion, pepper, and feta or chèvre goat cheese. Give the pie a jerk on the peel to loosen it before opening the oven door, then slide it onto the preheated stone or tiles. Bake for 10 to 15 minutes or until golden brown on the bottom and the top is bubbly.

PISSALADIÈRE

Makes two 12-inch pizzas in 3 hours and 30 minutes

Count on the French to try to improve on pizza. Cooking fresh Roma tomatoes into a sauce, sweating onions in butter until deliciously limp and golden, then layering the whole thing onto a rich egg dough makes a memorable pizza. If you wish, you can substitute our Plain Ole Pizza dough (see page 167) for the base, but whatever dough you use, be sure to give this pizza a thick pan crust. Serve for lunch with a green salad and a glass of decent Chianti, or cut into bite-sized pieces for a welcome addition to hors d'oeuvres.

1 recipe Beginner's Brioche (see page 267) prepared through micro-rising

6 Roma or 2 large Beefsteak tomatoes, coarsely chopped

2 tbsp. olive oil

2 cloves garlic sliced thin

2 tbsp. tomato paste

1/2 teas. sugar

Salt and freshly ground black pepper to taste

1 large yellow onion, coarsely chopped

1 1/2 tbsp. unsalted butter

1 C. freshly grated Parmesan

1/2 teas. rosemary needles, bruised in mortar and pestle

2-oz. tin anchovy fillets, drained

1 dozen very large ripe olives, preferably soft Italian or Greek, pits removed and cut into large pieces

1. While the brioche dough is working, prepare the filling.

2. Using a food processor, coarsely chop the tomatoes. Heat olive oil in an 8-inch skillet over medium-low heat, then add the tomatoes and garlic and simmer until the tomatoes have formed a paste, about 10 minutes, stirring occasionally. Now stir in tomato paste, sugar, and salt and pepper to taste. Cook 5 more minutes then set aside.

3. Meanwhile, in another saucepan, place chopped onions and butter. Over low heat, with a lid, sweat the onions until they are reduced and golden in color, about 15 minutes, then set aside.

4. After the first rising of dough, roll into two 9-inch circles about ⅜ inch thick. (Alternately, you can roll this into 1 rectangle, about 10 × 12 inches and ⅜ inch thick.) Place the dough in two 9-inch tart or cake pans (or in 1 oblong glass baking dish).

5. Sprinkle dough with Parmesan, then bruised rosemary needles. Now spread the tomato sauce over that, and the cooked onions atop. Arrange anchovy fillets on top in an artful pattern, and finish with pieces of olive.

6. Preheat the oven to 375°F. Set the pizza aside to raise while the oven heats, about 20 minutes, then bake 25 to 30 minutes until the crust is golden and the pizza is cooked through.

7. Remove immediately to a rack to cool. Serve hot or at

GARLIC-PEPPER BREAD

Makes one 1-pound loaf, basic bread setting

Serve this bread along with pasta entrées, or use it as the basis for an impromptu pizza (see Pissaladière for a fresh tomato topping). The aroma of this bread while baking or toasting is so laden with garlic, it will keep the vampires at bay. Cowards who wish to reduce the amount of garlic may need to compensate by adding a little more salt.

⅞ *C. warm water*
1½ *tbsp. fruity olive oil*
⅔ *teas. dried mixed Italian herbs*
¼ *teas. dried red pepper flakes*
¾ *teas. salt*
2 or 3 *large cloves garlic, pressed*
½ *tbsp. sugar*
¼ *C. freshly grated Parmesan*
2 *C. bread flour*
1½ *teas. active dry yeast*

1. Process according to the manufacturer's instructions for basic breads.

2. Turn out of pan onto a rack to cool. Wrap in foil to store.

Garlic Pepper ◇ Bread ◇

Makes 1½-pound loaf, basic bread setting

1½ *C. warm water*
2 *tbsp. fruity olive oil*
1 *teas. dried mixed Italian herbs*
½ *teas. dried red pepper flakes*
1 *teas. salt*
4 *large cloves garlic, pressed*
1 *tbsp. sugar*
⅓ *C. freshly grated Parmesan*
3 *C. bread flour*
2 *teas. active dry yeast*

◇ Onion Focaccia ◇

2 tbsp. unsalted butter or
  margarine
2 tbsp. fruity olive oil
2 medium yellow onions,
  sliced thin and separated
  into rings
1/2 teas. dried sage leaves

1. In a 10-inch skillet over medium-low heat, combine butter or margarine with olive oil and heat. Add onions and sauté until golden and just beginning to brown, about 15 minutes. Sprinkle sage leaves in and remove from the heat.

2. Dab olive oil on the flatbread. Spoon filling onto focaccia just before baking. Dimple with fingertips and bake as directed.

Focaccia ◇ Bianca ◇

1/2 C. freshly grated
  Parmesan
2 tbsp. pine nuts

Dab olive oil on flatbread. Sprinkle cheese and pine nuts over prepared focaccia and bake as directed.

Pear Focaccia ◇ Gorgonzola ◇

1/2 C. crumbled Gorgonzola
1 Comice pear, peeled,
  cored, and cut into thin
  slices

Dab prepared focaccia with olive oil, then sprinkle cheese on and arrange pear slices in a design. Bake as directed.

FINALLY FOCACCIA

Makes two 12-inch round flatbreads, dough setting

Let the bread machine do the work and all you have to do is remember to preheat the oven 30 minutes ahead so the pizza stone will be hot (for more on using a pizza stone, see pages 21–25). We cook these sequentially on the stone, so one gets a little puffier than the other, but that's OK. If you're using a cookie sheet, cook both flatbreads at once, and spritz the tops with plain water during the first 5 minutes to get the best crust.

3 C. bread flour
1 tbsp. yellow
  cornmeal
2 1/2 teas. active dry yeast
1 tbsp. sugar

1/2 teas. salt
2 tbsp. fruity olive oil
1 1/4 C. warm water
Olive oil, to dab on the
  top

1. Combine all the ingredients except the olive oil for the top. Process according to the manufacturer's instructions for the dough setting.

2. Meanwhile prepare the filling of your choice and preheat the oven to 425°F, with a pizza stone in place on the middle rack, for 30 minutes.

3. Once the dough cycle is complete, turn the dough out onto a lightly floured surface and punch down. Divide in 2 parts. Cover with the bread machine pan. Let the dough rest for 10 minutes.

4. Roll and stretch each piece into a 12-inch circle. Place on a pizza peel coated with cornmeal (see page 24). If you wish, you can top with nothing more than a dab of olive oil and kosher salt. If you prefer something fancy, try one of the toppings listed below. Set the dough aside to rise one final time until the dough looks puffy, about 10 minutes. Just before baking, dimple the dough with your fingertips.

5. Bake in the preheated oven 15 to 20 minutes or until golden brown. Cool on a rack. Cut into wedges and serve warm. Wrap in a brown paper bag to store.

CRUSTY CALZONE

Makes 2 large calzone or 4 small calzone, dough setting

Calzone, the folded and stuffed pizza, should be on the repertoire of every family who has teenagers. Calzone are more versatile than the traditional open-faced pie and can be basically made-to-order. Let each person form and fill a personal pizza with his or her favorite toppings. The most important thing to remember about filling calzone is that ingredients should not have a lot of liquid and all ingredients should be used sparingly. If too many ingredients are used, the crust will become soggy.

1 C. plus 1 tbsp. water
2½ teas. active dry yeast
3 C. bread flour
½ teas. salt
½ C. chopped fresh herbs, such as basil, oregano, rosemary, chives, or what have you that is fresh, or 2 tbsp. dried herbs (optional)

1 recipe calzone filling (see page 300)
Olive oil, for brushing on top

1. Process the water, yeast, flour, salt, and herbs, if using, according to your manufacturer's instructions for a dough setting. Preheat the oven to 400°F. for 20 minutes. Sprinkle cornmeal over a heavy-duty baking sheet that will not warp in the extreme heat. Assemble your chosen filling ingredients.
2. Remove the dough to a lightly floured surface and divide into 2 or 4 equal pieces. For 2 calzone, roll each piece into a 10-inch diameter circle, and place half of the filling on half of each circle, leaving a 1-inch border. For 4 calzone, roll each piece into an 8-inch circle, and place a quarter of the filling on half of each circle, leaving a 1-inch border. Fold the other half of the dough over the fillings and crimp the edges to seal. Brush lightly with olive oil.
3. Place the calzone on the prepared baking sheet and bake on the middle rack of the preheated oven for 20 to 25 minutes or until the calzone are golden brown. Remove from the baking sheet to a serving platter and let rest for 5 minutes. Slice into wedges and enjoy!

Breakfast ◇ Focaccia ◇

½ C. golden raisins
¼ C. fresh Queen Anne cherries, pitted and halved
½ C. turbinado sugar

Dab prepared focaccia with olive oil, then sprinkle with raisins, cherries, and turbinado sugar. Bake as directed.

◇ Olive Focaccia ◇

½ C. pimiento-stuffed green olives, sliced
½ C. Kalamata olives, pitted and sliced

Dab prepared focaccia with olive oil, then sprinkle with olives. Bake as directed.

Roasted Red Pepper ◇ Focaccia ◇

7 oz. jar roasted red peppers, drained and sliced

Dab prepared focaccia with olive oil, then sprinkle with roasted red peppers. Bake as directed.

Italian Sausage, Cheese, and Onion ◇ Filling ◇

Makes 2 large calzone, dough setting

1/2 pound mozzarella, shredded

1/2 pound sweet Italian bulk sausage or links, removed from the casing, crumbled, and cooked thoroughly

1 small sweet red onion, sliced thin

1/2 C. good-quality tomato sauce

Divide the ingredients into the appropriate proportions for each piece of dough and sprinkle the mozzarella on the dough first. (Cheese should always be placed on the dough first as it seals the dough and keeps the other liquids from seeping through.) Next, layer on the sausage and onion. Spoon on the sauce, seal, and bake.

Anchovy and Black Olive with Roma ◇ Tomato Filling ◇

Makes 2 large calzone, dough setting

Swimming with anchovy, snappy with balsamic vinegar, and suave with fruity olive oil, this one can't be missed.

1 C. sliced ripe Roma tomatoes

2 teas. balsamic vinegar

Coarsely ground black pepper to taste

1/2 pound mozzarella, shredded

1 2-oz. tin anchovy fillets packed in oil, drained and separated

1/2 C. coarsely chopped black olives

Season the tomatoes with balsamic vinegar and coarsely ground pepper to taste. Set aside. Layer the dough with the mozzarella and then the anchovies. Drain the vinegar from the tomatoes and layer on top of the anchovies with a sprinkling of black olives. Seal and bake.

Pesto, Cheese, and Sun-Dried Tomato ◇ Filling ◇

Makes 2 large calzone, dough setting

Fashioned after our favorite Pesto Torta with Tomatoes (see page 132), this one cannot be missed. Let it cool to room temperature before serving.

3/4 pound ricotta

1/4 C. drained and minced sun-dried tomatoes packed in olive oil

1/2 cup prepared pesto (for homemade see page 170)

Combine all the ingredients in a mixing bowl and blend well. Divide the cheese mixture into the appropriate proportion and spread over half of each calzone. Seal, bake, and cool.

Veggie Calzone ◇ Filling ◇

Makes filling for 2 calzones in 20 minutes

1/4 C. fruity olive oil

2 cloves garlic, sliced thin

1 large yellow onion, sliced thin

1/2 pound brown mushrooms, sliced thin

1 red bell pepper, seeded and sliced thin

1/2 teas. each salt, dried oregano, and dried marjoram

Grating of black pepper

In a medium soup pot, heat the olive oil, then sauté the garlic and onion until clear. Stir in the sliced mushrooms and continue cooking and stirring. Add the bell pepper and continue to cook for a total of 15 minutes. Season with salt, oregano, marjoram, and black pepper. Remove from the heat.

CALZONE NIÇOISE

Makes 2 calzone, dough setting

1 calzone recipe
1 recipe Fresh Roma
   Tomato Sauce
¼ C. fruity olive oil
2 large yellow onions,
   sliced thin
2 cloves garlic, sliced
   thin
½ teas. dried herbes de
   Provence
¼ C. snipped fresh
   parsley
2 C. (½ pound)
   shredded mozzarella
2 oz. tin anchovy
   fillets, drained
¼ C. small pitted
   Niçoise olives
2 tbsp. capers

1. While the calzone dough rises, make a recipe of Fresh Roma Tomato Sauce and set aside.

2. In a medium soup pot, heat the olive oil over moderate heat, add onions and sauté, stirring until barely browned, about 10 minutes. Remove from the heat.

3. Spoon a tablespoon of oil from the soup pot into a small bowl and combine with the garlic, herbes de Provence, and parsley. Set aside.

4. Roll the calzone dough as directed, spoon on fresh tomato sauce, then divide cooked onions over both calzones. Sprinkle evenly with cheese, then arrange anchovies, olives, and capers over that. Sprinkle with the garlic-herb mixture. Fold calzone circles in half and bake as directed.

Fresh Roma Tomato ◇ Sauce ◇

Makes 2 cups sauce in 30 minutes

1 pound fresh Roma
   tomatoes
2 tbsp. fruity olive oil
2 cloves garlic, minced
1 tbsp. minced fresh basil
   leaves
¼ teas. salt
¼ C. dry white wine

1. In the food processor fitted with the steel blade, coarsely chop the tomatoes, pulsing machine off and on.

2. In a medium saucepan, heat the olive oil, then add the garlic and sauté 2 minutes. Add tomatoes, basil leaves, salt, and wine and simmer for 15 minutes, stirring from time to time. Taste and adjust seasonings. Raise heat, cook, and stir until the sauce is thick and reduced to 1 cup. Remove from heat.

3. Spread sauce onto 2 calzone.

Makes one 10-inch torta, dough setting

Here's an alternate filling for the same whole wheat crust.

- 1 *recipe whole wheat dough (see Eggplant, Pepper, and Artichoke Torta)*
- 1 *bunch fresh spinach, thoroughly washed, stems removed*
- 2 *tbsp. fruity olive oil*
- 1 *medium yellow onion, chopped fine*
- 2 *cloves garlic, pressed*
- 1 *egg yolk*
- 1 *C. whole-milk ricotta*
- ½ *C. freshly grated Parmesan*

Salt and freshly ground black pepper to taste
Pinch of freshly ground nutmeg

Glaze
- 1 *egg, beaten with 1 teas. water*

1. While the bread is in the dough cycle, make the filling. Place spinach in a microwavable bowl, cover tightly with plastic wrap, and cook in the microwave on high power just until wilted, about 3 minutes. Remove from the microwave, squeeze out any remaining water, and chop in the food processor by pulsing off and on.

2. In a 10-inch skillet, heat the oil, then sauté finely chopped onion and garlic until just beginning to turn brown.

3. In a large mixing bowl, combine the egg yolk with the ricotta and Parmesan. Mix with a fork, then add salt, pepper, and nutmeg. Stir to mix. Add the spinach and onion-garlic mixture and mix thoroughly.

EGGPLANT, PEPPER, AND ARTICHOKE TORTA

Makes one 10-inch torta, dough setting

Serve a torta hot, warm, at room temperature. In your kitchen, from the tailgate, at the beach. This Italian sandwich, alongside antipasti, soup, and fruit, makes for a wonderful alfresco meal. If you're at the breakfast table, it brings the outdoors in. Don't forget the checkered tablecloth and the Chianti. See Italian Loaf Rustica (page 172) for another filling idea.

Whole Wheat Dough
- 1½ *C. bread flour*
- ½ *C. whole wheat flour*
- ½ *teas. salt*
- 2½ *teas. active dry yeast*
- ¼ *C. warm water*
- 1 *tbsp. mild honey*
- 2 *large eggs*
- ½ *C. (1 stick) unsalted butter or margarine*

Eggplant Filling
- ¼ *C. fruity olive oil*
- 1 *small eggplant (1 pound), unpeeled, cut into ½-inch cubes*
- 1 *medium yellow onion, chopped fine*
- 2 *cloves garlic, pressed*
- 1 *red bell pepper, seeded and cut into thin strips*
- ½ *C. pitted small whole black olives*

Juice and zest of half a lemon
- 1 *C. artichoke hearts, drained*
- 2 *tomatoes (1 pound), chopped fine*
- ¼ *C. pine nuts*
- 1 *tbsp. fine-chopped fresh basil leaves*
- ½ *teas. dried oregano*

Salt and freshly ground black pepper to taste
- 3 *eggs*
- 1 *C. (¼ pound) shredded Swiss cheese*

- ¼ *C. freshly grated Parmesan*

1. Make the torta dough in the bread machine on the dough setting following the manufacturer's directions.

2. Meanwhile, make the filling. In a medium soup pot, heat oil over medium heat, then add the eggplant, onion, and garlic. Cook and stir until the onion begins to brown. Add the

red pepper, and cook a few more minutes. Now stir in the black olives, lemon juice and zest, and artichoke hearts. Continue to simmer a few minutes, then stir in the tomatoes, pine nuts, basil, oregano, salt, and pepper. Simmer, uncovered, until the eggplant is tender and most of the liquid has evaporated, about 20 minutes. Remove from the heat and cool slightly.

3. Beat the eggs in a large bowl, then, for the glaze, reserve 2 tablespoons of beaten egg in a separate bowl. Combine a large portion of the eggs with the Swiss cheese and stir to mix. Now stir into the vegetable mixture.

4. When the dough cycle is complete, remove the dough to a lightly floured surface and punch down. Divide the dough into 2 unequal parts (about ⅔ and ⅓ portions), reserving the ⅓ portion of the dough for the top. Roll out the ⅔ portion into a 14-inch circle. Place it in a 10-inch springform pan. Roll the remaining dough into a 10-inch circle and cut 1-inch-wide strips, using a pizza cutter.

5. Fill the dough-lined pan with the vegetable mixture. Sprinkle with the Parmesan. Now weave the strips into a lattice atop the filling, pinching the edges to seal. Set the pie aside to rise until the lattice is puffy, while you preheat the oven to 375°F.

6. Just before baking, brush the reserved beaten egg onto the lattice. Bake on the middle rack of the preheated oven until the lattice is browned and the filling is set, about 50 minutes.

7. Cool in the pan on a wire rack 10 minutes before removing the sides of the pan. Cut into wedges and serve warm or at room temperature.

4. Form and fill the torta as directed in the above recipe, then brush the lattice with the egg glaze. Set the torta aside to rise until the lattice is puffy. Preheat the oven to 375°F.

5. Bake on the middle rack of the preheated oven until evenly browned and the filling is set, about 40 minutes.

6. Remove to a rack to cool. Leave in the pan 10 minutes, then remove the springform. Serve warm or at room temperature, cut in wedges.

You can ad-lib the fillings for tortas. Fontina cheese, fresh sliced Beefsteak tomatoes, whole basil leaves, cooked hot Italian sausage. Or how about mortadella, provolone, chopped tomatoes, and yellow peppers? See what sounds good to you.

These buns can be made and steamed ahead, then frozen. Reheat by steaming the frozen buns 30 to 35 minutes or defrosted buns for 15 minutes.

CHINESE STEAMED BUNS WITH BARBECUED PORK FILLING

Makes 1 dozen buns, dough setting

Straight from the dim sum tables of San Francisco's Chinatown comes Cha Siu Bau, small steamed buns with a sweet, spicy filling of barbecued pork and onions. We have speeded up the process by starting with take-out barbecued pork from our favorite Chinese restaurant. You might want to try fresh vacuum-packed barbecued pork available in the refrigerated case of many grocery stores.

Dough
- 3 C. bread flour
- 2 teas. sugar
- ½ teas. salt
- 2 teas. active dry yeast
- ¾ C. water
- 1 tbsp. peanut oil or vegetable oil
- 1 large egg

Barbecued Pork Filling
- ¼ C. minced onion
- ½ C. water
- 4 teas. oyster sauce
- 2 teas. sherry
- 2 teas. hoisin sauce
- 2 teas. catsup
- 1 teas. sugar
- ¾ teas. salt
- 1 tbsp. peanut oil or vegetable oil
- 1 teas. fresh minced garlic
- 1 teas. rice vinegar
- ½ teas. hot pepper sauce
- 2 tbsp. minced green onion (green part only)
- ½ teas. sesame oil (optional)
- 2 C. finely diced barbecued pork (½ pound vacuum-packed pork equals 2 C.)

Sesame seeds, for sprinkling on top (optional)

1. Add the flour, sugar, salt, yeast, water, oil, and egg to the bread pan. Process the ingredients according to your manufacturer's instructions for a dough setting. This cycle is approximately 2 hours long.

2. Meanwhile, prepare the barbecued pork filling. Combine all the ingredients except the pork in a medium skillet. Cook over medium heat for 10 minutes or until the onion is translucent and tender. Remove the skillet from the heat.

Add the pork to the skillet and stir to blend. Remove the pork mixture from the skillet and chill until the dough is ready. Cut twelve 4 × 4-inch pieces of aluminum foil and set aside.

3. When the dough cycle is finished, turn the dough out onto a lightly floured surface. Knead the dough for a few seconds to remove any remaining air bubbles. Divide the dough into 12 equal pieces. Pat or roll each piece of dough into a 4-inch round. Place the dough in the palm of your hand and fill with 1 heaping tablespoon of the chilled pork filling. Gather up the sides around the filling and twist the dough to seal. Place, twisted side down, on a piece of the aluminum foil. Repeat for all remaining.

4. Cover and let rise in a warm, draft-free place for about 15 minutes. (Buns will not be doubled.)

5. Place the buns on foil on a steamer rack or cake racks in a roasting pan or Dutch oven over boiling water. Leave at least 1 inch of clear space around each bun so the buns will steam properly. Cover and steam 15 to 18 minutes, until done. Sprinkle the tops of each bun lightly with sesame seeds, if desired. Serve with hot Chinese mustard.

BEEF AND POTATO KNISHES IN HALF THE TIME

Makes 2 dozen knishes, dough setting

Although the traditional knish is made from leftover roast beef brisket, mashed potatoes, and sautéed onions, we can make knishes fast by asking the bread machine to make the dough while we run to the store for a pound of deli roast beef and a couple of potatoes and onions that we can cook up quick in the microwave. Process the meat and cooked vegetables in the food processor. Then all you have to do is stuff and form the knishes. Now that is a job in itself.

What you are doing is enclosing a beef filling with bread to create a delicious fistful that makes a kosher-style sandwich. The best knishes are seasoned with schmaltz (chicken fat). If you make homemade chicken stock, you may have some fresh fat on top of your frozen broth. Otherwise, unless you live close to a kosher deli, substitute cooking oil. It won't taste quite as good, but it's not bad. *(continued)*

You can make the dough and the filling a day ahead if that suits your life better. One time, when we made them, we filled and cooked 1 roll, then stored the other 2 pieces of dough and filling covered in the refrigerator for the next day. We thought we had plenty. Little did we realize that when the monster dog sniffed over our day's labors, he'd choose the knishes for his taste test. Damn dog ate 6 knishes off the counter, whole plateful. His blue-ribbon winner for the day. We had to wait a day before we could tell him he was right. Delicious.

Knishes may also be deliciously filled without the beef. Double the potatoes and onions and you can make a wonderful vegetarian knish.

Dough

    3 C. bread flour
2 1/2 teas. active dry yeast
  1/2 teas. salt
    1 tbsp. sugar
  1/2 C. warm water
  1/4 C. melted chicken
        fat or salad oil
    2 eggs

Filling

    1 pound deli roast
        beef
    2 medium yellow
        onions, peeled
  1/2 C. melted chicken
        fat or salad oil
    1 pound russet
        potatoes
Salt and freshly ground
    black pepper to taste
    1 egg

1. Make knish dough in the bread machine set on the dough setting. The cycle takes about 2 hours.

2. Meanwhile, lightly grease 2 cookie sheets. Then make the filling. Chop the beef in the food processor fitted with the steel blade. Remove the beef to a large mixing bowl.

3. Chop the onions in the food processor fitted with the steel blade by pulsing on and off. Then sauté the onions in a 10-inch skillet in chicken fat or oil over medium heat, just until beginning to brown. Remove to the bowl with the beef.

4. Meanwhile, cook the potatoes in the microwave set on high power until tender, about 6 minutes. Peel, then pulse in the food processor fitted with the steel blade until grainy. Season to taste with salt and pepper, and add egg. Pulse to mix thoroughly. Now combine with the beef and onions and mix thoroughly.

5. Once the dough cycle is complete, turn the dough out onto a lightly floured surface and punch down. Divide the dough into 3 parts. Cover the dough with the bread machine pan and let it rest 10 minutes.

6. Roll out 1 piece of the dough into a 10 × 16-inch rectangle. Spoon a third of the filling onto the dough, making a long strip of filling down the middle. Roll the dough securely around the filling, making a long pipe of filling. Pinch the long edge to seal. Then roll the dough so that the edge is on the bottom. Repeat with the other 2 pieces of dough. Cover each roll with plastic wrap as you complete it so it won't dry out.

7. Now comes the hard part. Cut each filled roll of dough into 1-inch-thick slices. Holding a roll in your left hand, stretch the dough up and over the filling, crimping it to seal, then flip it over and pull the dough up over the bottom. Don't be distressed if these don't look like a Yiddish grandmother's knish. This takes practice! The idea is to enclose the filling on all sides, but don't worry if some of the filling seems to ooze out. It still tastes good. This is one of those labor-intensive products that remind us of making tamales. All we can say is—hold your mouth right and keep trying.

8. Arrange the knishes on prepared cookie sheets, leaving room between for them to rise. Brush lightly with chicken fat or oil and let them rise until puffy, about 15 minutes. Preheat oven to 350°F.

9. Bake in the preheated oven until golden brown, 15 to 20 minutes. Serve warm. Cover and store in the refrigerator.

15 ◆ SOUP AND SANDWICH BREADS

Dilly Bread 309

Red Onion–Nut–Bacon Bread 310

Tabasco Cheddar Bread 311

Gizzie's Grinder Rolls 312

Bettie Henry's Three-Seeded Cottage Bread 313

Crusty Tomato–Pine Nut Bread
  with Manhattan Clam Chowder 314

Dagwood's Picnic Sandwich on Walnut Bread 316

Hamburger Buns Flecked with Wheat Germ 318

DILLY BREAD

Makes one 1-pound loaf, basic bread setting

This bread makes a wonderful bowl cut in half, the insides pulled out leaving a 1-inch shell, then filled with your favorite chowder (see page 314). Salmon sour cream soup with corn or bourbon beef stew. Delicious.

You can reduce the cholesterol in this recipe by using low-fat cottage cheese, polyunsaturated margarine instead of butter, and 2 egg whites *only* in place of the egg.

2½ C. bread flour
½ teas. salt
2 teas. dried dillweed or 1 teas. minced fresh dillweed
2 tbsp. honey
3 tbsp. unsalted butter or margarine, room temperature

½ C. cottage cheese
½ C. water
1 large egg
1 teas. active dry yeast

1. Process the ingredients according to the manufacturer's instructions for a basic bread setting.

2. Remove the bread from the bread pan to a rack to cool. Wrap in aluminum foil to store.

◇ Dilly Bread ◇

Makes one 1½-pound loaf, basic bread setting

3 C. bread flour
1 teas. salt
2 teas. dried dillweed or 1 teaspoon minced fresh dillweed
2 tbsp. honey
3 tbsp. unsalted butter or margarine, room temperature
1 C. cottage cheese
½ C. water
1 large egg
1½ teas. active dry yeast

Red Onion–Nut–Bacon ◇ Bread ◇

Makes one 1½-pound loaf, basic bread setting

  1 *C. whole wheat flour*
  2 *C. bread flour*
1½ *teas. salt*
1½ *teas. sugar*
  1 *C. plus 1 tbsp. milk*
¼ *C. (½ stick) unsalted butter or margarine, room temperature*
½ *C. finely chopped red onion*
½ *C. chopped pecans*
¼ *C. chopped crisp cooked bacon (2 or 3 slices)*
2½ *teas. active dry yeast*

RED ONION–NUT–BACON BREAD

Makes one 1-pound loaf, basic bread setting

How about a little O-N-B bread for your next BLT? This is such an exciting and different combination for salads when cut into croutons or simply toasted as an accompaniment. We serve it as the bread-of-the-day with Senate Bean Soup. Delicious.

1 *C. whole wheat flour*
1 *C. bread flour*
1 *teas. salt*
1 *teas. sugar*
½ *C. milk*
3 *tbsp. unsalted butter or margarine, room temperature*

⅓ *C. finely chopped red onion*
¼ *C. chopped pecans*
¼ *C. chopped crisp cooked bacon (2 or 3 slices)*
2 *teas. active dry yeast*

1. Process the ingredients according to the manufacturer's instructions for a basic bread setting.

2. Remove the bread from the bread pan to a rack to cool. Wrap in aluminum foil or a paper bag to store.

◇ Senate Bean Soup ◇

Makes 12 cups in 4 hours

U.S. Senate Bean Soup was actually made famous in the House dining room, where decisions that really matter are made over lunch.

1 *pound dried navy beans*
8 *C. water*
1½ *pounds smoked ham, cut into small chunks*
1 *C. chopped onion*
3 *cloves garlic, minced*
2 *tbsp. paprika*
2 *teas. caraway seeds*
1½ *teas. salt*

1 *teas. freshly ground black pepper*
1 *C. sour cream*

Garnish
Chopped fresh parsley

1. Wash and pick over the beans. Place in a large heavy stockpot with 8 C. water and add the ham, onion, garlic, paprika, and caraway seeds. Heat over medium-high heat to boiling; skim off any foam that rises to the top. Reduce the heat to low; simmer, covered, until the beans are tender and the soup has thickened, about 3 hours.

2. When the beans are tender, add the salt, pepper, and sour cream. Heat for an additional 3 to 5 minutes to heat through, but *do not boil* or the soup will curdle. Garnish with chopped parsley and serve immediately.

If you live at a high altitude, you may need to soak beans, otherwise just cook 'em up. We haven't soaked beans in years. Draining water from soaked beans drains away vitamins we want in us, not down the drain.

TABASCO CHEDDAR BREAD

Makes one 1-pound loaf, basic bread setting

The cowboys of old would have yearned for a piece of this bread to go along with their Red River chili if they'd had bread machines. We suggest using a sharp cheddar for an intense cheese flavor (the cheese flavor in this bread reminds us of that burnt cheese on top of Mom's macaroni). The crust will be dark. If the crust is too dark for your taste and your machine has a light crust feature, try it.

2 C. bread flour	1 teas. Tabasco or cayenne pepper sauce, or to taste
2/3 C. grated sharp cheddar	
2 teas. fresh grated Parmesan	1/2 C. plus 2 tbsp. water
1 tbsp. sugar	1/4 C. instant nonfat dry milk solids
3/4 teas. salt	2 teas. active dry yeast
1 tbsp. unsalted butter or margarine, room temperature	

1. Process the ingredients according to the manufacturer's instructions for a basic bread setting.

2. Remove the bread from the bread pan to a rack to cool. Wrap in aluminum foil or a paper bag to store.

Tabasco Cheddar ◇ Bread ◇

Makes one 1½-pound loaf, basic bread setting

- 3 C. bread flour
- 1 C. grated sharp cheddar
- 1 tbsp. freshly grated Parmesan
- 1½ tbsp. sugar
- 1 teas. salt
- 1½ tbsp. unsalted butter or margarine, room temperature
- 1½–2 teas. Tabasco or cayenne pepper sauce, or to taste
- 1 C. water
- 1/3 C. instant nonfat dry milk solids
- 2½ teas. active dry yeast

Gizzie's Grinder ◇ Juice ◇

Makes 1 cup in 10 minutes, plus 4 hours to marinate

Let this sit for at least 4 hours before using to allow the flavors to blend.

- 1/2 C. olive oil
- 2 medium cloves garlic, minced
- 1/2 small onion, minced
- 1/2 teas. freshly ground pepper
- Juice of 2 medium lemons or 1/3 cup red wine vinegar
- Zest of 1 lemon
- 1 teas. dried oregano
- 1/4 teas. red pepper flakes
- 1 tbsp. freshly grated Parmesan

Combine all of the ingredients in a container with a tight-fitting lid and shake well. Let sit for 4 hours, allowing the flavors to blend. Sprinkle on grinder rolls before adding fillings. Keeps well in the refrigerator up to 2 weeks.

Gizzie's Grinder ◇ Rolls ◇

Makes 8 grinder rolls, dough setting

- 4 C. bread flour
- 1½ C. water
- 2 teas. sugar
- 2 tbsp. salt
- 2½ teas. active dry yeast

The directions for making 8 grinder rolls are the same as for making 4; however, you must divide the dough into 8 pieces instead of 4.

Gizzie's Cajun ◇ Shrimp Grinder ◇

Makes 4 grinders in 30 minutes

- 4 grinder rolls
- ¼ C. (½ stick) unsalted butter
- ¼ C. finely chopped green bell pepper
- ¼ C. finely chopped celery
- 4 green onions (white part only), finely chopped
- 1 medium tomato, chopped
- 1 pound medium shrimp, shelled and cleaned
- ½ teas. Tabasco
- ½ teas. dried mixed Italian herbs (a mixture of oregano, basil, parsley, etc.)
- Salt and freshly ground black pepper to taste
- 1 tbsp. Madeira (optional)
- Gizzie's Grinder Juice (see page 311) to taste

1. Warm the rolls wrapped in foil in a preheated 350° F oven for 10 to 15 minutes.

2. In a medium skillet, melt the butter and add the green pepper, celery, and green onion and sauté until the ingredients are soft and translucent, about 5 minutes. Stir

GIZZIE'S GRINDER ROLLS

Makes 4 grinder rolls, dough setting

With so many sandwich shops springing up, the competition for great grinders is fierce, and he who has the best bread wins. We find this simple recipe gets a blue ribbon. Some of our favorite fillings are: Black Forest ham, thinly sliced provolone and mild cheddar, sliced tomato, shredded lettuce, onion slices, shaved rare Italian beef. These rolls are best served the same day as baked or they may be wrapped in foil and frozen. To reheat, loosen one end of foil and bake at 375° F until hot and crisp.

- 2 C. bread flour
- ¾ C. water
- 1 teas. sugar
- 1 teas. salt
- 1½ teas. active dry yeast

1. Process the ingredients according to the manufacturer's instructions for a dough setting.

2. Remove the bread pan from the machine and let the dough rest in the pan for another 30 minutes. Remove the dough from the pan to a lightly floured surface, kneading in a little more flour as the dough will seem sticky. Lightly grease a baking sheet (microwavable if you plan to micro-rise).

3. Divide the dough into 4 equal-sized pieces and flatten and shape into oblongs about 6 inches long, 3 inches wide, and 1 inch high. Place on the prepared baking sheet and set

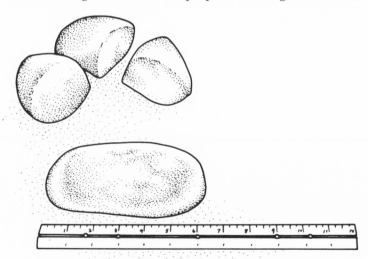

aside in a warm, draft-free place to double in volume, approximately 30 minutes, or you may micro-rise (see page 35). Meanwhile, preheat the oven to 425° F.

4. With a sharp knife or razor blade, slash the top of each roll from one end to the other about ¼ inch deep. Bake in the middle of the preheated oven for 15 minutes, reduce the heat to 375° F, and bake for an additional 10 to 15 minutes or until they are lightly browned. Remove from the oven to a rack to cool. Split and sprinkle with Gizzie's Grinder Juice and fill with your favorite grinder fillings.

in the tomato, shrimp, Tabasco, Italian herbs, salt, and pepper. Cook until the shrimp are cooked through, about 5 minutes. Stir in the Madeira, if using, and cook over high heat until the Madeira has just about evaporated, about 1 minute.

3. Split the rolls and sprinkle with grinder juice to taste. Spoon the shrimp mixture onto the rolls. Serve immediately with additional Tabasco if so desired.

BETTIE HENRY'S THREE-SEEDED COTTAGE BREAD

Makes one 1-pound loaf, basic bread setting

Made in the bread machine, this robust bread makes an ideal partner for stout cheese or hearty soup. Aromatic with the scent of dill, onion, poppy and sesame seeds, the bread has a light texture. The calcium level is boosted by the addition of cottage cheese.

¾ C. small-curd low-fat cottage cheese	2 C. bread flour
1 large egg	¾ teas. salt
1 tbsp. unsalted butter or margarine, softened	⅛ teas. baking soda
	1½ teas. dill seed
⅓ C. hot tap water	¼ teas. poppy seeds
2 tbsp. fresh minced onion or 1 teas. dried	1½ tbsp. toasted sesame seeds (see page 191)
	1½ teas. active dry yeast
	Pinch cayenne pepper (optional)

1. Combine the ingredients in the bread pan and select basic bread setting, following the manufacturer's directions.

2. When the cycle is complete and the bread is baked, turn it out immediately onto a rack to cool. Wrap in foil to store.

Bettie Henry's Three-Seeded ◇ Cottage Bread ◇

Makes 1½ pound loaf, basic bread setting

1 C. small-curd low-fat cottage

1 large egg

1 tbsp. unsalted butter or margarine, softened

½ C. hot tap water

¼ C. fresh minced onion or 2 tbsp. dried

3 C. bread flour

1½ teas. salt

½ teas. baking soda

2¼ teas. dill seed

¾ teas. poppy seeds

2¼ tbsp. toasted sesame seeds (see page 191)

1½–2 teas. active dry yeast

⅛ teas. cayenne pepper (optional)

Crusty Tomato–Pine Nut Bread with ◇ Clam Chowder ◇

Makes one 1-pound loaf, basic bread setting

- 4 C. bread flour
- 1/4 C. (1/2 stick) unsalted butter or margarine
- 1/3 C. pine nuts or sunflower seeds
- 3/4 teas. freshly ground black pepper
- 2 teas. salt
- 1 tbsp. grated lemon zest
- 1/3 C. milk
- 2 large eggs
- 3 tbsp. sugar
- 3/4 C. drained, canned plum tomatoes, pureed, or 3/4 cup tomato sauce
- 3 teas. active dry yeast

Manhattan ◇ Clam Chowder ◇

Makes 2 quarts in 30 minutes

There are 2 different schools of thought on clam chowder. One of us swears by New England with the cream base, the other adores Manhattan with the tomato base. We leave it up to you to decide which one is best. However, to save on calories and fat, we share with you the latter.

- 3 large baking potatoes
- 4 slices lean bacon, cut into 1-inch pieces
- 2 tbsp. unsalted butter or margarine
- 1 medium onion, chopped
- 2 medium carrots, chopped
- 2 stalks celery without tops, chopped
- 1/2 C. chopped red bell pepper

CRUSTY TOMATO–PINE NUT BREAD WITH MANHATTAN CLAM CHOWDER

Makes one 1-pound loaf, basic bread setting

Here on the West Coast we adore crusty bread "bowls" filled with chowders, soups, and stews. The bread machine is a natural for this endeavor. Either size machine will make 2 bowls, and you can save the middle and insides for croutons, crumbs, or the birds in the backyard.

- 2 1/4 C. bread flour
- 2 tbsp. unsalted butter or margarine
- 2 tbsp. pine nuts or sunflower seeds
- 1/2 teas. freshly ground black pepper
- 1 teas. salt
- 1 teas. grated lemon zest
- 1/4 C. milk
- 1 large egg
- 1 1/2 tbsp. sugar
- 1/2 C. drained, canned plum tomatoes, pureed or 1/2 cup tomato sauce
- 2 teas. active dry yeast
- Unsalted butter, for spreading in finished bread rolls

1. Process the ingredients according to the manufacturer's instructions for a basic bread setting.

2. Remove the bread from the pan to a rack to cool.

3. Preheat the oven to 350° F. To make the bread bowls, lay the loaf on its side and slice off one end, allowing about 3 inches for the depth of the bowl you're creating, and then slice the other bowl from the other end. Save the middle section for toast, croutons, or crumbs. Using a sharp knife, score 1-inch in from the crust. Then carefully remove the middles of the bowls, leaving a 1-inch thick shell. Place the bowls on a baking sheet and bake in the preheated oven for 10 to 15 minutes to toast lightly. Butter the inside of the bread bowls.

4. Slice a small section from the rounded top end so the bread will sit flat, and place the bread bowls in warmed soup bowls. Fill with Manhattan Clam Chowder and enjoy.

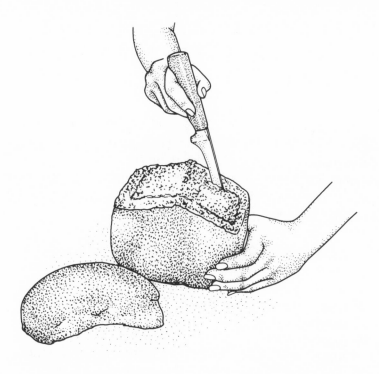

28-oz. can boiled baby clams, drained and liquid reserved
15-oz. can plum tomatoes, coarsely chopped
14¹/₂-oz. can chicken stock or 2 cups homemade chicken stock
¹/₂ teas. dried thyme or 1 teas. fresh
1 teas. salt
Freshly ground black pepper to taste

Garnish
Chopped fresh parsley

1. Wash the baking potatoes and pierce several times with a fork. Bake on high power in the microwave for 10 minutes or until they are not quite soft all the way through when pierced with a fork. Remove from the microwave and slice them open to cool. When they have cooled, peel and cut into large dice.

2. In a large soup pot over low heat, sauté the bacon until it is lightly browned and crisp, stirring frequently so that it does not burn. Remove the bacon from the pot and reserve.

3. Add the butter or margarine to the pot, and when it has melted, add the onion, carrots, celery, and red bell pepper. Cook over low heat until tender and translucent, about 10 minutes.

4. Add the reserved clam liquid, tomatoes, chicken broth, and the potatoes to the pot. Cover, and simmer for 15 minutes or until the potatoes are tender all the way through.

5. Add the clams, thyme, salt, and pepper. Heat just until the clams are heated through but do not boil.

6. Ladle into prepared soup bowls and garnish with parsley. Serve immediately.

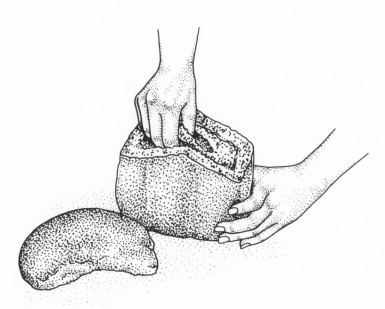

Dagwood
◇ Sandwich ◇

Nothing could be better than an oversize sandwich for a crowd. For this size sandwich you need approximately 1 pound thick-cut bacon, fried crisp and drained; 2 medium blood red ripe tomatoes; about 1 pound hand-carved turkey breast; lettuce, chicory, spinach, or your favorite greens; some first-rate mayo and mustard and perhaps a little cranberry chutney to go with the turkey; and at least 2 different kinds of cheeses (our favorites: Havarti and Muenster), about ¾ pound.

Spread the cut surfaces of the bread generously with the mayo and mustard and then layer the remaining ingredients. Such a feast.

DAGWOOD'S PICNIC SANDWICH ON WALNUT BREAD

Makes 1 large loaf, dough setting

There are times when a made-ahead sandwich for a crowd is the thing to serve. Picnics, beach parties, outdoor concerts, tailgate parties. The beauty of this bread is that it can be made ahead and filled right before you go. Make sure you store it properly in an ice chest with lots of ice to avoid the possibility of food poisoning.

2 teas. active dry yeast	**Glaze**
1 teas. sugar	1 egg white, lightly
1 C. milk	beaten
2 tbsp. unsalted	Sesame seeds, caraway
butter, room	seeds, poppy seeds,
temperature	coarsely grated
1½ teas. salt	Parmesan, kosher salt,
3 C. bread flour	or rolled oats, for
¼ C. ground walnuts	sprinkling on top
⅓ C. chopped walnuts	

1. Add the yeast, sugar, milk, butter, salt, flour, and ground walnuts to the bread pan. Process the ingredients according to the manufacturer's instructions for a dough setting.

2. Turn the dough out onto a lightly floured surface. Knead the dough for a few seconds to remove any remaining air bubbles. Knead the chopped walnuts into the dough.

3. Pinch off a quarter of the dough and reserve. Shape the remaining ¾ of the dough into a ball. Flatten the dough slightly and form into a 10-inch doughnut shape with a 2-inch hole in the middle. Place on a greased baking sheet (use a microwavable baking sheet if micro-rising).

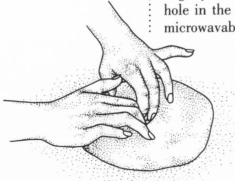

4. Divide the reserved dough into 5 equal pieces. Roll each piece between the palms of your hands to make a thin 10-inch-long rope. Fold each rope in half lengthwise and pinch to seal. Twist the rope several times, then arrange on top of the loaf, visually dividing the loaf into quarters. Tuck one end of each twisted rope into the hole and under the loaf, the other end across the loaf and under the outside edge. Cover the loaf loosely with a damp tea towel or plastic wrap and allow to rise until doubled in bulk (approximately 1 hour) in a warm, draft-free place, or you may micro-rise (see page 35). Meanwhile, preheat your oven to 400° F.

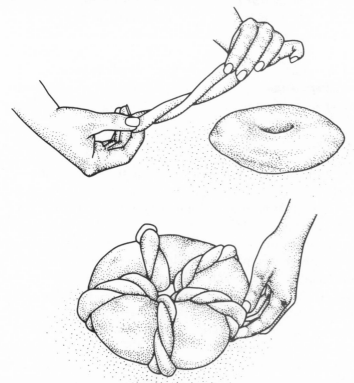

5. Brush the loaf with the beaten egg white. Sprinkle each quarter of the dough with your favorite topping from the above list. Bake the loaf in the preheated oven for 15 minutes. Lower the heat to 350° F and bake for an additional 15 to 20 minutes or until golden brown and the loaf sounds hollow when tapped.

6. Remove the bread to a rack to cool. After the bread has cooled completely, it may be sliced horizontally and filled with your favorite Dagwood fixin's.

To make hot dog buns, roll each ball with a floured rolling pin into a 6-inch long oval. Then starting on the long side, roll up tightly like a cigar, pinch the ends together and place seam-side down on the prepared baking sheet. Bake in a preheated 400° F oven for 12 to 15 minutes or until lightly browned. Let cool until just warm, split and fill. Try toasting on the grill next to the hot dogs for a slightly crunchy texture and good ol' fashioned barbecue taste.

HAMBURGER BUNS FLECKED WITH WHEAT GERM

Makes 6 to 8 buns, dough setting

With a fine crumb and moist texture, these buns have a nicely browned crust and an excellent flavor. A fine accompaniment to your hamburgers or hot dogs at the next picnic or barbecue.

3 C. bread flour	1 teas. salt
1/3 C. wheat germ	2½ teas. active dry yeast
1 large egg	
1/4 C. water	Glaze
3/4 C. milk	2 tbsp. butter, melted
1 tbsp. sugar	
2 tbsp. softened butter, or vegetable oil	

1. Process according to the manufacturer's directions for a dough setting.

2. Lightly grease a medium-sized baking sheet. Turn the dough out onto a lightly floured surface and knead a few times to remove any air bubbles. Divide the dough into 6 to 8 equal pieces. Form each piece into a ball and place on the prepared baking sheet. Press each ball lightly with the palm of your hand to flatten just a bit. Brush the tops with the melted butter. Cover the rolls with waxed paper or plastic wrap and set aside to rise in a warm, draft-free place until not quite double in size. Meanwhile, preheat the oven to 400° F.

3. When the rolls are almost double in size, bake in the preheated oven on the middle rack for 12 to 15 minutes or until they are lightly browned. Do not overbake or the crusts will become hard. Wrap in aluminum foil or place in a plastic bag to store or freeze.

16 ◆ FESTIVE SWEET, HOLIDAY, DESSERT, AND HIGH-TEA BREADS

Italian Angel Food 320

Lemon Dessert Bread 320

Apple Crumb Kuchen 321

Strawberry Savarin 322

Pineapple–Macadamia Nut Braid 324

Gram's Teddy Bear Bread 326

Christmas Bowknot Dinner Wreath 328

Christmas Sugar Canes 330

Pumpkin-Pecan Spice Bread 331

Cherry Bubble Coffee Cake 332

Challah 333

Italian Angel
◇ Food ◇

Makes 1½-pound loaf, basic bread setting

¾ C. warm water
3 large egg whites
6 tbsp. fruity olive oil
4 tbsp. sugar
¾ teas. salt
3 C. bread flour
1½–2 tbsp. active dry yeast

ITALIAN ANGEL FOOD

Makes one 1-pound loaf, basic bread setting

Light as an angel food cake but without all the sugar, this is a perfect ending to an Italian dinner. It's a sweet yeast cake, similar to French savarins (see page 322) and Babas au Rhum (see page 209); slice it thin and use as the basis for strawberry shortcake or serve it plain alongside a bowl of fresh fruit and soft cheeses.

½ C. warm water
2 large egg whites
4 tbsp. fruity olive oil
3 tbsp. sugar
½ teas. salt
2 C. bread flour
1–1½ teas. active dry yeast

1. Process according to the manufacturer's instructions for basic bread.
2. Turn out immediately onto a rack to cool. Wrap in foil to store.

Lemon Dessert
◇ Bread ◇

Makes 1½-pound loaf, basic bread setting

½ C. milk
2 eggs
¼ C. (½ stick) unsalted butter
¼ C. sugar
½ teas. salt
4 tbsp. fresh lemon juice
Zest of a lemon, minced
3 C. bread flour
1½–2 teas. active dry yeast

LEMON DESSERT BREAD

Makes one 1-pound loaf, basic bread setting

The texture of this bread is most like a fine sponge cake. Serve it sliced thin with fresh berries and whipped cream for dessert or, for tea, simply toasted, then layered with ricotta and a sprinkling of golden raisins. Vary the recipe by substituting orange or lime for the lemon.

⅓ C. milk
1 large egg
3 tbsp. unsalted butter
2 tbsp. sugar
¼ teas. salt
3 tbsp. fresh lemon juice
Zest of a lemon, minced
2 C. bread flour
1–1½ teas. active dry yeast

1. Process according to the manufacturer's instructions for basic bread.
2. Turn out immediately onto a rack to cool. Wrap in plastic to store.

APPLE CRUMB KUCHEN

Makes two 9-inch coffee cakes, dough setting

Apples top a not-too-sweet German cake with a light crumb topping. To really gild the lily, serve with barely sweetened whipped cream.

Cake
2¾ C. bread flour
2 tbsp. instant nonfat dry milk solids
2 tbsp. unsalted butter, room temperature
1 teas. salt
1 large egg
⅔ C. water
3 tbsp. sugar
2½ teas. active dry yeast

Apple Topping
5 C. cored, peeled, and thinly sliced Granny Smith or other tart cooking apples
(approximately 4 large apples)
1 C. sugar
2 tbsp. fresh lemon juice
⅓ C. golden raisins

Crumb Topping
⅓ C. all-purpose flour
3 tbsp. sugar
3 tbsp. light brown sugar
3 tbsp. unsalted butter or margarine, room temperature

Lightly sweetened whipped cream (optional)

1. Combine all of the cake ingredients in the bread pan and process according to the manufacturer's instructions for a dough setting.

2. Meanwhile, lightly grease two 9-inch cake pans and prepare your toppings. For the apple topping, combine all of the ingredients in a medium saucepan. Cook over high heat until the apples are soft and translucent, about 10 minutes, stirring occasionally so as not to burn them. Drain the apples, discarding the liquid, and let them cool.

3. For the crumb topping, mix the ingredients with a fork or pastry blender until crumbly.

4. Preheat the oven to 350° F. When the dough has finished the dough setting, remove it from the bread pan to a lightly floured surface and knead several times to remove any remaining air bubbles. Divide the dough in half and place

(continued)

each half in a prepared pan. Press the dough to the sides of the pan to cover the pan bottom completely. Spread half of the apple topping over each cake. Sprinkle half of the crumb topping over each cake. Set aside in a warm, draft-free place to rest for 15 minutes.

5. Bake the cakes on the middle rack of the preheated oven for 30 minutes or until the edges are lightly browned. Cool the kuchen in the pans on a wire rack. Serve with lightly sweetened whipped cream, if desired. Wrap in plastic wrap to store.

STRAWBERRY SAVARIN

Makes 1 large cake, dough setting

Savarin is a light French ring, a yeast cake soaked with spirited syrups and served as dessert. With the addition of strawberries, it takes on the characteristics of shortcake and Babas au Rhum (see page 209) all in one. You might also try changing the berries and matching them to their complementary glaze and spirit, such as blackberries with blackberry jam and *framboise*, raspberries with raspberry jam and *Chambord*.

Savarin
- 2 C. bread flour
- 4 large eggs
- 1 teas. salt
- ½ C. (1 stick) unsalted butter, room temperature and cut into 8 pieces
- ¼ C. water
- 2 tbsp. sugar
- 2½ teas. active dry yeast

Orange Syrup
- 1¼ C. sugar
- 1¼ C. water
- ½ C. fresh orange juice
- ½ C. Cointreau

Strawberry Glaze
- 1 C. strawberry jam

Strawberry Topping
- 3 C. strawberries, quartered
- ⅓ C. sugar
- ½ teas. coarsely ground black pepper

Whipped Cream
- 1 C. heavy cream
- 2 tbsp. confectioners' sugar
- 1 tbsp. Cointreau

1. Combine all of the ingredients for the savarin in the bread pan and process according to manufacturer's instructions for a dough setting. The dough will look like a batter, what Julia Child and the French bakers call a "paste."

2. Lightly grease a 9-inch ring mold or a 2-quart angel food cake pan (microwavable if you plan to micro-rise). When the dough has finished the dough setting, spoon the dough into the prepared pan. Cover the pan with plastic wrap or waxed paper and let rise in a warm place until the dough is level with the top of the pan (about 30 minutes), or you may micro-rise (see page 35). Remove the plastic wrap or waxed paper and let the dough rise for 20 more minutes. Meanwhile, preheat the oven to 375° F.

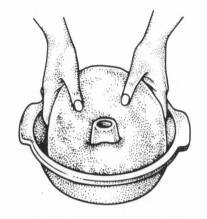

3. Bake the savarin on the middle rack of the preheated oven for 30 to 35 minutes or until light brown. Remove the pan from the oven and let the savarin cool in the pan for 5 minutes. With a knife, carefully loosen the edges and turn out onto a rack to cool completely.

4. For the orange syrup, combine the sugar and water in a large microwavable bowl and heat on low power until the sugar is dissolved, about 7 minutes. Add the orange juice and heat on medium power to a low boil. Remove from the microwave and add the Cointreau.

5. Place the cooled savarin in a bowl with deep sides large enough to accommodate it. Pour the orange syrup over the savarin and let stand until all the syrup is absorbed, about 15 minutes.

6. Process the strawberry jam in a food processor just until smooth. Brush the top and sides of the savarin with the jam to seal in the moisture. Slide the cake out of the bowl or gently turn the cake out of the bowl onto a platter and then turn right side up onto the serving platter.

7. For the strawberry topping, combine the berries, sugar, and pepper in a medium bowl and let stand for 15 minutes. Meanwhile, whip the cream until soft peaks form and add the confectioners' sugar, whipping until stiff peaks form. Fold in the Cointreau.

8. To serve, ladle the strawberries into the middle of the savarin and garnish with the whipped cream.

Fruit-filled breads are always a breakfast favorite. You may, however, want to try them for dessert. The same dough used for Pineapple–Macadamia Nut Braid may be used for different fillings. You might want to try the Kolacky fillings (see page 228–229).

Purple Prune ◇ Filling ◇

Makes 2 cups in 30 minutes

In a medium saucepan, combine 2 cups chopped prunes, 3 tbsp. sugar, 2 tbsp. fresh lemon juice, and bring to a boil. Boil 1 minute stirring occasionally; cool. Proceed with the assembly and topping instructions for the Pineapple–Macadamia Nut Braid, substituting the prune filling for the pineapple-nut filling.

PINEAPPLE–MACADAMIA NUT BREAD

Makes 1 large braided loaf, dough setting

Ideal for a busy schedule, this dough may be made the night before, stored in the refrigerator, filled, and baked in the morning. Even though the dough is made in the bread machine, we micro-rise it for the second raising period in 15 minutes.

2$\frac{1}{3}$ C. bread flour
$\frac{1}{8}$ C. sugar
$\frac{1}{2}$ teas. salt
$\frac{1}{2}$ C. milk
$\frac{1}{8}$ C. water
$\frac{1}{4}$ C. ($\frac{1}{2}$ stick) unsalted butter or margarine
1 large egg
2$\frac{1}{2}$ teas. active dry yeast

Filling
$\frac{1}{4}$ C. sugar
1 tbsp. cornstarch
1 C. crushed undrained pineapple, fresh or canned

1 C. coarsely chopped macadamia nuts
2 tbsp. unsalted butter or margarine

Topping
$\frac{1}{4}$ C. sugar
1 tbsp. unsalted butter or margarine, room temperature
2 tbsp. all-purpose flour

1. Process the flour, sugar, salt, milk, water, butter or margarine, egg, and yeast according to your manufacturer's instructions for a dough setting.

2. Meanwhile, prepare the pineapple–macadamia nut filling. Combine the sugar and cornstarch in a medium saucepan; blend well. Add the pineapple and nuts. Cook over medium heat until thickened, stirring constantly, about 3 minutes. Remove from the heat and add the butter or margarine, stirring until melted. Cool.

3. For the topping, blend the sugar, butter or margarine, and flour in a small bowl. Set aside.

4. Lightly grease a 10 × 12$\frac{1}{2}$-inch cookie sheet (glass if you plan to micro-rise). When the dough has finished the dough setting, remove it from the bread pan to a lightly

floured surface. Knead lightly a few times to remove any remaining air bubbles. The dough will be very soft. Roll the dough into a 10 × 12-inch rectangle and place it on the cookie sheet.

5. Spread the cooled filling in a 3-inch-wide strip lengthwise down the middle of the dough rectangle.

6. With a knife, cut the dough on the sides of the filling crosswise into 1-inch-wide strips. Fold the strips across the fillings alternately, resembling crossed arms.

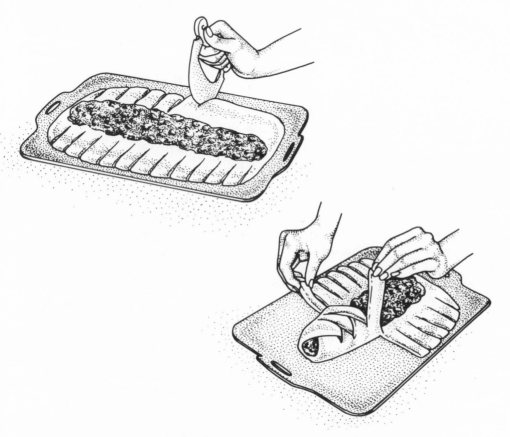

7. Cover loosely with a damp tea towel or plastic wrap and let rise in a warm, draft-free place for approximately 50 minutes or until doubled in bulk, or you may micro-rise the braid (see page 35). Meanwhile, preheat your oven to 375° F.

8. Sprinkle the topping mixture on top of the coffee cake. Bake on the middle rack in the preheated oven for 20 to 25 minutes or until golden brown. Cool on the baking sheet for 10 minutes and then remove to a rack to cool. Wrap in plastic wrap to store.

Gram's Teddy Bear
◇ Bread ◇

Makes 2 large bears, dough setting

2/3 C. sugar
3/4 teas. salt
3 teas. active dry yeast
1 C. graham flour
3 C. bread flour
1 C. milk
1/2 C. (1 stick) unsalted
  butter, room temperature
2 teas. ground cinnamon
1 large egg
1 tbsp. gluten flour
  (optional)

Garnish
6 raisins

Glaze
1 egg white, lightly beaten
  with 1 tbsp. water

The directions for 2 bears are the same as for 1 bear; however, you must first divide the dough in half before forming each half into equal numbers and sizes of balls.

GRAM'S TEDDY BEAR BREAD

Makes 1 large bear, dough setting

The perfect gift bread for children of all ages, this recipe is also suitable for underage helpers, because the dough can take whatever abuse kids dish out. They will think it's as much fun as modeling clay. Tasting somewhat like a graham cracker, this bread is great with a cold glass of milk. The dough can also be shaped into a variety of delicious beasts: turtles, crocodiles (sprinkled with green sugar), elephants. Try tying ribbons around the necks and giving as party favors.

1/3 C. sugar
1/2 teas. salt
1 1/2 teas. active dry yeast
1/2 C. graham flour
1 1/2 C. bread flour
1/3 C. plus 1 tbsp. milk
1/4 C. (1/2 stick) unsalted
  butter, room
  temperature
1 teas. ground
  cinnamon

1 large egg
1 tbsp. gluten flour
  (optional)

Garnish
3 raisins

Glaze
1 egg white, lightly
  beaten with 1 tbsp.
  water

1. Process the ingredients (except for the raisins and egg wash) according to your manufacturer's instructions for a dough setting.

2. Remove the dough from the bread pan at the end of the dough cycle. On a lightly floured surface, punch the dough down to remove any remaining air bubbles. Lightly grease a large baking sheet (glass if you plan on micro-rising).

3. Form the dough into one 5-inch ball for the body, one 3-inch ball for the head, four 2-inch balls for the legs, and three 1-inch balls for the ears and muzzle.

4. Lay the 5-inch ball on the baking sheet and lightly flatten to form the body. Lightly flatten the 3-inch circle for the head and tuck it under slightly at the top of the body. Lightly flatten the three 1-inch balls and place 1 in the middle of the head to form a muzzle and the other 2 slightly under the top of the head to form the ears. Lightly flatten the four 2-inch balls for the legs and tuck them under slightly around the outside of the body.

5. Push the 3 raisins deep into the dough to form the eyes and a belly button. With scissors, snip fingers and toes. Brush the bear lightly with the egg glaze; discard any leftover glaze.

6. Cover; let rise in a warm place away from draft, until doubled in bulk, about 40 minutes, or you may micro-rise (see page 35). Meanwhile, preheat the oven to 375° F.

7. Bake the bear on the middle rack of the preheated oven for 25 minutes. Let the bear cool completely on the cookie sheet before removing. Wrap in plastic wrap or bags to store.

CHRISTMAS BOWKNOT DINNER WREATH

Makes 18 bowknot rolls, dough setting

Let the bread machine do the kneading and first rising for your Christmas rolls, and you're free to prepare the rest of the Christmas dinner. Tie these rolls into bowknots, then form into a 12-inch ring, and you'll have the most festive Christmas wreath around. If you're serving more than 8 people, you'll probably want to make 2 batches. These rolls, tender with sour cream, melt in your mouth and get eaten up fast.

When you serve this Christmas wreath, place a small bowl of parsley butter in the center of the wreath (see pages 162–164) for fresh herb butters). If you'd like, you can vary this recipe by replacing ¾ cup of the bread flour with an equal portion of whole wheat flour.

½ C. plus 2 tbsp. sour cream	3 C. bread flour
½ C. water	2–2½ teas. active dry yeast
¼ C. (½ stick) unsalted butter, cut into pieces	
1 large egg	**Glaze**
2 tbsp. sugar	1 egg, beaten with 1 tbsp. water
½ teas. salt	Sesame seeds, for sprinkling on top

1. Combine all the ingredients except the glaze and the seeds in the bread pan and process on dough setting.

2. Meanwhile, prepare a 12-inch springform pan or cookie sheet by generously buttering a 12-inch circle of baker's parchment and placing it in the lightly greased baking pan.

3. When the dough cycle is complete, remove the dough to a lightly floured surface and punch down. Divide the dough into 18 equal-sized pieces. Roll each piece into an 8-inch-long rope and tie in a knot. Arrange the bowknots in a 12-inch ring on the baker's parchment in the prepared pan with the sides barely touching and the loose ends of the knots all pointing the same way. Cover and place in a warm, draft-free place to rise until double, about 20 minutes or micro-rise (see page 35).

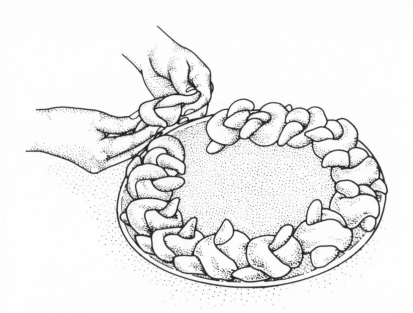

4. Meanwhile, preheat the oven to 400° F. Brush the egg glaze on raised rolls. Sprinkle generously with the sesame seeds. Bake the rolls 18 to 25 minutes on the middle rack of a preheated oven until golden brown.

5. Remove from the baking sheet and cool on the parchment on a rack for at least 15 minutes before serving. Serve warm with butter. Best eaten the day they're made.

CHRISTMAS SUGAR CANES

Makes 3 dozen sugar canes, dough setting

These delicious candy canes look great on a Christmas tree but won't last long. The Christmas elves at your house will likely eat them up. This is one job you won't have any trouble recruiting volunteers for, either. Who wouldn't like to spread luscious brown sugar–nut filling into rich bread dough, then cut and twist them into candy cane shapes?

⅓ C. sour cream
3 tbsp. unsalted butter
1 large egg
½ C. water
3 tbsp. sugar
1 teas. salt
3 C. bread flour
2½ teas. active dry yeast

Nut Filling
1 C. finely chopped hazelnuts or other nuts of your choice
⅔ C. packed brown sugar
6 tbsp. unsalted butter, melted

1 tbsp. lemon zest
1 tbsp. orange zest

Glaze
1 egg, beaten with 1 teas. water

Frosting
1 C. confectioners' sugar
2 tbsp. unsalted butter, softened
1–2 tbsp. milk
½ teas. vanilla extract

1. Process the first 8 bread ingredients on the dough setting of the bread machine.

2. Meanwhile, grease 2 cookie sheets and prepare the nut filling. Combine finely chopped nuts, brown sugar, melted butter, lemon zest, and orange zest in a small bowl. Stir to mix, and set aside.

3. Once the dough cycle is complete, remove the dough to a lightly floured surface, punch down, and divide the dough in 2 pieces. Roll each piece into a 12 × 9-inch rectangle. Top each piece with half the nut filling. Fold the dough in half lengthwise so that you now have a 12 × 9-inch filled rectangle. Pinch the long edge to seal. Cut each rectangle into 18 strips that are each 9 inches long.

4. Holding both ends, twist the ends of each strip in op-

posite directions 5 or 6 times. Place the strip on the prepared cookie sheet, forming into candy cane shape.

5. Cover loosely with waxed paper and place in a warm, draft-free place until risen almost double, about 20 minutes.

6. Meanwhile, preheat the oven to 375° F. Once the canes have risen, lightly brush the egg glaze onto the canes. Bake in the preheated oven 15 minutes or until golden brown.

7. Immediately remove the canes from the cookie sheet to a rack to cool.

8. Once the canes have cooled, mix confectioners' sugar icing in the processor using the steel blade. If you're patient, you can apply the white icing in candy cane stripes. If you or your elves are simply ravenous, slather the icing onto the candy canes and eat immediately.

PUMPKIN-PECAN SPICE BREAD

Makes one 1-pound loaf, basic bread setting

Linda remembers as a child a pumpkin-pecan quick bread that her mother made for lunches and snacks. Sweet, moist, and chewy, this is our yeast bread version. This bread would make a fragrant and colorful addition to your Thanksgiving breadbasket.

1 3/4 C. bread flour
1/2 C. whole wheat flour
1 tbsp. unsalted butter or margarine, room temperature
1/2 teas. salt
1/2 teas. pumpkin pie spice
1 large egg
1/3 C. milk
1/8 C. orange juice
1/4 C. canned pumpkin
1/4 C. sugar
1/3 C. pecan pieces
1 1/2–2 teas. active dry yeast

1. Process the ingredients according to the manufacturer's instructions for basic bread setting.

2. Remove the bread from the bread pan to a rack to cool. Wrap in aluminum foil or a paper bag to store.

Pumpkin-Pecan ◇ Spice Bread ◇

Makes one 1 1/2-pound loaf, basic bread setting

3 C. bread flour
1/2 C. whole wheat flour
1 1/2 tbsp. unsalted butter or margarine, room temperature
1 teas. salt
1 teas. pumpkin pie spice
1 large egg
1/2 C. milk
1/4 C. orange juice
1/2 C. canned pumpkin
1/3 C. sugar
1/2 C. pecan pieces
2–2 1/2 teas. active dry yeast

CHERRY BUBBLE COFFEE CAKE

Makes 1 large coffee cake, dough setting

Kids will love this!! A tasty blend of cherries and almonds. The bubble effect is created when the dough on top rises through the cherries like a bubble about to burst. Old-fashioned batter breads develop gluten by beating and were used by cooks-in-a-hurry when the only machine they had was a wooden spoon. Serve warm for an after-school snack.

3¼ C. bread flour
¼ C. sugar
1 teas. salt
½ C. milk
½ C. water
½ C. (1 stick) unsalted butter or margarine
2 large eggs
2½ teas. active dry yeast
21-oz. can cherry pie filling

Glaze
1 C. confectioners' sugar
2–3 tbsp. sour cream
½ teas. almond extract

Garnish
¼ C. sliced almonds

1. Process the flour, sugar, salt, milk, water, butter or margarine, eggs, and yeast according to your manufacturer's instructions for a dough setting. This will make a very thick batter instead of a dough. Meanwhile, generously grease a 13 × 9-inch baking pan (glass if micro-rising).

2. When the batter has finished the dough setting, spoon ⅔ of the batter into the prepared pan; spread evenly on the bottom of the pan. Top the batter with the cherry filling; spread evenly over the batter. Spoon the remaining batter by heaping tablespoonfuls over the cherries.

3. Cover and let rise in a warm, draft-free place until light and the cherries are just under the top of the pan, about 20 to 30 minutes, or you can micro-rise (see page 35). Meanwhile, preheat your oven to 350° F.

4. Bake the cake on the middle rack for 35 to 40 minutes or just until golden brown. Remove the pan to a rack and prepare the glaze. Blend the glaze ingredients in a small bowl until smooth. Drizzle the glaze over the cake while it is still slightly warm and sprinkle with the almonds. Serve the cake slightly warm. Cover the cake with plastic wrap to store.

CHALLAH

Makes one 1-pound braided loaf, dough setting

Challah, the Jewish Sabbath bread, a lovely braided yellow loaf of egg-rich dough with a golden crust speckled with poppy and sesame seeds, makes a fine centerpiece for a family supper and makes great bread pudding.

1 tbsp. sugar
1 teas. salt
2/3 C. water
1 large egg
3 tbsp. unsalted butter or margarine, melted and cooled
2¾ C. bread flour
2 teas. active dry yeast

Glaze
1 large egg, lightly beaten with 2 tbsp. milk

1 tbsp. poppy seeds and 1 tbsp. sesame seeds, for sprinkling on top

1. Add the sugar, salt, water, egg, butter or margarine, flour, and yeast to the bread pan. Process the ingredients according to the manufacturer's instructions for a dough setting.

2. Lightly grease a baking sheet (microwavable if you plan to micro-rise). Remove the dough from the bread pan to a lightly floured surface and knead several times to remove any remaining air bubbles. Divide the dough into 3 equal pieces. Roll each piece into a rope 12 inches long. Lay the 3 ropes parallel on the baking sheet and braid together. Pinch the ends together securely and tuck under. Brush the loaf with the beaten egg and milk glaze (discard any remaining glaze) and sprinkle with the seeds.

3. Cover loosely with a damp tea towel or plastic wrap and place in a warm, draft-free place to rise until doubled in bulk, or you may micro-rise (see page 35). Meanwhile, preheat the oven to 350° F.

4. Bake the loaf until golden and the bread sounds hollow when tapped, about 35 to 45 minutes. Remove from the baking sheet to a rack to cool. Wrap in a plastic bag or foil to store.

Bread Machine
◇ Challah ◇

Makes one 1½-pound loaf, dough setting

2 tbsp. sugar
1½ teas. salt
2/3 C. water
2 large eggs
¼ C. (½ stick) unsalted butter or margarine, melted and cooled
3½ C. bread flour
2½ teas. active dry yeast

Glaze
1 large egg, lightly beaten with 2 tablespoons milk
1 tbsp. poppy seeds and 1 tbsp. sesame seeds, for sprinkling on top

To braid the 1½-pound Challah, roll the 3 equal-sized pieces of dough into 14-inch-long ropes.

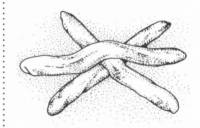

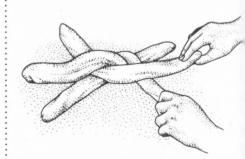

SOURCES FOR EQUIPMENT AND INGREDIENTS

Our sensibilities have been sharpened about the value of particular products for particular tasks during the testing of recipes for this book. We've become quite attached to the machines we use in our kitchens every day. These faithful friends have not let us down. We recommend them to you without reservation. If you can't find these products in local stores, give a call to the main office and they'll help you find the nearest retailer.

We've also gotten quite persnickety about supplies and ingredients. Professional bakers say time and time again that "it's the flour," so we've gotten fussy about using certain flours for certain jobs. Although we rely most often on bread flour from the supermarket, we do find that stone-ground whole wheat flour differs markedly from commercial "remixed" whole wheat. We offer this list of sources for specialized baker's supplies in the hope that you'll soon come to love baking so such that you'll be ordering specialty flours just for the play value of trying new recipes. We also love to try new yeasts. Different strains from different countries produce different tasting breads. Do try Dutch yeast, French yeast, and Italian yeasts.

There simply is no substitution for the right tool for the right job. We love our baking stones, our cloches, and our Chicago deep-dish pizza pans. We enjoy special pans and molds needed for specialty breads. Here's where to get them if you can't find them in your local shops.

FOOD PROCESSORS

Black and Decker (U.S.) Inc.
6 Armstrong Road
Shelton, CT 06484
203-926-3489

How did we ever keep house without our little Shortcut food processor? What a dandy countertop friend to chop an onion, or grate cheese, or even mix and knead a pizza dough.

Braun, Inc.
66 Broadway, Rte. 1
Lynnfield, MA 01940
617-596-7300

Our UK240 food processor kneads dough from the biggest recipes we have with ease. One thing we particularly like about this workhorse is that it comes with all the attachments. You don't have to buy them one by one after you've made the initial purchase.

Cuisinart Inc.
150 Milford Road
East Windsor, NJ 08520
800-726-0190

The grandmother of all food processors, call them for a retail outlet near you. Ask for the new model, 8-cup capacity, with a plastic dough blade and metal blade for doughs with fruits and for all other doughs.

BREAD MACHINES

MK Seiko
VSSI
7116 Sophia Avenue
Van Nuys, CA 91406-3912
818-785-5400

A reliable one-pound machine that's neat on the counter and quiet.

Panasonic
Matsushita Electronics Corp.
of America
1 Panasonic Way
Secaucus, NJ 07094
201-348-7000

Holding the lion's share of the market, this reliable machine comes in one and one-and-a-half pound sizes and is also marketed under the name National. We must have made a thousand loaves of bread in our Panasonics. We find them sturdy and dependable for turning out all sorts of breads. We're so glad they've made a whole wheat machine.

Sanyo
SFS Corporation, Chatsworth
  Division
21350 Lassen Street
Chatsworth, CA 91311
808-998-7322

A reliable one-pound machine that makes a vertical rectangular shaped loaf. We used this bread machine with ancillary cross testers who weren't heavy duty cooks. At the end of the testing period, they were so devoted to these machines we could hardly get them back.

Welbilt Corporation
3333 New Hyde Park Road
New Hyde Park, NY 11042
516-365-5040

Also known as R2D2, this machine makes an excellent quality cylindrical one-and-a-half pound loaf and has a good blower system to cool down the bread. A new model, well priced at about $100, is now available.

Zojirushi America Corp.
5628 Bandini Blvd.
Bell, CA 90201
213-264-6270

Last, but certainly not least, the one-and-a-half pound machine that we adore. The Zojirushi name means "elephant mark," and, believe us, this machine has made it's mark in our kitchens. We've worked it harder than elephants raising the circus tent. We like it.

MICROWAVE OVENS

Although there are many reliable microwave ovens on the market, we tested with Amana, Panasonic, Sharp, and Whirlpool. We recommend 650–700 watt ovens with or without a carousel. We tested in a small cavity 500 watt oven as well but found it less than ideal for micro-rising. (See introduction to Part One for more discussion.) Any of the national brands you find locally that fit the requirements for micro-rise should serve reliably.

GENERAL EQUIPMENT

The Chef's Catalog
3915 Commercial Avenue
Northbrook, IL 60062
312-480-9400

Good equipment and supplies for bakers including bread machines, pans, and stones.

Community Coffee
P.O. Box 3778
Baton Rouge, LA 70821
800-535-9901

Besides having specialty cooking supplies, they also sell bread machines.

Maid of Scandinavia
3244 Raleigh Avenue
Minneapolis, MN 55416
612-927-7996

Call for a baker's catalog. They sell both equipment and ingredients.

Planned Pottery
P.O. Box 5045
Eugene, OR 97405
503-345-2471

Wonderful unglazed terra cotta bread loaf pans, pizza bakers, a French bread baker, and tile squares to line the oven to create a fair approximation of a European brick oven for breads.

Sassafras Enterprises, Inc.
1622 West Carroll Avenue
Chicago, Illinois 60612
312-226-2000 or WATS
  1-800-537-4941

Here's where you can get a cloche or a pizza stone as well as a pizza peel, rectangular baking stones, and deep dish Chicago-style pizza pans. Good quality clayware.

Williams Sonoma
P.O. Box 7456
San Francisco, CA 94120
415-421-4242

Panasonic bread machines, stones, special pans and molds, La Cloche, special thermometers, and scales for those who want to begin weighing flour the way professional bakers do.

FLOURS

Arrowhead Mills
P.O. Box 866
Hereford, TX 79045
713-364-0730

Linda's hometown, and home of the famous mill that stonegrinds organically grown hard wheat and other grains into flour. They also produce durum flour, rice flour, pastry flour, and cornmeals.

Blue Corn Connection
8812 4th Street N.W.
Alameda, NM 87144
505-897-2412

In case you get a yen to make your cornbread blue, here's the place to order blue corn flour. When you get this flour, you'll see it's a nice shade of lavender. Add it to bread dough and don't be startled to see that the bread is shirt-flannel gray. Oh, well, remember, the Hopi Indians call it "strong food," Indian Chicken soup, Pueblo penicillin. At a hospital in Gallup, they keep blue corn on hand to feed to patients who refuse to eat anything else.

Brumwell Flour Mill
South Amana, IA 52333
319-622-3455

The Brumwell's stone grind flours using stones that, until recently, were turned by the motor they'd recycled from their daddy's Buick. For modest prices, you can order whole wheat flour, graham flour, rye meal and flour, unbleached white flour, buckwheat and whole wheat. The Brumwell's ship direct and don't warehouse their products, so you're getting quite fresh flours.

Butte Creek Mill
402 Royal Avenue North Box 561
Eagle Point, OR 97524
503-826-3531

Right up the road a piece from where we test breads is a mill that stone grinds flour be-tween stones that weigh 1,400 pounds. In addition to flours, meals, and cracked grains, they sell some interesting bread mixes you might want to try. Ask owner Cora Crandall to send you her recipe for whole wheat rolls with your flour order. It's great.

Falling Waters Stone-Ground
   Flours and Meals
1788 Tuthilltown Grist Mill
Albany Post Road
Gardiner, NY 12525
914-255-5695

If you live in the eastern half of the country, this may be the mill of choice for stone ground flours and meals. Their buckwheat is especially recommended.

Giusto's
241 East Harris Avenue
South San Francisco, CA 94080
415-873-6566

A prodigious list of grains and flours, organically grown and freshly milled. They also offer semolina and durum flours, graham, oat, rice, rye, and pastry flours.

Goldrush Enterprises
122 East Grand Avenue
South San Francisco, CA 94080
800-531-2039

Want sourdough but you don't want to make it? Order it dehydrated, then mix with water and begin baking right away.

SPICES, CHEESES, YEASTS, AND OTHER SPECIAL INGREDIENTS

American Spoon Foods
411 East Lake Street
Petoskey, MI 49770
616-347-9030

Dried cherries for your best breakfast breads as well as dried local mushrooms for pizzas or to dapple other flatbreads. They also make great jams and a rare, raspberry honey that's heaven with toast.

Balducci's
424 Sixth Avenue
New York, NY 10011
212-673-2600

Best quality imports. Write for their catalog.

Dean and DeLuca
121 Prince Street
New York, NY 10012
212-254-8776

Best quality imports for herbs, spices, sundried tomatoes, olive paste, olive oils and olives, porcini.

Fleischman's Yeast Inc.
Specialty Brands
222 Sutter Street
P.O. Box 7004
San Francisco, CA 94120-7004
800-777-4959

Call the Baker's Help Line for the answers to questions about yeast.

Kendall Cheese Co.
P.O. Box 686
Atascadero, CA 93423
805-466-7252

Sadie Kendall makes the best goat cheeses by hand to top a pizza or put in a calzone. She also makes lovely crème fraîche and chevredoux, made with half cow's and half goat's milk. Ask her for her cookbook. What a cook!

Muirhead
Box 189 RD 1
Ringoes, NJ 08551
201-782-7803

Doris Simpson makes interesting compound butters from her own garden-grown herbs, a great cranberry conserve, and apricot-jalapeño jelly you'll love.

Paprikas Weiss
1546 Second Avenue
New York, NY 10028
212-288-6117

Thousands of items; they import terrific spices, peppers, cheeses.

G. B. Ratto, International Grocers
821 Washington Street
Oakland, CA 94607
415-832-6503

Good selection of imported olive oils and other Mediterranean foods as well as grains and meals, seeds and nuts. An enormous catalog.

Rising Sun Farm
2300 Colestin Road
Ashland, OR
800-888-0795

Wonderful flavored honeys spiced up with Elizabeth Fujas's own organic herbs and spices. She also makes a nationally known, award-winning pesto torta with sundried tomatoes that, spread on a baguette, is heaven on earth. We have been known to buy a torta for two and eat the whole thing with our Sour Faux bread before the party begins.

H. Roth and Sons
1577 First Avenue
New York, NY 10028
212-734-1111

Flours, flavorings, essences. Crystallized baking sugar. Baking equipment.

S. E. Rykoff
P.O. Box 21467
Market Street Station
Los Angeles, CA 90021
800-421-9873

Great olives, chocolates, oils.

Sonoma Cheese Factory
2 Spain Street
Sonoma, CA 95476
707-938-JACK

For California-style pizza, use California Jack from Sonoma. Comes laced with garlic or peppers too. Smooth, velvety and low fat.

Todaro Bros.
557 Second Avenue
New York, NY 10016
212-679-7766

All things Italian. Cheese, olives, olive oils, porcini, prosciutto.

Universal Foods Corporation
P.O. Box 737
Milwaukee, WI 53201
414-347-3849

The Red Star yeast people have this help number so that you can call in if you're stumped by something the yeast in your house did today. Call them. We did. They're a big help.

Vella Cheese of California
315 Second Street East
P. O. Box 191
Sonoma, CA 95476
707-938-3232

Ignazio Vella makes by hand a nutty sweet, medium cure parmesan-like dry jack cheese that's heaven on a pizza. Get a wheel. It lasts about a year around here and is our choice for the all-purpose dry grating cheese for breads.

Williams Sonoma
P.O. Box 7456
San Francisco, CA
   94120-7456
415-421-4242

Excellent specialty yeasts, vanilla, chocolate, cocoa, olive oil, tomato paste: absolutely the best quality baker's supplies in the business. We love their French yeast for sweet doughs and their Italian Pizza yeast. Using it in the bread machines, we get the best tasting breads with no trouble at all.

◆ I N D E X

Bread machine recipe

Adding nuts and seeds to dough,
    33, 206
*After Church Angel Biscuits, 291
All-Star Calzone, 174–175
Almond Crumb Streusel, 229
Almond Spice Honey, 230
*Alpine Kaiser Rolls, 286
Amber Waves of Grain, 214
Anadama Dinner Rolls, 154–155
Anchovy-Garlic Crostini, 56
Anita's Sour Faux, 58–59
apple butter, 84
Apple Butter Bread, 84–85
Apple Crumb Kuchen, 321
appropriate micro-rise setting: a
    test, 35
*Apricot–Cream Cheese Braids,
    272
apricot filling, 228
apricot glaze for rolls, 229
Austrian Plunder Brot, 114–115

Babas Au Rhum, 209
**Bagels, Baguettes, Bread-
    sticks, Buns, and Rolls**
    Micro-Rise method, 137–164
    Bread Machine recipes, 281–
        292
bagels, water, 142, *282

baguettes
    *French, 257
    *Prosciutto, 278
    pumpernickel, 139
    sour faux, 58
    tomato-basil, 140
Baked Cinnamon Sugar Dough-
    nuts, 116–117
**Baking Equipment and Uten-
    sils,** 20–21, 25–26, 335
    Chef's Catalog, 335
    Community Coffee, 335
    Maid of Scandinavia, 335
    Planned Pottery, 335
    Sassafras, 22, 335
    Williams Sonoma, 335
*barbecued pork filling for
    steamed buns, 304
Basic Breads
    Micro-Rise method, 49–74
    Bread Machines, 251–259
batter breads
    garden, 204
    panettone, 222
*Beef and Potato Knishes, 305
beer breads
    Lager Bread, 193
    rye and kraut, 194
    Swedish Rye, 198
    Uncle Larry's, 73
    *Whole Wheat, 264

*Beginner's Brioche, 267
Bettie Henry's Three-Seeded Cot-
    tage Bread, 191, *313
Bing Hasty Pudding, 234
*Birdseed Bread, 266
biscuits
    low fat, 77
    *Angel, 291
black bread, 68–69
Black Olive Pesto, 70
*Black Walnut-Banana Bread, 271
*Blueberry-Granola Breakfast
    Bread, 270
bourbon sauce, 233
*bread and chocolate, 268
*Bread Machine Bagels, 282–283
Bread Machine Basics, 239–
    240
Bread Machine Features, 246–
    247
Bread Machines
    MK Seiko, 334
    Panasonic, 334
    Sanyo, 335
    Welbilt, 335
    Zojirushi, 335
bread puddings
    Bing and raspberry, 234
    breakfast, 100
    brioche, 233
    butterscotch, 235

orange, 230
tropical, 108
breadstick centerpiece, 147
breadsticks
herb, large, 146
Parmesan, 148
sweet, 150
Breadsticks Grande, 146–147
**Breakfast and Brunch
Breads**
Micro-Rise Method, 94–120
Bread Machine, 266–274
*brioche, 267
Brioche Bread Pudding, 233
Brown and Serves, 151–152
Buttermilk Bread, 60–61
butters, flavored
anchovy, 164
apricot, 163
avocado, 163
caper, 164
chili, 164
chocolate, 212
chocolate almond, 164
cinnamon sugar, 163
cracked pepper, 163
El Paso, 163
four pepper, 164
Herbes de Jardine, 163
Herbes de Provence, 164
honey-lemon, 285
horseradish-chive, 164
Los Angeles, 163
mustard-tarragon, 164
orange, 155
parsley-dill, 163
pesto, 163
Quatre Epices, 21
red pepper, 164
roasted red pepper, 164
rosemary, 163
saffron-leek, 164
shallot garlic, 164
Sonoma, 164
strawberry-honey, 164
Butterscotch Bread Pudding, 235
butterscotch sauce, 236

Cajun Shrimp Grinders, 312
calzone
All-Star, 174–175
*anchovy, olive, tomato, 300
cheddar and clam, 174
*crusty, 299
*fresh tomato sauce, 301
*Italian sausage, cheese,
onion, 300
*Niçoise, 301
*pesto, cheese, tomato, 300
tomato, chicken, cheese, 175
*veggie, 300
caponata, half-time, 124
Carrot-Currant-Wheat Berry
Bread, 86–87
Cheddar and Clam Calzone, 174
cheese
fondue, 218
watercress, 139
cheese breads
calzones, 174–175, *300–301
Chicago-style pizza, 168
cottage cheese, 190, *263,
*313
cracked pepper parmesan, 187
goat cheese pizza, 170
gorgonzola, 126
*Khachapuri, 275
Italian loaf, 172
*onion cream cheddar rolls,
292
Parmesan breadsticks, 148
pizza, 165–189, *293–307
Sedona, 180
Swiss and potato savarin, 195
Swiss-cheddar, 178
Tabasco-cheddar, 311
cheese fondue, 218
cheese soup, Canadian, 204
Cherry Bubble Coffee Cake, 332
cherry filling, 229
chicken and dumplings, 203
Chicago-Style Two-Crust Pizza,
168–169
Chinese Steamed Buns with Barbecued Pork Filling, 304

chocolate
*and bread, 268
cherry kugelhupf, 212
sauce, 230
Chocolate Cafe Au Lait, 224
Chocolate-Cherry Kugelhupf, 212
chocolate sauce, 230
choosing a crust, 46–48, 93
*Christmas Bowknot Dinner
Wreath, 328
*Christmas Sugar Canes, 330
cinnamon breads
baked doughnuts, 116
coffee cake, 109
crullers, 118
monkey bread, 98
pinwheel bread, 100
toast, 97, 104
Cinnamon Pinwheel Bread, 100–
101
Cinnamon Roll Coffee Cake,
112–113
Cinnamon Sugar Crullers, 118–
119
Citrus Avocado Salad, 232
clay baker, 24, 69
clay baking, 21, 24, 69
coffee cakes
*apricot cream-cheese, 272
*cherry bubble, 332
cinnamon roll, 112
German, 110
hazelnut, 220
*honey buns, 268
pecan praline, 224
*pineapple-macadamia nut
bread, 324
orange danish, 218
coffee drinks, 224
Columbus Circle Salad, 173
composed salad: roasted red/green
peppers, 123
Corn and Roast Pepper Gazpacho, 180
*cornbread, 253
cottage cheese
bread, 191, *263

*dilly bread, 309
sun-dried tomato pita sandwich
    filling, 189
three-seeded cottage bread,
    191, *313
cottage cheese filling, 228
Country Bread with Pears, Hazel-
    nuts, and Gorgonzola, 126–
    127
Country Raisin-Walnut Bread,
    128–129
*Country White Potato Bread, 254
Cracked Pepper Parmesan Bread,
    187–188
Cracked Wheat Bread, 79–80
cream cheese filling, 228
cream of cheese soup, 292
Crete Bread, 134–135
Crostini with Mushroom and Tar-
    ragon Cream, 74
croutons
    from breadsticks, 148
    herb seasoned, 130
    with Parmean, 257
crumpets, 102
*Crusty Calzone, 299
*Crusty Tomato–Pine Nut Bread,
    314
curried fruit, 120

Dagwood's Picnic Sandwich, 316
Dampfnudeln, 202–203
Deaf Smith Co. Wheat Bread, 72
*Dilly Bread, 309
Divine Butterhorn Rolls, 156–157
*Dr. Michael's Yeast Corn Bread,
    253
doughnuts
    baked, 116
    jelly, 116
*Dried Cherry Butterfly Rolls, 288
dumplings, raised, 202

Egg salad, 193
Eggs Sardou, 102

eggs
    custard, 110
    frittata, 118
    goldenrod eggs, 90
    in toast, 105
    huevos con salsa, 106
    milk toast, 101, 109
    salad, 193
    Sardou, 102
    scalloped, 114
    spinach-cheese torta, 133
Eggs with Frizzled Pastrami on
    Rye, 68
eggplant, pepper and artichoke
    torta, 302
English muffins, 103–104
English muffin loaf, 104–105

Featherweight White Bread,
    88–89
**Festive Sweet, Holiday, Des-
    sert, and High-Tea
    Breads**
    Micro-Rise method, 207–236
    Bread Machine, 319–333
Filled Breads
    *beef potato knishes, 306
    calzones, 174–175, *300–301
    Chicago-style pizza, 168
    *Chinese steamed buns, 304
    green onion and olive, 176
    Italian loaf rustica, 172
    orange danish, 218
    Swiss-cheddar, 178
Filled Swiss-Cheddar Bread,
    178–179
*Finally Focaccia, 298
finishing the loaf, 46–48, 93
**Fitness, Health and High-Fiber
    Breads**
    Micro-Rise Method, 75–93
    Bread Machine, 260–265
flatbreads
    *focaccia, 298
    green-olive fougasse, 182
    *pissaladière, 296

plain focaccia, 184
plain pizza, 167
rosemary-raisin focaccia, 185
sugar crusted galette, 210
fresh tomato pizza, 170
*West Coast pizza, 294
flour mills
    Arrowhead Mills, 335
    Blue Corn Connection, 336
    Brumwell Flour Mill, 336
    Butte Creek Mill, 336
    Falling Waters Stone-Ground
        Flours and Meals, 336
    Giusto's, 336
    Goldrush Enterprises, 336
flours
    all-purpose enriched white, 5
    bread, 4
    gluten, 6
    Graham, 6
    instant-blending, 5
    potato, 7
    self-rising, 5
    Semolina, 7
    unbleached white, 5
    whole wheat, 6
flours, storing, 7
focaccia
    anchovy, 184
    bacon, 184
    *blanca, 298
    *breakfast, 299
    *finally, 298
    green olive, 182
    *olive, 299
    onion, 184, 298
    pear-gorgonzola, 298
    plain, 184
    roasted red pepper, 299
    rosemary-raisin, 185
    sage, 184
    sun-dried tomato, 184
food processor kneading, 30, 32
food processors, 16–17, 334
    Black and Decker, 334
    Braun, 33, 69, 334
    Cuisinart, 334

forming rolls, 44–46
  bagels, 282
  butterfly, 289
  cinnamon snails, 46
  cloverleaf, 45
  crescents, 44
  fantans, 45
  *hamburger buns, 318
  *hotdog buns, 318
  *knishes, 307
  palm leaves, 46
  pan rolls, 44
  Parker House, 45
  pinwheels, 45
fougasse, green olive, 182
*free-form French baguette, 257
French bread
  *baguettes, 257
  *hands-off, 255
  hard rolls, 158
  pane all'olio, 54
  *petit prosciutto, 278
  sour faux, 58
French bread salad, 135–136
French Country Bread in a
    Cloche, 69–70
*French Filbert Bread, 279
French Milk Toast, 109
French toast, 109, 274
frittata, breakfast, 118
fruit breads
  *apple crumb kuchen, 321
  *apricot–cream cheese, 272
  Babas au rhum, 209
  *banana black walnut, 271
  *cherry bubble, 332
  kolacky, 226
  *lemon dessert, 320
  monkey bread, 99
  panettone, 222
  pear, hazelnut, gorgonzola, 126
  pecan-date swirl, 269
  orange danish, 218
  orange grove, 230
  *pineapple-macadamia nut
      braid, 324
  *strawberry, 322

fruits
  curried, 120
  method for adding, 129

Garden Batter Bread, 204–205
*Garlic Pepper Bread, 297
Garlic spread, 58–59
gazpacho, corn and red pepper,
    180
German Coffee Cake, 110
Gizzie's Grinder Juice, 311
Gizzie's Grinder Rolls, 312
glazing yeast breads, 48
Gloria's whole-meal bread, 81–82
gluten
  flour, 79
  formation, 50
Goat Cheese and Tapenade Pizza,
    170
Gold Dust Loaf, 92–93
Golden Egg Custard, 110
Golden Peach Jam, 53
Goldenrod Eggs, 90–91
*Gram's Teddy Bear Bread, 326
Green-Olive Fougasse, 182–183
Green Onion Market Bread with
    Italian filling, 176–178
grilled cheese sandwich, 195
Grissini Anise, 150–151

*Half-Time Granny's White Bread,
    252
*hamburger buns, 318
half-time jams
  apple butter, 84
  fresh berry, 143
  peach, 53
  strawberry, 52
Hands-Off French Bread, 255
hard rolls, 158–159
Hawaiian Sweet Bread, 108–109
Hazelnut Coffee Ring, 220–221
herb breads
  *dill rolls, 287
  *dilly bread, 309
  batter bread, 204
  *garlic pepper bread, 297

parsley, sage, rosemary, thyme
    pinwheel, 160
  *red onion-nut-bacon bread,
      310
  three-seeded, 190, 313
Herb's herbed croutons with
    cheese, 257
high altitude baking, 37
hollandaise, microwave, 103
home-style soft pretzels, 144–145
Honey-Swirl Raisin Bread, 96–97
Hors d'Oeuvres, Toasts, Crou-
    tons, and Salad Breads
  Micro-Rise Method, 121–136
  Bread Machine, 275–280
*Holiday Dinner Rolls, 285
Hot Anise Sweet Bread, 106–107
Hot Cross Buns with Orange, 290
hotdog buns, 318
huevos con salsa, 106

Idaho Potato Bread, 61–62
Irish Barley-Wheat Bread, 82–83
*Italian Angel Food, 320
Italian Loaf Rustica, 172–173

Khachapuri, 275
Kitchenaid mixing of bread
    dough, 34
kneading, machine, 29, 32
kolacky, 226–229

Lager Bread, 193–194
Lauren's Cinnamon Sugar Monkey
    Bread, 98–99
*Lemon Dessert Bread, 320
*Light White Bread, 261
liquids used in bread, 8–9, 50
  beer, 8
  buttermilk, 9
  evaporated milk, 9
  nonfat dry milk and water, 9
  yogurt, 8
low-fat buttermilk biscuits, 77
low-fat, low-cal breads
  black bread, 68
  buttermilk biscuits, 77

featherweight white, 88
French country, 69
*light white, 261
pane all'ollio, 54
pita, 124
*salt-free potato, 261
sour faux, 58
low-wattage microwave ovens,
    about, 35

*Machine Pain de Mie, 254
Manhattan Clam Chowder, 314
*McCully House Inn Fresh Dill
    Rolls, 287
Melba toast, 58
microwave ovens, 16–17, 35, 335
micro-rise method, 3, 15, 29–35,
    39–40, 50, 138
micro-rise setting and adjustment,
    35
milk toast, 101
millet bread, 92, *265
mixed grain breads
    barley wheat, 82
    *blueberry granola, 270
    Gloria's, 81
    rye wheat, 70
    rye-wheat-corn, 68
    *seven grain, 262
    wheat-oat, 65
Monkey bread, 98
muffins, 103
Muffulettta, 54

Narsai David's Light Rye, 256
No Pain Ordinaire, 52–53
nonfat dry milk, 9
Nuevo York Corn Rye, 200–201
nut breads
    *black walnut-banana, 271
    chocolate pecan, 212
    Crete with walnuts, 134
    *filbert, 279
    hazelnut, 220
    hazelnut-pear, 126
    *pecan date, 269
    pecan praline, 224

*pineapple-macadamia nut, 324
*pumpkin-pecan spice, 331
*tomato–pine nut, 314
*walnut, 316
*walnut-butter, 280
walnut-raisin, 128
nut filling, 229

Oat Bran–Oatmeal Bread, 89–90
oat bread
    oat-bran oatmeal, 89
    *Scotland, 264
Old Glory Sandwich, 57
Olive Oil Bread, 54
One Hundred Percent (100%)
    Whole Wheat Bread, 256
One-Rise Sauerkraut Rye, 205–
    206
*Onion-Cream-Cheddar Rolls, 292
Orange Bread Pudding, 230
Orange Danish from the Danes,
    218–219
Orange Grove Bread, 230
Our Daily Bread, 65–66
Ovens, 18
over-kneaded bread dough, 33

Pain de Mie, 56–58,
    *254
*Pain Perdu, 274
Pane all'Olio, 54–55
Panettone, 222–223
*Parker House Rolls, 284
Parmesan-Basil Toast, 123–124
Parsley, Sage, Rosemary and
    Thyme Pinwheel Loaf, 160–
    161
*Pecan Date Swirl Loaf, 269
pesto
    basic, 170
    black olive, 70
    torta, 132
*Petit Prosciutto Bread, 278
pickles, mushroom, 179
Pigs in a Blanket, 119–120
*Pineapple-Macadamia Nut Braid,
    324
*Pissaladière, 296

Pita bread, 124, 188
pizza
    Chicago-style two crust, 168
    *pissaladière, 296
    plain dough, 167
    sauce, everyday, 167
    sauce, fresh tomato, 301
    Summer in an hour, 170
    *West Coast New Wave, 294
Pizza, Focaccia, Flatbreads,
    and Filled Breads
    Micro-Rise Method, 165–189
    Bread Machine, 293–307
pizza peel, 23–24, 158, 168,
    171, 175, 178, 188, 258,
    295
pizza stone, 22, 158, 168, 171,
    175, 178, 188, 258, 295
Plain ole Focaccia, 184
Plain Ole Pizza Dough, 167–168
Popping Pitas, 124–125
Poppy-seed Bread, 66–67
poppy-seed filling, 229
Portuguese Sweet Bread, 231
*potato bread, 254
    Idaho, 61
    *salt-free, 261
Potted Shrimp, Leek, Dill on
    Toast, 65
pretzels, 144
prune filling, 228, 324
pumpernickel baguette, 139–140
*Pumpkin-Pecan Spice Bread, 331

Quarry tile, 24

Raisin bread
    Country with walnuts, 128
    honey-swirl, 96
    panettone, 222
Raleigh House Orange Rolls,
    162–163
raspberry sauce, 234
*red onion-nut-bacon bread, 310
reheating bread, 38, 52
reheating rolls, 151

Rich Dinner Rolls in an Hour, 153–154
Roasting Peppers, how-to, 123
rolls
    Anadama, 154
    *angel biscuits, 291
    *bagels
    brown and serves, 151
    butterhorn, 156
    *Christmas bowknot, 328
    *dill, 287
    dinner in an hour, 153
    *dried cherry, 288
    *holiday, 285
    *Hot Cross Buns, 290
    *Kaiser, 286
    *knishes, 306
    kolacky, 226
    *onion-cream-cheddar rolls, 292
    *Parker House, 284
    *petit prosciutto, 278
    *sugar canes, 330
    whole wheat, 78
Rosemary-Raisin Focaccia with Pine Nuts, 185
rye breads
    ale and kraut, 194
    black, 68
    *light with caraway seeds, 256
    Nuevo York corn, 200
    Pumpernickel baguette, 139
    sauerkraut, 205
    sour rye with dill, 197
    Swedish, 198
    Uncle Larry's Beer, 73

Saffron Challah, 216–217
salad dressings
    garlic vinaigrette, 173
    Gizzie's grinder juice, 311
    plain vinaigrette, 136
    Russian, 205
    tomato yogurt, 136
salads
    Caponata, 124
    citrus avocado, 232

composed, 123
French bread, 135
romaine and Parmesan, 173
Summer's bread, 280
*Sally Lunn, 253
salt, 11
*Salt-Free Potato Bread, 261
salt-free white bread, 91
*sandwich bread, 56, 254
sandwiches
    brie garlic, 159
    cocktail, 199
    cottage cheese, sun dried tomato, 189
    cucumber, 211
    Dagwood, 216
    grilled cheddar-turkey, 194
    Italian meat and cheese, 176
    muffuletta, 54
    pear fontina, 195
    peanut butter and jelly, 81
    One World, 200
    prosciutto and provolone, 140
    Rocket ribbon, 57
    Reuben, 205
    turkey-swiss on rye, 197
    Waldorf, 193
sauces
    bourbon, 233
    butterscotch, 236
    chocolate, 230
    raspberry, 234
*Scotland Oat Bread, 264
scalding milk, 9
scalloped eggs, 114
seasoned crouton bread, 130–131
Sedona Bread, 180–181
Senate Bean Soup, 310
setting the microwave, 35
*seven-grain wheat bread, 262
shaping bread dough, 40–46
    baguette, 42
    braided loaf, 43, 64
    breadsticks, 146, 149
    challah, 43, 64, 216
    coiled leaf, 42
    high round loaf, 41

Italian bread, 43
marble loaf, 42
pinwheel loaf, 41
pull-apart bread, 42
pullman loaf, 57
standard loaf, 40
wheat sheaf, 215
*Simple Sour English Muffins, 259
*Simple Sourdough Bread, 258
Skillet Breakfast Bread Pudding, 100
Soft Parmesan Breadsticks, 148–149
soup
    Canadian cheese, 204
    cream of cheese, 292
    gazpacho, 180
    Manhattan Clam Chowder, 314
    Senate bean, 310
Soup and Sandwich Breads
    Micro-Rise method, 190–205
    Bread Machine, 308–318
Sour Rye Bread with Dill, 197–198
*sourdough bread, 258
    English muffins, 259
    starter, 258–259
Spices, Cheeses, Yeasts and Other Special Ingredients, 336–337
    American Spoon Foods, 336
    Balducci's, 336
    Dean and DeLuca, 336
    Fleischmann's Yeast, 336
    Kendall Cheese, 337
    Muirhead, 337
    Paprikas Weiss, 337
    G. B. Ratto, International Grocers, 337
    Rising Sun Farm, 337
    H. Roth and Sons, 337
    S. E. Rykoff, 337
    Sonoma Cheese Factory, 337
    Todaro Bros., 337
    Universal Foods Corp (Red Star Yeast), 337

Vella Cheese of California, 337
Williams Sonoma, 337
Spiked-with-Ale Rye and Kraut
Loaf, 194–195
spinach-cheese torta, 133
sponge, micro-rise, 39, 50, 69
Standard for a perfect loaf of
basic bread, 51
storing bread, 38
strawberry jam, 52
*Strawberry Savarin, 322
streusel, almond crumb, 229
stuffing, bread
basic, 130
Dressed-to-the-Nines, 130
Sugar Crusted Galette, 210
*Summer's Bread Salad, 280
sugar, 11–12, 14
flat bread, 210
Summer Pizza in an Hour, 170–
171
Swedish rye bread, 198–199
sweet breads
*apple crumb kuchen, 321
Babas au Rhum, 209
chocolate-cherry kugelhupf,
212
*Christmas sugar canes, 330
crullers, 118
*Gram's Teddy Bear Bread, 326
Hawaiian, 108
*honey buns, 268
honey swirl, 96
hot anise, 106
kolacky, 226
*lemon dessert bread, 320
orange danish, 218
orange grove, 230
panettone, 222
*pecan date swirl, 269
pecan praline sugar loaf, 224
*pineapple-macadamia nut,
324
Portuguese pumpkin-pecan
spice, 331
*Sally Lunn
*Strawberry Savarin

sugar-crusted galette, 210
*Sweet Sunday Honey Buns, 268
Swiss cheese–potato savarin,
195–196

Tabasco Cheddar Bread, 311
tapenade, homemade, 171
testing for doneness, 37, 85
Thanksgiving Wheat Sheaf, 214
toasting hazelnuts, 220
toasting pine-nuts, 185
toasts
anchovy-garlic, 56
and egg, 105
banana peanut butter, 105
cinnamon, 97, 104
cups, 105
green-chili cheddar, 104
herbs, 81
Melba, 58
milk-, 101
mushroom-tarragon, 74
Parmesan-basil, 123
shrimp, leek, dill, 65
tomato-basil, 81
tomato-basil bruschetta, 255
Tuscan, 132
with goat cheese, 69, 81
Tomato-Basil Baguette, 140–141
Tomato, Chicken, Cheese Calzone, 175
tortas
*eggplant, pepper, artichoke,
302
pesto, 132
spinach-cheese, 133
*spinach-ricotta, 302
Rustica, 172
Tropical Bread Pudding, 108
troubleshooting the bread machine, 248–250
troubleshooting the micro-rise
method, 15–18, 29–35, 38–
40, 51, 61, 85, 90, 129,
156
Turtle Bread, 226
Tuscan Toasts, 132–133

Uncle Larry's Beer Bread, 73–74

Vegetables, micro-steaming, 136

*Walnut-Butter Loaf, 280
*walnut bread, 316
Waldorf Sandwich, 193
water bagels, 142
water sprayer, 25, 129, 158
Watercress Cheese, 139
*West Coast New Wave Pizza,
294–295
wheat kernel, 76
white bread—salt free, 91–92
white breads
buttermilk, 60
challah, 63
English muffin loaf, 104
featherweight, 88
*half-time Granny's white, 252
Italian olive oil bread, 54
*light, 261
no pain ordinaire, 52
*Sally Lunn, 253
salt-free, 91, *261
sandwich (Pullman), 56, *254
sour faux, 58
*whole wheat beer bread, 265
*whole wheat cottage bread, 263
whole wheat breads
apple butter, 84
barley-wheat, 82
*beer, 264
*blueberry granola, 270
carrot-currant-wheat berry, 86
*cottage, 263
cracked wheat, 79
daily, 65
Deaf Smith Co., 72
French Country, 69
Gloria's whole meal, 81
*100% whole wheat, 256
*seven grain, 262
whole wheat–style dinner rolls,
78–79
work space, 19, 91